The Handbook of Political Change in Eastern
Europe

The Handbook of
Political Change in
Eastern Europe

Edited by

Sten Berglund

Professor of Political Science, University of Örebro, Sweden

Tomas Hellén

Doctor of Political Science, Åbo Academy University, Finland

Frank H. Aarebrot

Associate Professor, University of Bergen, Norway

Edward Elgar
Cheltenham, UK • Northampton, MA, USA

Published by
Edward Elgar Publishing Limited
Glensanda House
Montpellier Parade
Cheltenham
Glos GL50 1UA
UK

Edward Elgar Publishing, Inc.
6 Market Street
Northampton
Massachusetts 01060
USA

A catalogue record for this book is available from the British Library

Library of Congress Cataloguing in Publication Data

The handbook of political change in Eastern Europe / edited by Sten
    Berglund, Tomas Hellén, Frank H. Aarebrot.
        Includes indexes.
        Includes bibliographical references and index.
        1. Europe, Eastern—Social conditions—1989—Congresses.
    2. Europe, Eastern—Politics and government—1989—Congresses.
    3. Social change—Europe, Eastern—Congresses. 4. Post-communism—
    Europe, Eastern—Congresses. I. Berglund, Sten, 1947–   .
    II. Hellén, Tomas. III. Aarebrot, Frank H., 1947–   .
    HN380.7.A8H36   1998
    306.2'0947—dc21   98–27169
                                                                                 CIP

ISBN 1 85898 840 3

Printed and bound in Great Britain by MPG Books Ltd, Bodmin, Cornwall

Contents

Tables and Figures

Tables

Figures

Notes on the Contributors

Frank Aarebrot (b. 1947) is associate professor of political science at the University of Bergen, Norway. He is the author and co-author of numerous articles and chapters within the field of comparative politics, among others: 'On the Structural Basis of Regional Variation in Europe' (in DeMarcchi and Boileau, eds, *Boundaries and Minorities in Western Europe*, Milan 1982), 'The Politics of Cultural Dissent: Religion, Language and Demonstrative Effects in Norway' (with Derek Urwin, *Scandinavian Political Studies* 2, 1979) and 'Analysis and Explanation of Variation in Territorial Structure' (in Stein Rokkan et al., eds, *Centre–Periphery Structures in Europe*, Frankfurt/M 1987).

Sten Berglund (b. 1947) is professor of political science at the University of Örebro, Sweden. His previous publications include *The Scandinavian Party Systems* (with Ulf Lindström, 1978), *Democracy and Foreign Policy* (with Kjell Goldmann and Gunnar Sjöstedt, 1985), *The New Democracies in Eastern Europe: Party Systems and Political Cleavages* (co-edited and co-authored with Jan Åke Dellenbrant, 1991 and 1994), and *The Political History of Eastern Europe: The Struggle between Democracy and Dictatorship* (with Frank Aarebrot, 1997).

William Crowther (b. 1952) is associate professor of political science at the University of North Carolina at Greensboro, and co-director of the Parliamentary Documents Center, USA. He is the author of numerous scholarly works on various aspects of Romanian and Moldovan politics, and is currently engaged in a comparative study of post-communist legislatures.

Marian Grzybowski (b. 1945) is professor of constitutional law and political institutions at the Jagiellonian University of Cracow and professor at the Maria Curie-Skłodowska University (Rzeszów Centre), Poland. His current research interests include: constitutional and political systems of

Scandinavia, Central Europe, the United States and Canada, electoral systems and voting behaviour. He is the author of twelve books, the most recent of which is *Electoral Systems of Central Europe* (1997).

Tomas Hellén (b. 1964, d. 1998) doctor of political science, Åbo Academy, Finland, and a writer at the *Hufvudstadsbladet* daily in Helsinki. He published widely on security policy and European integration and was the author of *Shaking Hands with the Past: Origins of the Political Right in Central Europe* (Helsinki 1996).

Georgi Karasimeonov (b. 1949) is professor of political science at the University of Sofia, Managing Director of the Institute for Political and Legal Studies in Sofia, and President of the Bulgarian Political Science Association. His main research interests and publications are in the fields of political parties, political institutions, post-communist transition and constitutional law.

Mikko Lagerspetz (b. 1963) is professor of sociology at the Estonian Institute of Humanities. His doctoral dissertation was *Constructing Post-Communism: A Study on the Estonian Social Problems Discourse* (Turku 1996), and he has co-authored, with Rein Raud, *Estonian Cultural Policy and its Impact* (Council of Europe, Strasbourg 1995). Currently, his research focus is on the construction and hegemonization of the new economic and political order in Estonia.

Zdenka Mansfeldová (b. 1950) is Senior Research Fellow at the Institute of Sociology, Academy of Sciences of the Czech Republic. Her current research interests include political parties, institutionalization of interest representation and social partnership. Her most recent books are *Pluralistic System of Interest Representation in Czech Society* (1996), *Zerfall der Tschechoslowakei: strukturelle Ursachen und Parteihandeln* (1995) and *Social Partnership in the Czech Republic* (1997).

Hermann Smith-Sivertsen (b. 1962) is assistant professor of political science at the Department of Business Administration and Political Science at Buskerud College in Kongsberg, Norway. His current research is focused on party systems, party organizations and mass politics in Latvia and Lithuania. His most recent publication is 'Towards parties of elites – or popularism', in *Revue Baltique* 8, 1997.

Gábor Tóka (b. 1962) is an assistant professor at the Department of Political Science of the Central European University, Budapest, Hungary. He is editor of *The 1990 Elections to the Hungarian National Assembly* (Sigma, Berlin, 1995), and has published articles on electoral behaviour, political parties and democratic consolidation, most recently in *Different but Similar* (Jan van Deth, ed, Routledge 1998).

Henri Vogt (b. 1967) is a researcher at the Department of Political Science, University of Helsinki, Finland, and a research student at St Anthony's College, University of Oxford, UK. He has written and published widely on issues related to the revolutions of 1989 and to subsequent developments in East Central Europe.

Drago Zajc (b. 1938) is professor at the University of Ljubljana, Slovenia, and president of the Slovene Political Science Association. His main fields of academic interst are human rights and parliamentary procedure. His most recent books are *The Role of the Slovene Parliament in the Process of Democratization* (1993) and *The Influence of the Electoral System on the Composition of Parliaments* (1996).

Darius Žeruolis (b. 1969) has degrees from the Central European University, Budapest, Hungary, and the London School of Economics and Political Science, UK, and is currently at the Institute of International Relations and Political Science, University of Vilnius, Lithuania. He has published widely on comparative politics and quantitative research methods.

Preface

This volume represents the successful conclusion of a research endeavour in progress since the early 1990s. Its roots can be traced back to the informal meetings between East and West European political scientists within the framework of the seminars on post-communist Eastern Europe organized at the Science Center (WZB) in Berlin by professor Hans-Dieter Klingemann. By the 1994 IPSA World Congress, the contours of a project organization were already visible, but the project did not gain momentum until after the ECPR research sessions in Tromsø, Norway, in June 1995. That meeting paved the way for a successful application for generous research funding from the Tercentenary Fund of the Swedish National Bank.

We are all indebted to the ECPR and the Tercentenary Fund. Tomas Hellén wishes to express his gratitude to the Ella and Georg Ehrnrooth Foundation, which made it possible for him to devote himself to the project on a full-time basis during the crucial final stages; and Frank Aarebrot is indebted to the Norwegian Research Council for providing research funding within the framework of its Central and East European programme.

The Science Center (WZB) hosted the two conferences – in December 1996 and January 1998 – which were needed in order to finalize the manuscript; and Hans-Dieter Klingemann graciously provided a spiritual home for all of us at the Science Center throughout the duration of the project.

In March 1997, the project was hit by a severe blow when professor Jan Åke Dellenbrant, who was to have been one of the co-editors, suddenly passed away. We think he would have liked the final product. It is a handbook offering in-depth analyses of the changing cleavage structures in the countries of Eastern Europe as well as hard facts about election results, government formation, electoral system and constitutional arrangements. This volume is dedicated to his memory.

Sten Berglund   *Tomas Hellén*   *Frank Aarebrot*

Postscript

The preceding preface was finalized by the editors on 25 March 1998. The following day Tomas Hellén was no longer with us. He had collapsed and passed away within hours of having completed his work on the book.

Tomas Hellén was a brilliant young political scientist with a strong interest in comparative politics and East European affairs. As a journalist he had a well developed feeling for style and format not only in his native Swedish tongue, but also in Finnish and English; he was a superb organizer, a hard worker and easy to get along with. He will be sorely missed for years to come by all the individual members of the research group to which he devoted what were to be the last few months of his life.

In retrospect, *The Handbook of Political Change in Eastern Europe* may be seen as a lasting tribute to the life and work of this talented young political scientist.

Sten Berglund   *Frank Aarebrot*

1. Foundations of Change

Sten Berglund, Tomas Hellén
and Frank Aarebrot

The topic of this book is cleavages in East European transitional societies. We are concerned with the transition to democracy and, even more, with the consolidation of democracy in a post-communist setting.

This volume is within the tradition of comparative macrosociology. As in the seminal book on cleavage structures edited by Seymour Martin Lipset and Stein Rokkan (1967), we focus primarily on the systems of contrasts and cleavages within national communities; on the factors important for development of a stable system of cleavages and opposition in national political life; and on the behaviour of rank-and-file citizens in the party-political systems. The historical dimension is important, as is the task of developmental comparison and the mapping of variations in the sequences of alternatives.

This introductory chapter, which will deal mainly with some issues of definition, is followed by a framework chapter, which sets out to formulate some crucial questions without necessarily providing the final answers to them. What is the relevance of the historical legacy? Which are the pre-requisites for consolidated democracy? What are the long-term prospects for democracy in Eastern Europe? The nine subsequent country-specific chapters address similar topics, albeit and obviously from slightly varying perspectives. The concluding chapter makes an attempt at synthesizing the results of the country-specific analyses.

What is Eastern Europe?

The term 'Eastern Europe' is ambiguous and in many ways outdated. It was the post-Yalta order which 'dictated a strict and single dichotomy by sub-suming under the label Eastern Europe all those parts of Central, East Central and South-eastern Europe that after 1945 came under Soviet domination' (Garton Ash 1989, 161). The term was not only an ideological precept pertaining to the East/West conflict, but also denoted the perceived homogeneity of the bloc of European states oriented towards the Soviet Union. The political systems of the socialist countries in Eastern Europe were initially copies of the Soviet model, and the rules of the political games were, in the final analysis, defined by Moscow until the very break-down of Soviet-style communism. After the 1950s, the East European leaders were more free to embark upon what was commonly referred to as a national road towards socialism, but some things were simply not condoned by the Soviet leaders. The leading role of the Marxist-Leninist party must not be eroded, democratic centralism must not be questioned, and the 'eternal' friendship and alliance with the Soviet Union must not be violated. These principles lent themselves to different interpretations – as demonstrated during the Prague Spring of 1968 – but Moscow had the final say and its interpretation tended to give the East European leaders a short rather than a long leash.

The ambitious Soviet programme of industrialization, urbanization and modernization also served as a model and source of inspiration of long-lasting consequences for the East European countries. They went through a rapid, profound and occasionally dramatic process of socioeconomic trans-formation under communism.

Even so, national traits were not eradicated by the communist regimes, which frequently exploited communalism, nationalism and xenophobia. By 1989–90, history had begun to repeat itself. Without instructions from the centre, the 'Soviet Bloc' in Eastern Europe almost immediately disinte-grated into historic sub-regions. In some respects, disintegration went even further, as the collapse of the Soviet Union, Yugoslavia and Czechoslovakia led to the establishment of several independent republics with little recent or, in some cases, no historical experience of statehood. If the USSR itself is included, the pre-1989 socialist bloc in Europe encompassed nine states. In 1992, one could find no fewer than twenty-seven independent states in the same area; fifteen arising out of the defunct Soviet Union, five out of Yugo-slavia, and two out of Czechoslovakia.

This book, however, deals with not all twenty-seven of these post-communist countries, but with a sample of ten: Estonia, Latvia, Lithuania, Poland, the Czech Republic, Slovakia, Hungary, Slovenia, Romania, and Bulgaria. The country-specific chapters are arranged in order of the geo-graphical north–south axis, starting off with Estonia and concluding with Bulgaria.

Several factors determine the inclusion of these states and the exclusion of others. There is the geographical argument: the newly independent Transcaucasian and Central Asian states are obviously beyond the scope of a book dealing with Eastern Europe. A cultural and historical definition comes into play: we deal with the 'interface' countries between the Baltic and the Aegean which are 'the East of the West and the West of the East' (Rupnik 1989, 4); the successor states of the German, Austrian, Russian and Ottoman empires which in the 1940s came under communist control. Moreover, the ten countries in the sample have a history of recent or continuous independence and clearer experiences of statehood and nation-hood than the (non-Baltic) successor states of the Soviet Union. These ten countries are at the core of the process of integration across the Cold War European divide. All have applied for membership of the European Union, and only Slovakia is currently hesitant about joining NATO.

Table 1.1: Freedom ratings of post-communist countries 1996–97 on a scale from 1 (most free) to 7 (least free). The freedom rating is a composite judgement based on survey results.

Country	Political Rights	Civil Liberties	Freedom rating
Estonia	1	2	Free
Latvia	2	2	Free
Lithuania	1	2	Free
Poland	1	2	Free
Hungary	1	2	Free
Czech Republic	1	2	Free
Slovenia	1	2	Free
Slovakia	2	4	Partly Free
Romania	2	3	Free
Bulgaria	2	3	Free
Croatia	4	4	Partly Free
Yugoslavia	6	6	Not Free
Bosnia-Herzegovina	5	5	Partly Free
Macedonia	4	3	Partly Free
Albania	4	4	Partly Free
Russia	3	4	Partly Free
Ukraine	3	4	Partly Free
Belarus	6	6	Not Free
Moldova	3	4	Partly Free
Georgia	4	4	Partly Free
Armenia	5	4	Partly Free
Azerbaijan	6	5	Not Free
Kazakhstan	6	5	Not Free
Turkmenistan	7	7	Not Free
Tajikistan	7	7	Not Free
Uzbekistan	7	6	Not Free
Kyrgyz Republic	4	4	Partly Free

Source: Kaplan, ed., (1997), *Freedom in the World: The Annual Survey of Political Rights and Civil Liberties 1996–1997*, New York, Freedom House. Also at: *http://www.freedomhouse.org/Political/frtable1.htm*

Most importantly, however, the ten-country sample forms a distinct group among the post-communist countries in terms of the state of the civil society, the market economy and the rule of law. As evaluated by Freedom House, all nine post-communist countries judged as 'free' are found within our ten-nation group; of the ten, only Slovakia does not merit that verdict, and even that country ranks higher in terms of political rights and civil liberties than any of the remaining seventeen post-communist states (*Table 1.1*). By way of example, the East European post-communist countries of Albania, Moldova and the successor states of the former Yugoslav federation – excepting Slovenia – are still very weak democracies in a state of political and social flux, at times even plagued by war and civil strife, a fact which renders an analysis of electoral politics and democratic consolidation extremely difficult, even pointless.

The ten East European countries may be further – and are in fact – divided into three sub-regions. The three Baltic states of Estonia, Latvia and Lithuania form one distinct and obvious group. The threesome is structurally cohesive not only because these three countries were all once part of the Soviet Union, but also due to their long-running common history at the cross-roads between Russia, Germany and Scandinavia.

Five countries in our sample are 'Central' or 'East Central' European: Poland, the Czech Republic, Slovakia, Hungary and Slovenia. This definition combines the criteria of pre-1914 Central Europe and post-1945 Eastern Europe: countries which went communist after the Second World War, once (wholly or mainly) were subsumed in the great multi-national Prussian-German and Habsburg empires, profoundly anchored in the Western tradition which entails Western Christianity, at least a measure of experience of the rule of law, the separation of powers, constitutional government and civil society (cf. Garton Ash 1989, 225). This sets them apart from the third sub-region in our sample, South Eastern Europe, with its traditions of Eastern Christianity or Islam, clientelism and Ottoman rule.

Indeed, the Central European and Balkan countries emerged from socialism in very different shape and with different prospects, particularly with respect to civil society. This has subsequently been demonstrated by very different reactions to the procedural shocks created by the post-1989 transition and democratic construction and reconstruction. This argument could, incidentally, be raised for including Slovakia in the Balkan sub-group rather than in the Central European one. Of the Balkan states narrowly defined, only Romania and Bulgaria merit country-specific analyses in this book. The other countries in the region – Albania, Bosnia-Herzegovina, Croatia, Macedonia and Yugoslavia – have not yet reached the level of political stability where divisions and cleavages are only, and freely, fought out in the electoral arena.

Theories of Transition?

The fundamental change which Eastern Europe underwent in the late 1980s and early 1990s had all the hallmarks of what political scientists commonly refer to as 'transition'. It was a transition not only from totalitarian or authoritarian rule to democracy, as had been the case in Southern Europe and Latin America in the 1960s and 1970s, but also a transition from plan to market. The literature on transition in the market in the late 1980s focused all but exclusively on the South European and Latin American transitions. Most Western area specialists on Eastern Europe agreed that communism was bound to fail, but they were nevertheless inclined to attribute an extremely high level of stability to the various communist regimes (cf. Brzezinski 1989), and later analyses of the events and the rationalization of the factors involved have had a distinct *ex post facto* character. Yet, of course, nothing said that real existing socialism would collapse in Eastern Europe when it did; it could just as well have happened twenty years earlier or twenty years later.

As Adam Przeworski has noted, it is not the lack of legitimacy but the presence of an opposition that threatens a dictatorship. When a dictatorial regime tolerates an opposition, it indicates that it is divided between reformers who want to broaden the power base and hard-liners who want to crush the opposition; no transition can be forced by internal opponents alone against a regime which maintains enough cohesion, capacity and willingness to apply repression. With the help of game theory, Przeworski proceeds to demonstrate how this process can generate a set of different outcomes depending on how hard-liners, liberalizers and the opposition interact. If the end result is a transition to democracy, one can conclude – but not predict beforehand – that liberalizers were first prepared to go all the way but had to hide their intentions from hard-liners; second, discovered in mid-course that repression was unlikely to succeed; third, found that they had not so much to lose as they had thought initially; or, fourth, had no choice and just put a good face on it (Prezeworski 1991; also O'Donnell and Schmitter 1986).

This approach is relevant, but it has little to say about the structural factors behind the appearance of a split in the regime and the emergence of an opposition viable enough to challenge it. For that, one may look at Stein Rokkan's discussion of the adoption of proportional representation (PR) in Continental Europe at the end of the 19th and start of the 20th century. He explains that PR came about 'through a convergence of pressures from below and from above. The rising working class wanted to lower the thresholds of representation to gain access to the legislatures, and the most threatened of the old-established parties demanded PR to protect their position against the new waves of mobilized voters created by universal suffrage' (Rokkan 1970, 157). Similar shifts to proportional representation in Latin America have also occurred simultaneously with major changes in the distribution of power: 'Parties expecting to decline ... want proportional representation as a means of insuring that they can continue to exercise some degree of influence' (Geddes 1990, 29). This is a 'rational-choice' explanation, related to Przeworski's game theory, but it has more to say about the relevance of socio-structural change. Although Rokkan's theory for Western Europe is far from a general social-science explanation, the hypothesis 'provides a theoretical point of departure for a theory-starved subject matter' (Lijphart 1992, 101).

In the East European context, the ruling communist parties might thus be substituted for Rokkan's 'old-established' parties, and the democratic opposition for his 'rising working class'. One may well argue that the ruling parties were prepared to opt for electoral reform in 1989, when the evaporation of Soviet support threatened to create a truly revolutionary situation which could have ended in their loss of all power and influence, a ban on their operations, and to lustration and criminal proceedings being instituted against their leaders and members. But the parallel is far from straightforward: Rokkan discussed the transformation of semi-democratic systems into fully-fledged democracies, while the communist regimes were driven by totalitarian ambitions founded on the Marxist-Leninist canon. The threshold against advocating and instituting even moderate change in the direction of pluralism was much higher.

Indeed, if there was a decisive split between regime liberalizers and hardliners – what brought it about? The argument of Soviet decline is not enough, as the 1989 terminal crisis was preceded by several serious but nonetheless non-fatal regime splits, notably in the GDR in 1953, in Hungary (and Poland) in 1956, in Czechoslovakia in 1968, and in Poland in 1980–81. O'Donnell and Schmitter (1986) minimize the importance of international pressure in transition processes, but that proposition is not borne out by evidence from Eastern Europe, where systemic crises in one country tended to spread rapidly throughout the region. In fact, the domino effect in 1989–90 testifies to the highly international nature of the transition from communism: the success of the first transitions provided a powerful demonstration effect, while the regional hegemony – the USSR – first removed its veto against democracy and then embarked on a process of self-reform (cf. Di Palma 1990). In fact, international influences had significant effects even earlier. Of particular importance were the human rights provisions in the Helsinki Final Act, which contributed towards legitimizing the East European opposition movements and greatly facilitated their work. The fact that the Socialist Bloc accepted the very concept of human rights transcending national interest and even Marxist-Leninist ideology 'wrought devastation in the internal coherence of the system' (Schöpflin 1993, 207–8).

When looking for impetuses for change, the impact of crises stands out. Two types of crisis are particularly pertinent: a crisis of failure, where the rulers are unable to solve pressing problems, and a crisis of leadership, where the regime faces problems related to leadership succession. Both these types of crisis were present in 1989. The socialist economies were increasingly strained by shortages, bottlenecks and inefficiencies; with the benefit of hindsight, it seems clear that the communist rulers had exhausted the once-abundant avenues for growth through industrialization, and failed to see the need to embark on a post-industrial path of development. Simultaneously, the reforms instituted in the Soviet Union by Mikhail Gorbachev's reform team paved the way for a serious leadership challenge to the East European old guards.

The different outcomes of the events in 1989–90 has much to say about the varying structures of the communist regimes. In the Central European countries, state- and nation-building had largely been completed – in this respect, Slovakia is yet again an outlier in the Central European group (cf. Chapter 7) – and the societies had all the attributes of modernity: e.g. high levels of industrialization, urbanization and secularization. The ruling communist parties of Central Europe came to rely increasingly on conventional co-optation and pragmatic management instead of Marxist-Leninist ideological maxims. In South Eastern Europe, the situation was very different. There, modernization had in some respects been every bit as dramatic as in Central Europe – in some ways even more so – but political culture had not been affected to the same extent. The communist regimes in the Balkan countries ruled with a much stronger reliance on patronage and repression than their Central European counterparts. They also put a considerably stronger emphasis on their state- and nation-building accomplishments and ambitions, as a legitimizing factor for their rule; an argument which was also widely accepted among the ethnic core populations. Indeed, in South Eastern Europe, the regimes often accused – and not without success – the democratic opposition of threatening state- and nation-building or even the states and nations themselves. By the 1980s, this option was no longer credible for the Polish communists; carried great foreign-policy costs for the communists in Hungary; and could not be safely used by the rulers in Prague due to the complicated Czech-Slovak relationship (cf. Hellén 1996). For leading Baltic communists, operating within the Soviet context, reference to state-building and nation-building was, of course, anathema.

One also has to bear in mind that the character of the ruling parties had changed dramatically between 1945 and 1989. What had once been revolutionary vanguard parties had gradually evolved into bureaucratic vehicles for career advancement. Obviously, this weakened ideological concord, eroded the ruling elites' cohesion and diminished the readiness to resort to repression. Analyses of the systemic crises indeed show a gradual decline of the regimes' ability and willingness to take immediate and harsh actions against their opponents; in 1956 it was a matter of days before the hard-liners had taken control of the Hungarian party, in 1968 it took weeks for their Czechoslovak counterparts; in Poland the liberalizers had the upper hand for several months in 1980–81; and in 1989–90 the hard-liners could not even put up a real fight.

Not all modern societies are democracies. And not all non-modern societies are dictatorships. The standard work on transition to democracy, the four-volume *Transitions from Authoritarian Rule* edited by O'Donnell, Schmitter and Whitehead (1986–87), concludes that there is little, if any, correlation between socioeconomic development and political structure; i.e. a certain socioeconomic structure can generate and coexist with a number of political systems. Yet there is a good case to be made for the notion that modernity facilitates the transition to democracy. Economic development is often cast as a necessary, if not sufficient, prerequisite for democracy – this is in fact one of the underlying notions of the so-called convergence theory – and it would be entirely plausible to draw the somewhat paradoxical conclusion that the prospects for democracy are particularly bright in those former communist states where the ruling Marxist-Leninist parties were especially successful in promoting socioeconomic development and state-building. It is no easy task to sort out the 'successful' communist regimes from the less 'successful' ones, but some general observations are in order.

The communist call for modernization was universal, but as a rule it was more successful in Northern than in Southern Europe. The communist campaign against organized religion made itself felt throughout the Soviet bloc as well as in Yugoslavia, to say nothing of Albania, which proclaimed itself an atheist republic, but it was less than successful in predominantly Catholic countries like Poland and Lithuania. The managerial style of communist Eastern Europe required a powerful state machinery capable of mobilization as well as social control, but the kind of clientelism which had been practised for centuries in Southern Europe does not disappear during a few short decades. The many references to the sultanistic features of the Ceauşescu regime in Romania, and to the feudal heritage of post-communist Bulgaria, testify to the resilience of old patterns of governance (Linz and Stepan 1996).

The argument that socialism had run its course by 1989, having built more modern societies, should not be construed to mean that the transformation itself or its timing were predestined and inevitable in all, or any, of the East European states. Nor does it imply that the countries of Eastern

Europe had become duplicates of Western societies. It takes time for modernization to change political culture. As Slavenka Drakulic notes: 'Romania, like most ex-Communist countries, remains a country of peasants ... The values of a civil society are values created by citizens, and one or two generations of peasants living in the cities under a totalitarian regime had no chance of becoming citizens, politically or culturally' (Drakulic 1994). In particular, the socialist societies did not include a middle class in the traditional sense; the middle strata were defined not by ownership but by educational achievement and access to state and party power structures. This fluidity of the class cleavage has indeed proved a destabilizing factor after the introduction of multi-party democracy.

Nevertheless, it remains true that the East European revolutions were the result of an alliance between intellectuals and the working class. The turning point came when the middle strata – even segments of the privileged *nomenklatura* – lost faith in the system. This was a gradual process, starting long before 1989; during the 1980–81 Polish crisis every third member of the communist party joined the Solidarity opposition movement, and the Hungarian and Czechoslovak crises of 1956 and 1968 witnessed large-scale defections from the ranks of the ruling parties. This loss of faith was particularly debilitating due to the nature of the ruling parties; by reference to Marxist-Leninist dogma, they defined themselves as leading parties, but now increasingly found themselves in a position where they could command the support, or even the compliance, of but a minority of the population. Without the backing of the Soviet Union, their fate was sealed.

As Linz and Stepan point out in their recent book (1996), a transition to democracy is not everything; democracy also has to be consolidated. A consolidated democracy, they argue, requires that five arenas are represented in the state, and that these arenas interact and mutually reinforce one another, creating a situation where democracy is not challenged – 'in a phrase, democracy has become the "only game in town"' (Linz and Stepan 1996, 5).

The five arenas are as follows: civil society, political society, economic society, rule of law, and state bureaucracy. These arenas will be familiar from previous standard works on democracy (cf. Putnam 1993) and their relevance is beyond doubt. It is, however, an open question how the arena concept can be used in systematic comparative studies. How much political consensus among the ruling elites is needed and what level of economic regulation is acceptable? How many independent voluntary associations, and what kind of voluntary associations, are required to make democracy work? Clearly, not only the number of organizations, but also their quality is relevant. Analyses of transitional societies must also take into account the fact that what is functional for crushing a communist system is not necessarily functional for consolidating democracy.

Cleavage Politics

This volume is based on the assumption that cleavages matter. They structure the behaviour of voters and parties alike and they determine the number of parties and the nature of partisan conflict; they are of obvious importance for the way democracy works. Indeed, the cleavage concept is crucial to the study of parties, party systems and regime change. And like many key concepts, it is subject to many different interpretations.

In their classic account, Lipset and Rokkan (1967) portray parties as the principal agents of transforming societal conflicts into political divisions. This is in contrast to the more traditional representation of parties as 'outgrowths' of social forces (cf. Knutsen and Scarbrough 1995). Chemists use the term 'cleavage' to depict the tendency of crystals to split in certain directions, and Lipset and Rokkan argue that political parties translate group interests to political oppositions by crystallizing and articulating conflicting interests, constructing alliances, setting up organizational networks, and devising electoral strategies. Thus, 'cleavages do not translate themselves into party oppositions as a matter of course' (Lipset and Rokkan 1967, 26).

Lipset and Rokkan identified four classical cleavages in Western Europe: those of state versus church and centre versus periphery, which arose during the era of nation-building, and those of land versus industry and employers versus workers, arising from the industrial revolution. These cleavage dimensions have since been reformulated and empirically operationalized with reference to late-20th-century society. The church/state cleavage is now commonly recast as secularized versus religious, and the employer/worker cleavage as middle-class versus working-class, while the centre/periphery cleavage captures resistance to the state – often based on ethno-religious conflicts – and the urban/rural cleavage is recast as sectoral conflicts.

Cleavages go beyond issues, conflicts and interests of a purely economic or social nature. They are in a sense more fundamental, as they are founded on culture, value orientations and ideological insulation; they constitute deep-seated socio-structural conflicts with political significance. A cleavage is rooted in a persistent social division which enables one to identify certain groups in society: members of an ethnic minority, believers of a particular denomination, residents of a particular region. A cleavage also engages a certain set of values common to members of the group; group members share the same value orientation. And finally, cleavages are institutionalized in the form of political parties and other associational groups.

It follows from Rokkan's argument that the 'freezing' of a party structure needs a coupling to the cleavage structure. Electoral behaviour becomes more predictable when, and only when, parties find voters and voters find parties corresponding to their respective positions in the same cleavage structure.

Indeed, the political quietude in Western Europe during the 1950s and 1960s indicated that the party systems had frozen along the lines of the cleavage structure. Conversely, the much higher degree of electoral mobility and emergence of new party-political forces thereafter – an 'unfreezing' of party systems – can be seen as the result of the erosion of old cleavage lines and the emergence of new ones. Some studies even argue that cleavage politics in the West is in the process of being replaced by 'new politics', anchored not in cleavages but in more fluid relationships between social groups, value orientations and party preferences (Inglehart 1984). In fact, an appropriate description of 'new politics' would be 'politics without cleavages' or 'post-cleavage conflicts' (Knutsen and Scarbrough 1995, 497).

Eastern Europe emerged from socialism with what Wessels and Klingemann (1994) have described as 'flattened societies'. As a result of the communist regimes' levelling and modernizing policies they were much less socio-politically structured than the Western democracies or, for that matter, the pre-communist societies. The low level of socioeconomic differentiation had the consequence that citizens' party preferences after 1989 were largely determined by 'cultural politics' rather than by interests related to their individual positions in the social structure. It has indeed been argued that the political parties which operated in the period immediately following the political transition may have articulated only theoretical interests of social groups that did not exist at the time. Class certainly was a weak predictor of electoral behaviour, far behind the factors of age, education, union membership and, in particular, religion.

The volatility of electoral behaviour since the transition from communism seems to confirm the notion that the class cleavage remains weakly articulated. This does not, however, imply that the East European societies have moved directly from socialism to a 'new politics' mode. Indeed, the predominance of cultural politics over interest politics at the early stages of transition seems to testify to the existence of fairly strong cleavages particularly in the centre/periphery, ethnic, secular/religious and, in some cases, urban/rural dimensions. As indicated by the country-specific Chapters 3–11, the East European parties which have managed to garner stable support have often done so by articulating and exploiting these cleavages.

The country-specific chapters in this volume will provide an overview of how cleavages have made themselves felt after communism. Of particular interest is the extent to which there is a link between the cleavage structure and the emerging party systems. As mentioned above, Rokkan has pointed out that the link between parties and cleavages is crucial for the development of stable party systems. The following chapters will demonstrate that most, if not all, East European countries are still far from having established a cleavage-party linkage to dominate the electoral arena. The party systems in the region are still in a state of flux, and electoral behaviour is characterized by a great deal of volatility. This makes the political systems vulnerable to various kinds of populist movements, including those of an anti-democratic hue. Even so, a historical perspective tells us that the prospects for consolidated democracy have never been better in Eastern Europe than they are today.

REFERENCES

Brzezinski, Zbigniew (1989), *The Grand Failure: The Birth of Communism in the Twentieth Century*, New York, Praeger.

Di Palma, Giuseppe (1990), *To Craft Democracies: An Essay in Democratic Transitions*, Berkeley, University of California Press.

Drakulic, Slavenka (1994), 'Lav Story: Romania's dirty little secret' *The New Republic*, 25 April

Garton Ash, Timothy (1991), *The Uses of Adversity*, London, Granta and Penguin.

Geddes, Barbara (1990), 'Democratic institutions as a bargain among self-interested politicians', paper presented at the *APSA Annual Meeting*, San Francisco.

Hellén, Tomas (1996), *Shaking Hands with the Past: Origins of the Political Right in Central Europe*, Helsinki, The Finnish Society of Sciences and Letters and the Finnish Academy of Science and Letters.

Inglehart, Ronald (1984), 'The Changing Structure of Political Cleavages in Western Societies', in R.J. Dalton, S.C. Flanagan and P.A. Beck, eds., *The Electoral Change in Advanced Industrial Democracies: Realignment or Dealignment?*, Princeton, Princeton University Press.

Kaplan, Robert, ed., (1997), *Freedom in the World: The Annual Survey of Political Rights and Civil Liberties 1996–1997*, New York, Freedom House 1997.

Knutsen, Oddbjörn and Elinor Scarbrough (1995) , 'Cleavage Politics', in Jan W. van Deth and Elinor Scarbrough, eds., *The Impact of Values*, Oxford, Oxford University Press.

Lijphart, Arend (1992), 'Democratization and Constitutional Choices in Czecho-Slovakia, Hungary, and Poland, 1989–1991', in György Szoboszlai, ed., *Flying Blind: Emerging Democracies in East-Central Europe*, Budapest, Hungarian Political Science Association

Lipset, Seymour Martin and Stein Rokkan (1967), 'Introduction', in Lipset, Seymour Martin and Stein Rokkan, eds., *Party Systems and Voter Alignments*, New York, Free Press.

Linz, Juan and Alfred Stepan (1996), *Problems of Democratic Transition and Consolidation: Southern Europe, South America and Post-Communist Europe*, Baltimore and London, Johns Hopkins University Press.

O'Donnell, Guillermo and Philippe Schmitter (1986), *Transitions from Authoritarian Rule: Comparative Perspectives*, Baltimore, Johns Hopkins University Press.

Przeworski, Adam (1991), *Democracy and the Market: Political and Economic Reforms in Eastern Europe and Latin America*, Cambridge, Cambridge University Press.

Putnam, Robert D. (1993), *Making Democracy Work: Civic Traditions in Modern Italy*, Princeton, Princeton University Press.

Rokkan, Stein (1970), *Citizens, Elections, Parties: Approaches to the Comparative Study of the Process of Development*, Oslo, Universitetsforlaget.

—— (1975), 'Dimensions of State Formation and Nation-Building: A Possible Paradigm for Research on Variations within Europe', in Charles Tilly, ed., *The Formation of National States in Europe*, Princeton, Princeton University Press, 562–600.

Rupnik, Jacques (1989), *The Other Europe*, London, Weidenfeld and Nicholson.

Schöpflin, George (1993), *Politics in Eastern Europe 1945–92*, Oxford, Blackwell.

Wessels, Bernhard and Hans-Dieter Klingemann (1994), 'Democratic transformation and the prerequisites of democratic opposition in East and Central Europe', Wissenschaftszentrum Berlin für Sozialforschung, FS III, 94–201.

2. The Challenge of History in Eastern Europe

Tomas Hellén, Sten Berglund and Frank Aarebrot

In the past century, Central and Eastern Europe has experienced three major political transformations: in 1917–19, after the First World War; in 1944–48; after the Second World War; and in 1989–91, after the demise of the Soviet Union and the end of the Cold War. External forces and sources have played a major role in all three of them, but the transformations were clearly also a product of domestic divisions and cleavages.

This chapter sets out to identify social divisions and political cleavages at work in Eastern Europe throughout the 20th century. Some of these divisions and cleavages have their roots in the individual societies, others are linked to the broad international environment; the urban/rural cleavage would be an example of the former type; the divide between communists and their opponents highlights the latter family of cleavages. The roots of the cleavages are, however, of limited significance for our analysis. Our ambition is to describe the full set of cleavages at various critical junctures in the history of Eastern Europe, for the additional purpose of evaluating the prospects for democratic consolidation in the most recent attempt at democracy in the region. Much has changed in Eastern Europe over the past hundred years, but this should not make us oblivious to the importance of historical heritage. Indeed, history sometimes rebounds with a vengeance when and where least expected. Social and political changes of a large magnitude often include an initial element of overshooting that tends to be corrected in the long run. The French Revolution is, of course, a classic case in point, but so too is the gradual adaptation of the Soviet puppet regimes in Central and Eastern Europe to their respective national constituencies. History clearly matters and must be taken into account by those who build political institutions and by those who analyse them.

The present chapter is structured first to provide the reader with a rough overview of the foremost social divisions and political cleavages in Eastern Europe between, as well as after, the two World Wars. This predominantly historical section serves as a background for one more analytically cast sub-chapter on the prospects for consolidated democracy in Eastern Europe today.

The Imperial Heritage

The First World War (1914–18) resulted in a cataclysmic shift in the power structure on the European continent. The German, Habsburg, Russian and Ottoman empires came out of the war fatally weakened, and as the victorious Western allies – the United States in particular – propagated the idea of national self-determination, the 'captive nations' of these empires were able to break free of their empires into independence, statehood and the first of three experiments in democracy thus far.

Already, in the mid-19th century, the quest for statehood and independence was attached to calls for social regeneration: in less-developed areas, by demands for land reform and an eradication of feudal and semi-feudal structures; in the more developed ones, by rising middle classes and industrial working classes. Thus, socioeconomic conflicts and cleavages were often directly linked to ethnic and cultural ones; indeed, most mainstream theories of nationalism see it primarily as a function of different aspects of modernization (Deutsch 1953; Gellner 1983; Hobsbawm 1990). In any case, both nationalism as an ideology and the nation state as a mode of societal organization are incarnations of modernity.

The political culture in the newly independent states was strongly marked by the legacy of the past. The region, taken as a whole, had been an interface between East and West since at least the 10th century, when it became part of Christian European civilization. But with the onset of proto-industrialization in the 15th and 16th centuries, the distance to the European core again began to broaden. Since then, the bulk of Eastern Europe has remained relegated to the periphery or at least the semi-periphery of the European economic system; only some parts (in particular, Bohemia) have occasionally been within the core (Wallerstein 1974, 99). There is no doubt that all of Eastern Europe has been part of the broad pattern of European civilization and culture for at least a millennium, but 'slightly differently, less intensively, less fully' than the West, 'with the result that East European participation in the European experience was only partial' (Schöpflin 1993, 11). In political terms, Eastern Europe has been a transitional zone between the Western tradition of division of power and the Eastern tradition of concentration of power. This fault-line coincides with that between Western and Eastern Christianity; the Eastern tradition is at its strongest in territories once under Ottoman rule, and the Western tradition is strongest in areas marked by Lutheranism.

Figure 2.1: The main historical religious cleavage lines in Eastern Europe

The history of Eastern Europe in the modern era is in many respects the history of the great empires. But these empires were different in character. By the late 19th century, the German and Habsburg empires had most of the trappings of a modern *Rechtsstaat,* and although they were far from being model democracies, civil society and representative democracy were developing fast. After 1871, Prussia developed into a great German power based on the mono-national principle, but within the Habsburg empire, nation-building accelerated during the decades prior to the First World War, just like state-building in the case of Hungary after the 1867 *Ausgleich* or Compromise with Austria. In contrast, the territories once subjected to the Russian and Ottoman empires reached independence almost totally void of state- and nation-building traditions.

This dichotomy between the German and Habsburg empires and their Russian and Ottoman counterparts, neatly coincides with the East/West fault-line between Central and Eastern Europe. The Western group shares traditions of Roman law, feudalism and relatively early national awakening; the Eastern group has a Byzantine heritage and a lack of strong feudal traditions, enabling ancient local authority relationships such as kinship and clientelism to survive longer. This tendency is stronger in the South than in the North. The North/South dichotomy is reinforced by the strength and autonomy of political authority versus religious leadership. The North/ South dimension separates the Protestant and substantially secularized states from the Counter-Reformation Catholic states, non-secularized Orthodox states, and the Muslim states (Berglund and Aarebrot 1997).

The Baltic states are characterized by their position at the crossroads of German, Russian, Polish and Scandinavian culture. Nevertheless, they are not a culturally homogenous group. In the late pre-modern and early modern era, the Lithuanian heartland was part of the Polish–Lithuanian commonwealth, at times ruling over vast tracts of land stretching down to the Black Sea; thus it has a tradition of itself being an imperial centre. Estonia and most of Latvia, on the other hand, have no pre-20th-century traditions of independence. They were ruled by the Teutonic Order, Denmark, Poland, Sweden and eventually by aristocratic Germanic agents of the Russian Tsar. This gave them a more Western cultural tradition, and a mainly German nobility and bourgeoisie, as opposed to Lithuania's mainly Polish and Russian landowners and Jewish artisan, merchant and professional classes. For these same historical reasons, Latvia and Estonia are predominantly Protestant while Catholicism is dominant in Lithuania. In linguistic terms, however, the cleavage runs otherwise: Estonian is a Fenno-Ugric language distinct from Latvian and Lithuanian, which both represent relatively distant branches of the Baltic family of languages.

The Structure of Conflicts in the Inter-War Era

The states formed in Eastern Europe as a result of the First World War did not settle once and for all the issue of state- and nation-building. In fact, in many cases they were as ethnically diverse as, or even more than, the empires from which they emerged. In the inter-war era (1919–39), all East European states had significant national minorities and/or substantial diasporas. Problems of state-building and nation-building were thus at the very top of the political agenda. Topics such as democracy, the rule of law and the distribution of wealth also played a prominent role in the Central and East European inter-war political debate, but the emphasis was more frequently than not on the survival of state and nation in what was felt to be a hostile environment. The odds were, in that sense, tilted against the survival of the new democracies, and by the end of the inter-war era Czechoslovakia was the only democratic survivor.

In Czechoslovakia, the Czech core nation constituted less than half of the total population; and the arguably artificial 'Czecho–Slovak' nationality added up to only two-thirds in the 1920 and 1930 official censuses. In Yugoslavia, similar figures applied to the core Serb and 'Serbo-Croat' nationalities, respectively; all in all, no less than fourteen different languages were widely spoken in the State of the Southern Slavs. Moreover, of Poland's inter-war population, fewer than 70 per cent were ethnic Poles, and of Romania's, only about three-quarters could be defined as ethnic Romanians – what constitutes a 'Pole', 'Romanian', 'Macedonian' etc., has, of course, always been the subject of both controversy and manipulation (cf. Rothschild 1974, 1989; Crampton and Crampton 1996). Even in the most ethnically homogenous states in the region – the Baltic states, Albania, Bulgaria and Hungary – the proportion of the core populations were only in the 80–90 per cent range during the 1920s and 1930s (*Table 2.5*).

The ethnic mosaic also had a territorial dimension. In particular, the entire Hungarian polity was shell-shocked by the loss of no less than two-thirds of the territory and three-fifths of the population ruled from Budapest during the Habsburg era. While rump Hungary was by and large ethnically homogenous, one Magyar in three was left outside the country's borders – in Romania, Czechoslovakia and Yugoslavia – as territories were transferred to her neighbours by the Western allies of the First World War. This was done partly on strategic grounds, but also as a result of the Magyars' bad record on minority rights and because Hungary – like Austria proper, but as opposed to the Slavic nations of the Dual Monarchy – was considered a defeated aggressor nation. Not surprisingly, revanchist feelings became the determining force in Hungarian politics from the very outset of independence. Poland, which almost miraculously re-emerged as a sovereign state after a hundred and twenty years of partition, had territorial grievances with all her neighbours, some of which were settled by force during a confusing and violent process reminiscent of the conflicts that erupted after the break-up of Yugoslavia in 1991. All of Bulgaria's borders were disputed, and the post-1920 demarcation line between Lithuania and Poland cut right through an ethnically very mixed area; as did the borders between Poland and the USSR, between Lithuania and Germany, between Yugoslavia and Italy and between Albania and Yugoslavia. Czechoslovakia did, thanks to successful lobbying among the Western powers, hit a territorial jackpot and walked off with an extravagant settlement. In Eastern Europe, Czechoslovakia was alone in being solely on the defensive when it came to territorial conflicts.

All the new states in Eastern Europe, save Bulgaria and Albania, retained substantial and/or influential German-speaking minorities – even when it came to the exclusively German-speaking areas in Austria and Bohemia directly bordering on Germany proper, the Western allies had refused to apply the nationality principle, since that would have left the *Reich* bigger and stronger than before the war. Jewish minorities were also present in great numbers throughout the region, Estonia, Bulgaria and Albania excepted. Polish Jewry counted about three million, equal to 9–10 per cent of the total population; of Carpatho-Ukraine's population, some 12 per cent were Jewish; of Lithuania's, 7 per cent; of Hungary's, 6.5 per cent; of Slovakia's, Romania's, and Latvia's, 3–5 per cent. With no outside power to protect them, the Jews were particularly vulnerable to the rising tide of xenophobia. Most countries in the area introduced anti-Jewish legislation, such as quotas in higher education, during the 1930s.

Given the ethnic mix, the regimes were faced with two alternatives: either create multi-ethnic, consociational states (Lijphart 1968; 1980) or embark on a policy of national assimilation and/or exclusion. All eventually went for the latter alternative – even Czechoslovakia, where escalating German, Magyar and Slovak separatism and Czech hegemonic ambitions dashed Tomás Masaryk's hopes that the democratic process would eventually bring all ethnic components into a political nation. All over Eastern Europe, national and state consolidation were seen as prerequisites for each other.

The imposed policies of ethnic integration and ethnic exclusion had much to do with the absence of autonomous sub-system structures. During the Habsburg era, the cultural and linguistic integration of Jews, Slavs and Romanians into the politically dominant German and Magyar communities was welcomed and encouraged, while imperial Germany and Russia used much stiffer methods to impose their hegemony over Poland and in the Baltic states. Because this process encouraged both the integrators and those subjected to integration to perceive political structures and conflicts in national rather than in economic, social or class terms, genuinely autonomous structures had experienced great difficulties in forming. Here, the imperial centre of Hungary and the economically more advanced Bohemia and Moravia proved exceptions: already, by the late 19th century the Czechs had won the ethnic struggle for hegemony in Prague and Moravia. Long thereafter, the local German nobility remained in control in Estonia and Latvia, where national awakening was slow to commence; Germans, Magyars, Jews, Greeks, Italians and Armenians dominated urban life in the Balkans; Slovakia was ruled as any province of Hungary; and Poland was administered from the imperial centres of St Petersburg, Berlin and Vienna.

If the peace settlements and establishment of new states were intended to ease communal tension, defuse national conflicts and, in general, set the successor states on a path towards democracy and prosperity, this failed miserably. Even though national self-determination was a straightforward enough concept in theory, its practical application to Eastern Europe as things stood in 1919, created an abundance of new intra-state and inter-state conflict dimensions. The nation-states created were far from perfect, with borders designed to accommodate the victors and their protégés, and very little protection for the minorities, whose calls for cultural autonomy were considered seditious by the new ruling ethnic groups. Germans and Magyars in Czechoslovakia, Ukrainians, Germans and Jews in Poland, and Magyars, Jews and Ukrainians in Romania were among those who experienced harassment or even persecution (Tismaneanu 1993, 6).

In newly-independent Poland, Marshal Józef Piłsudski and the moderate left championed a multi-ethnic Polish state, but were, however, not prepared to grant any significant amount of autonomy to the minorities, particularly not to some five million ethnic Ukrainians and 1.5–2 million Belorussians who lived in the Eastern borderlands, which nationalist Poles perceived as the bastion of Western Christianity, the *przedmurze*. The failure to create a political state led to the eventual victory of Roman Dmowski's vision of a state founded on national kinship. President Beneš envisaged that Czechoslovakia would develop into an 'Eastern Switzerland', but others saw only a mini-replica of the Habsburg concoction – the difference being that Czechoslovakia, like the other successor states, lacked the Habsburg supra-national ideology which helped national minorities to feel included. And even for the ethnic groups that had not been content with that prospect, the imperial policy of ethnic favouritism had at least been more reversible than that of the successor states constructed around nation-building ethnic majorities.

The imperfect application of the nationality principle guaranteed that nationalism would remain the dominant issue in inter-war Eastern Europe.

The widespread irredentism encouraged states to intervene in their neighbours' affairs to protect minorities belonging to their own core nationality, and, as a counter-reaction, caused the host states to attempt forceful integration of their minorities, or even to deny their very existence. Social policies were strongly influenced by attempts at ethnic assimilation, economic policies drifted towards economic nationalism and competitive striving for autarky, and attempts at land reform were primarily motivated by the glory of expropriating 'alien' landlords. Moreover, resilient irredentist tension pre-empted the development of regional political and economic co-operation, and enabled Germany and the USSR, the revisionist great powers, to exploit the situation to their own advantage.

Ethnic cleavages often coincided with religious ones. Multi-ethnic and multi-denominational Poland was, despite its secular constitution, for all intents and purposes a state of and for Roman Catholics, just as Romania and Bulgaria were states of and for Orthodox believers. In Yugoslavia, an Eastern Orthodox dynasty ruled over not only Catholic Croatia and Slovenia but also over predominantly Muslim areas in Bosnia, Herzegovina and Southern Serbia. In Czechoslovakia, Slovak dissatisfaction was fuelled by the strong Catholic heritage, as opposed to the Protestant or secular outlook of the politically dominant Prague and Bohemian elites. Latvia was an amalgamation of three historical regions of which Livonia and Courland were mainly Protestant and Latgale mainly Catholic.

Apart from the ethno-religious cleavage, conflicts between the centres and the peripheries were also rife, due to the centralizing ambitions of the new elites. Czechoslovakia, where Prague was pitted against the rest of the country is a case in point. Hungary was divided between cosmopolitan Budapest and the countryside with feudal estates and subsistence farmers. In Romania, the anti-Magyar and anti-Jewish policies were complemented by Walachian chauvinism. Polish political life in the inter-war era was characterized by tensions between the formerly Russian areas, which provided most of the bureaucracy and military officers, and the previously German and Austrian territories, which dominated industry and commerce. In Yugoslavia, the relationship between politically dominant Serbia and the economically more advanced Northwest was of a similar nature.

The ethnic cleavage
Party formation in immediate post-independence Eastern Europe was co-determined by ethnicity, class, ideology and religion, but as Table 2.1 indicates, ethnicity was the defining cleavage, to which other cleavages – including left/right – were subordinated. Typical in inter-war Eastern Europe was the existence of parallel party systems for each ethnic group, a tendency which was reinforced by constitutional arrangements which had

Table 2.1: Relevant parties and their main ethnic bases

	Social Democratic	Agrarian	Liberal	Conservative	Nationalist/ Ethnic Defence
Estonia					
Estonian	x	x	x	x	x
Russian					x
German					x
Swedish		x		x	x
Latvia					
Latvian unitary	x	x	x	x	
Latgalian	x	x	x	x	x
Semgalian		x			x
Russian	x	x		x	x
German					x
Jewish	x				x
Polish	x				x
Lithuania					
Lithuanian	x	x	x	x	x
Polish	x	x			x
German	x				x
Jewish	x				x
Poland					
Polish	x	x	x	x	x
Ukrainian	x	x			x
Belorussian	x	x			x
German	x	x	x	x	x
Jewish	x	x	x		x
Czechoslovakia					
Czecho-Slovak	x				
Czech		x	x	x	
Slovak		x		x	x
German	x	x	x	x	x
Magyar	x	x	x	x	x
Ruthenian					x
Jewish					x
Polish					x
Hungary					
Magyar	x	x	x	x	x
Romania					
Romanian	x	x	x	x	x
Magyar	x	x	x	x	x
Jewish	x				x
German	x				x
Bulgaria					
Bulgarian	x	x	x	x	x

paved the way for extreme multi-partyism, particularly in the northern half of the region. The matrix depicts the party systems classified according to ethnicity and party families. The parties included in the matrix may have operated for only a short period in time or only as voting lists or parliamentary clubs.

As Derek Urwin (1980, 195) has noted:

[w]e find in these imperfectly integrated European states with substantial minorities that either the ethnic cleavage coincided with other cleavages, especially religion, or that the linguistic groups generated complete party systems of their own. This is generally the case in Eastern Europe, examples being the Germans and Magyars in Czechoslovakia, and the Jews and Ukrainians in Poland. These sub-cultural party systems often included an agrarian party.

Indeed, agrarian parties were almost universally ethnically based (the Yugoslav Peasant Union was one exception), as were many of the liberal and conservative parties, and – for obvious reasons – the radical nationalist formations. But fragmentation according to ethnicity also applied to the left. The social democrats, faced by the bewildering ethnic array of the Austro–Hungarian empire, had already by the 1890s abandoned the territorial basis of nationality for a 'personal' principle. By the end of the First World War, the social democratic parties in the German, Habsburg and Russian empires had formally split into their national branches, and the disintegration continued within the newly independent states.

The main exception to the ethnic principle of party organization was the communist movement, which remained staunchly internationalist. This was only natural, since the one defining moment of the Marxist movement was the outbreak of the First World War, when the overwhelming majority of European social democrats rallied behind the respective governments and only a minority remained committed to supra-nationalism. In 1942–43, however, the communist strategy changed, and the communist parties founded or co-founded 'national' or 'patriotic' fronts which proved able to attract broad public support.

Table 2.1 strongly suggests an extremely high level of ethnic compartmentalization and political fragmentation particularly in the Northern tier of East European countries. In Czechoslovakia, there were moderate socialist, agrarian, liberal, Christian democratic and conservative parties catering to almost every single ethnic group. By way of example, Poland had a total of 92 registered parties by 1925, about half of which were ethnically Polish; in Latvia, ethnic fragmentation resulted in separate party systems for Latvians, Russians, Germans, Poles and Jews, while regional fragmentation prompted the emergence of parochial Latgalian and Semgalian parties (cf. Crampton and Crampton 1996). In Yugoslavia, the party system was also structured along ethnic lines, with the National Radical Party being dominant in Serbia proper and the Democratic Party among Serbs elsewhere, and the Croat People's Peasant Party, the Slovene People's Party and the Yugoslav Muslim Organization dominant within their respective ethnic constituencies; over 40 parties participated in the November 1920 election for the constituent assembly.

The new states invariably chose or were endowed with formally Western-style constitutions, albeit that Bulgaria and Romania were monarchies since the 19th century and Yugoslavia and Hungary emerged as kingdoms in 1918–19. The constitutional formats were conducive to extreme multi-partyism. The problem was that these new, modern political systems largely had no base of autonomous spheres and power-centres. The nation-builders inevitably had to turn to the state, and paradoxically the state thus came to perform or organize many of the functions of civil society. These attempts to create a civil society from above were not entirely unsuccessful, but they also resulted in a high degree of state control of social and political interaction. The process of enforced social modernization formed the basis of the statism often mentioned as the main characteristic of inter-war Central and Eastern Europe. And even when the state did succeed in building structures of civil society, it often proved unwilling to relinquish control.

The Balkans were a special case. Bulgaria, Serbia and Romania had been ruled by local proxies of the Ottoman empire, and when independence arrived by instalments beginning in 1817, they simply cut their remaining ties with Constantinople. Contrary to their tight hold at the state level, the Turks allowed local governments considerable autonomy. After conquering an area, the Ottomans preferred to rule through intermediaries. Under the *millet* system, the Turks eliminated any residual local secular government and replaced it with a religious authority of local origin, or at least of local confession, with civic responsibilities. In the Balkans, the Orthodox Church came to serve as the Ottomans' agent for regional and local government, and the Church became strongly identified with the Ottoman state. When nationalism began to emerge within the region, non-Orthodox groups saw the Orthodox Church as an obstacle to their ethnic and nationalist goals. Religion thus tended to reinforce ethnic differences, exacerbating social divisions and complicating political development (cf. Jelavich and Jelavich 1965; Jelavich 1983a; 1983b).

As the Ottomans had eradicated the local aristocracies, the Balkan elites were not landed but rather military and clerical, and relative late-comers to political power, heavily reliant on the state and on clientelist relationships.

Albania was even worse off than the other Balkan countries when it became autonomous in 1913, as it had only a rudimentary state administration; the country was in practice ruled by tribal structures dominated by the Muslim clans of the north and was reduced to an economic and political client of Italy.

As George Schöpflin has argued (1993, 24–25), the attempts by the weakly grounded semi-authoritarian or fully fledged dictatorships – in the Balkans as well as elsewhere in Eastern Europe – to build loyalty to the state through the promotion of nationalism raised two problems: it left open or exacerbated the national issue, and nationalism as a political doctrine provided answers to very few questions of political organization and the distribution of power.

> It created strong identities and a sense of belonging to the state for members of the dominant group, but said next to nothing about political structures, the resolution of conflicts of interests, the allocation of resources and values, participation and representation, i.e. the day-to-day problems of political, economic and social life. [...] The comparative vagueness of the nationalist message, together with its emotional intensity, produced a somewhat contradictory result. East European nations in the inter-war era reached a fairly high state of national consciousness of their political identities as members of a nation and as those excluded as non-members. At one and the same time the implicit promise of equality and justice, encapsulated in the nationalist message, was left unfulfilled, with inevitable frustration and resentment at the social-political closures enforced against society by its rulers.

From fragmentation to strongman rule

The institution of the government party operating in a pseudo-parliamentary system was common to all the post-independence polities of the successor states: the governing parties (or coalitions) were incarnations of the bureaucracies and the technocratic and military elites. Prime ministers tended to emerge from the administrative elite and then proceeded to 'elect' a parliament to serve them. This system was, however, hegemonic, not totalitarian, and parliamentary opposition both on the left and on the right – even radical opposition – was tolerated as long as it did not threaten the fundamental stability of the regime in power. Hungary was a case in point: the ruling Unity Party was an instrument for administration rather than an association of like-minded people, and as the electoral system – with suffrage restricted to less than 30 per cent and an open ballot in rural areas – virtually guaranteed it a permanent majority, most of the formal requirements of democratic rule could be observed. Likewise, Romania and Bulgaria had vocal parliaments, but their function was to legitimize the governments designated by the monarchs. In Poland and the Baltic countries, the representative systems also took on a façade character after the post-independence constitutions, modelled on Weimar and the French Third Republic, had shown the dangers of extreme multi-partyism.

Another effect of the marriage between the bureaucratic and administrative élite and the government was the personal, rather than ideological, nature of conflicts and of party loyalties. The influence of informal 'old-boy networks' – such as the Polish and Czech Legionnaires, the Estonian Freedom Fighters, the Lithuanian Light Infantry Association, the IMRO in Bulgaria and Macedonia – sometimes resembling secret societies, marked the clientelistic nature of political loyalties and encouraged opportunistic defections and sudden shifts in coalitions.

In Eastern Europe of 1900–39, 'governments did not lose elections' (Schöpflin 1993, 12). The exceptions, Hungary in 1905 and Bulgaria in 1932, both resulted from divisions within the elite rather than being expressions of the popular will. Strong state control of the administrative machinery enabled the elites, when united, to produce the desired election outcomes. But while there was a strong element of façade politics, a large amount of outward and genuine respect for constitutional probity was observed; sensitivity to international opinion also put a lid on the most outrageous authoritarian ambitions.

The authoritarian systems which emerged after the experiment with Western-style parliamentarism were often based on a similar ideological cocktail as in Poland after 1935, when the 'Government of Colonels' united the rival forces of left and right into the Camp of National Unity: '40 per cent nationalism, 30 per cent social radicalism, 20 per cent agrarianism, and 10 per cent anti-Semitism' (Wandycz 1992, 226). In many cases one could add technocratism, as the modernization of industry and infrastructure was hailed as the programmatic solution to the problems of the states and the regimes, regardless of the social mobilization which rapid industrialization always entails (Rothschild 1974, 71–2). The rise of fascism in Italy and Nazism in Germany provided East European strongmen and nationalists with an outside blueprint for authoritarianism which they were increasingly eager to embrace – but only up to a point. In fact, the authoritarianism of the 1930s was as much directed against the radical, mass-based right as against the Marxist or utopian–agrarian left. The presidential coups in Poland and the Baltic states and the tightening of the Balkan royal dictatorships were prompted by – or at least said to be prompted by – the threat from anti-regime fascist or fascist-style movements: Estonia had its Freedom Fighters, Poland its *Falanga*; Czechoslovakia had the (Hlinka's) Slovak People's Party, the Czech National Party and the Sudeten subsidiary of the *Reich* NSDAP; Hungary the Arrow Cross; Romania the Iron Cross.

By the mid-1930s, the principle of parliamentary rule had been discarded and replaced by strongman rule almost throughout Eastern Europe (*Table 2.2*). Czechoslovakia's experiment in democracy proved the most success-ful; despite strong centrifugal forces, it had a functioning parliamentary system, rule of law and separation of powers until the 1938 Munich agreement – as a result of Masaryk's and Beneš's vision that social and economic development would pave the way for ethnic harmony. But even in Czechoslovakia, the political system was rigid, bureaucratic and non-participatory: in the inter-war era, the country was dominated by the *Pětka* or 'Committee of Five', a loose cartel of five major Czech-dominated parties (Zeman 1976; Bankowicz 1994).

Table 2.2: The breakdown of democracy

Country	Date	Strongman	Authoritarian orientation
Estonia	1934	Konstantin Päts	Centrist, corporatist
Latvia	1926	Kārlis Ulmanis	Centrist, corporatist
Lithuania	1926	Antanas Smetona	Corporatist, semi-fascist
Poland	1926	Józef Piłsudski	Initially left-oriented; then rightist and nationalist
Czechoslovakia			
Czech lands	1939		Corporatist, modelled on Italy
Slovakia	1938	Jozef Tiso	Clerico-Fascist, German puppet
Hungary	March 1919	Béla Kun	Soviet Republic
	August 1919	Miklós Horthy	Reactionary, semi-authoritarian
	November 1944	Ferenc Szálasi	Fascist, German puppet
Yugoslavia	1928	King Alexander	Royal coup
Romania	1920	King Ferdinand, Alexandru Averescu	Royal coup, fascist-leaning military junta
Bulgaria	1934	King Boris	Royal coup

The argument that the ruling elites of inter-war Eastern Europe were pursuing state-building rather than nation-building may seem surprising, given their exploitation of nationalism. But as Józef Piłsudski put it para-phrasing Massimo d'Azeglio, one of the founding fathers of the Italian state: 'It is the state which makes the nation and not the nation the state'; the first task of the rulers of the newly independent countries was to consolidate state structures, so as to be able to counter external and internal threats. Moreover, these ruling elites did not emerge from nowhere; there was indeed a marked continuity of the state-building elites, as witnessed by the strong military and aristocratic element.

The elites were socially and economically conservative, and the truly revolutionary force in predominantly rural Eastern Europe before, during and after the First World War was the peasantry – not the working class.

There were only pockets of industrialization in inter-war Eastern Europe – Bohemia, Silesia, Warsaw, Łódź, Riga, parts of Budapest, the Romanian oil district – and worker radicalism on issues other than wages and working conditions was ill-supported by the shallow roots of the working class.

Modernization and the rural problem

The elites were aware of the dangers of rural backwardness, and the main concern of the state-builders became the issue of how to counter it through accelerated social modernization. There were land reforms and ambitious industrialization schemes in almost every East European country, and the depression of the 1930s prompted many of the regimes to further step up modernization. Poland built from scratch the gigantic Gdynia harbour complex, and in 1935 introduced a six-year plan which called for state intervention, capital regulation, nationalization of key industries and the creation of a Central Industrial Area to the east of Warsaw. The Hungarian government also experimented with Polish-style state planning and micro-management, spearheaded by the armament and investment programme centred on the city of Györ between Budapest and Vienna. Even so, the efforts at socioeconomic modernization focused on rural life, which was characterized by insularity, rigid structures and a negative egalitarianism which sought to equalize downwards (Schöpflin 1993, 26). Agriculture, the dominant livelihood in Eastern Europe, was backward and unproductive, and at subsistence level, almost everywhere.

The national independence project was initiated by the urban elites, and the majority of the East European peasantry remained deeply sceptical of the state-building efforts. Only a small portion of the peasantry was entrepreneurial, within the sphere of the money economy and aware of the possibilities and limitations of politics. The overwhelming majority, with very small or no land-holdings, either only occasionally or never entered into commodity production. It was deeply suspicious of the state, which was seen as a manipulator of the market or as an agent of the alien, parasitic 'city' that depleted the countryside of its resources. This was the world of the *Gemeinschaft*, resisting the emerging *Gesellschaft* (Schöpflin 1993, 26–8). In some of the cases, the urban/rural cleavage coincided with the ethno/religious one, as in Eastern Poland where the peasantry was mostly Orthodox or Uniate Catholic Ukrainian and Belorussian, but the landlords Roman Catholic Poles; also in Transylvania and the Banat, where the Orthodox Romanians were concentrated in rural areas and German and Magyar Catholics and Protestants dominated the towns and cities; or in Slovakia with its staunchly Catholic Slovak peasantry pitted against Jewish town-dwellers, largely Protestant Magyar landowners and the secular Czech political elite.

Peasant parties were strong already at the outset of independence. Some of the peasant movements were what Rokkan (1975) would have called 'parties of rural defence', while others had a more distinct class profile. The former had a reactionary touch as they tended to idealize the past and present it as a model for the future. The latter tended to be radical in the sense that they questioned and challenged the social order in the countryside as well as in the cities. Its targets were both the landed gentry and the urban bourgeoisie with Jewish, German or Magyar elements, thus creating a link between radical agrarianism and radical nationalism.

In post-First World War Bulgaria, the Agrarian Patriotic Union (BAPU) of Alexandr Stambolisky dominated the stage with its calls for land reform and social equality. Romania had a populist movement extolling traditional rural values. Poland had a strong, but divided, peasant movement with parliamentary offshoots. Hungary was confronted with agrarian socialism at an early stage and the Smallholders Party was to remain one of the dominant political forces throughout the inter-war era. Similar comments apply to the Agrarian Party in Czechoslovakia and the agrarian parties in the Baltic states (Berglund and Aarebrot 1997, 16). Most of the peasant movements, however, were unable to translate the numerical strength of their constituencies into political influence. The organizations were not strong enough and their leaders prone to co-optation by the ruling elites.

The elites could successfully play the game of divide and rule as the opposition was from opposite quarters: the national minorities, opposed mainly to the nation-building project, and the rural population opposed to the state-building project. For instance, the peasant movement in Yugoslavia was deeply divided between centralist and autonomist forces.

The radicalization of the peasantry is largely explained by the adverse economic circumstances, particularly the impoverishment brought on first by the agricultural crisis in the early- and mid-1920s, and later by the depression. The experience was particularly debilitating as the villages had only just initiated their integration into commodities production and the monetary economy; the adverse effects were thus largely interpreted as yet another example of urban society's efforts and ability to exploit the peasant. The experiences of the First World War had of course also whetted the appetites of millions of peasants to benefit from modernization, and demonstrated the dependence of urban societies on the fruits of rural labour. As their relative deprivation and exclusion from the general progress in Europe was ever more clearly exposed, large parts of the peasantry chose to identify groups outside 'the peasant way of life' as their enemies. This juxtaposition was both class-based – directed against the land-owners, the urban bureaucracies, industrialists and the socialist proletariat – and ethno-racial – directed at 'national outsiders' such as Jews, Gypsies and Magyars. In many instances these identifications coincided, such as the equation of Jews with both finance capitalism and internationalist, godless Bolshevism, or of Magyars in Slovakia with feudalism and cultural imperialism. At times the right proved their radical credentials to the peasants, as in Hungary where a second bill on land reform was pushed through on the eve of the Second World War.

The legacy of radicalism

Pressure arising from rapid and turbulent modernization has been identified as a source of popular radicalism in rural, backward and peripheral regions. This 'emerging radicalism' has often been left-oriented, not only in post-war Eastern Europe but also in Scandinavia where support for communism has traditionally had two bases: in the established industrial regions and in the poorest rural areas. Support for the rural, emerging variety of left radicalism has been found to be consistent with the prevalence of economic and social instability (high unemployment or underemployment, large differences in living standards, wide fluctuations in income, and a high level of migration); rapid and widespread socioeconomic change; weak socio-political traditions and norms; rootlessness and weak group identification; and expressive and momentary political activity (Allardt 1964; 1970).

In contrast to industrial communism, the rural variety of left-wing radicalism tends to emerge where individuals without strong class identification experience deprivation. But this deprivation is not relative and insti-tutionalized, as is the case within the established urban working class. It is 'diffuse', an effect of the modernization process which breaks down the traditional rural groups of reference and comparison. Rapid arrival at modernity opens up vistas to which isolated individuals cannot relate, while simultaneously obscuring their rural roots. In general terms, 'isolation and lack of opportunity to participate in social life tend to increase radicalism' (Allardt 1964, 55). This theory ties in neatly with the socioeconomic dynamics in inter-war Eastern Europe.

Even so, the communist opposition could not make itself felt in any significant way after the early 1920s. This may be attributed partly to the strategy and organization of the communist parties: they were cadre-driven, dogmatically proletarian and extremely suspicious of alliances with other social formations. The industrial working class itself was small almost everywhere, and among the peasantry, communism was strongly identified not only with 'soulless', materialistic industrialism and an urban way of life, but also with 'alien' social and ethnic groups and with a foreign power – the Soviet Union – which was seen as threatening the hard-won national free-dom. In Hungary, the rural *Lumpenproletariat* initially rallied behind the 1919 Soviet Republic, but support fizzled out once the revolutionaries had demonstrated their contempt for the peasantry. The other inter-war Bolshevik uprisings – in conjunction with the Soviet invasion of Poland in 1919–20, in Bulgaria in 1923 and in Estonia in 1924 (as well as the wave of communist-led strikes in Romania in 1921–3) – were based on severe overestimations of potential public support. Subsequently, the communists were marginalized throughout almost the entire region. The Czechoslovak Communist Party which consistently polled some 10 per cent of the vote was the main exception from this rule. This deviant case is generally seen as a by-product of a number of circumstances: Czechoslovakia had not experienced Soviet or Russian aggression; there was a substantial and class-conscious working class in Bohemia and Moravia; and an anomic rural Slovak proletariat formally included in the national core but *de facto* excluded from influence. In Bulgaria, with its long-standing identification with Russia, the Communist Party also had a spell of success at the polls before it was banned in 1925, and it did quite well as it resurfaced under a new label in the early 1930s. Pockets of fairly stable communist support also existed in some blue-collar worker milieus (such as the Tallinn docks, the Romanian oilfields and some Budapest districts), and in backward areas in Yugoslavia, particularly in Montenegro.

Only occasionally did the communists manage to combine their internationalist critique of nation-building and socialist critique of state-building. 'Irredentist communism' had an appeal within minority Slavic communities in Eastern Europe, notably in Eastern Poland, Eastern Estonia, Latvia, Slovakia, Ruthenia and Romania. This phenomenon linked rural discontent and ethnic separatism with the external challenge of the Russian Revolution. But this discontent rarely translated into real influence because of formal barriers – the Communist Parties were eventually banned everywhere except in Czechoslovakia.

The link proposed by Allardt and others between *anomie* and relative deprivation to account for early left-wing radicalism can indeed be generalized. In Eastern Europe, communist parties were not the sole beneficiaries of such sentiments. In fact, the general radical mood in the immediate wake of the First World War is almost a dominant feature throughout Central and Eastern Europe, from Germany to Russia to Turkey. At this point in time, the entire region was marked by general fatigue, or even exasperation, with a war that everybody had lost. The imperial regimes, which had mobilized the masses for war but not succeeded in winning it, were felt to have lost their legitimacy. In a sense it may be argued that personalities with such different backgrounds or ideological outlooks as Hitler, Lenin and Piłsudski, all derived their initial political support from this anomic mode of exasperation. One country, Hungary, saw a pattern of revolution parallel to that in Russia, but in many other countries too, political actors had to consider these forces: the Legionnaires of Poland and Czechoslovakia, the agrarian radicals in Bulgaria, the semi-fascist or nationalist veterans' movements of the Baltic and Balkan states were all tributaries of the same river.

The possibilities for democratic survival were closely linked to the ability of civil society to integrate these forces. Hence, in Czechoslovakia – the socioeconomically most advanced country in the region – discontent was channelled into social democratic and trade union movements, which, however, were ethnically divided. In Finland, democracy survived the onslaught first of left-wing and then of right-wing radicalism as a result of the Nordic traditions of civil society. But Finland and Czechoslovakia were the exceptions, not the rule. Most of the newly independent countries were marked by the failure to develop a modern civil society to replace the clientelistic structures of the imperial era. It may seem paradoxical that whereas populist radicalism – whether left-wing, right-wing, agrarian or royalist – in itself represented a rebellion against the old clientelistic networks, it offered no real alternative to them. Therefore, as the new states of Eastern Europe moved from an era of democratic idealism towards a period when they were gradually reduced to buffer states squeezed between the new secular mass movements of communism and fascism, most of them did not succeed in developing participatory systems conducive to democratic consolidation. Instead they moved towards a new form of clientelism, where parties strongly associated with and linked to the state apparatus became the focal points of new clientelistic networks. When the Iron Curtain came down in 1946–47, the new Soviet-backed regimes simply took over the function as the nodal point in these new clientelistic networks.

So it should come as little surprise that the inter-war experiment in democracy failed, as did the following experiment in the immediate wake of the Second World War. Between 1919 and 1939, very little happened in terms of social and political regeneration. Nationalism and economic modernization served as instruments of political mobilization rather than as attempts at solving the problems of nation-building and economic reform. Ethnic diversity remained very high, rural economic development did not fulfil its promises and expectations, and industrialization remained largely confined to the industrial areas of the old empires. The democratic regimes of the early inter-war period, faced with populist challenges of almost every conceivable ideological shade, responded by ever grander promises of a swift entry into the modern world. But as they did not have the capacity to come through on most of these promises, they harvested dissatisfaction and disillusionment. This created a climate that played readily into the hands of non-democratic forces, which went on to develop a modern form of clientelism rather than a true civil society.

The Post-War Cleavage Structure

With the exception of the Baltic states which found themselves forcefully integrated into the Soviet Union, the arrival of the Red Army in Eastern Europe at the end of the Second World War spelled the return of partial political pluralism and provided for a second experiment in democracy. But it was a pluralism that was closely monitored by Moscow and its allies in Central and Eastern Europe. By 1949, the so-called popular democracies had been reduced to mere carbon copies of the supposedly superior Soviet model of democracy. The pluralism that remained was of a purely formal character, featuring domesticated non-socialist parties whose leaders had pledged allegiance to the Soviet model of government.

War and occupation was to leave a lasting imprint on the nation-states of Central and Eastern Europe. The map of Europe was drawn and redrawn several times, first by Nazi Germany and subsequently by the victorious anti-Hitler coalition (Berglund and Aarebrot 1997). In parallel with territorial revisions on a vast scale, the new rulers opted for policies of population transfers, inspired by Nazi and Soviet examples of ethnic cleansing, but with an additional antecedent in the 1923 Lausanne settlement after the Graeco–Turkish War of 1919–21.[1] Between 1936 and 1956, an estimated 22 million people were transferred from, to or within Poland, equalling no less than 70 per cent of the 1939 population (Davies 1986, 82). Throughout Central Europe, these drastic policies went a long way towards creating ethnically almost homogenous states (*Figure 2.2*). However, the Balkan states remained strongly multi-ethnic, and in the Baltic republics multi-ethnicity was reinforced by emigration, deportations and Slavic immigration. The USSR itself, of course, remained a multi-ethnic empire, albeit that Moscow pursued its own nation- and state-building agenda through Russification and attempts to create a *homo sovieticus*, with a Balkan parallel in the proclamation of a 'Yugoslav' nationality.

In 1947, when Europe had been divided by the allies into stable spheres of interest, millions of people – Poles, Russians, Latvians, Estonians, Lithuanians, Magyars and last but not least, Germans – had been driven away from their traditional settlement areas into truncated or redefined homelands by consecutive waves of ethnic cleansing. Estonia, Latvia and Lithuania were wiped out as independent states by the Soviet Union in 1940 and again – after an interlude under German domination – in 1944, when the German *Wehrmacht* had to give in to the advancing Soviet Red Army; and in the aftermath of the Soviet occupation, they were subjected to such an intensive process of Russification that the viability of a return to the pre-war formula was questionable, at least in Estonia and Latvia with the obvious majority potential of their large Russian-speaking minorities.

Figure 2.2: Ethnic cleansing and resettlement, 1945–49

Source: Crampton and Crampton 1996

The other states of Central and Eastern Europe did return to the pre-war formula of national sovereignty, but under conditions dictated and closely supervised by the one remaining great power in the region. These conditions included acceptance of the border changes and the concomitant population transfer imposed and/or encouraged by the Soviet Union, and whatever else might be required to promote the 'friendly relations' between the Soviet Union and its Central and East European neighbours presupposed by the Yalta and Potsdam agreements among the allies of the Second World War; these constraints were imposed on friends and foes alike. Though technically an ally of the anti-Hitler coalition, Poland was not treated any more gently than Hungary which had fought the war as an ally of Nazi Germany. It was in fact the other way around, and probably for the simple reason that Hungary needed less monitoring by Russia than Poland (Hellén 1996). Hungary had been pushed back to the borders imposed on it by the Trianon Peace Treaty of 1919 and thus had to resign itself to the loss of the Magyar-dominated province of Transylvania on the border with Romania.

This was a serious blow to long-standing Hungarian national aspirations, but it was much less of a threat against the *Pax Sovietica* imposed on the region than the chaos that existed in Poland, in the wake of the massive border changes which had compensated Poland for the loss of its eastern provinces to the Soviet Union by extending Poland deeply into what had recently been Germany, east of the rivers Oder and Neisse. The border changes were accompanied by truly large-scale population transfers, involving tens of millions of refugees of German, Polish and Russian nationality. The task of implementing and supervising this social experiment – to say nothing about the actual integration of the new territories into Poland proper – made it imperative for the Polish provisional government not only to rebuild the war-torn state apparatus but also to improvize a state machinery, where there was none at all. The stage was clearly set for identity politics and state-building in early post-war Poland.

Poland was admittedly an extreme case of the turmoil that gripped all of post-war Central Europe. Czechoslovakia was restored to its pre-war boundaries with the exception of Ruthenia (Carpatho-Ukraine) which was handed over to the Soviet Union upon the request of the war-time Soviet ally. This was in no way comparable to the Polish post-war trauma, but Czechoslovakia faced the dual task of overcoming the social, political and economic consequences of the expulsion of the some three million German-speaking residents in the Sudetenland along the German–Czechoslovak border, and of welding the Czech and Slovak parts of the republic together after war-time separation under German domination. The stage was set for a revival of the inter-war concept of a Czechoslovak nationality and, needless to say, for the resurgence of a strong Czechoslovak state.

The victory of the anti-Hitler coalition of the Second World War had put Hungary back to square one. The loss of predominantly ethnic Hungarian Transylvania to Romania, and the return of the Magyar-dominated southern rim of Slovakia to Czechoslovakia, reintroduced the well-known diaspora problem of the inter-war period into Hungarian politics and confronted Hungary with a refugee problem, albeit of limited magnitude. This was an open invitation to identity politics. With the economy in a shambles and the state apparatus partly dismantled by the retreating Germans, state-building was also of paramount importance to the post-war Hungarian authorities.

Romania regained Transylvania, which was hers by virtue of Trianon, but was deprived of Bessarabia, which had been occupied by the Soviet Union in accordance with the Molotov-Ribbentrop Pact and in defiance of the First World War peace treaties (Crampton and Crampton 1996). Moscow was – it turned out when it came to negotiations – no more willing to give up Bessarabia than any other territory seized within the framework of the ill-fated treaty with Nazi Germany. In the case of Romania, however, the transfer of territories was smooth without large-scale accompanying population transfers, but – as will be demonstrated later – this was to have a lasting impact on Romania's political agenda (cf. Chapter 10). The other countries of South Eastern Europe were only marginally affected by border changes and ethnic cleansing in the wake of the Second World War, but this should not be construed to imply that they were somehow safely beyond identity politics and state-building. The original ethnic mosaic had been preserved, with all which that entailed, by way of instability and the pre-war state apparatus often had to be rebuilt literally from scratch.

Yugoslavia is a case in point. The restoration of Yugoslavia to its pre-war borders spelled the revival of the inter-war concept of Yugoslav nationality as opposed to and as a substitute for Serb, Croat, Slovene and/or Macedonian nationalism, and the return to political centralization in a heterogeneous setting that might have called for far-reaching decentralization. But the bottom line was that the contradiction between nation-building elites and ethnically diverse populations had been markedly reduced, particularly in Central Europe. As the process of ethnic homogenization was largely instituted by the Soviet Union, the communist parties could claim credit for having, at least to an extent, solved the national problem, and as ethnic tension had built up during the inter-war era, this was a source of popular support and legitimacy.

The resilience of historical cleavages

The stage was set not only for a identity politics and ethnic cleavages, but also for a revival of the religious–secular dimension. But this dimension – it will be remembered – was not independent of identity politics. The Catholic Church, and the political parties close to it, had in fact been at the very centre of nation-building processes in Central and Eastern Europe ever since the Habsburg, Russian and German empires (Berglund and Aarebrot 1997;

Hellén 1996). Similar comments apply to the highly salient urban/rural dimension in Central and Eastern Europe of the inter-war era. The social structure of the region had hardly changed since the First World War. With the exception of Czechoslovakia which belonged to the leading industrial nations of the inter-war era, Central and Eastern Europe remained basically rural and agrarian with pockets of industrialization in major cities and urban conglomerations. The countryside provided fertile ground for organized religion and for all kinds of agrarian movements, from the utopian to the pragmatic, which were likely to re-emerge with the backing of neat political majorities once democracy had been re-introduced.

The left/right dimension, however, did not seem to have particularly bright prospects in post-war Central and Eastern Europe. The parties of the left have traditionally been working-class parties and, with the exception of Czechoslovakia, there was not much of a working-class base in this basically rural region. The parties of the right have traditionally had a middle-class and/or entrepreneurial background which was yet another scarce commodity in the prevailing social structure of Central and Eastern Europe. The region had had its share of communist, social democratic, liberal and conservative parties in the 1920s and 1930s, but as a rule they had not performed particularly well. The liberal and conservative parties were successful only to the extent that they managed to link up to the strong and vocal nationalist and religious constituencies; the communists and the social democrats did not have an equivalent fall-back option.

The cleavage structure of the pre-war era had survived the Second World War intact, but with one important addition. War against and/or occupation by Nazi Germany had introduced a fascist/anti-fascist cleavage. By the end of the war, few, if any, Central and East Europeans were openly professing fascist sympathies; the overwhelming majority of them now pledged allegiance to anti-fascism. The day of reckoning had come for the fascists, the Nazi collaborators and other suspected war criminals. The methods ranged from lynchings, summary executions, and trials for war crimes, to political disenfranchisement of large segments of the population. There was only one drawback: how to define fascists and how to separate criminal fascists from mere Nazi fellow-travellers? These were questions with which the governments and courts of liberated Western Europe grappled for years after the war without producing any clear-cut answers. As a rule, the West European approach to the problem was cautious rather than rash and legal rather than political. In Soviet-dominated Central and Eastern Europe, however, justice and retribution was frequently meted out in a way that made sense only from the vantage point of political expediency. The initial Soviet concept for the so-called popular democracies in liberated Eastern Europe called for these countries to be governed by broad 'anti-fascist' coalitions with their roots in the national fronts that had been part and parcel of the underground resistance against the German occupiers. The small and in many cases insignificant communist parties were cast for a major role within these anti-fascist coalitions. It was to the advantage of the communists and their allies, if part of the competition could be disqualified on real or trumped up charges of harbouring pro-fascist sympathies; and the Soviet authorities actually did not agree to local or national elections until the old ruling elites and their potential followers had been barred from taking part in the electoral process.

The election results were in all likelihood a source of great concern to Moscow. Polling 38 per cent of the vote in the general elections in Czecho-slovakia in May 1946, the local communists had done very well, particu-larly considering that this gave them, and their long-time social democratic coalition partner, a parliamentary majority (Broklová 1995). But this was all there was by way of reassuring electoral reports for Moscow.

In the Hungarian general elections of November 1945, almost two-thirds of the voters had come out in favour of the Smallholders Party (Hellén 1996); in Poland, the Polish Peasant Party of Stanisław Mikołajczyk had apparently done considerably better than officially reported in the rigged plebiscite of November 1946 and the even more tightly controlled elections in February 1947 (Grzybowski 1994); in Bulgaria, the communist-dominated Patriotic Front had carried the general elections of November 1945 due to the boycott of several non-communist parties, including the majority faction of the Bulgarian Agrarian Union (BAU) of Nikola Petkov, which had unsuccessfully called upon the Allied Control Commission to supervise the election carefully so as to avoid fraudulent practices (Fowkes 1995); and in Romania, it took yet another openly fraudulent election to provide the communists and their allies with a majority in the 1946 parliament (Dellenbrant 1994).

These elections were followed by other elections which reduced the space for political pluralism until it had been eliminated altogether. The social democrats were forced to merge with the communists, and the non-socialist parties were either infiltrated by the communists or banned. Many of the popular democracies formally preserved the multi-party format, but the surviving non-communist parties were permanent allies of the ruling Marxist-Leninist parties, totally reconciled with operating within the framework of the fundamental principles of the world communist move-ment. These principles included unconditional acceptance of the leading rule of the Marxist-Leninist party, the consistent application of the principle of democratic centralism with its distinctly authoritarian components, and the unwavering support of the notion of eternal friendship and alliance with the Soviet Union (Berglund and Dellenbrant 1994).

Communism as a modernizing force

Within a few short years, the popular democracies of Central and Eastern Europe had been transformed into mere carbon copies of the Soviet political system. The party space was dominated by one single force, and the dominant Marxist-Leninist force was itself constrained by the Soviet mentor. The social and economic programme on which the new regimes embarked was one of radical modernization, inspired by the Soviet crash programme for industrialization of the 1920s and 1930s. The means of production were socialized; the agricultural sector was collectivized and a number of gigantic industrial projects – like the Nowa Huta steelworks in Poland – were initiated throughout the Soviet bloc. The long-term consequences were manifold. The traditional middle-class and rural constituencies of the liberal, conservative and agrarian parties were wiped out and the traditional working-class and urban constituencies of the left-wing parties were substantially strengthened; the countryside was impoverished and the role of traditional religious values was sharply reduced; illiteracy was wiped out or sharply reduced; the average level of education jumped upwards as dramatically as industrial output and the standard of living.

Several inferences may be drawn on the basis of the socioeconomic indicators in Table 2.3. It is readily seen that communist Eastern Europe trails behind the industrial nations of the West. The East European countries rarely come out at the very top of the list of socioeconomic indicators and they surpass West Germany, which entered the post-war era in a state of devastation and destruction, much like that of Central and Eastern Europe. Hence, when the East European countries actually rank at the top of the list, it is not necessarily an indicator that they are ahead of Western Europe, the United States and the British Commonwealth. The large share of industrial workers in the Hungarian labour force in 1978 (58 per cent) and the huge industrial output in the GDR, Bulgaria and Romania as of 1978 (62, 55 and 58 per cent of the GDP, respectively) testify to rapid social transformation and economic development, particularly compared to pre-war conditions (Hellén 1996) and also compared to the first decades of the post-war era. The data also serve as a reminder that Eastern Europe did not provide fertile ground for what is sometimes referred to as the post-industrial society, with its emphasis on service production and small-scale enterprises.

The Soviet model of modernization, with its emphasis on industrialization, urbanization, collectivization and secularization, lost part of its attraction even for the local communists who had promoted it, when – after Stalin's death – the Soviet leaders openly admitted that there might be more roads than one leading to socialism, but the model was never entirely abandoned. Industry in general, and huge industrial conglomerates in particular, were promoted at the expense of the agricultural sector;

collective farming was at the very least preferred to whatever there was left of private farming, and religion was at best tolerated. The net result was an unprecedented social transformation of Eastern Europe, with the exception of Albania which rejected one socialist partnership after the other – first with Yugoslavia (1948), then with the Soviet Union (1961) and subsequently with China (1977–78) – only in order to withdraw into splendid and self-imposed isolation as the only 'true exponent of socialism'.

Table 2.3: Socioeconomic indicators for Central and Eastern Europe

	Poland	CSSR	Hungary	GDR	Bulgaria	Romania	Albania	FRG	Highest
Urban pop. % in									
100,000+ cities									
1950	23	14	38	20	9	10	0	48	71 UK
1960	27	14	22	21	14	16	8	51	72 UK
1976	20	17	28	24	24	25	8	35	72 US
Labour force,									
% in industry									
1960	29	46	35	48	25	21	18	48	48 FRG
1977	38	49	58	51	38	31	24	48	58 Hun
GDP,									
% in industry									
1960	51	65	58	–	–	–	–	54	56 CSSR
1978	52	60	47	62	55	58	–	42	62 GDR
GDP,									
% in agriculture									
1960	23	13	20	–	–	–	–	6	n/m
1978	16	9	15	10	18	15	–	3	18 Bulg
Literacy rate, %									
1960	98	99	98	99	85	99	–	99	100
1970	98	n/a	99	99	91	98	-	99	100
Telephones									
per 1,000 pop.									
1966	41	105	56	75	–	–	–	108	481 US
1975	76	177	100	150	88	56	–	318	697 US
Newspaper circ.									
per 1.000 pop.									
1960	145	236	143	456	182	147	47	307	477 Swe
1975	248	300	233	463	232	129	46	312	572 Swe
TV receivers									
per 1.000 pop.									
1965	66	149	81	188	23	26	1	193	362 US
1975	180	249	223	302	173	121	2	307	571 US

Note: Dates may be approximate. The most recent Romanian data on urbanization were gathered in 1971 and not in 1976 and the East German data on newspaper circulation were collected in 1965 rather than 1960. The Bulgarian data on literacy were gathered in 1965 rather than 1960 and the Romanian and Albanian data on newspaper circulation are from 1974 and 1965 respectively.
Source: Taylor and Hudson, (1972), Taylor and Jodice (1983a, 1983b).

By the end of the 1980s, Central and Eastern Europe was closer to Western Europe than ever before in terms of modernity, but with a class structure marked by the equalizing impact of almost fifty years of 'real socialism' (Wessels and Klingemann 1994). As indicated by Table 2.3, tremendous socioeconomic changes took place under communism, mainly in favour of industry to the detriment of the agricultural sector. An almost equally important change, which is not shown in the table, is the change in life-style in rural areas due to collectivization. Briefly, collectivization entailed the introduction of an industrial life-style for agricultural workers. In sum, many of the advantages of a modern and urban organization of labour, such as fixed working hours, regulated holiday periods, pensions and fixed wages, were introduced without consideration for anything like cost-benefit analysis. Thus, politics in the 1990s has inherited a new cleavage: the desirability of retaining a modern, urban-type life-style in agriculture and declining industries, as opposed to an understanding of the adaptation of life-styles to such uncomfortable facts of life as profit margins.

Another feature of communist policies education was a marked increase in investment in education on all levels, particularly in technical fields. This produced large middle classes, but not middle classes structured in the same way as in Western Europe. Income distribution was weakly, or not at all, linked to education. Nor was political and social stratification only a matter of education. Who belonged to the ruling class, the so-called *nomenklatura*, was defined by the ruling party and in terms of access to this party. But to the extent that education can be used as an indicator of modernity, the relative size of the population with a middle-class education has never been larger in Eastern Europe than it is today. This is clearly a legacy of communist policies, and ought to be conducive to the establishment of a civil society and, in a similar vein, detrimental to the continuation of clientelistic relationships. The poor development of civil society in some East European countries today may be attributed to two interrelated factors: the harsh realities of daily life in transitional societies, and the lingering effects of professional specialization originally intended to fit the requirements of the communist system. We would, however, argue that the possibilities for developing a stable civil society to complement democratic institutions is better now than ever before.

The social transformation on which the communist regimes embarked called for a strong government presence; and there is indeed a case to be made for the notion that the communist regimes of Central and Eastern Europe had state-building as a top level priority (Berglund and Aarebrot 1997). The concept of a liberal state with the emphasis on individual rights and freedoms and rule of law was obviously alien to the communist leaders, but they definitely needed a strong and efficient state machinery capable of levying taxes, mobilizing the masses and supervising the individuals. Nation-building or identity politics was also of obvious importance for the leaders of communist Central and Eastern Europe, particularly for the leaders of countries affected by large-scale border changes and population transfers. But identity politics in many ways represented a Pandora's box of horrors and had to be handled with great care. The territorial revisions and population transfers had, after all, been initiated by the Soviet Union; and, to the extent that the Soviet Union did not itself benefit from the changes, the beneficiary was a neighbouring socialist country also aligned with the Soviet Union.

The West German card could, however, be played with impunity. The refusal by West Germany to recognize the Oder–Neisse line *de jure* prior to a comprehensive peace settlement, was frequently used by the Polish United Workers' Party in its attempts to mobilize support for Poland's alliance with Russia (Hellén 1996); and Moscow was relentless in its references to German militarism and revanchism. The Jewish card could also be played with relative impunity, once Israel had been written off as a potential ally of Soviet Russia in an otherwise hostile Arab world. The history of the Soviet Union and communist Eastern Europe is in fact full of thinly veiled anti-Semitic campaigns, from Stalin's aborted crusade against Jewish doctors in the early 1950s to the recurrent verbal attacks on Zionism and cosmopolitan tendencies all over Central and Eastern Europe. The verbal abuse frequently carried over into outright punitive actions purges of the party rank and file, imposed exile and stiff and summary sentences – which further reduced the importance of the survivors of Hitler's racial war against the European Jewry. The notion of an overarching Czechoslovak national identity – which the leaders of post-war Czechoslovakia used to combat Czech and Slovak nationalism just as the pre-war leaders had done – was an acceptable form of nationalism in the new Central and East European setting. Similar comments apply to the idea of a Yugoslav nationality aggressively promoted by the post-war leaders of this multi-ethnic state and, for that matter, to the anti-Turkish undercurrents of Bulgarian nationalism. The Romanians had a licence to engage in anti-Magyar rhetoric ever since the Soviet Union had decided to hand over Transylvania to Romania. The communist regime in Bucharest was to use this option quite frequently in its attempts to come out as the true defender of the nation. The loss of Moldavia and Bessarabia was a more sensitive issue, but, by the end of the 1980s, this did not stop the beleaguered Ceauşescu regime from suggesting that this region be reincorporated into Romania.

The forty years of communism in Central and Eastern Europe included successive waves of political and economic liberalization, but – with Poland

and Hungary as the two major exceptions – the fundamental features of the Marxist-Leninist system remained intact until the very end. The first (almost) free parliamentary elections in Poland in June 1989 and the gradual return to genuine political pluralism in Hungary in the late 1980s set a dangerous precedent for the hibernating Stalinist and neo-Stalinist regimes in Central and Eastern Europe and served as a source of inspiration for dissidents throughout the region. Marxist-Leninist tradition would have called for Soviet intervention sooner rather than later. Stalin would not have condoned free elections and the return to genuine political pluralism anywhere within the Soviet bloc, nor would Khrushchev, nor Brezhnev. But Gorbachev was willing to take a chance on reform communism in Central and Eastern Europe and thus paved the way for the breakdown of Soviet-style communism throughout the entire region. The countries of Central and Eastern Europe found themselves thrust into their third experiment in democracy in the 20th century.

A Third Try at Democracy

The focus of the present volume is on the current and most recent experiment in democracy. It has been going on for less than a decade, but we nevertheless perceive it as the most successful and most promising democratic experiment ever seen in Central and Eastern Europe. This is due to a number of factors:

- the existence of an international climate defined by the US, NATO and the European Union so as to promote the development of democracy in Central and Eastern Europe;
- the relatively high level of socioeconomic development in contemporary Central and Eastern Europe with all which that entails by way of industrialization, urbanization and secularization;
- a historical legacy that favours inclusion and co-optation of the spiritual heirs to Marxism-Leninism;
- the development of the Central and East European countries towards the ethnic homogeneity presupposed by the nation-state model; and
- the skilful use of creative electoral engineering in order to put an end to political fragmentation and promote stable government as opposed to the political immobilism of the inter-war years.

There are factors pulling in the opposite direction, most notably the uncertain economic prospects in several East European countries; the strongly clientelistic heritage particularly in South Eastern Europe; the inclination towards populism of the nationalist variety and pronounced generational differences in the approach towards democracy, market economy and market reform as evidenced by the recent Central and East European Eurobarometers; and, last but not least, more than a nagging suspicion by Eastern Europeans that their respective governments have no interest in promoting human rights (Berglund and Aarebrot 1997).

Survey research is a post-Second World War phenomenon, but there is no reason whatsoever to assume that the Central and East Europeans of the inter-war era were less ambivalent in their approach towards democracy and more optimistic about the government's willingness and ability to respect human rights than the Central and East Europeans of today. Similar comments apply to the economic crisis, the clientelistic heritage and the inclination towards populism and strongman rule. If anything, the depression between the two world wars was probably stronger than the economic crisis that accompanied the transition from plan to market. A clientelistic heritage is probably more strongly felt in underdeveloped than in developed or developing societies. And populism is likely to be a more attractive option in underdeveloped countries with a long-standing imperial heritage, with its authoritarian appeal, than it is in developed or developing countries which have recently emerged from communist rule, with its formally egalitarian ideology.

We would be inclined to conclude that the negative factors are of lesser – and definitely not greater – magnitude today than they were during the inter-war era. We therefore limit ourselves to a discussion of the five factors we believe favour the development of democracy in contemporary Central and Eastern Europe.

The international climate
The First World War (1914–18) was supposedly fought 'to make the world safe for democracy'. But with all due respect to President Wilson, it is probably fair to say that the architects of the Versailles world order, including the British and the French, struck a delicate balance between democracy on the one hand and national self-determination on the other. And with all due respect to the East European inter-war leaders, there is little doubt that they were under the sway of nation-state ideologies which tended to relegate the defence of democracy to a secondary position. Democracy was a beleaguered form of government throughout the inter-war era. It was questioned by the far left as well as by the far right; and the gradually increasing competition between the Soviet Union and Nazi Germany for political influence in Central and Eastern Europe certainly did not make things easier.

In the early 1990s there were no dictatorships left in the new European house, and the emphasis in Central and Eastern Europe was on democracy and on co-operation with the West which was seen as the only safeguard against a possible revival of Soviet imperial ambitions. This West European and Atlantic orientation was not only the gut reaction of recently liberated states, marked by the anti-communist backlash of the early 1990s, but the considered opinion of nations most of which have since seen government by reform communists as well as by right-wing forces. The East European commitment to the European Union and to NATO is in fact one of the most important factors – perhaps the single most important factor – accounting for the continued allegiance to the democratic format in countries with a turbulent past and a clientelistic legacy.

Modernity makes for democracy

In their *Political History of Eastern Europe in the 20th Century*, Sten Berglund and Frank Aarebrot (1997) analyse the outcome of the inter-war struggle for democracy (read: breakdown versus survival of democracy) in Western as well as Eastern Europe in terms of two explanatory factors: state-building, and religious autonomy or secularization (*Figure 2.3*). The model is clearly inspired by Stein Rokkan's (1975) seminal conceptual map of Europe and the outcome could hardly have been more neat. With only two exceptions, democracy survives in countries with a strong state-building tradition which are either predominantly Protestant or secularized Catholic or Orthodox. The two deviant cases – Germany and Eire – can be accounted for in terms of another factor of general importance: structural or practical co-optation. The literature on inter-war Czechoslovakia – the sole democratic survivor in Central and Eastern Europe by the end of the inter-war era – emphasizes the dynamics of an intricate system of consociational devices (Lijphart 1968, 1980). The authors therefore conclude:

> Where the state-building tradition was weak and the legacy of empire strong, or where secular nation-building was still impaired by deeply rooted religious sentiments, or where significant segments representing major cleavages were not co-opted into a constitutional compromise, the chances for democratic survival in inter-war Europe were slim indeed. (p. 36)

Strictly speaking, this finding only pertains to the inter-war era, but the implications are nevertheless manifold. In the long run, even the most stable macrosociological relationships are bound to change. The communists who were to take over Central and Eastern Europe after the brief semi-democratic interlude of 1945–49 had state-building and socioeconomic change at the very top of the their political agendas; and the primacy of politics, industrialization, urbanization and secularization became the catch-words of the day in the 1950s and 1960s.

Figure 2.3: Democratic survival: a classification of European countries in inter-war Europe (short-lived and semi-independent state formations are parenthesized)

	State-building tradition	
Religious autonomy from state authority	*The City Belt, empire states and states devolved from these empire states: The Charle-magne Heritage*	*External Eastern historical empires and states devolved from these historical empires: The External Challengers*
Predominantly Protestant countries: State and Church integrated	Denmark Sweden Norway Finland Great Britain The Netherlands Switzerland	*Estonia* *Latvia*
&	*Germany*	
Secularized Catholic or Orthodox countries: Domi-nant state	France Belgium Czechoslovakia	*Russia (USSR)* *(Ukraine)*
Catholic counter-reformation countries, non-secularized Orthodox countries and Muslim countries: Continued dualism between Church and State	Eire *Spain* *Portugal* *Austria* *Hungary* *Italy* *(Croatia* *(Slovakia)*	*Lithuania* *Poland* *Romania* *Bulgaria* *Yugoslavia (Serbia)* *Greece* *Albania* *Turkey*

Co-optation and democracy

Yet another difference between the inter-war era and the post-communist period, perhaps too obvious to be mentioned, has to do with the readiness of leaders and voters to integrate or co-opt parties and movements across the entire political spectrum. The fate of the former ruling parties is a case in point. With two notable exceptions – Czechoslovakia and the GDR – the initial call for de-communization and lustration did not make a lasting impression on the political system, and, in fact, the former communist parties were accepted as legitimate contenders for political power within the political system, once they had pledged themselves to parliamentary demo-cracy. This policy of inclusion rather than exclusion was endorsed not only by the new political elites but also by the voters. The inter-war era was characterized by a tendency of exclusion rather than inclusion, as evidenced by the presidential coups in the Baltic states, which served to exclude the extreme left as well as the extreme right, or by the inverted power relationship between governments and parliaments in Poland, Hungary, Bulgaria and Romania. The particularly harsh nature of this Czechoslovak and East German approach to the instruments of the former communist regime may be attributed to a number of factors: a strong civil society, the democratic legacy from the inter-war era, and the weak reform credentials of the defunct regimes. Nevertheless, the political systems of these two countries have gradually adopted more integrative features.

It is a moot question whether it is good or bad for democracy that reform communism remains a viable political alternative in Eastern Europe. We would, however, be inclined to say it is good rather than bad. Exclusion of political elites is always conducive to instability of democratic regimes; and, other things being equal, circulation of power among competing political elites is preferable to the monopolization of power by one single political force, whether communist or not.

Stability and ethnic homogeneity
The ideals of what constitutes nation-states are often constant over time and across regimes, but they may also vary. It is indeed indicative of the fluid and adaptable nature of nationalism (Anderson 1991) that the very definition of nationality may be changed by political regimes in an effort to create new super-nationalities more suitable for the transformation of a multi-ethnic society into a 'national' society. The deliberate attempts to that end by Tsarist Russia in the 19th century, and by Soviet rulers in the 20th century, are good examples, as are the notions of Czechoslovak and Yugoslav nationalities advocated by the inter-war and the post-war leaders of these mini-empires.

In Poland, Bulgaria, Hungary, Romania and Albania, the nation-state ideals remained largely unchanged under communist rule. The anti-Semitic campaigns in the People's Republic of Poland and the systematic denial of the existence of a German community in post-war Poland testify to this (Hellén 1996). The Bulgarian communist regime also adopted the traditional nation-state concept. Todor Zhivkov's persecution of the Turkish-speaking minority and the pressures brought to bear on the Bulgarian-speaking Muslims – the Pomaks – are cases in point (Crampton and Crampton 1996). The communist regimes of Romania and Hungary maintained their respective nation-state ideals, which were reinforced by the constant conflicts between the two countries over the plight of the Magyar minority in Transylvania (Hellén 1996). Finally, in Albania, open enmity towards Yugoslavia over the Albanian majority in the Kosovo province of Serbia served as one of the pillars of the sultanistic and isolationistic Hoxha regime.

Table 2.4: Ratings of ethnic homogeneity in terms of the relative size of the regime-proclaimed majority nationality (percentages of total population)

	Country	Majority Population	Censuses * 1920	1930	1993
Stable approximate nation-states: stable definition of the majority nationality, large majorities	Lithuania	Lithuanians	81_{1923}		80_{1992}
	Hungary	Magyar		97_{1992}	
	Bulgaria	Bulgarians	83	87_{1934}	85-90**
	Albania	Albanians			
Newer approximate nation-states: stable definition of the majority nationality, large majorities today but smaller majorities in the inter-war era	Poland	Poles	70***	70***	99
	Romania	Romanians		72	89
Recent approximate nation-states: devolved from dissolved 'Mini-Empires': large or medium-large majorities today, small majorities or minorities prior to the recent dissolution of the 'Mini-Empire' states	Czechoslovakia	'Czechoslovaks'	66_{1921}	67	
	The Czech Rep.	Czechs			81
	Slovakia	Slovaks			86
	Yugoslavia	'Serbo-Croats'	74_{1921}	77_{1931}	
	Slovenia	Slovenes			99_{1991}
	Croatia	Croats			78_{1991}
Former approximate nation-States with a decreased majority population today	Estonia	Estonians		86_{1934}	62_{1992}
	Latvia	Latvians		77_{1935}	53
	Macedonia	Macedonians			65_{1991}

* The censuses of the inter-war period are generally unreliable in their estimates of the size of ethnic minorities. The figures are, nevertheless, interesting as expressions of perceived size of regime-proclaimed core populations. ** For Bulgaria's current ethnic population our source only indicates that national minorities exceed 10 per cent. *** The Polish inter-war estimates are highly questionable. Polish nationality was at last partly determined by the ability of the respondent to understand the census-taker when addressed in Polish.
Source: Berglund and Aarebrot 1997, 161; data from Crampton and Crampton 1996.

With the demise of the Czechoslovak and Yugoslav mini-empires, a new definition of nationhood was instated. This new definition is very similar to the ideals of the nation-state found in countries which have retained a constant concept of nationhood across regimes throughout the 20th century. This is brought out in the official Czech and Slovak statistics on the ethnic composition over time. In the Czechoslovak censuses of 1921 and 1930, the core group was widely defined as people of 'Czechoslovak' nationality. No more than 65 per cent of the population could be subsumed as belonging to the artificial national core of this 'nation-state'. The minorities, i.e. those citizens who were not considered 'Czechoslovak', included Germans, Poles, Ruthenes, Magyars and Jews. The nationalities excluded from the core thus consisted of Slavic as well as non-Slavic speakers, and one excluded group, the Jews, was not linguistically defined at all. Gypsies were not even listed. The Czechoslovak core population counted Czechs, Moravians and Slovaks. The 1991 censuses list Czechs and Slovaks as the largest groups of the Czech and Slovak republics respectively. The definition of the core group is apparently much narrower today, but with more than 80 per cent of the national grand totals, these narrowly defined majority groups nevertheless account for considerably more than the 65 per cent reported for the Czecho-slovak nationality in the censuses of 1921 and 1930. Similar observations can be made upon comparing the official statistics of Yugoslavia in the inter-war period with current censuses in the successor states. The old Serbo-Croat nationality has been discarded.

In this context, Estonia, Latvia, and maybe Macedonia, are deviant cases. Until the early 1990s, these have been countries with decreasing ethnic homogeneity, but with a linguistically defined, and thus limited, definition of nationhood which has remained stable across previous regimes. Moreover, the possibilities of increasing the core populations of these countries are hampered by the fact that the new large minorities mainly consist of a diaspora population of a former imperial ruler, or – in the case of Macedonia – of a potentially irredentist Albanian minority.

Table 2.4 classifies the Central and East European countries into four groups, using as a measure of ethnic homogeneity the percentage of the population which has been reported by the different regimes in the censuses as belonging to the regime's proclaimed core – or majority – populations. It should be noted that the main purpose of the table is classification of countries. Estimates in terms of percentages have only been included where relatively reliable international sources are available.

The European house that emerged in the aftermath of the breakdown of communist totalitarianism had more rooms in it than the old and familiar Cold War European building of states. In this sense, the unification of Germany in October 1991 was unique. All the other recent border changes in Central and Eastern Europe have been by-products not of amalgamation but of secession and/or breakdown. Sometimes this process resulted in new, ethnically homogeneous entities – sometimes it did not. The Czech and Slovak republics are clearly more homogeneous than the federal Czecho-slovak republic from which they seceded, which in its turn had been more homogeneous than Masaryk's inter-war Czechoslovak republic. Due to a continuous and systematic influx of ethnic Russians into the Baltic region, Estonia and Latvia came out of the Soviet Union with much more by way of ethnic diversity than they had ever had before. On the whole, however, contemporary Central and Eastern Europe stands out as distinctly more homogeneous than its inter-war counterpart.

Electoral engineering

It may also be argued that the current experiment in democracy in Eastern Europe benefits from the laboratory provided by the inter-war era. Inspired as they were by the German Weimar constitution, the inter-war East European constitutions had encouraged multi-partyism to the point of creating a high degree of political fragmentation which resulted in government instability and political immobilism. The post-communist democracies of Eastern Europe have opted for a variety of oligopolistic devices designed to exclude minor political parties from parliamentary representation. Hungary did so prior to the founding elections in March/April of 1990. Poland held on to the Weimar notion of fair representation for a while, and then followed suit, like the other East European latecomers to adopt oligopolistic devices such as strict thresholds of registration and parliamentary representation, as well as proportional representation tempered by distinctly majoritarian features, like French-style two-stage elections and the introduction of single-member constituencies. The net result is that political fragmentation has been all but wiped out in Eastern Europe. There is nothing to prevent parties already in parliament from breaking up between elections, but there is a definite price tag, in the form threshold requirements, attached to hasty and ill-considered political divorces to be met in the upcoming elections.

Not all Cats are the same Shade of Grey

The perspective which we have applied in this historical overview has been macrosociological. We have taken a bird's-eye view on an entire region. This is a legitimate endeavour, but it should not be seen as a licence to neglect the between-country variations. As mentioned in the previous chapter, there are in fact at least three groups of countries in contemporary Central and Eastern Europe, all marked by distinctive historical heritages.

We have the five Central European countries of Hungary, Poland, the Czech and Slovak republics, and Slovenia, for all intents and purposes successor states of the German and Habsburg empires and firmly embedded in the Western tradition. They have all benefited from the improved international climate that has prevailed in the 1990s. They all have some, if not all, the attributes of modernity, including an emerging class cleavage which appears to have the makings of being a dominant factor in electoral behaviour and party structuring. With the exception of Hungary, ethnically homogeneous ever since 1919, they have all been on a conspicuous historical journey of nation-building. With Slovakia as the deviant case, they have all but completed the transition from plan to market and co-operate closely with NATO, the EU and other structures of European integration.

The three Baltic countries of Estonia, Latvia and Lithuania form yet another cluster. They have also benefited from the disintegration of the Soviet empire which resulted in the re-establishment of sovereignty. They have oriented themselves towards the West, and embarked on a course of radical – and largely successful – transformation from plan to market economy. But with Russia as next-door neighbour and with minorities of hundreds of thousands of Russian-speakers who are not yet fully integrated into their societies, Estonia, Latvia and – to a lesser extent – Lithuania find themselves in a potentially explosive situation. It is explosive not only from a domestic point of view, but also by virtue of the foreign policy implications, since Russia sees itself as the guardian of the some 20 million diaspora Russians now living outside the borders of Russia proper. This goes a long way towards accounting for the preoccupation of Estonians and Latvians with identity politics (cf. Chapters 3 and 4). Identity politics is no less important in Lithuania, but has a somewhat different background: it does not only revolve around Russia and the Russians, but also around the historically problematic relationship to Poland. In the Baltic countries, the nation-building and state-building processes are far from complete.

Finally, we have the countries of South Eastern Europe or the Balkans. They still find themselves in the middle of political and economic transition processes, the outcomes of which are far from clear. The relatively slow transition in these countries is a result of a clientelistic political culture with its roots in the era of Ottoman rule; a tradition skilfully manipulated, exploited and reinforced by the communist rulers. They are also up against ethnic problems which might possibly destabilize the democratic regimes introduced after 1989. The fate of the former Yugoslav federation gives ample evidence as to the severity of ethnic problems in a clientelistic setting. The cleavages likely to emerge in South Eastern Europe constitute a mixture of what Georgi Karasimeonov, in Chapter 11, refers to as 'residual' and 'transitional' cleavages. In the Balkans, the modern cleavages are likely to remain latent for quite a while yet.

The regionalization of Eastern Europe which we have introduced should not make us oblivious of the within-group variations. Hungary cannot be substituted for Poland, nor can Poland be substituted for the Czech Republic, or, for that matter, for Slovenia – not to mention Slovakia, which is indeed somewhat of an outlier in the Central European group. The point, however, is that the five Central European countries have more in common with one another than with the Baltic or Balkan countries. Similar comments apply to the Baltic countries and the countries of South Eastern Europe. The country-specific data in Chapters 3–11 are therefore vital for the comparative analysis of the entire region in Chapter 12.

Politics Makes for Strange Bedfellows

In the following country-specific chapters, the reader will notice that two extreme positions are possible when evaluating the effect of historical cleavages on present-day politics in Eastern Europe. Some authors choose to interpret the emerging party systems mainly as functions of stable historical cleavages. This approach is similar to that applied in Lipset and Rokkan's seminal article on Western Europe (1967); in this volume, the contributions by Zdenka Mansfeldová, Marian Grzybowski and Gábor Tóka testify to the resilience of historical cleavages in the Czech and Slovak republics, in Poland as well as in Hungary. The opposite position would be to argue that historical cleavages are of little or no importance and the structure of the current party systems must be explained by reference to new cleavages derived from new social structures. The argument would then be that the democratic development started in the 1920s and 1930s has been interrupted for a long period of time by authoritarian and totalitarian regimes, and that the societies have changed dramatically during the subsequent period. In this volume, this position is most strongly represented by Hermann Smith-Sivertsen and Darius Žeruolis in their eminent chapters on Latvia and Lithuania, respectively. Considering that the Estonian experience is largely similar, as evidenced by the fascinating analysis by Mikko Lagerspetz and Henri Vogt, it is tempting to infer that we have encountered an effect of more than forty years of forced integration with the Soviet empire. In the broader East European perspective, the Baltic countries nevertheless are outliers.

On the issue of historical continuity, the editors of the present volume would take an interim position. The basic dimensions of change in Central and East Europe appear to follow three patterns, as illustrated by Figure 2.4:

The pattern of ethnicity The old empires with their ethnic fragmentation have been replaced by states which today can legitimately refer to themselves as nation states, with the notable exceptions of some countries in South Eastern Europe and on the Baltic rim. The pivotal role of the national cleavage in a situation where nation-building has not run its full course is indeed one of the main themes in William Crowther's enlightening contribution on Romania (Chapter 10);

Modernity All countries covered by this book have undergone a fundamental process of modernization which entails industrialization at the expense of the previously predominant agrarian economy, as well as industrialization of the agrarian sector itself. The gap between urban and rural areas, both in terms of economic production and in terms of life-style, has narrowed;

Clientelism and civil society The 20th century has entailed vast changes in the patterns of social authority from imperial clientelism via clientelistic one-party states towards patterns conducive to the establishment of civil society.

Figure 2.4: Three dimensions of continuity and their impact on the cleavage structure

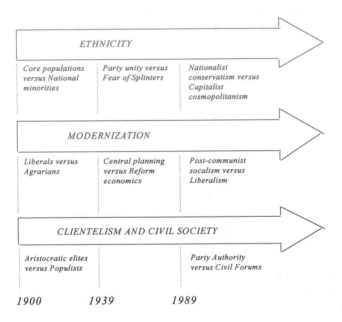

It is admittedly difficult to document a continuation of the manifest cleavages based on ethnicity, modernization and authority from the inter-war era to the present day. It is difficult to establish this linkage across time, it can even be difficult to document it contextually within the same time period – as evidenced by Drago Zajc's highly illustrative chapter on Slovenia. Even so, we would argue that there is an indirect continuity in the salience of the patterns within each of three crucial areas of ethnicity, modernity and pattern of social authority, but that a juxtaposition of the political forces surrounding the three domains might indeed be dramatically different today than it might have been in the 1920s and 1930s.

Thus, in the case of ethnicity, after the First World War parties were formed in order to protect ethnic minorities or, conversely, to mobilize national core populations in defence of a real or imagined threat from such minorities. In some cases there is a continuity, as shown, amongst others, by the post-1989 organization of Magyar parties in Slovakia and Romania. But in most cases, ethnicity has been transformed into an instrument for the political elites in a general nation-building project. Even though the Jewish minority in contemporary Poland is numerically insignificant, a Polish political leader may use anti-Semitic innuendo in order to position his party in relation to the cleavage between nationalism and cosmopolitanism.

In the inter-war period, most East European party systems included agrarian parties for rural defence (Urwin 1980). In Hungary and Romania, the old agrarian parties have re-emerged in the 1990s, sometimes even under their former labels, but they have a totally different function in post-communist society than they had in the inter-war era. Paradoxically, one may argue that many parties which label themselves 'agrarian' or 'green' actually work in favour of maintaining an industrial life-style among farmers and indeed, resist the dismantling of collective farming.

In the inter-war period, clientelism served to prevent the formation of strong, modern, mass-based organizations and to hinder the development of marked ideological conflicts between parties with different clienteles. Contemporary Eastern Europe clearly is not a region where rivalling patrons can mobilize followers with any set of policies. Yet clientelism can account for a difference in mentality between a rent-seeking electorate, mainly concerned with extracting resources from the state, and a wage-earning electorate whose interest lies in minimizing taxes and expanding the space for individual initiative.

In short, ethnicity, modernization and clientelism have all played an important role in political life in Eastern Europe throughout this century, but there is only a limited degree of direct continuity in the manifestation of cleavages if we compare the regimes of the 1920s and 1930s with the regimes of today.

NOTE

1. The peace settlement, which replaced the 1920 Peace Treaty of Sévres, gave Turkey all of Anatolia and Eastern Thrace. To prevent any future disputes, it also called for a compulsory population exchange; some 1.3 million Greeks and some 380,000 Turks were forced to emigrate (Jelavich 1983, 172).

REFERENCES

Allardt, Erik (1964), *Social Sources of Finnish Communism: Traditional and Emerging Radicalism*, University of Helsinki, Publications of the Institute of Sociology, 22.
—— (1970), 'Types of Protest and Alienation', in Erik Allardt and Stein Rokkan, eds., *Mass Politics*, New York, The Free Press.
Anderson, Benedict (1991), *Imagined Communities: Reflections on the Origin and Spread of Nationalism*, Verso Books.

Bankowicz, Marek (1994), 'Czechoslovakia: From Masaryk to Havel', in Sten Berglund and Jan Åke Dellenbrant, eds., *The New Democracies in Eastern Europe: Party Systems and Political Cleavages,* Aldershot, Edward Elgar.

Berglund, Sten and Frank Aarebrot (1997), *The Political History of Eastern Europe in the 20th Century: The Struggle Between Democracy and Dictatorship,* Aldershot, Edward Elgar.

Broklová, Eva (1995), 'Historical Roots for the Restoration of Democracy in Czechoslovakia', in Ivan Gabal, ed., *The Founding Election in Czechoslovakia: Analyses, Documents and Data,* Berlin, Edition Sigma.

Crampton, Richard and Ben Crampton (1996), *Atlas of Eastern Europe in the Twentieth Century,* London and New York, Routledge.

Davies, Norman (1986), *Heart of Europe: A Short History of Poland,* Oxford, Oxford University Press.

Deutsch, Karl (1953), *Nationalism and Social Communication: An Enquiry into the Foundations of Nationality,* New York, MIT Press–Wiley.

Fowkes, Ben (1995), *The Rise and Fall of Communism in Eastern Europe,* London, Macmillan, 2nd ed.

Gellner, Ernest (1983), *Nations and Nationalism,* Oxford, Blackwell.

Hellén, Tomas (1996), *Shaking Hands with the Past: Origins of the Political Right in Central Europe,* Helsinki, The Finnish Society of Sciences and Letters and the Finnish Academy of Science and Letters.

Hobsbawm, Eric (1990), *Nations and Nationalism since 1780: Programme, Myth, Reality,* Cambridge, Canto, 2nd ed.

Jelavich, Barbara (1983a), *History of the Balkans Volume 1: Eighteenth and Nineteenth Centuries,* Cambridge, Cambridge University Press.

—— (1983b), *History of the Balkans Volume 2: Twentieth Century,* Cambridge, Cambridge University Press.

Jelavich, Charles and Barbara Jelavich (1965), *The Balkans,* Englewood Cliffs, NJ, Prentice Hall

Lijphart, Arend (1968), *The Politics of Accommodation: Pluralism and Democracy in the Netherlands,* Berkeley, University of California Press.

—— (1980), *Democracy in Plural Societies: A Comparative Exploration,* New Haven, Yale University Press.

O'Donnell, Guillermo, Philippe Schmitter and Lawrence Whitehead, eds. (1986–87), *Transitions from Authoritarian Rule*: Baltimore, Johns Hopkins University Press, 4 Vols.

Rothschild, Joseph (1974), *East Central Europe between the Two World Wars,* Seattle and London, University of Washington Press.

—— (1989), *Return to Diversity: A Political History of Eastern Europe since World War Two,* New York, Oxford University Press.

Taylor, Charles Lewis and Michael C. Hudson, eds. (1972), *World Handbook of Political and Social Indicators,* 2nd ed., New Haven, Yale University Press.

—— and David A. Jodice, eds. (1983a), *World Handbook of Political and Social Indicators: Cross-National Attributes and Rates of Change,* Vol. 1, 3rd ed., New Haven, Yale University Press.

—— (1983b), *World Handbook of Political and Social Indicators: Political Protest and Government Change,* Vol. 2, 3rd ed., New Haven, Yale University Press.

Tismaneanu, Vladimir (1993), *Reinventing Politics: Eastern Europe from Stalin to Havel,* New York, Macmillan.

Urwin, Derek (1980), *From Ploughshare to Ballotbox: The Politics of Agrarian Defence in Europe,* Lommedalen, Universitetsforlaget.

Wallerstein, Immanuel (1974), *The Modern World System: Capitalist Agriculture and the Origins of the European World-Economy in the Sixteenth Century,* London, The Academic Press.

Wandycz, Piotr S. (1992), *The Price of Freedom: A History of East Central Europe from the Middle Ages to the Present,* London, Routledge.

Zeman, Z.A.B (1976), *The Masaryks: The Making of Czechoslovakia,* London, Weidenfeld & Nicholson.

3. Estonia

Mikko Lagerspetz and Henri Vogt[*]

This chapter aims to open up different levels of or perspectives into Estonia's society and politics. In the first part, we attempt to reconstruct the background of the country's present politics by trying to explain the Estonian public's seemingly minimal interest in politics, a trend also found in other former communist countries. In the second part, our perspective is purely historical: we will review the main patterns of development in Estonia's party system since the advent of the independence process. In the third part, we are more concerned with policies and actual cleavages in Estonian society, the most important of them being the division between native Estonians and other nationalities. However, the most crucial question appears to be why some key areas of Estonian politics have displayed continuing stability and decisiveness despite the many cleavages and controversies inherent in the process of change.

Indifference Towards Politics

The prevailing conviction in the Estonia of today (1997) is that politics suddenly lost its aura, its popularity, its legitimacy, after – or probably even before – the long-desired end of communist rule in August 1991, and that it has remained utterly unpopular ever since. A young Estonian's plain words are very much to the point: 'Politics doesn't interest me, I've had enough of it! All those XXs [name of a politician] and their nonsense simply disgust me!' (Lagerspetz 1997, 2249). It is not difficult to find empirical evidence to support this general thesis of indifference towards politics. For example, according to the figures presented by Vihalemm, Lauristin and Tallo (1997, 203), in January 1990, 90 per cent of the population was interested in politics, but by October 1993 this figure had already dropped to 43 per cent. By November 1996 the figure did not climb above 62 per cent at any stage (cf. Rose 1997, 17). It therefore seems there are at present two large groups in Estonian society: those interested in politics and those not interested, and that the 'cleavage' between these two is much more profound than all other political cleavages. This division moreover makes it significantly more difficult to speak of other cleavages that might materialize in people's electoral behaviour.

However, one could claim that a figure of 60 per cent representing those interested in politics is not that low, at least not lower than corresponding figures might be in the West – in Sweden, for example, it was 58 per cent in 1994 (Weibull and Holmberg 1997, 217). Indeed, the situation is much more complex than it seems at first sight, as it is not clear what kind of politics the general indifference thesis refers to. This in turn begs the question: what exactly is the meaning of 'politics' in post-communist Estonia?

Figure 3.1: Three concepts of Estonian politics: a conceptual scheme

Type of politics	*'Building process'*	*People's present attitude*	*Main questions and factors*
Institutional politics	State-building	Negative exclusion; very few partisans; will improve in the future as the system becomes less turbulent	Too-high expectations after independence; political scandals; small political elite and few fresh faces; instability of the party structure
Identity politics	Nation-building	Latent importance; inde-pendence and the new political system approved as such; leads to extraordinary politics (see the conclusion)	Relations with Russia; future of non-Estonians; position in Europe and membership in the EU and Nato; *'longue durée'*
Politics as such	Society-building	Scepticism towards political processes and ideologies; no true alternatives to be found in politics or to be achieved through politics	Crucial for the creation of civil society; individual-ism; business versus politics; successful economic transition

Three different concepts of politics seem to be significant, concepts that are by no means applicable to the Estonian case alone – of the countries dealt with in this volume, Latvia and Slovakia are probably the best parallel examples. We will call them 'institutional politics', 'identity politics', and 'politics as such'[1]. Up to a certain point, these three forms are analogous to the processes of state-building, nation-building and society-building that have been extremely important for all post-communist countries: insti-tutions form the basis of state-building; nation-building is essentially a question of national identity, and the position politics conquers and guards in a society, the way politics is understood, is indistinguishable from the nature of that society itself. The difference is that whereas 'building' denotes the whole process of creating a societal entity, politics in its various forms is more of a tool in that process. In any case, just as the processes of 'building' are partly overlapping, so, too, are these three forms connected to each other in many ways. For example, many decisions made by the government have potential impacts on the nation's understanding of itself, and once these become articulated in public debate, we will have entered the world of identity politics. It is also important to note that two of these three, institutional politics and politics as such, seem to advance the thesis that people are indifferent to politics, whereas the third, identity politics, defiantly negates the existence of any such indifference.

Institutional politics
By 'institutional politics' we simply refer to predominantly state-level politics, encompassing the parliament, government, the presidency, political parties, corporate groups, and sometimes even the legal system; other possible names might be 'official' or 'high' politics. This is, without doubt, the kind that first comes to most people's minds when they hear the term 'politics'. Political conflicts and their resolution, the actual politicking as well as policy-making, are included in our definition; all the actions and manners of the polity (or how it is perceived to act) must also be considered. On the other hand, political institutions, as well as the idea of democracy as such, are excluded.

It goes without saying that it is this form of politics that has been so unpopular in the country during the past six or seven years, actually even more unpopular than the percentage of those interested in politics, mentioned above, might suggest. The way the central institutions of the polity has worked has clearly disappointed many people. For example, only about half of the population had trust in the *Riigikogu* and the government in successive polls in 1996 and early 1997 (Lauristin and Vihalemm 1997, 337; cf. Rose 1997, 30–32.) Above all, the critical attitudes towards politics are a by-product of the pessimism regarding political parties. This is so clear that it allows David Arter – in his excellent book on Estonian politics, *Parties and Democracy in the Post-Soviet Republics: the Case of Estonia* – to call Estonia an anti-party system[2]. Arter also argues that in the light of electoral behaviour in the first and second parliamentary elections in 1992 and 1995, the main characteristics of this anti-party system remained more or less constant. Our own evidence also suggests that in this respect the situation has not changed markedly since 1995.

In order to illustrate how deep this distrust towards parties actually is, let us examine the traditional division between partisan, non-partisan or anti-party views. In Estonian circumstances, which are still in many ways turbulent, it is fairly difficult to estimate how widespread these attitudes are, but, in any case, it is obvious that few people at present can be labelled partisan. According to Arter (1996, 263–4), in the period of 1992–95, only 20 per cent of Estonians considered themselves supporters of a specific political party (cf. Rosimannus 1995, 30–31). The survey evidence that Arter refers to also shows that in 1994, as many as 67 per cent of the voters would have made their electoral choices on individual rather than on party grounds. The situation has not changed since: in the New Baltic Barometer Survey III of 1996, only one per cent of the population felt 'complete trust' and 15 per cent 'general trust' in political parties (Rose 1997, 30). With this in mind, it is not surprising that parties are still very small, and, one could also claim, underdeveloped. The Centre Party, *Keskerakond*, led by one of the heroes of the independence struggle, Edgar Savisaar, is the largest party in Estonia in terms of membership, but even so, it has only about 2,100 members (*Postimees,* 24 August 1997); there are six other parties with more than one thousand members each.[3]

It is even more difficult to assess the extent to which people can be called non- or anti-partisan than it is to estimate the number of partisans. In the New Baltic Barometer III survey mentioned above, 59 per cent of respondents had 'general distrust' and 25 per cent 'complete distrust' in parties. About one third of voters did not cast their vote in the first two *Riigikogu* elections (turnout was 66.7 and 68.9 per cent, respectively). According to a survey published in the *Postimees* on 29 August 1997, about the same proportion – 30 per cent of respondents – was not able to answer the question as to which party they would vote for if the elections were to be held the following day. This proportion might represent those who are predominantly anti-partisan – but then again, they might choose a protest group to channel their sentiments. In fact, the role of protest groups has been significant in both parliamentary elections held so far. In the 1992 elections, Jüri Toomepuu, a retired American Estonian and US Army veteran, won the highest individual number of votes, without doubt largely because of his anti-party political views (Arter 1996, 202). The protest groups of the 1995 elections – the Country People's Party *(Eesti Maarahva Erakond)* and the Reform Party *(Eesti Reformierakond)* – were not anti-party in the same sense as Toomepuu – they had prominent political figures as their leaders.[4] Nevertheless, although both parties were founded only a couple of months before the elections, they achieved very good electoral results. Together they received over 30 per cent of the votes cast.

There are, of course, several reasons for this scepticism towards insti-tutional (or party) politics in Estonia. First of all, there was the initial shock of entering the new world, the wounds of which have probably never entirely healed in the realm of politics. The real – or rather, the material – consequences of change in Estonia were very different from what people had expected. In the winter of 1991–92, prices went up very rapidly – fuel prices by 200 to 300 per cent – there was a serious shortage of goods, and food coupons were introduced. At the same time, quite naturally, support for the Supreme Council, the then parliament, dropped dramatically. Only after the introduction of the Estonian national currency, the kroon, in June 1992, was trust in Estonia's economy re-established – but trust in the parliament remained at a fairly low level (Kask 1996, 199). Another aspect of this initial shock was the lamentable turn from national unanimity to a day-to-day political tug-of-war; the 'movement society' became the 'party society'. Many former heroes and friends from the independence struggle suddenly became members of different political camps; something which undoubtedly surprised and irritated many people.

Secondly, the actual record of parties has not been flattering. Numerous political scandals have stained the escutcheon of politics at the highest level of decision-making. The past five years have seen two prime ministers being forced to step down on three occasions as a result of such scandals (see Appendix 3.2). Moreover, no attractive new faces have appeared in politics; many politicians who have been in the spotlight ever since the independence struggle have been unable to renew themselves; people probably simply think that these politicians have already done their job. Thus, politics is often seen as the nasty game of a very exclusive group of present or former friends – in a small country like Estonia this is, of course, also predictable: everybody tends to know everybody else. This system of exclusion has had detrimental consequences, especially in the case of young people: apart from a handful of young intellectuals (Mart Laar, Jüri Luik and others) who were active already in the revolutionary process, young people have preferred to stay outside political life.

Finally, party politics is still a new phenomenon; people are simply not used to it. The short democratic exercise of the inter-war period did not create any lasting traditions of party politics. As shown, the party structure has been rather turbulent for most of the time covered in this chapter, and it is still fairly fragmented (*Figure 3.1*). It has not been easy for voters to follow party system development. In 1997, however, it seemed that some sort of stability had finally been achieved, but, of course, this may still change very quickly. However, stability is a two-edged sword; stability may also mean stagnation. Indeed, in newspaper debates in 1997, the Centre Party was often accused of having stagnated. The obvious counter-argument put forward by the party's defenders was that it was a stable political party – in fact, the only one in Estonia – and thus represented a safe option for voters.

Identity politics

The second category in our tripartite division of politics, 'identity politics', represents all the questions that somehow refer to the role of Estonia as a country, and as a state among other states. We do not refer to identity politics in the sense in which it is often used today to denote the politics of various under-represented groups: sexual minorities, women, and refugees; our starting point is simply the Estonian nation. The construction of a nation's identity is, of course, a never-ending story and one that pertains to all modern societies: a country's position in the world is a matter of continuous redefinitions. Institutional politics may be – and in the case of Estonia, usually is – a self-regulating process exclusive to political elites. But identity politics, although it may often be expressed through these same elites, always needs to be connected in some way to the population at large.

It is obvious that the whole revolutionary process in Estonia started in the field of identity politics – that is, in the field that could not develop freely under the Soviet regime as long as Moscow's bear's paw was still strong. When the new era dawned in the mid-1980s, the nation had to be redefined in both time and space. The first thing was to reveal and reformulate the 'true' history of the nation, the whole cultural heritage of Estonia, in a manner suitable for the new political conditions (see later references to the National Heritage Society, and the Estonian Group for Making Public the Molotov-Ribbentrop Pact).[5] Simultaneously, it was deemed imperative to preserve and defend the soil that Estonians had inhabited from time im-memorial. The major movements during the independence struggle – *Rahvarinne* (the Popular Front) and the Citizens' Committees – can also initially be seen as identity political movements. Although all of these organizations gradually moved towards institutional politics (they did play a decisive role in the formation of a multi-party system when it truly started during the latter part of 1989), they did not entirely lose their nature as identity-political groupings before the declaration of independence in August 1991.[6] But as the advent of independence became more and more apparent, the need for identity politics greatly diminished and institutional politics quite naturally started to dominate the public sphere.

More important still, as long as identity politics prevailed, with its emphasis on the future of the nation, people were politically very active. But as soon as politics became a matter of the state – i.e. when institutional politics gained precedence – people turned away politics; or, rather, they did want to stick to identity politics, but since that was not so crucially important any more, it became latent or invisible.

This is not only a phenomenon of the present, however, it has deep historical roots. We claim to be able to discover a historically determined sentiment in Estonia that glorifies the nation but condemns the state. Indeed, this may be the reason for the survival of this small nation, whose lands have been regularly conquered throughout history; Estonia has had the ability to exist outside the realm of institutional politics, that is, outside of the state. One could, of course, claim that the first experience of independence in the inter-war period made a difference in this sense. Alternatively, it might be more accurate to describe it as the final confirmation of the inability of the state to protect the nation: democracy could not be preserved and many people thought that President Konstantin Päts, the embodiment of the state, simply handed over the country to the Soviet Union. Be this as it may, the documented criticism of, and indifference towards, institutional politics mean only a return to the traditional historical path, to scepticism towards the state.

It is also important to note here that regaining independence, gaining democracy, a parliament, a president, political parties, was – and is – very important from the perspective of identity politics; acquiring all these was essential for the Estonian identity. This has obviously not changed. Although people may criticize the present parliament and laugh at the parties, they still believe in the multi-party system, in the parliamentary system and particularly in democracy in general; people do not want to go back to a system that lacks these. To give an example, according to the 1995 Eurobarometer East, only some 15 per cent of Estonians were very dissatisfied with democracy in their country; the corresponding figure for Italy was 25 per cent, and 12 per cent for France and Britain a year earlier (Berglund and Aarebrot 1997, 172; cf. also the chapter on Lithuania in the present volume). So, if politics is defined essentially as the process of maintaining democracy (and freedom), people's attitudes towards politics could actually be termed fairly positive.

It is no easy task to give any exact empirical evidence as to what the substance of identity politics is currently. Obviously, Estonia is still not a ready-made society; it remains open to many kinds of definitions. Identity politics inevitably plays a central role in this regard. Indeed, and as will be seen in the final section of this chapter, Estonians' relations with Russia and Russians still define the course of Estonian politics in many ways. Similarly, the question of Estonia's identity in relation to the West, e.g. membership in the EU and/or NATO, is of crucial importance. In addition, if Estonia is compared with many Western countries, i.e. to countries where national identity seems to be more or less secure and self-evident, some aspects of Estonian societal discussions and debates look fairly striking. For example, surprisingly, on many occasions it is still important to use the label *Eesti Vabariik*, The Republic of Estonia, instead of merely 'Estonia'; in Britain one can talk of the Prime Minister whereas in Estonia it is still necessary to refer to the Prime Minister of Estonia (cf. Lagerspetz 1997). As these examples show, the country is still very political if seen from an identity political perspective. Of the 60 per cent of the population who still dare to confess that they are interested in politics, a significant part may be people who are interested in politics only in so far as it is a question of identity. Conversely, institutional politics has still not become part of identity politics; being an Estonian is not shaped by the acts of political institutions (as is the case in, say, Britain). But the popular wisdom, or hope, is that such a day will arrive in the years to come.

Politics as such

Our third major category of politics, 'politics as such', is undoubtedly even more difficult to analyse, or even recognize, than identity politics. Our definition can probably be traced back to an Arendtian understanding of politics (Arendt 1958): it is how the role of politics is understood in society, the space that the business of politics is able to retain in society, the possibilities people perceive in political action. In this sense it is the precondition for any actual form of politics.

Three points regarding politics as such are significant here. First of all, we have to ask how the unsuccessful attempt at communism (and, why not, other great political utopias) and the realization that not even the new system was perfect, have affected people's willingness to participate in any kind of political process. As many social thinkers have claimed, it is obvious that such experiences have led to a general disillusionment with all-embracing political projects; scepticism in this sense may be the most profound political feature of today's East Europeans (Vogt 1996). But scepticism can be interpreted positively; turning away from big political projects could mean turning towards small ones. Thus, on a very practical level, the way people perceive politics is decisive for the creation and development of civil society, and for the ability of the organizations of this civil society to create a functioning political realm, a *polis*. People should learn that being political, which includes a conflictual component – to be able to fight for, say, the future of a local school – makes a difference. Here our idea is probably not too far away from what Vihalemm, Lauristin and Tallo (1997, 200) call the critical–rational stage of political culture, into which they argue that Estonia has not really yet entered.

Secondly, we have to analyse the way politics is understood in relation to general societal trends, particularly in Estonia and in Europe generally. The most significant of such trends is probably the Western-type individualism that may also be emerging in Estonia. Indeed, according to Marju Lauristin (1997), this is a fairly clear tendency in the country, both among ethnic Estonians and non-Estonians, and especially among the young and well-educated. They have seen much more alluring prospects in the world of business; business signifies opportunities to fulfil one's individualism. Lauristin claims that Estonia now lives simultaneously in three different times: in the pre-modern time shaped by clear national values; in the industrial time shaped by economic rationality; and in the post-modern time, where people greatly emphasize free time and pleasure (interview with Lauristin in *Eesti Ekspress*, 29 August 1997). However, we would like to return to what was said above about the *longue durée* of Estonian national sentiment. It is still very much there; if necessary it could easily overcome the emerging individualism. Even so, the shift towards more individualistic value orientations may prove to be invaluable in solving the country's ethnic problems.

Finally, and very much related to the first point, it seems that the range for political manoeuvring has become extremely narrow and the variation of political possibilities has been dramatically reduced. In economic policy, Estonia has followed a fairly straight course despite the constant changes of government – Mart Siimann's moderate-right minority cabinet, which took office in March 1997 was the seventh government since the declaration of independence in August 1991 (see Appendix 3.2). No realistic alternatives to the current policy have been put forward with regard to the most important economic decisions, and this absence of alternatives has probably made people believe that change may not be brought about through politics. This reduction of space for political manoeuvring is also interesting in the sense that there were clear ideological differences between different movements during the transformation process. Now, however, ideological differences between parties have become minimal. We will have to come back to the question of Estonia's economic success and to the present-day ideological similarity between parties, but before that we will briefly review some of the major structural developments of the political parties in contemporary Estonia.

The Development of the Party System

Estonia's return to full sovereignty started in 1987, on 25 February to be precise, when the issue of an increase in phosphorite mining came to the fore[7], and lasted until 31 August 1994, when the last Soviet troops finally left the country.

This period can be subdivided into two parts: the first lasted until 20 August 1991, when the Supreme Council and the Estonian Committee (the executive body of the Estonian Congress) declared Estonia's independence. The Soviet Union recognized the independent Republic of Estonia less than three weeks later, on 6 September 1991.

Before independence

How many people really supported the Soviet regime in Estonia – or in other Baltic states, or even in Russia? It is one of those questions that will forever remain unanswered; we only know that support was never high and that it gradually decreased and crumbled (Lagerspetz 1996, 50; 103). Be that as it may, it was the attitude towards the Soviet regime that paved the way for the development of a political spectrum in Estonia. During the first years of the transition period, the main conflict was whether to seek full independence or only extended autonomy within the Soviet Union. Yet after the March 1990 Supreme Council elections at the very latest, it was clear that an overwhelming majority of Estonians and all major ethnic Estonian-led movements were in favour of the former alternative. Even among ethnic Russians this was not an entirely illegitimate goal, although in the independence referendum of March 1991, the majority of 'no' votes (totalling 21.4 per cent) came from predominantly Russian-speaking areas. In Tallinn, however, at least one-third of Russians were in favour of independence.[8]

In Estonia, as in every corner of Eastern Europe, there were always dissident voices that could not be completely silenced. After Mikhail Gorbachev came to power in Moscow and initiated the policies of *perestroika* and *glasnost*, these voices became more co-ordinated. The decisive moment, however, was the Phosphorite War, an ecological issue[9] that did not look too confrontational, too political, on the surface. For the first time on such a scale, critical factions could coalesce around a single issue. A new counter-elite was born, and the ability and willingness of the Estonians to mobilize became apparent. By way of example, it may be noted that students at the University of Tartu played an active role in these early events. But equally important was the fact that many prominent members of the Estonian Communist Party, including Edgar Savisaar and Arnold Rüütel joined the protests against the new phosphorite mines (Laar et al. 1996, 164).

These prominent personalities also played a decisive role in the formation of *Eestimaa Rahvarinne*, the Popular Front, on 13 April 1988. This movement was, from the very beginning, meant to serve as an umbrella organization for various critical groups[10]; it never became a party. In practice, most of the groups that joined (or stayed in) *Rahvarinne* belonged to the moderate left or centre. Therefore, and surely also because of the background of many of its leaders, *Rahvarinne's* policy was relatively cautious; dramatic confrontations with the Soviet Communist Party were avoided. The initial primary goals were to provide a platform for democracy and to achieve more autonomy, especially economic autonomy, for Estonia within the Soviet Union.[11] In any case, *Rahvarinne* was able to win a very large following among Estonian citizens, so that it has even been claimed that 'a dual Communist Party–Popular Front power existed at that period in Estonia' (Park 1995, 295). With respect to the Supreme Council, this state of affairs cannot be overstated: there, *Rahvarinne*-minded politicians, or at least its sympathizers, formed a majority from the very outset. This is why many decisions made by the Supreme Council, such as the Declaration of Sovereignty in November 1988, were possible.

The rewriting of Estonia's history was one of the first major tasks for the builders of independence. Two organizations were of particular importance: the Estonian National Heritage Society *(Eesti Muinsuskaitse Selts,* EMS), a merger of several small heritage groups, composed mainly of intellectuals, and founded in December 1987; and the Estonian Group for Making Public the Molotov–Ribbentrop Pact *(Molotovi–Ribbentropi Pakti Avalikustamise Eesti Grupp,* MRP–AEG), which was brought to the public's attention in August 1987, when this group organized a demonstration – the first clear manifestation of national self-consciousness – in a park in downtown Tallinn; on 10 August the next year the leading Estonian daily, *Rahva Hääl*, published the secret protocols to the Pact. In January 1988, the leaders of the MRP–AEG founded the *Eesti Rahvusliku Sõltumatuse Partei* (ERSP), the Estonian National Independence Party. Many of the founding fathers were well-known radical dissidents, and some, e.g. Lagle Parek and Enn Tarto, had even been incarcerated in Soviet prisons in the mid-1980s. It is no wonder that the policy of *Rahvarinne* appeared far too cautious to these radical dissidents. In February 1989, they founded the Estonian Citizen's Committees (*Eesti Kodanike Komiteed*) along with activists from the National Heritage Society, for whom the restoration of the pre-1940 Republic was the primary, indeed, the only acceptable goal (Laar et al. 1996, 558). The major task of the Citizens' Committees was the organization of a census of those who had been, or were descended from, citizens of pre-1940 Estonia, and to have them elect an Estonian Congress. This was designed to become the only true Estonian parliamentary institution, responsible to an ethnically defined Estonian constituency.

Thus, there were two major political players on the Estonian side, the moderate *Rahvarinne* and the radical Citizens' Committees. The third major actor in the political arena might have been the Communist Party of Estonia (EKP), but the communists had rapidly lost clout despite the backing they received from Moscow. It is very likely that less than 10 per cent of the ethnic Estonians supported the EKP in 1989 (Taagepera 1993, 150). The majority of the ethnic Estonian communists started to support *Rahvarinne* – even Vaino Väljas, the newly-chosen pro-reform First Secretary of the EKP spoke at its inaugural congress in October 1988 – or other anti-regime movements. After the EKP split in January 1990, many of those who were still members joined pro-independence Free Estonia *(Vaba Eesti).*

Practically no ethnic Estonians remained loyal to the Soviet Union.

The attitudes among non-ethnic Estonians were different; they reacted with irritation to the nationalist elements of the Estonian movements. The most important counter-independence movement, the Inter-Movement *(Internatsionalnoe dvizhenie)*, was actually founded as a direct response to the emergence of *Rahvarinne*, only two months after the latter, in July 1988. The founders were mainly Russian-speakers who had moved to Estonia during the forty years of Soviet rule. It is hard to estimate the true level of support for the Inter-Movement, but many non-Estonians definitely did not support it. Inter-Movement itself claimed that it had 150,000 to 200,000 supporters in 1989 (Arter 1996, 140), but according to Taagepera (1993), who refers to a May 1989 survey, it had the support of some 50,000 people, or approximately 11 per cent of the non-ethnic Estonians. Hence, the only reliable figure for illuminating the mood among the non-Estonian population, may be the one from the independence referendum of 1991, in which approximately two-thirds of non-Estonians voted in favour of staying within the Soviet Union.

Three important elections were held in 1989 and 1990: the elections to the Congress of the USSR People's Deputies (26 March 1989); the elections to the Estonian Congress (24 February–1 March 1990); and the elections to the Estonian Supreme Council (18 March 1990). The 1989 elections were the first almost free elections in Estonia since the inter-war era. Turnout was surprisingly high, 87.1 per cent, and the victory of *Rahvarinne* clear; it received 29 out of 36 seats. This was an open manifestation of the mood prevailing in the country against the Soviet system. As Tiina Raitviir (1996, 353) notes, the elections to the Estonian Congress and to the Estonian Supreme Council were, not only 'held almost simultaneously but they were also essentially interrelated. They reflected the competition between the pro-independence groups on the ground of rightist and leftist [in our terminology: radical and moderate] ideals'. *Rahvarinne* had considered the creation of the Estonian Congress too confrontational; it wanted to use existing bodies for proceeding towards independence. However, only a week before the elections to the Estonian Congress, *Rahvarinne* finally decided to participate. This was crucially important: it was the final confirmation of the radicalization of *Rahvarinne* in favour of full independence.[12] However, from the point of view of electoral success, *Rahvarinne's* decision obviously came too late; groups associated with the Citizens' Committees won an electoral victory. So, 174 out of the 499 seats (464 in Estonia plus 35 abroad) went to candidates close to the Citizens' Committees (the EMS got 104 seats, the ERSP 70). *Rahvarinne* won 107 seats; independents 109; and the EKP 39 *(Helsingin Sanomat*, 6 March 1990; quoted in Arter 1996, 257).[13]

The Estonian Congress never acquired the decisive role that its founders had hoped for, although the radical example it showed was undoubtedly a major factor in making full independence a real alternative (Raitviir 1995, 186). From May 1990 onwards, the Congress became increasingly marginalized, no doubt because its policy was too much dominated by the ERSP – many people simply chose to channel their political influence through the Supreme Council (over 40 individuals were members in both bodies). Many confrontations between these two bodies occurred until the first *Riigikogu* elections in September 1992, but the Supreme Council was able to dominate the political scene. However, thirty members were nominated by both the Council and the Congress to the Constitutional Assembly that started the preparation of a new constitution in September 1991.[14]

In the Supreme Council elections, *Rahvarinne* emerged as the victor; the Citizens' Committees movement was critical about the very legitimacy of the elections. It is difficult to provide exact information about electoral behaviour in these elections due to the peculiarities in the electoral system. For example, a candidate could run for two different lists without even knowing it, and no party labels were used. In this sense, these elections were not yet really party-political, although nine registered parties or popular movements participated. In any case, 43 out of 105 seats went to candidates supported by *Rahvarinne*; the Joint Council of Work Collectives, which represented the Russian population and was close to the Inter-Movement, won 23; Free Estonia and its rural allies gained 27 seats and other groups (e.g. greens and liberals) eight mandates; 4 seats were reserved for the military. This put the number of 'nationalist-inclined' representatives at between 70 and 80 (cf. Dellenbrant 1994, 99–100; Arter 1996, 257; Gerner and Hedlund 1993, 122; Raitviir 1996, 190). Two weeks later, on 3 April, the leader of *Rahvarinne*, Edgar Savisaar became prime minister.

The referendum on independence of 3 March 1991 was the final major political event before the declaration of independence. As mentioned earlier, 21.4 per cent of the permanent residents of Estonia voted against independence in a referendum with a turnout of 83 per cent. Voting behaviour in urban and rural areas was remarkably dissimilar. In the predominantly ethnic Estonian countryside, only 4.1 per cent were against independence, whereas the corresponding figure in the ethnically much more heterogeneous cities was 28.5 per cent (Raitviir 1996, 446).

After independence
Party formation started long before the final declaration of independence, but once the leading role of the Communist Party in Soviet Estonia had been terminated by an amendment on 23 February 1990, the number of parties immediately mushroomed. The declaration of independence did not

produce any change in this respect; however, before the elections of September 1992, these numerous parties started to reorganize into electoral alliances, not least as a result of the 5 per cent electoral threshold which had been introduced. Later on, these alliances often became parties, but the party system has nevertheless remained fairly fragmented (Figure 3.1). In actual parliamentary work, parliamentary factions, frequently significantly different from the electoral alliances, have also played an important role (Kask 1996). We shall concentrate on the question of what became of the movements that had had the largest role in the struggle for independence, namely *Rahvarinne* and the Citizens' Committees.

Rahvarinne had lost its function as an umbrella organization by the time of the elections of 1992, mainly due to the defection of three important political formations: the social democrats, the liberal democrats and the agrarians. The loose structure of *Rahvarinne*, which never set out to become a political party itself, probably facilitated the break-up, but the split has also been attributed to Edgar Savisaar's allegedly authoritarian leadership style. An electoral alliance called *Rahvarinne* did participate in the first elections, but it obtained only 12.4 per cent of the votes and 15 seats out of 101 in the first *Riigikogu*. The most important component of this *Rahvarinne* alliance was the People's Centre Party *(Eesti Rahva Keskerakond)*, led by, among others, Savisaar himself, Mati Hint, and Jaan Kaplinski. The prefix 'People's' was removed from the party label in 1993, and in the elections of 1995, which it contested on an independent platform, the Centre Party came in second. In April 1996, a new party, the Progress Party *(Arengupartei)*, was founded by those who opposed the re-election of Savisaar as the leader of the Centre Party. In the presidential elections of 1992, held simultaneously with the parliamentary elections, Professor Rein Taagepera was supported by the Centre Party (see Appendix 3.1). The Centre Party's popular image is that of a party for those for whom the transformation has not been a success story in all respects. The party has also received significant support among the Russian-speakers.

The Moderates *(Mõõdukad)* was the only *Rahvarinne*-derived electoral alliance to become part of the government which was formed after the elections of September 1992. The coalition of Moderates consisted of two parties: the Social Democratic Party *(Eesti Sotsiaaldemokraatlik Partei)* – itself a merger of several social democratic groups and led by Marju Lauristin, one of the central figures of the independence struggle – and the Rural Centre Party *(Eesti Maa–Keskerakond)* led by Ivar Raig. In the first elections, the Moderate alliance polled a respectable 10 per cent of the votes and got 12 seats. After the 1995 elections, in which their support dropped to 6 per cent, the two parties merged and took the name of their electoral alliance. It still remains to be seen whether the Moderates will be able to take on the cloak of Scandinavian-style social democracy, but at present the party is the most likely candidate for this. There is definitely room for some kind of social democracy in Estonia.

Kindel Kodu, Secure Home (crime rates were skyrocketing at the time), which got 17 representatives elected to the first *Riigikogu* of 1992, was a joint platform for three party formations. The most important of these formations was (and remains) the Coalition Party *(Eesti Koonderakond)*, named after the Finnish conservative party but having as its key figures many reform communists (several of whom had a Free Estonia background) along with a number of former managers of small and medium-sized state companies (Arter 1996, 181). The other two groups were considerably smaller: the Estonian Rural Union *(Eesti Maaliit)* got four seats in the first *Riigikogu* and the Estonian Democratic Justice Union *(Eesti Demokraatlik Õigusliit)* two. In 1994, the latter was renamed the Union of Pensioners and Families *(Eesti Pensionäride ja Perede Liit)*, and, as the name implies, this party has had a fairly clear image ever since. In the 1992 presidential elections, *Kindel Kodu* supported the popular incumbent President, Arnold Rüütel. In the 1995 elections, the electoral alliance of the Coalition Party and the Rural Union became a clear winner. This alliance also included the Country People's Party led by Rüütel, who polled the highest individual number of votes.

Among the five (main) parties that formed the electoral alliance *Isamaa* (Pro Patria, literally 'Fatherland'), the clear winner of the 1992 elections[15], the Liberal Democratic Party *(Eesti Liberaaldemokraatlik Partei)* was the only one with a *Rahvarinne* background. Otherwise *Isamaa* originated from Citizens' Committees or groups close to them. Interestingly, two Christian parties, both founded as early as the summer of 1988, belonged to *Isamaa*. The most important one, and the core of *Isamaa*, was the Estonian Christian Democratic Union *(Eesti Kristlik Demokraatlik Liit*; the other called itself the Estonian Christian Democratic Party), whose leaders, Mart Laar, Trivimi Velliste and Illar Hallaste had also been active in the National Heritage Society. In the *Isamaa*-led government that was formed after the 1992 elections, Laar became prime minister – aged 32 years, the youngest prime minister in Europe. Of the remaining two *Isamaa* parties, the Republican Coalition Party *(Eesti Vabariiklaste Koonderakond,* EVKE) was particularly important in formulating the ultra liberal policies of Laar's government (Arter 1996, 169); the Conservative People's Party *(Eesti Konservatiivne Rahvaerakond,* EKRE) was a radical right-wing party. All the parties in the *Isamaa* bloc merged in January 1993 under the name of the electoral alliance, but soon thereafter, their new party started to disintegrate.

Figure 3.2: Main patterns of party developments in Estonia

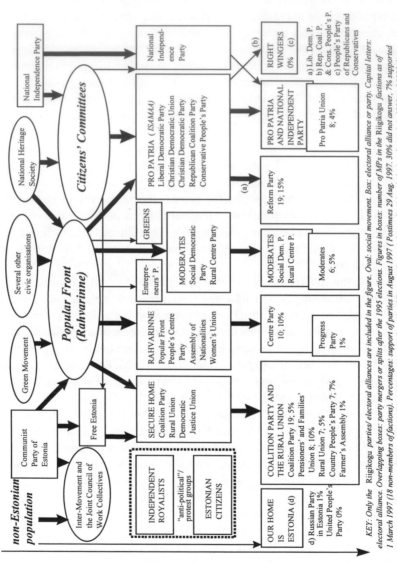

The Movement Society in 1989   Elections of September 1992   Elections of March 1995   1997

KEY: *Only the Riigikogu parties/ electoral alliances are included in the figure. Oval: social movement. Box: electoral alliance or party. Capital letters: electoral alliance. Overlapping boxes: party mergers or splits after the 1995 elections. Figures in boxes: number of MPs in the Riigikogu factions as of 1 March 1997 (18 non-members of factions). Percentages: support of parties in August 1997 (Postimees 29 Aug. 1997. 30% did not answer, 7% supported non- Riigikogu parties). The placement of the 1989 groupings reflects the differences between the 'radicals' and the 'moderates'; in 1992 and 1995 the placement reflects the cleavage between the 'young professionals' and the 'old guard'.*

In June 1994, some EVKE and EKRE groups left *Isamaa* to found a *Riigikogu* faction called the 'Right-Wingers', which gained considerable support in 1995 when it got five MPs elected. On the other hand, the remnants of *Isamaa* only got eight representatives when it ran together with the Estonian National Independence Party (ERSP). On 2 December 1995, *Isamaa* merged with the ERSP to form *Isamaa Liit,* the Pro Patria Union.[16]

Finally, to complete this presentation of Estonia's party system, the new-comer to Estonian politics, the Reform Party, is a party primarily catering to young businessmen, in other words to the winners in the transformation process. The party did well in the elections of 1995 when it received 19 seats. According to opinion polls conducted in 1997, the Reform Party had become the single most popular party in Estonia, with a steady electoral support of more than 15 per cent (*Postimees*, 29 August 1997).

Cleavages but Consensual Policies

In the two previous sections we have tried to show how, on the one hand, the clear ideological cleavages of the early days of the independence process have been transformed into a fairly fragmented party system, and on the other hand, how this fragmentation has failed to appeal to the population at large, leaving the majority of voters indifferent towards party politics. But a few more bricks are needed in order to make full sense of the pattern of Estonian politics.

The cleavage between the 'old guard' and the 'young professionals', is the only major cleavage that can be derived from the party structure presented above. Of fundamental significance for an accurate interpretation of Estonian political life today, however, are the situation of the Russian minority and the consensual but successful economic policy.

Old guard versus young professionals

Writing about party politics in the Baltic states, Anatol Lieven (1993, 214–9) comes to the conclusion that an analysis in terms of the conventional left–right ideological pattern makes little sense. Tiina Raitviir (1996, 117–23) confirms this view from an Estonian domestic perspective when she states that the great number of political parties and their ideological vague-ness are the most fundamental problems of the Estonian party system. Characteristically, Tiit Vähi, the leader of the Coalition Party, then the strongest opposition group, made a statement in March 1993 denying any ideological differences between his party and *Isamaa,* the party of Prime Minister Mart Laar: 'There are actually no ideological differences between the parties. Both parties have supported independence and both strive for a market economy' (quoted in Park and Ruutsoo 1995, 197). Indeed, the striking fact in Estonian politics is that all major parties seem to claim that they are either rightist, centrist or right-centrist; nobody wants to be unequivocally leftist. Instead, and as Lieven (1993, 215) also notes, the significant dividing lines between parties are their attitudes regarding history and national culture – in one word, the past.

Post-1991 Estonian politics clearly reflect this. The issue of the restoration of the pre-1940 Republic of Estonia – the main demand of the Citizens' Committees – interacts with the varying attitudes towards the achievements of, and traditions inherited from, the Soviet era. Here, the interests of the Soviet-period elite, and those of the previous owners of nationalized property and their heirs, are understandably in opposition. The Estonian expatriate community has shared the views of the latter, as have often the domestic young professionals, given that their career prospects are furthered by the replacement of Soviet-era senior officials and by the reorganization of the formerly state-owned enterprises.

At the same time, however, even the old guard of the Soviet era has not opposed privatization or market reforms. The difference between the two groups – the young professionals along with previous owners of nationalized property on the one hand, and the 'old guard' on the other – may thus be attributed to group-specific interests which they have tried to protect in the course of the privatization and marketization processes. With some reservations, it could be said that the development expected by some commentators (e.g. Raitviir 1996, 116–7) towards two large coalitions of parties – the 'right-centrist' coalition around *Isamaa* and at the moment, probably also the Reform Party (although many of its leaders are former prominent communists), and the 'centrist' coalition around the Coalition and Centre Parties – would, first and foremost, reflect this cleavage. Obviously, it could also be seen as an ideological vestige from the original dispute between the Citizens' Committees and *Rahvarinne*. Be that as it may, the importance of politicians' personal relations to the old Soviet administration will diminish eventually. A future consolidation of party structures towards bipolarity is still only one out of several alternatives, and, as we see it, not even the most likely one.

The ethnic cleavage

A much more important – probably the most important – cleavage is that of the relationship between native Estonians and immigrant Russian-speakers. As is well known, this is also the question of particular interest to outside observers. When Estonian democracy is being evaluated by such observers, the position of non-Estonian residents sometimes puts Estonia's democratic character in doubt. Here, only a couple of facts are presented – the question is put into the overall political context in the concluding section.

Of Estonia's 1.49 million inhabitants, approximately 64 per cent were native Estonians in 1995 (Statistical Yearbook 1996, 55); the remainder belonged to a number of different nationalities, of which the 430,000 Russians formed the largest group. When the Law on Citizenship was enacted in February 1992, citizenship was automatically granted only to the pre-1940 citizens and their descendants, irrespective of ethnicity. The people who had arrived during the Soviet era were supposed to apply for citizenship and pass a language test (for a further analysis of Estonian citizenship policy, see Everly 1997). This law effectively disenfranchised a majority of non-Estonian residents, who were (and are) allowed to vote only in local elections. However, having the idea of legal continuity of the pre-1940 Estonian state as its point of departure, the Law on Citizenship is strictly logical and not in conflict with international law (Öst 1994). The *jus sanguinis* principle applied is no different from that of some other countries, notably Germany. The Aliens Law of 1993 obliges non-citizens to seek residence permits.

Russians have not had many opportunities to make themselves heard in party politics. Before the 1992 elections, the Russians were divided into two groups on the basis of their relationship with the Soviet Union, subsequently Russia. The 'Russian Community in Estonia' was more sympathetic to its big Eastern neighbour, while the 'Representative Assembly of the Russian-Speaking Community' was more liberal and oriented towards Europe. In any case, in the elections of September 1992, no Russian representatives were elected to the *Riigikogu*. In the 1995 elections, however, the Russian population was able to enter the parliament within the electoral alliance of Our Home is Estonia (*Meie kodu on Eestimaa*), which received a total of six seats. As the name implies, the group is in favour of Estonia's statehood, but it has heavily criticized the human rights record in the country.

The future of the non-Estonian inhabitants has by no means been solved yet. From 1990 to 1993, the non-Estonian population was notably reduced, as almost 80,000 people left Estonia, mostly for Russia and other countries of the Commonwealth of Independent States, the CIS (Statistical Yearbook 1994, 79). However, this large-scale migration has evidently come to an end – Estonia simply offers better chances for improving one's living standards than Russia. The integration of those remaining in Estonian society is an issue that politicians have been rather reluctant to discuss and Estonian-language political parties have treated it only in very vague terms (Raitviir 1996, 109–10). Due to the Soviet policy of promoting Russian as the main language of communication between different nationalities, many non-Estonians' knowledge of Estonian is still poor (*Table 3.1*). The situation is obviously improving, but due to insufficient funds for Estonian language teaching and the psychological constraints of the old Russian-speaking majority, integration is not likely to be a rapid process. As the figures in Table 3.1 demonstrate, there are also considerable differences in the way Estonians and non-Estonians interpret the process of change.

Table 3.1: Differences between Estonians and non-Estonians in Estonia

	Estonians	Russians
'Where on the scale from –100 to 100 would you put the former communist regime?' (mean)	–38	23
'Where on this scale would you put our system of governing at present / in five years time?' (mean)	18/42	–3/22
'Where on this scale would you put our economic system at present / in five years time?' (mean)	16/86	1/71
What was the total household income in the past month (mean in EEK)?	4,333	3,548
'We would be better off if we were still part of the Soviet Union'; strongly agree/strongly disagree (%)	1/87	15/29
'Everyone who is resident of Estonia' (%)		
– should learn the national language, always / usually	82/16	33/53
– respect the nation's flag, always / usually	78/20	49/42
– should definitely be educated in language of parents	78	80
'Who should be a citizen?' (%)		
– those whose families were citizens before 1940	44	0
– everyone who was born in the country	34	27
– everyone who has lived here for more than ten years	19	21
– everyone living here at the time of independence	2	28
– any former citizen who is now living in the country	1	23
'Do you think that the Russian state is a threat to peace and security in this country?'		
– Definitely / possibly / probably not / definitely not (%)	33/48/18/1	4/16/48/32
'If a referendum took place tomorrow on joining the EU, how would you vote?'		
– In favour/ against (%)	59/41	78/22
'How would you describe the relations between nationalities and ethnic groups in this country?'		
– All right/not so good (%)	74/23	62/30
Able to carry on a conversation in Russian (Estonians) or in Estonian (Russians) (%)	81	43
'This country offers better chances for improving living standards in future that Russia does'; agree (%)		74
'Are you generally satisfied or not satisfied with your way of life?' ('completely' and 'somewhat' satisfied, %)?	61	57

Source: New Baltic Barometer III (Rose 1997). The survey conducted in November 1996 by Saar Poll. N = 682 Estonians and 389 Russians (residents). Face-to-face interviews.

The consensual area: economic policy

Despite the cleavages mentioned above, and given the destabilizing effects of the ongoing transformation processes, some crucial areas of policy seem amazingly stable. Estonia's economic performance since independence compares favourably with that of all the post-Soviet republics, with that of the two other Baltic states, and, notwithstanding Estonia's more awkward point of departure, even with that of many of the countries in East Central Europe. The radical and decisive nature of Estonian economic reforms, and especially its monetary policy, are often proposed as the main factors accounting for this relative success (Grennes 1997). The total and extremely rapid orientation towards the West of Estonian foreign trade is among the most impressive developments. In 1991, the republics of the Soviet Union, including Latvia and Lithuania, took 95 per cent of Estonian exports. In the following year, the corresponding figure was 47 per cent, and it has continued to drop: in 1995, 54 per cent of Estonian exports went to the EU, and a mere 25 per cent to the CIS countries, including Russia (Statistical Yearbook 1994, 221–2; 1996, 235–6).

It should be borne in mind, however, that macroeconomic success often seems to be reached at the cost of worsening economic conditions for certain segments of the population. In Estonia, the stubbornly high inflation rate, together with the monetarist budgetary policies applied since the monetary reform of 1992 have made the situation very difficult, especially for people dependent on fixed transfers from the state budget – i.e. pensioners, large families, and those with working disabilities; also for people working for the state and the municipalities, e.g. teachers and medical staff. Indeed, the fundamental socioeconomic cleavage in Estonia can easily be traced: young, urban, well-educated, private sector employees are those who are best off within the new system.[17] The reorientation of Estonia's foreign trade towards the West, along with the government's refusal to subsidize exports or to support state-owned industries with public funding, has led to growing unemployment in remote rural areas of the Southeast, and in the large industrial region of the Northeast. The heavy industry in this area, as well as Estonia's large agricultural sector, used to be closely integrated with the Soviet all-Union economy.

The desire to avoid developments of this kind, and also the political risks involved in letting some branches of the economy suffer because of radical restructuring, usually restrains post-socialist governments from opting for economic 'shock therapy'. In Estonia, however, there has been almost no opposition at all to the cornerstones of the present economic and foreign policies – that is, the fixed exchange rate of the Estonian kroon, the need to keep the budget balanced, and the economic and political orientation towards the West. According to a survey undertaken in November 1996 (cf.

Rose 1997, 32), a total of 75 per cent of native Estonians and 61 per cent of ethnic Russians in Estonia had 'complete trust' in the National Bank. The figure is much higher than the corresponding figure in the other Baltic countries and, in fact, in any of the ten new democracies surveyed by Rose and Haerpfer (1996, 81). Interestingly enough, since the first parliamentary elections of 1992, governments have resigned only as a result of highly personal scandals – the change of government after the 1995 elections is the one exception from the rule. It may also be noted that incoming governments have made a point of continuing the policies pursued by their predecessors.

Still Extraordinary Politics

How, then, could one explain this absence of opposition? First of all, it must be remembered that one potential opposition group, the unemployed industrial workers of the Northeast, are mainly immigrant Russians and thus non-citizens without direct influence on national politics. But the present economic and foreign policies have not been seriously questioned neither by the rural population nor by the state-employed professionals, in spite of their representation in the *Riigikogu*. In fact, Estonians show remarkable patience.

Here, one could apply the concept of 'extraordinary politics' introduced by Polish economist Leszek Balczerowicz (1993, 31). According to his argument, 'great changes' in a country's history create a reserve of political capital at the disposal of the government in charge. This reserve enables the government to apply radical and drastic measures of economic reform, if concentrated in the period of 'extraordinary politics' shortly after the historical change.[18]

We may be accused of extending the meaning of extraordinary politics too far; nonetheless, we argue that this particular era has yet not ended in Estonia. This may be attributed to what in the domestic debate is sometimes referred to as 'The Russian Question' *(Vene küsimus)*, with all which that entails by way of interrelated problems. In spite of its apparent absence from everyday politics, this question creates the background against which the consensual nature of some key areas of Estonian policy-making should be judged. In Estonian political discourse, reference is made both to the perceived continuing colonial ambitions of the Russian state (see *Table 3.2*), and to the unresolved question of the integration of non-Estonian residents into Estonian society. Estonia's currency reform and orientation towards membership of the EU,[19] have above all been presented as a means of distancing Estonia from Russia's sphere of influence. In his straightforward way, President Lennart Meri has expressed this view by arguing that

Estonia has a choice of either joining the EU or becoming a Russian *oblast* (Interview for Estonian television, 21 January 1996).

Figures help to make the Estonian perspective even clearer. According to the Estonian Human Development Report, in early 1997 approximately 116,000 Russian citizens lived in Estonia, along with 170,000 stateless former citizens of the former Soviet Union; 130,000 ethnic Russians had Estonian citizenship (Estonian Human Development Report 1997, 63).[20] Non-citizen residents cannot influence the political process directly, but the number of non-Estonian people who adopt Estonian citizenship is steadily growing. What their predominant political orientation will be is still an open question that causes concern among many Estonians. An even more delicate question is the growing number of Estonian residents who have adopted Russian citizenship. The problem is that the presence of a large settlement of Russian citizens in Estonia gives Russia a pretext for intervening in Estonia's internal affairs.

When confronted with these facts, the choice which an ordinary native Estonian will make is clear. Although the Estonians were able to cut loose from the Soviet Empire, history has taught them not to take for granted national independence, or indeed, their very existence as a people. This attitude serves as a strong incentive for overcoming internal social divisions – people are simply postponing their demands for better living standards because of the perceived Russian threat. This attitude has given the governments a free hand to implement radical economic reform policies, without having to fear powerful protests from the social groups most negatively affected. In short, the Estonians' emphasis on identity politics has made it possible to pursue consensual policies. This is what we consider the key factor explaining the radical nature of Estonia's post-socialist economic reforms.

But if we interpret the recent and present developments as 'extraordinary politics', when can we expect this era to come to an end? If the 'Russian Question' is regarded as the key issue, any answer should take into account the development of Estonia's international situation, the pace of integration of the non-Estonians and even Russia's own internal political development. Membership of the EU (and maybe of NATO), and a reduction of the number of stateless residents and Russian citizens in Estonia to acceptable proportions (however defined), will certainly change the overall picture of Estonian internal politics.

Even so, once initiated, the policy-making style described above may well dominate, even after the situation has changed in this respect. The pattern of consensual policy-making could become a permanent feature of Estonian politics. Here, one is tempted to draw a parallel with Finnish political life during Urho Kekkonen's presidency (1956–81). He regarded the formation of broad-based coalition governments as crucial for a small state neighbouring a superpower. One may even see this pattern of internal politics as something typical of small European states. Shmuel N. Eisenstadt (1985, 47–48) has argued that such states have historically developed two complementary patterns of political organization and activity. The 'real' decisions tend to crystallize in the course of negotiations between the executive, the bureaucracy, the parliamentary commissions and the relevant interest groups, while the 'open' parliamentary debate tends to be more of a symbolic and illusory nature. The function of the latter is to create legitimacy for the ground rules of the political system, while the first form of policy-making ensures smooth co-operation between different elites.

As it turns out, Eisenstadt's description of the internal politics in small European states is surprisingly well-suited to the actions of the seemingly fragmented and scandal-ridden, but, in fact, unequivocally 'centrist-rightist' Estonian political elite – despite the fact that the interests of different social groups are still clearly under-represented in the polity within the realm of institutional politics.

NOTES

*Acknowledgement: The authors wish to express their gratitude to the following for their generous financial assistance: the Open Society Institute (OSI/HESP Research Support Scheme, grant No. 1256/1997), which supported Mikko Lagerspetz's research; the Finnish Cultural Foundation, which assisted Henri Vogt's research; and, finally, the Finnish Kone Foundation, for its kind support of both researchers.

1. In his widely discussed article, *The Reinvention of Politics*, Ulrich Beck makes a distinction between politics and sub-politics. Politics simply refers to the traditional area of interest of political science, composed of the three aspects of policy, politics and the polity, whereas sub-politics means, very generally, 'shaping society from below' (1995, 23). In our formula, institutional politics is roughly equivalent to 'politics', and identity politics and politics as such bear some resemblance to Beckian sub-politics.

2. Arter defines his anti-party system in terms of three parameters: first, 'partisan allegiance provides the basis of candidate choice for only a minority of voters at general elections'; second, 'abstentionism should exceed one in three of those entitled to cast a ballot'; third, 'there exist numerically significant anti-parties' (Arter 1996, 252).

3. On the other hand, one has to bear in mind that becoming a party member can be characterized as a rarity all over Europe, a fact of great concern for all parties and especially newer ones. For example in Finland – often a good point of comparison in the case of Estonia – the Green Party, which has had some ten out of 200 MPs throughout the 1990s, only has approximately 1,000 members. It is also more than well documented that old-established parties are becoming smaller because of recruitment problems among the young (Pekonen 1997).

4. For the Rural People's Party, former President Arnold Rüütel, and for the Reform Party the former head of the Bank of Estonia, Siim Kallas.

5. A more thorough discussion of the role of history in the revolutionary process can be found in Lagerspetz 1996, 66–79.

6. Vihalemm, Lauristin and Tallo (1997, 202) refer to the first stage of the new political culture as

'the mythological stage' (1988–1989/91). One of its most important characteristics was that '[l]arge mass demonstrations united the participants with an emotionally high voltage. Symbols, myths and rituals had a heyday, and the function of words during the mass rallies was magical. Speeches, songs and slogans represented a collective witchcraft, the symbolic fight of a small nation against the totalitarian machinery'. The next stage, when political differentiation started, was the ideological stage; the third would be the critical–rational stage.

7. On that day, the popular *Panda* TV show revealed Moscow's plans to expand phosphorite mining in Estonia (Lagerspetz 1996, 58; Gerner and Hedlund 1993, 70).

8. In Narva, with its solid ethnic Russian majority of more than 90 per cent, 72.7 per cent voted 'no'. In Tallinn, the Pearson correlation between the number of Russians in a given area and the number of 'no' votes was no less than 0.96 (Data provided by Raitviir 1996, 448).

9. Due to the 'Phosphorite War', environmentalism was an important force in the early stages of the independence process. The Green Movement, *Rohelised*, was officially founded on 23 May 1988, and the first green party in August 1989. However, 'greenness' as a political alternative gradually lost its popularity and in the first elections the Green Party only gained one seat in the *Riigikogu*.

10.The political background of the delegates at *Rahvarinne's* founding congress, on 1 October 1988, were as follows: EKP members 28 per cent, National Heritage Society 19 per cent, *Rohelised* 10 per cent, religious organizations 2 per cent, Estonian National Independence Party 0.2 per cent and others 40 per cent (Lauristin, Marju, Peeter Vihalemm and Rein Ruutsoo 1989, *Viron vapauden tuulet*, Helsinki and Jyväskylä, Gummerus; quoted in Arter 1996, 131).

11.This idea of economic autonomy became a force to be reckoned with in September 1987, when four members of the Estonian Communist Party (EKP) published the IME programme, which accepted the basic principles of capitalism and called for economic institutions to be put under Estonian control (IME is an abbreviation of *Isemajandav Eesti*, 'self-management of Estonia'; the term IME also means 'miracle'; Gerner and Hedlund 1993, 79).

12.This radicalization of *Rahvarinne* obviously did not take place overnight. Mati Hint has claimed that it had already started in May 1989. 'After the Baltic Assembly people spoke about full independence – before that there had been only considerations' (Quoted in Laar et al. 1996, 556)

13.The COE election in February 1990 was probably the only privately run general election ever staged (Arter 1996, 137).

14.The new constitution was accepted in a referendum on 18 June 1992. Voter turnout was 66.9 per cent.

15.Lennart Meri was originally *Isamaa's* candidate when he became President in 1992.

16.Interestingly enough, the name alludes to *Isamaaliit* (the Fatherland League), the ruling party subsequent to the coup of 1934.

17.They tend to support *Isamaa* and the Reform Party. A survey published by the *Postimees* on 30 August 1997 comparing the Reform and Centre parties, gives an indication of this. 29 per cent of those aged between 18 and 24 supported the Reform Party, as opposed to the meagre 9 per cent in favour of the Centre Party; among those aged between 50 and 64, the figures were 9 and 12 per cent, respectively. Of those economically well-off (earning more than 2,000 kroons a month), 31 per cent supported the Reform Party, as against only 12 per cent in favour of the Centre Party. The survey estimated the support for the Reform Party at 22 per cent of the entire population, and that of the Centre Party at 15 per cent.

18.Balczerowicz's term has also been applied to politics in the Baltic states by Nørgaard (1996, 3). Perhaps slightly shifting the meaning of the concept, he suggests that the period of extraordinary politics lasted in Estonia until the final departure of the Russian troops in late August 1994 (p. 220). Russian troops were an issue which continued to mobilize people across social divides even after the restoration of independence, to the point of relegating other possible political issues to a subordinated position.

19.Interestingly enough, non-ethnic Estonians are more favourably disposed towards joining the EU than ethnic Estonians (*Table 3.2*). This could be attributed to the fact that non-Estonians are inclined to believe that membership in the EU would help solve Estonia's ethnic problems. But it

may also be noted that most non-ethnic Estonians are urban dwellers and thus belong to a segment of the population which tends to be more pro-EU than the rural strata.
20.Kirch et al. (1997, 54) present significantly lower figures for the number of Russian citizens in Estonia. They emphasize that the exact number is not known, but refer to recent surveys and other data which seems to suggest that 12–20 per cent of the ethnic Russians in Estonia carry Russian passports.

REFERENCES

Arendt, Hannah (1958), *The Human Condition,* Chicago and London, Cambridge University Press.
Arter, David (1995), 'Estonia after the March 1995 *Riigikogu* election: still an anti-party system', *The Journal of Communist Studies and Transition Politics*, Vol. 11, No. 3.
—— (1996), *Parties and Democracy in the Post-Soviet Republics: the Case of Estonia*, Aldershot and Brookfield, Darthmouth.
Balczerowicz, Leszek (1993), 'Common fallacies in the debate on the economic transition in Central and Eastern Europe', *Working paper* No. 11. London, European Bank for Reconstruction and Development.
Beck, Ulrich (1995), 'The Reinvention of Politics: Towards a Theory of Reflexive Modernization', in Ulrich Beck, Anthony Giddens and Scott Lash, eds., *Reflexive Modernization Politics, Tradition and Aesthetics in the Modern Social Order*, Cambridge, Polity Press.
Berglund, Sten and Frank Aarebrot (1997), *The Political History of Eastern Europe in the 20th Century: The Struggle Between Democracy and Dictatorship,* Aldershot, Edward Elgar.
Dellenbrant, Jan Åke (1994), 'The Re-Emergence of Multi-Partyism in the Baltic States', in Sten Berglund and Jan Åke Dellenbrant, eds., *The New Democracies in Eastern Europe: Party Systems and Political Cleavages*, 2nd ed., Aldershot, Edward Elgar
Eisenstadt, Shmuel N. (1985), 'Reflections on Centre–Periphery Relations and Small European States', in Risto Alapuro, Matti Alestalo, Elina Haavio-Mannila and Raimo Väyrynen, eds., *Small States in Comparative Perspective: Essays for Erik Allardt,* Oslo, Norwegian University Press.
Estonian Legislation in Translation, Legal Acts of Estonia No. 1, January 1996, Estonian Translation and Legislative Support Centre.
—— No. 7, July 1996, Estonian Translation and Legislative Support Centre.
Estonian Human Development Report 1997, United Nations Development Programme.
Everly, Rebecca (1997), 'Ethnic Assimilation or Ethnic Diversity? Integration and Estonia's Citizenship Law', in Aksel Kirch, ed., *The Integration of Non-Estonians into Estonian Society. History: Problems and Trends*, Tallinn, Estonian Academy Publishers.
Gerner, Kristian and Stefan Hedlund (1993), *The Baltic States and the End of the Soviet Empire*, London and New York, Routledge.
Grennes, Thomas (1997), 'The economic transition in the Baltic countries', *Journal of Baltic Studies*, Vol. XXVIII, No. 1.
Kask, Peet (1996), 'Institutional Development of the Parliament of Estonia', in David M. Olson and Philip Norton, eds., *The New Parliaments of Central and Eastern Europe.* London and Portland, Frank Cass.
Kirch, Marika, Aksel Kirch, Ilvi Rimm and Tarmo Tuisk (1997), 'Integration Processes in Estonia 1993–1996', in Aksel Kirch, ed., *The Integration of Non-Estonians into Estonian Society: History, Problems and Trends*, Tallinn, Estonian Academy Publishers.
Laar, Mart, Urmas Ott and Sirje Endre (1996), *Teine Eesti,* Tallinn, Meedia- ja Kirjastuskompanii SE & JS.
Lagerspetz, Mikko (1996), *Constructing Post-Communism: A Study in the Estonian Social Problems Discourse*, Turku, Annales Universitatis Turkuensis, Series B, 214.
—— (1997), 'Oleneb, millisesse paati satun... Noorte eestlaste mustad stsenaariumid', *Akadeemia,*

Vol. 9, No. 11.

Lauristin, Marju (1997), 'Contexts of Transition', in Marju Lauristin and Peeter Vihalemm, eds., *Return to the Western World. Cultural and Political Perspectives on the Estonian Post-Communist Transition*, Tartu, Tartu University Press.

Lieven, Anatol (1993), *The Baltic Revolution: Estonia, Latvia, Lithuania and the Path to Independence*, New Haven and London, Yale University Press.

Nørgaard, Ole (1996), *The Baltic States after Independence*, Cheltenham and Brookfield, Edward Elgar.

Öst, Anna-Carin (1994), *Medborgare eller främling? En studie av medborgarskapsregleringen i Estland, Lettland och Litauen*, Åbo, Institutet för mänskliga rättigheter, Åbo Akademi.

Park, Andrus (1995), 'Ideological dimension of the post-communist domestic conflicts', *Proceedings of the Estonian Academy of Sciences*, 44/3.

—— and Rein Ruutsoo, eds., (1995), 'Visions and policies: Estonia's path to independence and beyond, 1987–1993', *Nationalities Papers*, Vol. 23, No. 1, Special Topic Issue.

Pekonen, Kyösti (1997), 'Puoluevastainen mieliala Suomessa', *Politiikka*, No. 1.

Raitviir, Tiina (1996), *Eesti Üleminekuperioodi valimiste (1989 1993) võrdlev uurimine; Elections in Estonia During the Transition Period (1989 1993): A Comparative Study*, Tallinn, Teaduste Akadeemia Kirjastus.

Rose, Richard (1997), *New Baltic Barometer III: A Survey Study*, Glasgow, University of Strathclyde.

—— and Christian Haerpfer (1996), *New Democracies Barometer IV: A 10-Nation Survey*, Glasgow, University of Strathclyde.

Rosimannus, Rain (1995), 'Political Parties', *Nationalities Papers*, Vol. 23, No. 1.

Statistical Yearbook of Estonia 1994, Tallinn, Statistical Office of Estonia.

Statistical Yearbook of Estonia 1996, Tallinn, Statistical Office of Estonia.

Taagepera, Rein (1993), *Estonia: Return to Independence*, Boulder, San Francisco and London, Westview Press.

Vihalemm, Peeter, Marju Lauristin and Ivar Tallo (1997), 'Development of political culture in Estonia', in Marju Lauristin and Peeter Vihalemm, eds., *Return to the Western World: Cultural and Political Perspectives on the Estonian Post-Communist Transition*, Tartu, Tartu University Press.

Vogt, Henri (1996), 'The return of Svejk and the detemporalisation of politics in Eastern Europe', Paper presented at the conference of the *Nordic Political Science Association*, Helsinki, August 1996.

Weibull, Lennart and Sören Holmberg (1997), 'Two Young Democracies and an Old One', in Marju Lauristin and Peeter Vihalemm, eds., *Return to the Western World. Cultural and Political Perspectives on the Estonian Post-Communist Transition*, Tartu, Tartu University Press.

APPENDIX 3.1: ELECTION RESULTS

PARLIAMENTARY ELECTIONS

1992 Elections
Date: 20 September
Turnout: 66.8%

Electoral Alliance/Party	%	Seats
Pro Patria *(Isamaa)*	22.2	29
Secure Home *(Kindel Kodu)*	12.4	15
Popular Front *(Rahvarinne)*	12.4	15
Moderates *(Mõõdukad)*	9.8	12
Estonian National Independence Party		
(Eesti Rahvusliku Sõltumatuse Partei, ERSP*)*	9.8	12
Independent Royalists *(Sõltumatud Kuningriiklased)*	7.2	8
Estonian Citizens *(Eesti Kodanik)*	7.0	8
Estonian Entrepreneurs' Party *(Eesti Ettevõtjate Erakond)*	2.2	1
The Greens *(Rohelised)*	2.5	1
Others	14.1	0
Total		101

Electoral Alliances:

Pro Patria *(Isamaa)*: Christian Democratic Party, Christian Democratic Union, Liberal Democratic Union, Estonian Liberal Democratic Party, Conservative People's Party, Republican Coalition Party *(Eesti Kristlik-Demokraatlik Erakond, Eesti Kristlik-Demokraatlik Liit, Eesti Liberaaldemokraatlik Liit, Eesti Liberaaldemokraatlik Partei, Eesti Konservatiivne Rahvaerakond, Eesti Vabariiklaste Koonderakond).*

Secure Home *(Kindel Kodu)*: Coalition Party, Rural Union, Democratic Justice Union *(Eesti Koonderakond, Eesti Maaliit, Eesti Demokraatlik Õigusliit).*

Popular Front *(Rahvarinne):* Popular Front of Estonia, People's Centre Party, Assembly of Nations in Estonia, Women's Union *(Eestimaa Rahvarinne, Eesti Rahva-Keskerakond, Eestimaa Rahvuste Ühendus, Eesti Naisliit).*

Moderates *(Mõõdukad)*: Social Democratic Party, Rural Centre Party *(Eesti Maa-Keskerakond, Eesti Sotsiaaldemokraatlik Partei).*

Independent Royalists *(Sõltumatud Kuningriiklased)*: Royalist Party, Royalist Association 'Free Toome' *(Eesti Rojalistik Partei, Rojalistik ühendus Vaba Toome).*

Estonian Citizens *(Eesti Kodanik)*: Party of the Republic of Estonia, 'Fair-minded Owners in Tartu', 'Association of Healthy Life' *(Eesti Vabariigi Partei, Tartu Õigusjärgsete Omanike Ühendus, Noarootsi Tervisliku Eluviisi Selts).*

Greens *(Rohelised):* Green Movement, Green Party, European Youth Forest Action in Estonia, Maardu Green League, Green Regiment, *(Eesti Roheline Liikumine, Erakond Eesti Rohelised, Keskkonnakaitse- ja noorteühendus Euroopa Noorte Metsaktsioon Eestis, Ühedus Roheline Maardu, Roheline Rügement).*

1995 Elections
Date: 5 March
Turnout: 68.9%

Electoral Alliance/Party	%	Seats
Coalition Party and the Rural Union *		
(Koonderakond ja Maarahva Ühendus)	32.2	41
Reform Party *(Eesti Reformierakond)*	16.4	19
Centre Party *(Eesti Keskerakond)*	14.2	16
Pro Patria and Estonian National Independence Party		
(Rahvuslik Koonderakond 'Isamaa')		
ja Eesti Rahvusliku Sõltumatuse Partei)	7.9	8
Moderates *(Mõõdukad)* **	6.0	6
Our home is Estonia *(Meie Kodu on Eestimaa)***	5.9	6
Right Wing *(Parempoolsed)* ****	5.0	5
Others	12.4	0
Total	100.0	101

* Coalition Party, Rural Union, Country People's Party, Pensioners' and
Families' Union, Farmers' Assembly
** Social Democratic Party, Rural Centre Party
*** United People's Party of Estonia, Russian Party in Estonia
**** People's Party of Republicans and Conservatives

PRESIDENTIAL ELECTIONS

1992 Elections
First direct round
Date: 20 September
Turnout 67.9%

Candidate	% Nation-wide	Tallinn	Tartu	Kohtla-Järve
Arnold Rüütel	41.8	37.8	27.8	50.4
Rein Taagepera	23.4	22.4	17.1	31.6
Lennart Meri	29.5	33.8	49.8	14.2
Lagle Parek	4.2	4.8	3.9	2.3
Invalid ballots	1.1			

Second Round
Votes in the Riigikogu
Date: 5 October

Candidate	Votes
Arnold Rüütel	31
Lennart Meri	59
Invalid ballots	11

1996 Elections
Votes in the Riigikogu

Candidate	1st Round 26 August	2nd Round 27 August	3rd Round 27 August
Lennart Meri	45	49	52
Arnold Rüütel	34	34	32

Votes in the Electoral Body

Candidate	1st Round 20 September	2nd Round 20 September
Lennart Meri	139	196
Arnold Rüütel	85	126
Tunne Kelam	76	
Enn Tõugu	47	
Siiri Oviir	25	

Note: Before the 1992 presidential elections, the Chairman of the Supreme Council was effectively 'president' and sometimes even called so. That office was held by Arnold Rüütel from 8 May 1990 until 5 October 1992.

APPENDIX 3.2: GOVERNMENT COMPOSITION

Time	Prime Minister (party)	Parties; number of cabinet seats	Political orientation	Reason for change of government
3 Apr 1990–30 Jan 1992	Edgar Savisaar	Primarily non-party	Caretaker government with majority support in the Supreme Council.	Savisaar stepped down because of accusations he had not anticipated the cuts in fuel supply from Russia.
30 Jan 1992–21 Oct 1992	Tiit Vähi	Primarily non-party	Caretaker government with majority support in the Supreme Council.	*Riigikogu* elections.
21 Oct 1992–4 Nov 1994	Mart Laar (Pro Patria)	Pro Patria 4 Nat'l Ind. Party 3 Moderates 3 No affiliation 4 (as of 21 Oct 1994)	'Right–centre' oriented majority government.	Vote of no confidence in Laar because of the roubles sale scandal. *
4 Nov 1994–17 Apr 1995	Andres Tarand (No party affiliation; later to lead Moderates)	Caretaker government on same basis as above; premature elections not desired.	'Right–centre' oriented majority government.	*Riigikogu* elections.
7 Apr 1995–6 Nov 1995	Tiit Vähi (Coalition Party)	Coalition Party, 5 Centre Party, 4 Country P.P. ,1 No affiliation, 4	'Centre' oriented majority government.	Vähi stepped down because of the 'Tape scandal' **
6 Nov 1995–Mar 1997	Tiit Vähi Coalition Party	Coalition Party, 4 Reform Party, 4 Country P.P., 2 No affiliation, 4	'Right-centre' oriented majority government until 21 Nov 1995, when the Reform Party quit the coalition.	Vähi forced to step down because of 'Real estate scandal' ***
Mar 1997 –	Mart Siimann (Coalition Party)	Coalition Party, 6 No affiliation, 6 Country P'.P., 2 Progress Party, 1	'Right-centre' oriented minority government.	

* 2.3 billion roubles that had been obtained when Estonia introduced its national currency; the kroon, had been sold clandestinely for 1.9 million US dollars.
** Edgar Savisaar had allegedly organized the taping of conversations with other political leaders during the government negotiations in April.
*** Vähi was accused of having arranged a cheap flat for his daughter in the centre of Tallinn

APPENDIX 3.3: THE ELECTORAL SYSTEM

According to the *Riigikogu* Election Act of 11 July 1994, an Estonian citizen who has reached the age of eighteen by election day has the right to vote, and an Estonian citizen who has attained twenty-one years of age by the election day may run as a candidate.

Regular Riigikogu elections are held every fourth year – the first *Riigikogu*, however, was elected for only three years. Regular and extraordinary *Riigikogu* elections are called by the President of the Republic. The President may call extraordinary elections upon the request of the Government, or upon expression of no confidence either in the government or in the Prime Minister, pursuant to the Constitution.

Estonia is divided into eleven multi-member electoral districts. The 101 seats are distributed among electoral districts in proportion to the number of citizens with the right to vote.

An independent candidate or candidate list may be nominated by a political party or by an electoral alliance. An independent candidate may be nominated by any Estonian citizen with the right to vote, including the prospective candidate himself or herself. If a political party or an election coalition nominates candidates in more than one electoral district, a national list of candidates specifying the rank order of candidates must be presented to the National Election Committee.

The distribution of mandates in the electoral districts is determined by three rounds of counting:

1. *First round of counting.* A simple quota is calculated for each electoral district by dividing the number of valid votes cast in the electoral district by the number of mandates. A candidate is elected in favour of whom the number of votes exceeds or equals the simple quota.

2. *Second round of counting.* In the lists competing for the national pool of equalizing mandates, the candidates are ranked according to the number of votes received. The votes cast in favour of all candidates running on the same list are added up. A list receives as many mandates as the number of times the votes it receives exceeds the simple quota, but an individual candidate on the list must receive at least 10 per cent of the simple quota in order to be elected.

3. *Third round of counting.* Mandates which are not distributed in the electoral districts are distributed as compensation mandates among the national lists of political parties and election coalitions, the candidates of which receive at least 5 per cent of the votes nationally, but not between fewer than two lists. A modified d'Hondt distribution method with the distribution series of $1, 2^{0.9}, 3^{0.9}$, etc., is used.

Political parties, election coalitions and independent candidates shall, within one month after the announcement of the election results, submit a report to the National Election Committee concerning expenses incurred and sources of funds used for the election campaign.

The electoral system used in the 1992 elections was similar to the current electoral system, with the exception that the number of electoral districts was twelve.

According to the President of the Republic Election Act of 18 May 1996, the President of the Republic is elected by the *Riigikogu*. If the *Riigikogu* fails to elect the President, an electoral body shall convene to elect the President. Anyone born an Estonian citizen and at least forty years of age, may be nominated as candidate for the presidency. The right to nominate a candidate for the presidency rests with no less than one-fifth of the 101 members of the *Riigikogu*. A member of the *Riigikogu* may nominate only one candidate. A person can be elected President only for two consecutive five-year terms. In 1992–96, however, a four-year term was applied.

In all three rounds in the *Riigikogu*, a candidate who receives a two-thirds majority of the full caucus of the Riigikogu (i.e. at least 68 votes) is elected President. If no candidate receives the required majority in the first round, a second round of voting is held on the following day, preceded by a new round of nomination of candidates. In the case of a third round of voting, the members of the *Riigikogu* have a choice between the two most successful candidates in the second round of voting.

If no candidate receives the required majority in the third round, the Chairman of the *Riigikogu* convenes an electoral body for the election of the President of the Republic. The electoral body consists of the members of the *Riigikogu* and of representatives of the local government councils (in 1996, there were 273 representatives; thus the total number in the electoral body was 374). A minimum of 21 members of the electoral college has the right to nominate a candidate for election. No member of the electoral body may nominate more than one candidate. A candidate obtaining a majority vote in the electoral body is considered elected. If no candidate receives a majority, a second round of voting shall be held on the same day between the two candidates who received the greatest number of votes in the first round.

Source: Estonian Legislation in Translation. Legal Acts of Estonia. No. 7, July 1996. Estonian Translation and Legislative Support Centre.

APPENDIX 3.4: THE CONSTITUTIONAL FRAMEWORK

Adopted in a referendum on 28 June 1992, the Constitution of the Republic of Estonia vests legislative power in the *Riigikogu.* The *Riigikogu* shall: pass laws and resolutions; decide on the holding of a referendum; elect the President of the Republic; ratify or reject international treaties; authorize the candidate for Prime Minister to form the Government of the Republic; pass the state budget and approve the report on its implementation. Upon the initiative of the President, it appoints the Chief Justice of the Supreme Court, the Chairman of the Board of the Bank of Estonia, the Auditor General, the Legal Chancellor and the Commander or the Commander-in-Chief of the Defence Forces; upon the proposal of the Chief Justice of the Supreme Court, it appoints Justices of the Supreme Court. The *Riigikogu* decides upon the expression of no confidence in the Government, the Prime Minister or individual Ministers. Upon the proposal of the President, it is entitled to declare a state of war, and order mobilization and demobilization.

The President of the Republic shall: represent the Republic of Estonia internationally; initiate amendments to the Constitution; designate the candidate for Prime Minister; appoint to and release from office members of the Government; serve as the Supreme Commander of the Defence Forces; and appoint the President of the Bank of Estonia on the proposal of the Board of the Bank.

The President shall, within fourteen days after the resignation of the Government of the Republic, designate a candidate for Prime Minister. The candidate for Prime Minister shall, within seven days, present his/her government to the President, who shall appoint the government within three days. If a candidate for Prime Minister does not receive a majority of votes in the *Riigikogu*, or is unable to or declines to form a government, the President has the right to present another candidate for Prime Minister within seven days. If the President does not present a second candidate or if the second candidate is rejected by the *Riigikogu*, the right to nominate a candidate for Prime Minister is transferred to the *Riigikogu*. The *Riigikogu* shall then nominate a candidate for Prime Minister who shall present his/her government to the President. If the membership of a government is not presented to the President within fourteen days after the transfer to the *Riigikogu* of the right to nominate a candidate for Prime Minister, the President of the Republic shall declare extraordinary elections to the *Riigikogu*.

The Government shall resign upon: the convention of a newly elected *Riigikogu*; the resignation or death of the Prime Minister; the expression of no confidence in the government or the Prime Minister by the *Riigikogu*. The *Riigikogu* may express no confidence in the Government of the Republic, the Prime Minister, or an individual Minister. If no confidence is expressed in the Government or in the Prime Minister, the President may, upon the proposal by the Government and within three days, call extraordinary elections to the *Riigikogu*. The Government may tie the approval of a bill it introduces to the issue of confidence. If the *Riigikogu* does not approve the bill, the government shall resign. An individual member, faction, or committee of the *Riigikogu*, and the Government of the Republic have the right to initiate laws. The President of the Republic may only initiate amendments to the Constitution. The majority of the *Riigikogu* has the right to call upon the Government to initiate legislation desired by the *Riigikogu*.

The *Riigikogu* has the right to refer a bill or any issue to a referendum. A law which is passed by a referendum shall promptly be proclaimed by the President. If the referendum does not produce a majority for the bill, the President shall declare extraordinary elections to the *Riigikogu*.

Laws shall be proclaimed by the President of the Republic. The President may refuse to proclaim a law passed by the *Riigikogu;* within fourteen days, he must return the law the to *Riigikogu* for a new debate and decision, along with his/her reasoned resolution. If the *Riigikogu* again passes the law unamended, the President shall proclaim the law or propose to the Supreme Court to declare the law unconstitutional. If the Supreme Court declares the law constitutional, the President shall proclaim the law.

Source: Estonian Legislation in Transition. Legal Acts of Estonia. No. 1, January 1996. Estonian Translation and Legislative Support Centre.

4. Latvia

Hermann Smith-Sivertsen

In this chapter we will argue that Latvia around 1997 has developed four basic cleavages of political relevance. The first is the independence cleavage. The second is the ethnic inclusion/exclusion cleavage. The third is the rural/urban cleavage. The fourth emerging cleavage is that between the disadvantaged strata versus the managing, occupational elites.

The proposal that current Latvian mass politics – to a large extent expressed as popular participation through elections and parties – could be analysed in terms of these four cleavages, will require a few notes on the concept of cleavages. After only three national elections, each of which drastically changed the party system, it can be argued that the short time span and the instability of the party system make possible only the observation of political divisions of a temporary nature, not cleavages.

Even so, the four divisions or cleavages treated here are likely to remain important – those who opposed independence and those who struggled for it at the critical historical junctures will be remembered for a long time to come. Besides, the incorporation process of the non-citizens will probably be a lasting feature. The linguistic interests of the Russophones in Latvia are also fundamentally different from those of the Latvian-speakers, and this too will be a lasting feature. Also, rural dwellers have different economic needs from those in the metropolitan areas. The introduction of a market economy in a society in which most people are poor and egalitarian by outlook, creates a setting in which some groups are more adaptable and other groups come out as losers. When trying to make sense of political participation in Latvia from the late 1980s to the late 1990s, political contradictions embedded in socioeconomic interests or related to specific social groups, are increasingly identifiable.

The cleavage approach applied on Latvia in this chapter is primarily a model of electoral behaviour. The model is based on the assumption that a certain degree of correlation exists between the main policy messages of the parties and the social and ethnic characteristics of the parties' electorates. Even so, the cleavage model of Latvian mass politics that we propose is a tentative one: the cleavages are weakly institutionalized as the parties' memberships are small and the interest organizations are not powerful. We also lack data about the level and quality of the diffusion of mass consciousness about cleavages in Latvia. Furthermore, our cleavage model may later be corroborated or challenged by new electoral data.

The Relevance of History

From the point of view of the perspective applied by Lipset and Rokkan (1967), cleavages become significant at different stages in history; they are developed over time; and the historical roots of current manifest and latent cleavages are often regarded as important in explaining the nature of the current cleavages. Thus, a cleavage model should be related to history. Yet in fact, the social and political similarities between Latvia of the 1990s and Latvia of the inter-war era are few. During the previous period of independence, Latvia was predominantly agrarian: in 1935, farming accounted for more than two-thirds of the labour force (Spekke 1951). Today, less than one-fifth of the Latvian labour force is employed in farming, fishing and forestry, while two-thirds of the population live in towns and urban areas. In inter-war Latvia, the social democrats were always the largest and the Farmers' Union the second largest party. Party fragmentation was extreme, with 22 to 27 parties gaining representation in the 100-seat *Saeima* in the four elections from 1922 to 1931. Regional parties proliferated, and the German, Jewish and Russian ethnic minorities had their own parallel party systems. Grand coalitions were a rare occurrence. All these political features have been absent since Latvia regained independence. The introduction of an electoral threshold of 4 per cent in 1993 – raised to 5 per cent in 1995 – can probably account for some features of the new party system.

So what is left of inter-war Latvia? The constitutional framework and the political–institutional model were resurrected after independence was regained in 1991, and the legitimacy of the republic has its foundation in the inter-war republic. The core body of citizens is defined by their or their families' status before 1940. Two other current traits can be traced back to the inter-war era. One is the absence of large parties: even the two largest parties can not form an absolute parliamentary majority. This was the case during the inter-war era, and again after 1995. The second quality is the apparent weakness of Russian ethno-political mobilization. In 1925, 12.6 per cent of Latvia's citizens were ethnic Russians, yet in the inter-war years the Russians never had more than 6 per cent of the seats in the *Saeima* despite the highly proportional electoral system. The small German minority of 3.8 per cent in 1925 normally won 6 per cent of the seats, and there were always at least as many German as Russian *Saeima* deputies (Garleff 1976).

Other historical periods than the inter-war era are arguably more important for current cleavage formation. The crucial phase of Latvian nation-building took place in the 19th century when Latvia was an integral part of the Russian empire. The nation-building effort was a two-front struggle against linguistic Russification and Baltic German economic dominance. Current disagreements regarding the capacity of the Latvian nation and state to integrate ethnic non-Latvians can probably be traced back to this period, but even so, developments during the Soviet era are probably more important for recent cleavage formation. The current economic problems in Latvia are rooted in the industrialization and urbanization processes which took place during the Soviet era. The fundamental change in the ethnic balance in Latvia also took place in these years, mainly due to immigration and deportation.

The influx of Russian-speakers was reinforced by the extensive purge of the Latvian national communists from the party in 1959–60 (Misiūnas and Taagepera 1993); in Soviet Latvia, the Communist Party was thereafter dominated by Russians and Russian-born Latvians. As Darius Žeruolis points out in the following chapter, such a purge did not occur in Lithuania and the Lithuanians were allowed to take full control of the local Communist Party. The destiny of the national communists in Latvia was probably also important for the later transition to democracy. In the late 1980s, the national communists found themselves too weak to sustain a significant political party, and chose to join or endorse the main independence movement. As opposed to Poland, Hungary and Lithuania, Latvia has not experienced a return to power of the communist successor parties. This is partly due to the fact that the prominent national communists of Latvia have aligned themselves with many different parties and groups. The diverse political career patterns of the former members of the Latvian *nomenklatura* paved the way for a party system dominated by dimensions other than the pro- versus anti-communist division, prevalent in many other post-communist East European countries (cf. Chapters 6 and 11).

A Tentative Model of Cleavages and Parties

In this chapter, four cleavages – pertaining to independence, ethnic inclusion/exclusion, rural versus urban, and the disadvantaged strata against the occupational elites – are presented according to the sequence in which the conflict became manifest in the party system. The most salient cleavages around 1997 were those of ethnic inclusion/exclusion and of the socio-economically disadvantaged versus the occupational elites. With these two cleavages as our point of departure, we may suggest a tentative model of cleavages and parties of current Latvia:

Figure 4.1: Party positions on the national and socioeconomic cleavages

	Parties with over-representation of the adaptable and the emerging middle classes in the electorate	*Parties with over-representation of the disadvantaged strata in the electorate*
Latvian nationalist parties	For Fatherland and Freedom (LNNK)	
		Latvian Farmers' Union and Latvian Christian Democratic Union *
Socio-economic parties	Latvia's Way Democratic Party–*Saimnieks*	People's Movement for Latvia (Siegerist Party) Latvian Unity Party
		Social Democratic Alliance LSDP/LSDSP **
Russophone-friendly parties		National Harmony Party Latvian Socialist Party

* The 1995 electoral alliance between the Farmers' Union and the Christian Democrats took an intermediate position between the nationalist parties and the socioeconomic parties.
** Exit poll data from the 1995 elections show that those voting for the social democratic alliance 'Labour and Justice' were in a socioeconomically intermediate position. In Figure 4.1, this coalition is listed as belonging the 'disadvantaged strata' category due to the type of voters it seems to have attracted when it had its electoral breakthrough in the local elections of 1997. However, survey data to corroborate this assumption is not available.

Everyone who has read political science studies of post-Soviet Latvia must have noticed that ethnic Latvians now only constitute a rather small majority of the residents there. About 40 per cent of the current inhabitants are Russophone. Of the latter group only about a third possess Latvian citizenship while the bulk of the Russian-speakers are stateless.

So to ask if 'class' matters to current and future Latvian politics can indeed seem bold and/or irrelevant. Party names tell a story too. In Latvia, not a single party claiming to be socialist, social democratic, workers' or representing the underprivileged or defrauded, won significant support in the 1993 and 1995 elections. None of these parties entered parliament in 1993, and in 1995 only one of them, the Latvian Socialist Party, won parliamentary representation after having polled 5.6 per cent of the vote.[1] In these two elections, no parties in Latvia labelled themselves 'leftist' or 'communist'.

This quick glance at party labels corroborates Anton Steen's suggestion (1997, 8) that the emergence of class-based parties seems unlikely in Latvia. Steen asserts that this is due to the dominance of the issue of ethnic cohesion. He argues that the socioeconomic cleavages are unlikely to depoliticize ethnic tensions by cutting across ethnic groups, and that a party system along ethnic divisions is gradually emerging. In this case, Russian-speaking citizens will vote for Russophone parties to the extent that they vote at all (Steen 1997, 8). Steen builds this claim on the argument put forth by Graham Smith (1996), that the Russian-speakers in Latvia opted for ethnically distinct political parties in 1995. However, Smith does not corroborate his argument with survey data. As opposed to Smith, others observers (Kolstø and Tsilevich 1997, 376) claim that Latvia is a special case in Eastern Europe due to the absence of ethnic-minority political parties of significance. A voter survey of the 1995 general election suggests that the picture of ethnic voting is too simplistic. Ethnicity does matter, but so do other factors. By way of example, the NORBALT living conditions project concluded that, as far as mass attitudes go, 'ethnic affiliation does not play the dividing role we may have anticipated' (Jacobsen 1996).

In a 1996 research report, Steen (1996, 196) concludes that the 'deep ethnic cleavages' between the Russians and the Latvians have been the 'overriding basis of conflict' in Latvia (and also in Estonia). When state-building and nation-building processes dominate the agenda, such a statement can be true. Also, empirical research on the elite level can provide other impressions than research on the mass level. We would chose to maintain that severe socioeconomic hardship strongly affects the everyday lives of most of the residents regardless of ethnicity, and many difficult political decisions must be made on pressing socioeconomic issues. When the socioeconomic conflicts of interest become clarified, these questions can also cause increased tensions inside the core nation and sooner or later demonstrate a significant mobilizing power. Nørgaard et al. (1996) suggest that the parties in Latvia should be placed within a two-dimensional matrix, with a radical/moderate dimension on the ethno-political issue and a 'political/economic left/right cleavage'. The Nørgaard model is indeed helpful, but it was constructed without corroboration by voter survey data. The model seems to be founded solely on the author's evaluation of the policy positions of the parties before the election campaign of 1995 started.

This chapter will offer another perspective than that of Steen and Smith. Our position is closer to that of Nørgaard: we will argue that the dominant conflict issues in Latvian politics have changed in recent years. From 1988 until 1991, the relationship to the Soviet Union was the dominant issue.

Between 1991 and 1994, economic hardship was a significant issue, but the political-cultural inclusion/exclusion issue regarding the Soviet-era Russo-phone immigrants and the Citizenship Law created the most heated debate. Since 1995, however, the socioeconomic predicaments have constituted the most important issues in Latvian politics. The issue of cultural and political inclusion/exclusion remains an important but less heated political conflict. It will be argued here that the inclusion/exclusion or 'ethnic' issue is not only a Latvian/Russophone conflict but also a Latvian/Latvian conflict.

The Independence Cleavage

The dominating conflict from 1988 to 1991 was the question of inde-pendence. In the single-seat constituency elections to the Latvian Supreme Council in March–April 1990, the pro-independence side needed to win a minimum of 134 seats. Under Soviet statutes, a two-thirds majority was required to enact constitutional changes. At a time when the Latvian share of the electorate was only about 52 per cent, with an 81.3 per cent turnout, 68.2 per cent of the votes cast were for the pro-independence Latvian People's Front. It elected 144 deputies, of whom 138 voted for the reso-lution of independence in May 1990. Without Russophone support or indifference, this outcome would not have been possible (Lieven 1993; Dreifelds 1996). But ethnicity did matter. Opinion polls conducted in March 1991 showed that 38 per cent of the non-Latvians and 94 per cent of the ethnic Latvians supported independence. The independence referendum that month resulted in 73.7 per cent of the participants voting in favour, with an impressive 87.6 per cent turnout. The result would have been much more ambiguous if significant Russophone support for independence had not been forthcoming. According to Dreifelds (1996, 69), the pro-Soviet Communist Party and the Interfront attracted 20–30 per cent of non-ethnic Latvians in 1990, while an equal share of that group supported the Latvian People's Front *(Latvijas tautas fronte,* LTF).

The struggle for independence created the strongest political mass movements Latvia has seen in decades. The Latvian People's Front mus-tered a membership of 110,000 in October 1988 (Dreifelds 1996), and Karklins claims that the Front's membership had grown to 230,000 regis-tered members by the spring of 1989 – i.e. one member for every ninth inhabitant (Aasland 1996). The more radical independence activists organ-ized themselves within the framework of the National Independence Movement (LNNK) – which had joined forces with the Front – and of the Congress Movement. The independence issue mobilized and unified the Latvians and divided the Russophones; thus it both was and was not a contradiction defined by ethnicity. Yet the over-representation of Russian-speakers on the losing side may have fostered suspicions about loyalty to the state among the Russophones, thereby legitimizing their non-inclusion.

Was the independence cleavage a transitional cleavage which determined political divisions only at an early stage? Soon after independence, the LTF started to disintegrate into factions and nascent political parties. In the pro-independence camp, this cleavage was indeed transitional, but it divided the Russophone group more permanently. Russia recognized Latvia's independence in late August 1991. Some years later, those parties in Latvia which were most dependent on the Russophone vote and which advocated citizenship rights to non-citizens, were split by the independence cleavage. The Equal Rights movement and the Socialist Party are the political heirs to the groups which resisted independence. The pro-independence National Harmony Party attracts support from Russophone groups and from some anti-nationalist Latvians. The independence cleavage contributes much to prevent the creation of one significant, unified party which advocates citizenship for stateless residents and is sympathetic to Russophone interests. With a potential constituency of nearly 20 per cent of the post-1991 electorate, a successful Russophone party could have had an impressive parliamentary impact. However, even if the independence cleavage loses its significance, the Russian-speaking electorate may still split along at least two dimensions: rejection of or compliance with Latvian nation-building policies, as well as along a socioeconomic axis.

The independence cleavage also seems to brand the Equal Rights movement and the Socialist Party as pariahs in Latvian politics. This reduces the likelihood of mutual co-operation between the Russophone-friendly parties and the ethnic-Latvian leftist and centre-left parties.

A Single Dominant Ethnic Cleavage?

The citizenship issue became crucial in Latvian politics when the bulk of the resident Russophones – the Soviet-era settlers – were legally defined as non-citizens in October 1991. The Latvian Supreme Council ruled that citizenship should be granted to pre-1940 citizens and their descendants; other residents could be naturalized contingent upon a set measure of knowledge of spoken Latvian, sixteen years of residency and the renouncement of non-Latvian citizenship. These guidelines for naturalization were not passed into law because of opposition from Latvian nationalists who thought this policy was too inclusive. A cleavage between moderate Latvians and radical nationalist Latvians started to develop. The legislation regulating the mode and pace of naturalization was not enacted until 1994, and actual naturalization began only early in 1995. Latvian moderates advocated limited, slow and strict naturalization with a quota to be decided annually. This had been the policy of the 1993–94 ruling elitist-liberal Latvia's Way and the Farmers' Union. The Latvian nationalist position was to oppose any naturalization of Slavic non-citizens or to create a quota regime which would make naturalization virtually impossible. It was proposed that the annual quota should not exceed 10 per cent of the natural growth rate of the Latvian population, a proposal which left virtually no room for naturalization given the low birth rate in Latvia. The 'For Fatherland and Freedom' movement and the Latvian Independence Movement (LNNK) proposed such policies in 1993 (Røeggen 1997). Being a part of the ruling grand coalition from December 1995, these two parties have gradually learned to live with the policy of Latvia's Way, as well as with the liberalizing international pressures in this regard. Due to pressure from the latter, quotas were rejected and instead, annual application windows were introduced from 1996 to 2003 for different age groups. Until 1 January 1998, a modest 6,993 individuals had been naturalized. There are many reasons why so few of the eligible residents have applied for naturalization: the language proficiency requirement; the military draft; the visa regime between Latvia and Russia; and the high naturalization fee (Hendra 1997).

Since the naturalization process started, the political conflict over the citizenship question has gradually become less heated (Dreifelds 1996, 98). In January–February 1996, during the early months of the Šķēle grand coalition, the leading nationalist 'Fatherland and Freedom' party initiated a petition for a more strict citizenship law. But the party failed, although only just, to mobilize 10 per cent of the electorate to sign the proposal which would have set annual quotas equivalent to a maximum of 0.1 per cent of the citizenry to be naturalized. If the parliament had rejected a petition for stricter citizenship legislation with the required number of signatures attached to it, the proposal could have become the object of a popular referendum. From the governing coalition's point of view, it was fortunate that the issue was not reopened.

In 1997, 28 per cent of the registered residents of Latvia were non-citizens, and these were mainly Russian-speaking. The gradual integration of these Russian-speakers may make for political tensions for a number of years to come. However, tensions can also be managed. In the co-operation agreement of the ruling grand coalition, consensus among the ruling parties is required for any amendments to the legislation on citizenship and naturalization. This agreement has provided the nationalist parties with a veto; they can in fact veto legislation which would speed up naturalization. The climate of the grand coalition partly stabilized and partly postponed the citizenship issue, and this paved the way for the socioeconomic issues to attract more of the political attention of the population.

This inclusion/exclusion question could be understood as a disagreement

over the nature of the Latvian nation and its relationship to the sur-
roundings. The liberal nationalists in Latvia's Way, other moderate Latvian
parties, and the patriotic nationalists who in 1997 united in the 'For Fatherland and Freedom' (LNNK) all agree that Latvia should be a 'one-commu-
nity nation state giving the traditional minorities the right of cultural
autonomy'. The disagreement is more a question of optimism or pessimism
regarding the prospects of assimilation of the Russophones in the one-
community state. This sentiment is probably influenced by the view of the
nation as a prospective victim or victor. In the Soviet epoch, Latvians had to
be bilingual while the resident Russian-speakers were mainly monolingual.
For Latvian schoolchildren, English has now become the first and compulsory foreign language while the study of the Russian language is no
longer required. Russophone schoolchildren face a different emerging
situation. The minority education system is now only taking shape, but it
seems as if they will be taught both in Russian and Latvian. In the future,
the residing Russophones will have to be bilingual while the Latvians may
act as monolinguals in domestic public life. Other trends also favour this
vision of one community. Differences in birth-rates between ethnic Latvians
and Russian-speakers will probably increase the ethnic Latvian share of the
population from 56.7 per cent in 1997 to about 60 per cent in 2007.

Moreover, more residents regard themselves as Latvians than public
statistics display (Aasland et al. 1996, 34). The 1995 Eurobarometer survey
also found that 60.1 per cent of the population of Latvia reported themselves as of Latvian nationality, which gives a ethnic Latvian share more
than three percentage points higher than the officially reported share
(Berglund and Aarebrot 1997). This is probably due to the fact that some
people speak Latvian at home, but may be registered as ethnic Lithuanians
or ethnic Poles in their passports. The fact that Latvian passports state the
holders' ethnicity contributes to the complications for Latvian-speaking
citizens, but officially allows ethnic non-Latvians to feel co-opted into the
nation; Latvian national identity is basically ethnic (Kruks 1997). However,
in 1991 citizenship was granted on the 'First Republic' option which was
somewhat more inclusive to non-Latvians than an ethnic definition of
citizens would have implied.

The Russophones

Do the Russophones react strongly when their language loses status due to
the strict language laws? A thorough Latvification of the ministries and
government agencies was carried out in 1992–93 through mandatory
language tests for those with a non-Latvian education (Kolstø and Tsilevich
1997), and as a result, almost all jobs in the state apparatus have been

occupied by Latvians. Language tests were also carried out in the private sector. Despite this, the Russophones responded with political inactivity. Indeed, in the parliamentary elections of 1993 and 1995 the proportion of non-Latvians elected were less than half the non-Latvians' share of the electorate. Kolstø and Tsilevich (1997) argue that ethnic mobilization of Russians and other Russian-speakers is largely absent in Latvia.

The human rights situation for non-citizens in Latvia was particularly serious in 1992–94; when the status of non-citizens was legally defined in 1995, the human rights situation improved. By the mid-1990s, the number of restrictions on non-citizens had decreased; by way of example, they no longer receive 90, but 100 per cent of the basic pension which all Latvians are entitled to. Opinion polls also suggest that there has been a significant decline in ethnic tensions after 1993 (Hendra 1997).

The Salience of the Ethnic Inclusion/Exclusion Dimension

So far, Latvian politics in the 1990s has mainly been a product of two sets of conflicts. The first to become manifest pertained to the processes of state-building and nation-building, i.e. issues regarding independence, ethnicity and power, citizenship and language. The second set of conflicts, which has a distinct socioeconomic flavour to it, has gained in importance since naturalization proceedings opened up and, particularly, since the approach to ethnicity by the nationalist parties became tempered by their need to maintain working parliamentary coalitions. Anti-elitist sentiments and the emerging social stratification are increasingly making themselves felt; and the socioeconomic conflicts between ethnic Latvians are mainly independent of their attitudes towards naturalization and citizenship.[2]

Indeed, it is very hard to explain Latvian elections only in terms of state-building and nation-building conflicts, such as independence and inclusion/exclusion. The victors in the 1993 and 1995 *Saeima* elections and in the 1997 local elections were neither the Latvian nationalist parties nor the Russophone-friendly parties. Instead, parties stressing socioeconomic issues and downplaying inter-ethnic issues came out on top. The popularity of the individual candidates, campaign funding and success in attracting the media obviously played a role in facilitating the electoral success or failure of the parties, but it would be too cynical to disregard the main policy messages of the parties at the time when they made their electoral breakthroughs.

Socioeconomic issues were already important in the 1993 elections. In fact, the failure of the ruling Latvian People's Front to win any seats at all may be attributed to two factors related to this dimension: the deteriorating living standards and the increasing gaps between social strata (Cerps 1994,

89). Income differentiation is not popular in Latvia. In the mid-1990s, more than 80 per cent of the population had the opinion that the income differences 'should be less' (Jacobsen 1996, 180). The victor of the 1993 election, Latvia's Way, was heterogeneous, composed of both radicals and moderates from the Latvian People's Front, and held together by basic agreement on economic reform (Lieven 1993, 301). Latvia's Way included some former members of the *nomenklatura* as well as Latvian *émigré* organizations in the West. The most successful electoral lists in 1993 were those which were most seriously preoccupied with the socioeconomic area (Freimanis and Semanis 1994, 66). Surveys conducted in 1993 indicated that the issues which had the highest priorities among the voters were economic problems, unemployment and agriculture; citizenship was only the seventh important issue.

The 1993 electoral programme of Latvia's Way was basically concerned with economic questions. It was also helpful that this electoral list had the most popular politicians and the biggest campaign budget (Dreifelds 1996). Centre-right Latvia's Way won 36 per cent of the seats in 1993. The nationalist-oriented Latvia's National Independence Movement (LNNK), which won 15 per cent of the seats, was one of medium-sized parties to make an electoral breakthrough. The LNNK changed its name to Latvia's National Conservative Party (LNNK) which in 1995 and in 1997 it merged with the other main nationalist party. The Russophone-friendly, centre-left 'Harmony for Latvia–Revival for the Economy' was yet another successful, newcomer, winning 13 per cent of the seats. In 1994, this party split the National Harmony Party and the Political Union of Economists, of which the latter participated in the Gailis cabinet and did not survive the 1995 elections. The Farmers' Union was the fourth largest party in 1993. Four more parties each obtained 5–7 per cent of the seats in 1993. Of the eight parties represented in parliament, The Equal Rights was alone in not endorsing independence; the bulk of the remaining seven were offshoots from the People's Front.

The ethnicity of the respondents categorized as ethnic majority or ethnic minority, was recorded in a 1993 opinion poll on electoral preferences. The results indicate that 44 per cent of the ethnic Latvians would vote for moderate parties, such as Latvia's Way, the Democratic Centre and the Harmonists, while 39 per cent expressed preference for the parties which in 1994 formed the 'National Bloc' (the LNNK, Fatherland and Freedom, the Christian Democrats and the Farmers' Union). Among the ethnic minorities, 25 per cent expressed a preference for the Equal Rights Movement and 19 per cent for the Harmony party – i.e. the two main Russophone-friendly parties had a total share of 44 per cent among the non-ethnic Latvians. But 36 per cent of the non-ethnic Latvians responded that they would vote for

Latvian parties, mainly Latvia's Way and the Farmers' Union (Klingemann et al. 1994). This data corroborates the theory that ethnic mobilization among the minorities was quite weak in 1993, and that a very sizeable proportion of the ethnic Latvians did not endorse the least inclusive parties even in 1993, when the citizenship law was undecided.

Exit-poll data on ethnic voting is not available for the 1993 *Saeima* elections, but for the 1995 elections, the voting behaviour of ethnic Latvians can be compared with that of the Russophones. The 1995 election was a serious blow both for the ruling 'Latvia's Way and for the main opposition parties, the LNNK and the Farmers' Union. These elections were the break-through for the Democratic Party–*Saimnieks*. It advocated support for Latvian industry, emphasized professionalism, and at the time seemed centre-left. The populist parties (the Siegerist Party and the Unity Party) and the nationalist-oriented 'Fatherland and Freedom' party also fared well. After the election, Maris Grinblats of 'Fatherland and Freedom' was nominated as Prime Minister, but failed to win the vote of confidence. He was supported by the nationalist parties, the Farmers' Union and the Christian Democrats as well as by Latvia's Way. President Guntis Ulmanis then proposed Ziedonis Čevers of the DP–*Saimnieks* for Prime Minister, but the coalition of the DP–*Saimnieks* and the Unity, Siegerist and Harmony parties fell one vote short of obtaining the confidence of the *Saeima*. Eventually, a grand coalition was formed including the former governing party, Latvia's Way, as well as the nationalist parties, DP–*Saimnieks*, the Unity Party and the Farmers' Union. The Russophone-friendly parties and the largest populist party were left in the cold.

This raises the question to which degree the Russian-speakers in the electorate mainly supported Russophone-friendly and non-citizen inclusive parties in the 1995 elections.

Table 4.1 indicates that some 52 per cent of the Russophones voted for the three parties that rank at the very top as regards inclusion of non-citizens and integration of Russian-speakers: the Socialist, the Harmony and the Russian parties. The communist successor Socialist Party offers the voters the option of a symbolic 'exit' (cf. Hirschman 1972), while the centre-left Harmonists provides a 'voice' option. It will be remembered that the Russophone-friendly parties of Latvia do not express support for the current state-building and nation-building efforts; thus Russian-speaking voters concerned about socioeconomic issues while at the same time accepting the ongoing state-building and nation-building have to turn to other parties. Indeed, no less than 46 per cent of the Russian-speakers opted for predominantly Latvian parties, most of them campaigning on a socio-economic platform, including issues such as the mode and pace of the transition from plan to market and of privatization, the plight of workers and the poor, anti-elitism, local industry and rural economic interests, and, last but not least, the importance of international trade and EU membership. The data would seem to suggest that the proportion of Russian-speakers supporting Latvian parties increased by 10 percentage points between 1993 and 1995. A collective wish among Russian-speakers to strengthen moderate ethnic Latvians against radical ethnic Latvians may partly explain this voting pattern.

Table 4.1: The Russophone vote in the 1995 Saeima *election (%)*

Latvia's Socialist Party	23.4
National Harmony Party	21.7
Party of Russian Citizens of Latvia	6.8
Latvian Unity Party	7.8
People's Movement for Latvia (Siegerist Party)	12.4
Democratic Party–*Saimnieks*	12.6
Alliance 'Latvia's Way'	8.0
Coalition 'Labour and Justice' (LSDSP/LDDP)	3.4
Farmers' Union/Christian Democrats	2.2
Union 'For Fatherland and Freedom'	0.0
Latvian National Conservative Party (LNNK) and Latvian Green Party	0.0
Other lists	1.7

Calculated from the exit-poll survey by the Baltic Data House as well as from official electoral data.[3] Estimated number of Russophone voters: 175,656

Table 4.2: The ethnic Latvian vote in the 1995 Saeima *election (%)*

Alliance 'Latvia's Way'	16.2
Democratic Party–*Saimnieks*	15.8
People's Movement for Latvia (Siegerist Party)	15.4
Union 'For Fatherland and Freedom'	15.0
Latvian. National Conservative Party (LNNK) and Latvian Green Party	8.0
Farmers' Union/Christian Democrats	7.5
Latvian Unity Party	6.8
Coalition 'Labour and Justice' (LSDSP/LDDP)	4.9
National Harmony Party	1.8
Latvia's Socialist Party	1.6
Party of Russian Citizens of Latvia (est.)	0.0
Other lists	7.0

Calculated from the exit-poll survey by the Baltic Data House as well as from official electoral data.[3] Estimated number of Latvian voters: 758,469

In the 1995 elections, 23 per cent of the ethnic Latvians voted for the main Latvian nationalist parties: 'For Fatherland and Freedom' and the

LNNK. Thus, ethnic Latvian support for the parties of the 'National Bloc' fell from 39 per cent in 1993 (Klingemann et al. 1994), to 30.5 per cent in 1995. This phenomenon was paralleled by an increased Russophone tendency to vote for ethnic Latvian parties, which would seem to suggest that ethnicity had lost salience between 1993 and 1995. Table 4.2 shows that 3.4 per cent of the ethnic Latvians opted for one of the Russophone parties. This was of crucial importance: neither Socialists nor Harmonists would have overcome the 5 per cent electoral threshold without some ethnic Latvian support. Moreover, one should note that more than half of the ethnic Latvians voted for those predominantly Latvian parties which also enjoyed significant support among the Russian-speakers.

Some parties had an equally strong base of support among Russian-speakers and ethnic Latvians: the agrarian-oriented, rural-populist Unity Party; the anti-elite populist People's Movement for Latvia led by Joachim Siegerist; and the Democratic Party–*Saimnieks* for the support of local industry. These three parties made an electoral breakthrough in 1995, together polling no less than 37.4 per cent of the total vote. The electorally less successful social democratic coalition for 'Labour and Justice' also enjoyed similar levels of support among Latvians and Russian-speakers. Moreover, about 10 per cent of those who voted for the liberal/elitist, centre-right Latvia's Way in 1995 were Russian-speakers, and Latvia's Way can be added to the list of the other four socioeconomic parties. In 1995, these parties accounted for 56.7 per cent of the total vote, scoring 44.2 per cent among the Russian-speakers and 59.1 per cent among the ethnic Latvians.

We may thus conclude that Latvia has an inclusion/exclusion cleavage that defines three groups: Russophone-friendly and Russophile parties, Latvian nationalist parties, and socioeconomic parties which enjoy support among ethnic Latvian as well as among Russian-speakers.

The Urban/Rural Cleavage

In the inter-war era, Latvia had several significant rurally-based parties. The leading one of these parties was reborn when Latvia regained her independence and today several parties vie for the rural vote. In 1993, the Farmers' Union with its rural appeal (Freimanis and Semanis 1994, 67), became the fourth largest party, which does indeed raise the topic of importance of the rural/urban cleavage in modern Latvia.

Economic reforms took off in the countryside. Legislation on land reform was passed by the Supreme Council as early as June and November 1990. In 1991, 92 per cent of all agricultural land in Latvia was held by collective and state farms: four years later, this proportion had fallen to a mere 17 per cent. In 1996, private farmers controlled 80 per cent of the agricultural land. There are two kinds of individual farms: 64,000 family farms accounting for 47 per cent of the farmland in 1995, and part-time farms and private subsidiary plots accounting for 32 per cent (Zecchini 1996). By 1997 privatization was almost complete. Agriculture, forestry and fishing are important job providers, accounting for 18.5 per cent of employment in 1995 (European Commission 1997).

The Farmers' Union has been included in all governments save one since the 1993 elections. The exception was the 1994–95 Gailis cabinet dominated by Latvia's Way; the Farmers' Union left the government in the summer of 1994 after controversy over import tariffs and farming subsidies (Dreifelds 1996). Following independence, Latvia adopted a liberal trade regime, but the agricultural sector remained sheltered from international competition, albeit that Latvia's free trade agreements with Estonia and Lithuania were extended to agricultural products in January 1997 (European Commission 1997). Latvia's limited financial resources restrict the scope for agricultural subsidies and credits for farming. Due to lack of investment, agriculture is backward and in decline (Hendra 1997).

Farmers have their own interest organization, the Farmers' *Saeima*. *Lauku Avize* (Rural Newspaper), a biweekly with the highest circulation of any newspaper in Latvia, is close to the Farmers' *Saeima* (Prikulis 1997), but sceptical of all parliamentary parties, including the Farmers' Union.

An urban/rural cleavage normally manifests itself in the form of parties with distinct rural constituencies and an equally distinct rural platform catering to farmers' interests. In Latvia, it still remains to be seen which political parties will occupy the rural end of an urban/rural spectrum. In 1995, the electoral coalition of the Farmers' Union and the Christian Democrats stood out as strongly rural-oriented by polling 71.5 per cent of its votes in rural constituencies. The more populist Unity Party had 70 per cent of its voters in the countryside (Ikstens 1997). The People's Movement for Latvia (also known as the Siegerist Party) had a high share of rural votes – 60.5 per cent – but it also had strongholds in the urban environment of small towns, although not in metropolitan Riga. It is worth noting that only 31 per cent of the total population lived in rural areas as of 1995 (European Commission 1997); the rural areas, however, accounted for a slightly higher proportion of the electorate.

The main Russophone-friendly parties and the ethnic Latvian nationalist parties clustered towards the urban end of the urban-rural continuum. The leading nationalist party, 'For Fatherland and Freedom', received only 22.5 per cent of its votes from rural constituencies as opposed to 40.5 per cent from Riga, which accounted for 26 per cent of Latvia's electorate. The Democratic Party–*Saimnieks* and Latvia's Way both had mixed urban-small town-rural support (Ikstens 1997). In 1995, the parties of socioeconomic protest came out strongest in the countryside, while Latvian nationalist and Russian-speaking protest voters were mainly found in urban areas.

The data from the 1995 election testify to the emergence of an urban/rural cleavage. This can be interpreted as an actual cleavage or, for that matter, as a historical cleavage (cf. Chapters 2 and 12).

The Disadvantaged Against Occupational Elites

Latvia has a historical labour/capitalist cleavage. Between 1922 and the 1934 *coup d'état,* the Latvian Social Democratic Party consistently came out as the strongest party controlling 20–31 per cent of the parliamentary seats. In the 1990s, however, it is an open question whether, how or when this cleavage will reappear. In 1993, the historical Latvian Social Democratic Workers' Party (LSDSP) won only 0.7 per cent of the vote, while the former Latvian nationalist Communists – now campaigning on a social democratic platform as the Democratic Labour Party (LDDP) – obtained an equally disappointing 0.9 per cent of the vote. Andris Siliņš, the chairman of the most important trade union, LBAS, ran together with the Pensioners' Association and received only 0.4 per cent (Cerps 1994). Two years after the 1993 electoral debacle, the two social democratic parties LSDSP and LDDP, joined the tiny Justice Party and Siliņš (who by then had resigned as LBAS leader) in an electoral coalition. This coalition just fell short of the five per cent threshold. To the extent that the disadvantaged strata voted differently than other strata in 1995, they must have preferred parties other than those of a social democratic flavour. But the Latvian party system is still in a state of flux, and several opinion polls from late 1997 suggest that support for the social democrats is on the increase.

Employment and Trade Unionism

Already in early 1993, the majority of the total work force was privately employed. At the beginning of 1997, the private sector accounted for 64 per cent of employment and for 55 per cent of the GDP (Hendra 1995; 1997). Privatization of large-scale industrial enterprises was remarkably slow as compared to the swift privatization of the agricultural sector and small-scale businesses (European Commission 1997). The position of labour is weak in Latvia. According to official statistics 7.2 per cent of the economically active were unemployed in 1996 (Hendra 1997), but using ILO methodology the real unemployment rate at the end of that year was estimated at 18.3 per cent (European Commission 1997). LBAS, the most important trade union, has 300,000 members, including pensioners and unemployed, but no central strike fund. Only a few of the LBAS member organizations have started to collect such funds. Some LBAS officials co-operate with political parties, but LBAS leaders are expected to be non-partisan. As LBAS sees it, strikes are very rare in Latvia due to the fact that striking workers risk losing their jobs, and the union itself tends to prefer demonstrations or negotiations with the government to strikes.

The labour/capital cleavage may be reinforced if the LBAS becomes wealthy enough to finance significant political parties. The People's Movement For Latvia (the Siegerist Party) has stood out as closest to LBAS, when it comes to willingness to act in support of union interests, than any other of the parties represented in the 1995–98 *Saeima*.[4] Even so, there are no formal connections between the Siegerist party and LBAS. A labour/capital cleavage is unlikely to become manifest until trade unions are strong enough to carry out effective strikes, and several unsuccessful strikes bear witness to the current weakness of organized labour.

In 1997, no less than 26.3 per cent of Latvia's population were pensioners, who have experienced a dramatic drop in living standards in the wake of the economic transition. The real income of pensioners declined between 1994 and 1996; according to a 1997 report from the United Nations Development Program (UNDP), the average income of pensioners covers only 74.3 per cent of the 'crisis subsistence level'. The average monthly pension in November 1997 was 46 lats, the equivalent of 78 US dollars. The Socialists, the Siegerist Party and the social democrats (LSDSP/LSDP) are among the parties strongly advocating the cause of pensioners and other people with fixed incomes (Ikstens 1997, Prikulis 1997).

According to the 1997 UNDP report on Latvia, households with children or with unemployed members account for the bulk of the disadvantaged strata. Poverty is more widespread in the countryside than in urban areas, and particularly common in eastern Latgale province. Between 44 and 67.9 per cent of Latvia's population is estimated to live in poverty. In 1995, per capita GDP adjusted for purchasing power was among the lowest in Eastern Europe and the lowest among the three Baltic states (Hendra 1997). In this light, it would be unrealistic to expect poor people to vote mainly according to conflicts related to state-building and nation-building in one election after the other, to the detriment of their own economic interests.

Social Strata and Voting

The Baltic Data House exit poll of 1995 contains data about the income, education, occupation and age of the surveyed voters. An analysis of the data indicates that voters in households with a monthly per capita income of less than 20 lats were over-represented among the supporters of the Harmony Party, the People's Movement for Latvia (Siegerist Party), the Unity Party and the Farmers' Union–Christian Democratic alliance. 40.5 per cent of Siegerist Party voters belonged to this group, compared with only 21 per cent of those voting for 'Fatherland and Freedom'. The Russophone-friendly parties, the rural parties and anti-elite populist Siegerist Party were the most successful among voters with 30 lats or less income per household member. On the other end of the income axis, the better-off voters preferred Latvia's Way and 'Fatherland and Freedom'.

Latvia's Way and the DP–*Saimnieks* had the highest shares of entre-preneurs among their voters: 15 and 9 per cent, respectively. On the other hand, the two Russophone-friendly parties – the Harmonists and the Socia-lists – and the two populist protest parties (the Siegerist and Unity parties) obtained 14–29 per cent of their votes from among the unemployed – a category which did not include the retired, students and housewives.

Not surprisingly, voters with gloomy prospects in the transition from plan to market were over-represented among the voters of the Unity, Harmony and Siegerist parties. These parties were particularly successful among the 50 to 64-year-olds. Pro-market Latvia's Way was strongest among voters aged 18 to 24 years. In a similar vein, it may be noted that the Siegerist and Unity parties had strong bases of electoral support among voters with little education. The two nationalist parties, 'Fatherland and Freedom' and LNNK, were popular among university graduates, while the Siegerist and Unity parties found very little support within this group (Ikstens 1997).

The bottom line is that stratification probably mattered in the polling booth, but in a way that benefited not only more or less leftist parties but also protest-populist parties such as the Siegerist Party and the Unity Party. Latvia's Way and the DP–*Saimnieks* may be developing into class parties capable of attracting ethnic Latvians as well as Russian-speakers. Both these parties have provided some prominent former communists with a new political platform, which makes them vulnerable to populist, anti-elitist attacks. The support for protest-populist parties indicates an inclination of disadvantaged groups – Latvians and Russophones alike – to join together in protest against social and economic hardship. The disadvantaged strata may later choose other parties, but as long as they tend to vote for the more socioeconomically-oriented parties and do not split their vote along ethnic lines, a pattern of class-based voting may emerge in Latvia.

Indeed, a division between the emerging middle class and the disad-vantaged strata may be developing. In 1995, however, the tensions between the disadvantaged and the occupational elites were more dependent on age, education and place of residence than on position in the capital/labour dimension. The younger, the well-educated, the well-off and the urban tend to vote differently from the old, the unemployed, those with the lowest levels of education, the low-income groups and the rural population. The emerging middle classes can accept the hardships of the transition to market with relative ease, due to their professional positions, their education, or their youth, and the time horizon deriving from youthfulness. The disadvantaged strata have pronounced difficulties in coping with the transition, and the bleakest prospects in the market economy.

In their chapter, Mikko Lagerspetz and Henri Vogt point to a similar socioeconomic cleavage in Estonia: the young, the city-dwellers, the well-educated and private-sector employees are those best off in the new system. However, this socioeconomic cleavage has not yet had a fundamental impact on the Estonian party system. What makes Latvia a special case is the widespread anti-elitism in the country. This sentiment may reinforce the pattern of protest voting among the disadvantaged. It must not be forgotten that voter turnout in Latvia has surpassed that of Estonia and Lithuania for several consecutive parliamentary elections.

Emerging Socioeconomic Cleavages in Riga

Of Latvia's five multi-seat *Saeima* electoral constituencies, Riga has shown the clearest signs of Latvian/Russophone political polarization. Of Riga's inhabitants, the majority of whom are Russian-speakers, the ethnic Latvians dominate the electorate with a share of 70 per cent (Kolstø and Tsilevich 1997); of all Latvian regions, Riga has the highest proportion of non-citizens among the local non-Latvian population (Aasland et al. 1996, 37). The stage is, in a sense, set for ethnic confrontation. In the 1995 parliamentary elections, Riga stood out as the stronghold of the two main Latvian nationalist parties ('Fatherland and Freedom' and LNNK); together they polled 27.7 per cent of the Riga vote, as compared to 18.3 per cent of the total national vote. Surpassed only by Eastern Latgale, Riga was also a stronghold for the Russophone-friendly parties, which won 18.8 per cent of the Riga vote as against 12.4 per cent nation-wide.

Riga municipal politics provides additional cues about the developing polarization between Latvian nationalists and Russian-speakers. In the 1994 city council elections, 14 parties gained representation on the council; three years later, 17 parties entered. These parties may be divided into three groups with respect to their main policy objectives at the time of their electoral breakthrough. One group consists of Latvian nationalist parties with a manifest non-inclusive policy as regards non-citizens. The parties in this group were successful, even when their socioeconomic policies were not well-defined. The second group of parties includes those which are favourably inclined towards the Russian-speakers and have a socio-economic orientation. The third group counts parties with vague inter-ethnic political profiles but with strong views on a variety of socioeconomic issues, such as market reforms, privatization, promotion of business, the plight of the disadvantaged, poverty, crime, pensions and taxes. Some of these 'socioeconomic' parties are pro-market and pro-business; others are populist and/or centre-left. What they have in common is that they leave it to others to campaign on inter-ethnic issues.

In the 1994 city council elections, the Latvian nationalist parties conquered 52 per cent of the Riga votes, the Russophone-friendly parties 9.1 per cent, and the socioeconomic parties 31.5 per cent with the centre-left *Saimnieks* as the largest in this group. Three years later, however, the picture had changed. In the March 1997 local elections, the nationalist parties obtained 28.5 per cent of the Riga votes, the Russophone-friendly parties 14.3 per cent, and the socioeconomic parties 49.8 per cent. Within the latter group, tensions increased as the centre-left social democrats took ·the lead with an 18.7 per cent share of the vote – up from a modest 4.7 per cent in 1994 – while centre-right pro-market Latvia's Way also improved strongly, from 3.5 per cent in 1994 to 14.1 per cent in 1997. The main issues in the 1997 campaign were social and economic. The social democrats attempted to appeal to low-income groups on issues such as rent control, heating and housing subsidies (*The Baltic Times,* Vol. 2, No. 49). The social democrats also set out to 'rid Riga of corruption and mafia influence', another pressing social problem. The social democrats were not alone in raising these socioeconomic issues, but their pay-off was the best.

This changing centre of political gravity from nationalist to socioeconomic parties in ethnically divided Riga is an important demonstration of how political cleavages in Latvia have developed. The most successful populist parties as of 1995 – the Siegerist and Unity parties – together polled a meagre 3.7 per cent of the Riga vote in 1997, down from to 13.5 per cent in 1995. The populist failure and the social democratic success story were probably connected; it is not unlikely that many economically hard-pressed voters moved from the populists to the social democrats.

Conclusion

The Latvian parties do not have stable bases of electoral support. In 1995, more than 40 per cent of the voters postponed their voting decision until the very last week prior to the elections (Zepa 1996). Besides, the electorally successful parties of 1995 have a very small membership base; the three parties that did best in 1995 had a mean membership of only 561 (Smith-Sivertsen 1996). Even so, Latvian mass politics is not completely unstructured. The independence cleavage and the ethnic inclusion/exclusion cleavage currently seem to be clearly linked to the party system. The rural/urban cleavage seems significant, but the relationship between rural parties and rural voters is less stable. The emerging cleavage between the disadvantaged strata versus the occupational elites is also unstable. This fourth cleavage might be interpreted as protest voting, but it has a strong socioeconomic component to it that might be reinforced in the future.

NOTES

1. The post-communist ballot not endorsing independence was labelled 'Equal Rights Movement' in 1993 and 'Latvia's Socialist Party' in 1995. The former is a movement and was allowed to run in 1993; in 1995 only registered parties could submit lists. All in all, the same political groups stood behind these two ballots in 1993 and 1995.

2. A correlation between ethno-political cleavages and socioeconomic stratification may be present or may emerge, as the economic conditions of various ethnic groups are influenced by the ethnic distribution of political power. The NORBALT living conditions project found that the rate of unemployment among citizens of Latvia was 16 per cent, as opposed to 20 per cent among the non-citizens in the labour force as of September 1994. However, the NORBALT report on Latvia claimed that the differences between the two groups were too small to be considered systematic (Priede 1996, 135). The NORBALT project maintained that non-citizens were not much worse off than citizens, and that gender, age and geography were stronger variables in influencing living conditions (Aasland et al 1996, 212).

3. The percentages were calculated by the author from the Baltic Data House (BDH) exit poll at the 1995 *Saeima* elections published by Brigita Zepa. The BDH data report the share of ethnic Latvians, Russians and 'other nationalities' for parties with more than 4 per cent of the votes. Of the electorate, 78.7 per cent were Latvians and 16.3 per cent Russian. 'Other nationalities' includes Poles (2.2 per cent), Belorussians (1.2 per cent), Lithuanians (0.4 per cent), Jews (0.4 per cent), Roma (0.4 per cent) and Ukrainians (0.2 per cent). The majority of the Lithuanians speak Latvian at home, the Roma speak their own language, while the other minorities usually use Russian. In this case, the estimate is that two-thirds of the respondents counted as 'other nationalities' are Russian-speaking, as are all Russians. The tiny 'Party of Russian Citizens of Latvia' was not included in the BDH data, but is estimated to have a 100 per cent Russophone electorate, as suggested by Kolstø and Tsilevich (1997, 376). The Russophone share of the electorate of the category 'Other lists' is not provided by BDH; here other minor parties (gaining less than 1.5 per cent of the vote) are estimated to have some 5 per cent Russian-speaking voters.

4. Interview with Lilija Babre, International Secretary of the Free Trade Union Federation of Latvia (LBAS), 25 March 1997.

REFERENCES

Aasland, Aadne et al., eds., (1996), 'Latvia: the impact of the transformation', *The NORBALT Living Conditions Project, Fafo report 188*, Oslo

Cerps, Uldis (1994), 'The Leftist Parties in Latvia and Their Performance in the 1993 Parliamentary Elections', in Jan Åke Dellenbrant and Ole Nørgaard, eds., *The Politics of Transition in the Baltic States*, Umeå, Umeå Universitet.

Dellenbrant, Jan Åke (1994), 'The Re-Emergence of Multipartyism in the Baltic States', in Sten Berglund and Jan Åke Dellenbrant, eds., *The New Democracies in Eastern Europe, Party Systems and Political Cleavages*, 2nd ed., Aldershot, Edward Elgar.

Dreifelds, Juris (1996), *Latvia in Transition*, Brock University, Cambridge University Press.

European Commission (1997), *Agenda 2000: Commission Opinion on Latvia's Application for*

Membership of the European Union, Brussels, European Commission.
Freimanis, Aigars and Einars Semanis (1994), 'The Transition of the Political Regime in Latvia', in Jan Åke Dellenbrant and Ole Nørgaard, eds., *The Politics of Transition in the Baltic States,* Umeå, Umeå Universitet.
Garleff, Michael (1976), *Deutschbaltische Politik zwischen den Weltkriegen: Die parlamentarische Tätigkeit der deutschbaltischen Parteien in Lettland und Estland,* Bad Godesberg.
Hendra, John (1995), *Latvia Human Development Report 1995.* Riga, UNDP.
—— (1997), *Latvia Human Development Report 1997,* Riga, UNDP.
Hirschman, Albert O. (1972), *Exit, Voice and Loyalty: Responses to Decline in Firms, Organizations, and States,* Cambridge, Harvard University Press.
Ikstens, Janis (1997), *Cleavage-related information about Latvia.* Mimeo.
Jacobsen, Birgit (1996), 'Political Attitudes', in Aadne Aasland et al., eds., 'Latvia: the impact of the transformation', *The* NORBALT *Living Conditions Project, Fafo report* 188, Oslo.
Klingemann, Hans-Dieter, Jürgen Lass and Katrin Mattusch (1994), *Nationalitätenkonflikt und Mechanismen politischer Integration im Baltikum,* FS III 94–205, Wissenschaftzentrum Berlin für Sozialforschung, Berlin November 1994.
Kolstø, Pål and Boris Tsilevich (1997), 'Patterns of nation building and political integration in a bifurcated postcommunist state: ethnic aspects of parliamentary elections in Latvia', *East European Politics and Societies,* Vol. 11, No. 2.
Kramins, Atis (1995), *Latvijas Republikas 6. Saeimas Velesanas,* Riga, Centralas velesanu komisijas.
Kruks, Sergei (1997), *Identity Discourse in Contemporary Latvia,* Dept of Media and Communication, University of Oslo.
Lieven, Anatol (1993), *The Baltic Revolution. Estonia, Latvia and Lithuania and the Path to Independence,* Yale University Press.
Lipset, Seymour Martin. and Stein Rokkan (1967), 'Cleavage Structures, Party Systems and Voters Alignments: An Introduction', in Seymour Martin Lipset and Stein Rokkan, eds., *Party Systems and Voter Alignments: Cross-National Perspectives,* New York, The Free Press.
Misiūnas, Romuald and Rein Taagepera (1993), *The Baltic States: Years of Dependence 1940–1990,* London, University of California Press, expanded and updated edition.
Nørgaard, Ole with Dan Hindsgaul, Lars Johannsen and Helle Willumsen (1996), *The Baltic States after Independence,* Cheltenham, Edward Elgar.
Priede, Zaiga (1996), 'Employment and Working Conditions', in Aadne Aasland et al., eds., 'Latvia: the impact of the transformation', *The* NORBALT *living conditions project, Fafo report* 188, Oslo.
Prikulis, Juris (1997), *Latvian Political Parties and Their Electorate 1995–1997,* Mimeo.
Røeggen, Vidar (1997), *Statsborgerskapspolitikk i Latvia: et spørsmål om suverenitet,* Hovedoppgave, Inst. for Administrasjon og Organisasjonsvitenskap, Bergen, Univ. i Bergen.
Smith, Graham (1996), 'The ethnic democracy thesis and the citizenship question in Estonia and Latvia', *Nationalities Papers,* Vol. 24, No. 2.
Smith-Sivertsen, Hermann (1996), 'Mot elitepartier eller massepartier?', *Nordisk Østforum,* Vol. 10 (3).
Spekke, Arnolds (1951), *History of Latvia: An Outline,* Stockholm.
Steen, Anton (1996), 'Elites, democracy and policy development in post communist states: A comparative study of Estonia, Latvia and Lithuania', *Research Report* 02/96, Department of Political Science, University of Oslo.
—— (1997), 'Cleavage Structures, Elites and Democracy in Post Communist Societies. The Case of the Baltic States', in Anton Steen, ed., *Ethnicity and Politics in Estonia, Latvia and Lithuania.* Forskningsrapport 02/97. Departement of Political Science, University of Oslo.
Zecchini, Salvatore (1996): *Review of Agricultural policies: Latvia,* Paris, OECD
Zepa, Brigita (1996): Veletaju uzvedība Saeimas un pasvaldību velesanas 1990–1995, *Sociologijas un Politologijas Žurnals,* No 7 maijs.

APPENDIX 4.1: ELECTION RESULTS

PARLIAMENTARY ELECTIONS

1990 Elections to the Supreme Council of the Republic of Latvia
Date: 18 March (first round; 170 deputies elected);
      25 March, 1 April and 29 April (run-off elections)
Turnout: 81.3 %

Party/list/caucus	%	Mandates May 1990 [*]	Mandates Aug. 1990 [**]
Latvian People's Front *(Latvijas Tautas fronte)*	68.2		131
Independents	10.3		8
Communist Party members and sympathizers [***]	21.5		59
Deputies not belonging to any faction			3
'Latvian People's Front and associated deputies' [*]		144	
'Equal Rights faction and associated deputies' [*]		53	
Total	100.0	197	201

Sources: [*] Lieven 1993; [**] Dellenbrant 1994, Misiūnas and Taagepera 1993, Dreifelds 1996.
Note: [***]'Members of the Communist party and its sympathizers' is a category proposed by Dellenbrant (1994); this group was mainly defined by its opposition to the Latvian People's Front (LTF). It should be noted that the LTF contained many former members of the Communist Party of the Soviet Union. Lieven (1993) labels the category of candidates which received 21.5 per cent of the vote as 'opponents of independence'.

1993 Elections to the 5th Saeima
Date: 5 and 6 June
Turnout: 89.9%

Party/list	%	Seats
Latvia's Way *(Latvijas Ceļš)*	32.4	36
Latvian National Independence Movement-LNNK *(Latvijas Nacionalas Neatkarības Kustība-LNNK)*	13.4	15
Harmony for Latvia–Revival for the Economy *(Saskana Latvijai–Atdzimšana Tautsaimniecībai)*	12.0	13
Latvian Farmers' Union *(Latvijas Zemnieku Savienība)*	10.6	12
Equal Rights Movement *(Lidztiesība)*	5.8	7
For Fatherland and Freedom *(Tevzemei un Brīvībai)*	5.4	6
Latvian Christian Democratic Party *(Latvijas Kristīgo Demokratu Savienība)*	5.0	6
Democratic Centre Party *(Demokratiska Centra Partija)*	4.8	5
Latvian People's Front *(Latvijas Tautas fronte)*	1.2	–
Others	9.5	–
Total	100.0	100

1995 Elections to the 6th Saeima
Date: 30 September–1 October
Turnout: 71.9%

Party/coalition	%	Seats
Democratic Party 'Saimnieks'		
(Demokratiska partija Saimnieks)	15.2	18
People's Movement for Latvia (Siegerist Party)		
(Tautas kustība Latvijai [Zigerista partija])	15.0	16
Alliance 'Latvia's Way' *(Savienība 'Latvijas ceļs')*	14.7	17
Union 'For Fatherland and Freedom'		
(Apvienība 'Tevzemei un Brivībai')	12.0	14
Latvian Unity Party *(Latvijas Vienības partija)*	7.2	8
United list of Latvian Farmers' Union, Latvian Christian		
Democrat Union and Latgale Democratic Party		
(Latvijas Zemnieku savienibas Latvijas Kristīgo		
Demokratu Savienība un Latgales Demokratiskas		
partijas apvienotais saraksts)	6.4	8
Latvian National Conservative Party-LNNK and Latvian		
Green Party *(Latvijas Nacionali konservativa partija-*		
LNNK un Latvijas Zala partija)	6.4	8
Latvian Socialist Party *(Latvijas Socialistiska partija)*	5.6	5
National Harmony Party *(Tautas saskanas partija)*	5.6	6
Coalition 'Labour and Justice': Latvian Democratic		
Labour Party, Latvian Social Democratic Workers		
Party, Party for the Defence of Latvia's Defrauded		
People 'Justice' *(Latvijas Demokratiskas darba*		
partijas [LDDP], Latvija Socialdemokratiskas		
stradnieku partijas [LSDSP] un Latvijas Apkrāpto		
cilvēku aizstavības partijas 'Taisnība' [Taisnüiba]		
koalicija 'Darbs un taisnīgums')	4.6	–
Latvian People's Front *(Latvijas Tautas fronte)*	1.2	–
Others	6.3	–
Total	100.0	100

Comparison of parliamentary election results over time

Party/electoral coalition	1990	1993	1995
Latvian People's Front	68.2	1.2	1.2
Communists and Interfront	21.5	–	–
Alliance Latvia's Way	–	32.4	14.7
Latvian National Independence Movement (LNNK) *	–	13.4	–
Latvian National Conservative Party (LNNK) and Latvian Green Party**	–	–	6.4
Harmony for Latvia–Revival for the Economy *	–	12.0	–
National Harmony Party **	–	–	5.6
Latvian Farmers' Union *	–	10.6	–
Latvian Farmers' Union, Latvian Christian Democrat Union and Latgale Democratic Party **	–	–	6.4
Equal Rights Movement *	–	5.8	–
Latvian Socialist Party **	–	–	5.6
Union For Fatherland and Freedom	–	5.4	12.0
Christian Democratic Union***	–	5.0	–
Democratic Centre Party*	–	4.8	–
Democratic Party 'Saimnieks'***	–	–	15.2
People's Movement for Latvia (Siegerist Party)	–	–	15.0
Latvian Unity Party	–	–	7.2
Coalition 'Labour and Justice' (LSDSP/LDDP)	–	–	4.6
Others	10.3	9.4	6.2

Note: Each electoral list from 1993 marked with one asterisk (*) has its main successor in the 1995 election marked with two asterisks (**). The Democratic Centre Party relabelled itself the Democratic Party and in 1995 merged with *Saimnieks*, which had won 17.8 per cent of votes in the 1994 Riga local elections. The word 'Saimnieks' can be translated as 'host', 'master', or 'in charge'.

*** The Christian Democratic Union ran jointly with the Latvian Farmers' Union in 1995.

Percentage of seats in the 1993 and 1995 Saeima *elections
and* Saeima *party caucuses in the autumn of 1997*

Party/electoral coalition	1993	1995	1997
Latvian People's Front	0	0	–
Alliance Latvia's Way	36	17	16
Latvian National Independence Movement (LNNK)	15	–	–
Latvian National Conservative Party (LNNK) and			
Latvian Green Party*	–	8	–
National Reform Party and the Greens*	–	–	6
Harmony for Latvia–Revival for the Economy	13	–	–
National Harmony Party	–	6	5
Latvian Farmers' Union	12	–	–
Latvian Farmers' Union and Latvian Christian			
Democrat Union and Latgale Democratic Party	–	8	13
Equal Rights Movement	7	–	–
Latvian Socialist Party	–	5	4
Union For Fatherland and Freedom*	6	14	–
Fatherland and Freedom/LNNK*	–	–	17
Christian Democratic Union	6	–	–
Democratic Centre Party	5	–	–
Democratic Party 'Saimnieks'	–	18	20
People's Movement for Latvia (Siegerist Party)**	–	16	9
Latvian Unity Party**	–	8	1
Coalition 'Labour and Justice' (LSDSP/LDDP)***	–	0	1
Freedom faction**	–	–	5
Independents	0	0	3

* The LNNK merged with 'Fatherland and' Freedom in 1997. The National Reform Party is primarily a platform for those of the old LNNK (Andrejs Krastins, Alexander Kirsteins and others) who did not want to merge with the Fatherland and Freedom.

** The Unity Party lost most of its *Saeima* members in March 1997; the bulk of them went over to the Farmers' Union–Christian Democratic caucus. The Freedom faction is composed of three former Siegerist party deputies, one ex-Fatherland and Freedom deputy plus one ex-Unity Party deputy. Ex-Siegerist party deputies are also to be found in the DP-*Saimnieks*, Fatherland and Freedom/LNNK, and National Reform party caucuses (Ikstens 1997).

*** The historic social democratic party LSDSP got one deputy in 1996 when *Saeima* deputy Janis Adamsons defected from Latvia's Way. In the autumn of 1997 Adamsons became chairman of the LSDSP. Adamsons was one of the most popular candidates of Latvia's Way in the 1995 elections: among the party's candidates, only Anatolijs Gorbunovs obtained a higher number of personal votes.

PRESIDENTIAL ELECTIONS

1993 Elections
In the Saeima

Candidate	Party	1st Ballot 6 July	2nd Ballot 7 July	3rd Ballot 7 July
Gunars Meierovičs	Latvia's Way	35	did not run	did not run
Aivars Jerumanis	Christian Democratic Union	14	10	–
Guntis Ulmanis	Latvian Farmers' Union	12	46	53
Against all		no option	no option	26

Guntis Ulmanis won an absolute majority among the 100 *Saeima* deputies in the 3rd ballot and was duly elected. Gunars Meierovičs recalled his candidature after the first ballot and endorsed the candidacy of Guntis Ulmanis. 'Harmony for Latvia' boycotted the *Saeima* vote; the party wanted direct elections to the presidency.

Sources: Dreifelds (1996) and the *Saeima* Interparliamentary Relations Bureau.

1996 Elections
In the Saeima

Candidate	Party	1st Ballot 18 June
Guntis Ulmanis	Incumbent	53
Ilga Kreituse	DP–*Saimnieks*	25
Imants Liepa	People's Movement for Latvia (Siegerist Party)	14
Alfreds Rubiks	Latvian Socialist Party	5
Did not vote		3

Incumbent State President Guntis Ulmanis won an absolute majority among the *Saeima* deputies in the first ballot, and was duly elected for a second three-year term.

Source: OMRI Newsletter No. 118, 1996.

APPENDIX 4.2: GOVERNMENT COMPOSITION

Date of inauguration	Prime Minister	Party of PM	Parties in Cabinet	Left–Right position
May 1990	Ivars Godmanis	Latvian People's Front	Latvian People's Front	Centre
July 1993	Valdis Birkavs	Latvia's Way	Latvia's Way, 10 Farmers' Union, 3	Centre
Sept. 1994	Māris Gailis	Latvia's Way	Latvia's Way, 10 Pol. U. of Economists, 2 Independent, 1	Centre
Dec. 1995	Andris Šķēle	No affiliation	DP–*Saimnieks*, 4 Fatherland & Freedom,4 Latvia's Way, 3 LNNK, 2 Unity Party, 1 Farmers' Union, 1	Centre
Feb 1997	Andris Šķēle	No affiliation	DP–Saimnieks, 3 Fatherland & Freedom, 4 Latvia's Way, 3 LNNK, 2 Farmers' Union, 2	Centre
Aug. 1997	Guntars Krasts	Fatherland and Freedom/LNNK	Fatherland and Freedom/LNNK, 4 DP–Saimnieks, 4 Latvia's Way, 3 Farmers' Union, 2 Christian Democrat, 1	Centre

APPENDIX 4.3: THE ELECTORAL SYSTEM

The Supreme Council of the Republic of Latvia elected in March–April 1990 established a transitional period for restituting independent state power, and this period terminated with the convening of the first post-Soviet *Saeima* (parliament), which since the election of the Fifth *Saeima* on 5 and 6 June 1993 is the highest legislative body in Latvia. The one-chamber *Saeima* comprises of 100 deputies and is elected in direct, proportional and secret elections by citizens 18 years of age and over. Until the term of the 6th *Saeima* expires in 1998, the *Saeima* deputies serve for three years; a constitutional amendment, valid from the election of the 7th *Saeima* in 1998, extends the term of the *Saeima* to four years.

The 100 members of *Saeima* are elected proportionally on party candidate lists or electoral coalition candidate lists in five multi-seat constituencies: In the 1995 elections, Riga had 27 seats, Vidzeme province 25, Latgale province 19, Zemgale province 15 and Kurzeme province 14 seats. The allocation of mandates to the constituencies is made 100 days before each election; the number of mandates is proportional with respect to the constituency's relative share of the total electorate. In 1993 there was a 4 per cent national electoral threshold; the threshold was raised to 5 per cent in 1995. The draft election law proposes that the threshold for parties shall remain at 5 per cent in the 1998 elections, but that it shall be raised to 7 per cent for electoral coalitions.

The *Satversme* (constitution) of Latvia proscribes the *Saeima* to be elected in 'general, equal, direct and secret elections, on the basis of proportional representation' but it does not mention the method for achieving proportional representation nor any electoral threshold. The 1995 Election Law prescribes the St. Lagües method of distributing mandates among parties, with the divisors being 1, 3, 5, 7, 9, etc. The individual voter can give a plus sign to candidates on the ballot list, or delete the names of candidates. Parties can enhance the possibilities of candidates to be elected by putting them on the ballot in several constituencies.

Citizens over 21 years of age are eligible for election to the *Saeima*. The 1995 election law rules that several groups were not eligible to run as candidates, among them prison inmates, former KGB employees, those who had been active in certain communist pro-Soviet organizations after 13 January 1991, and those who do not master the national language of Latvia to the highest (third) level of competence.

The President is elected by the *Saeima* by secret ballot. For a candidate to be elected, he or she must receive a minimum of 51 votes. The President serves a maximum of two consecutive terms. Persons aged 40 or over are eligible for the office of President. When Guntis Ulmanis' second term expires in 1999, the presidential term of office will be extended from the current three years to four years.

APPENDIX 4.4: THE CONSTITUTIONAL FRAMEWORK

Latvia is a parliamentary republic first established on 18 November 1918. Its *de jure* independence was recognized on 26 January 1921. The *Satversme* (Constitution) was adopted on 15 February 1922, and it was reintroduced in full, with amendments, on 6 July 1993, when the 5th *Saeima* (Parliament) was elected.

The main function of the *Saeima* is law-making and adopting the state budget, but it also elects the President of State, the State Auditor, and the Central Election Commission, and ratifies international agreements. The *Saeima* may give a vote of confidence or non-confidence in the government. Draft laws may be presented to the *Saeima* by the President of State, the Cabinet, the Committees of the *Saeima*, no less than five individual members of the *Saeima* or, in cases and in a manner provided for in the Constitution, by one-tenth of the electorate.

The members of the *Saeima* shall be exempt from judicial, administrative and disciplinary prosecution, in connection with in the fulfilment of their duties, although not for the dissemination of defamatory information with the knowledge that it is false, or the dissemination of defamatory information about private or family life. Members of the *Saeima* may not be arrested or searched, nor may their personal liberty be restricted in any way, without the sanction of the *Saeima*. According to the Rules of Procedure of the *Saeima*, a deputy may be expelled from the *Saeima* by a *Saeima* decision if he or she during the period of a current session has been absent from more than half of all the *Saeima* sittings without a valid excuse. A deputy can also be expelled due to a lack of command of the State language.

According to the *Satversme*, executive power is held by the Cabinet of Ministers. The Cabinet consists of Prime Minister, full Ministers and State Ministers, the latter resembling junior ministers in other countries. State Ministers cannot be regarded as fully-fledged Cabinet members, but have voting rights in the issues concerning their field. An incoming Prime Minister must be nominated by the President. A nominated Prime Minister must then receive a vote of confidence in the *Saeima*, in which an absolute majority among those deputies present is required. The Prime Minister nominates the members of Cabinet, who also must receive a vote of confidence in the *Saeima*. All decrees of the President shall be countersigned by the Prime Minister, or by the Minister concerned, who thereby assumes full responsibility for the decrees.

If the *Saeima* expresses a vote of no confidence in the Prime Minister, the whole Cabinet shall resign. If the *Saeima* expresses a vote of no confidence in a particular minister, the Minister shall resign and the Prime Minister shall nominate another person to take his or her place. According to the *Saeima* Rules of Procedure, draft resolutions about a vote of no confidence in the Cabinet, the Prime Minister, Ministers or in Ministers of State, may be submitted by at least ten deputies or by a *Saeima* Committee. A question to any member of Cabinet in the regular *Saeima* 'questions and answers' sittings must be submitted in writing by no fewer than five deputies. Five deputies is also the minimum size of a *Saeima* faction.

The President promulgates laws passed by the *Saeima*. He may suspend the promulgation of a law for a period of two months at the request of not less than one-third of the members of the *Saeima*. A law thus suspended shall be submitted to a referendum if a minimum of 10 per cent of the electorate so requests. A referendum shall not be taken if three-quarters of the *Saeima* members pass the law once again, or, generally, on budget matters and foreign policy. The President (1) represents the State in an international capacity; (2) carries out the decisions of the *Saeima* concerning the ratification of international treaties; (3) is Commander-in-Chief of the Armed Forces and in time of war appoints a Commander-in-Chief; (4) declares war on the basis of a decision of the *Saeima*; (5) pardons criminals; (6) has the right to convene extraordinary meetings of the Cabinet and presides over such meetings; (7) has the right of legislative initiative; (8) has the right to propose the dissolution of the *Saeima*. A proposal to dissolve the *Saeima* shall be followed by a referendum. If, in the referendum, more than one-half of the votes are cast in favour of dissolution, the *Saeima* shall be considered as dissolved and new elections shall held within two months. If, in the referendum, the dissolution of the *Saeima* is opposed by a majority, the President shall be regarded as dismissed and the *Saeima* shall elect a new President of State for the remaining period of office of the President.

On the motion of not less than one-half of the members of the *Saeima*, the *Saeima* may at a secret sitting decide by a two-thirds majority to dismiss the President and immediately appoint a successor. Should the President resign, die or be dismissed, the duties shall be carried out by the Chairman of the *Saeima* pending the election of a new President of State.

5. Lithuania

Darius Žeruolis

Since Lithuania regained independence in 1990, it has become recognized by the international community as a consolidated and stable democracy. As regards the first Copenhagen criterion for accession to the EU, Lithuania was among the most successful candidate countries. The European Commission's Agenda 2000 (1997) reported that:

> Lithuania's political institutions function properly and in conditions of stability. They respect the limits on their competences and co-operate with each other. [...] The Opposition plays a normal part in the operation of the institutions. [...] Lithuania demonstrates the characteristics of a democracy, with stable institutions guaranteeing the rule of law, human rights and respect for and protection of minorities.

Also, following the second report of the special monitoring mission on human rights of September 1997, the Council of Europe ceased monitoring Lithuania, as well as the Czech Republic, because democratic practices in the sphere of human rights were judged to be well entrenched (*Lietuvos rytas*, 24 September 1997). Elections have become a routine feature in the political process. Lithuanian scholars and politicians no longer compare Lithuania and Western Europe on the assumption that Lithuania is underdeveloped in comparison with Western models of party system development and electoral processes.

All this implies that Lithuanian party and electoral politics have entered a 'dull' phase. Indeed, the level of political stability in Lithuania has been remarkable, especially when juxtaposed with the turbulence in the economic field.

When analysing the characteristics of post-communist party systems, scholars typically employ a dual design. First, they use Lipset's and Rokkan's classic 'freezing hypothesis', according to which societal conflicts predominant at the time of party system formation and reflected in the initial configuration of party positions, will be carried over into the later stages of party system development, even as the principal instrument shaping party alternatives. According to the freezing hypothesis, changes in the original structure of conflicts in society do not necessarily affect the party system. Secondly, post-communist party system formation clearly reflects the supremacy of politics over economy. So parties are formed as agents of potential interests, only gradually accommodating the emerging interest groups. Hungarian scholar Attila Agh has neatly summarized this phenomenon as 'quick systemic change', i.e. the rapid establishment of political parties in a democratic setting, followed by a 'long structural adaptation' to emerging interests (Agh 1995).[1]

The Lithuanian party system has gone through a freezing of party alternatives, based on party attitudes towards independence and Lithuania's Soviet past as well as on the primacy of politics over economy. As will become evident below, these processes may, however, have culminated by the end of 1997.

The 'capture' of the main conflict lines in Lithuanian politics and the subsequent mushrooming of new political parties occurred in 1988–93. The starting point was the formation of the *Sąjūdis* on 3 June 1988. It was initially a movement for restructuring *(perestroika)*, but it soon transformed itself into the main organizational vehicle for Lithuania in her struggle for independence. In May 1993, *Sąjūdis* was converted into a right-wing party, the *Tėvynės sąjunga (Lietuvos konservatoriai),* (TS[LK], Homeland Union [Lithuanian Conservatives]).

The transformation of *Sąjūdis* into TS(LK) marked the closure of important niches in the Lithuanian party system. Apart from contributing to Lithuania's independence on 11 March 1990, *Sąjūdis* also played a crucial role in democratizing the *Lietuvos komunistų partija* (LKP, Lithuanian Communist Party); it was a forerunner to several political parties, whose leaders acquired political experience working within the *Sąjūdis* framework

The transformation of the LKP from a hard-line communist party[2] into a democratic leftist party was largely driven by the controversy between *Sąjūdis* and LKP on the question of Lithuania's independence. *Sąjūdis* did act as a locomotive in this process, but the competitive nature of party politics and Lithuania's traditions of soft, national communism (Misiūnas and Taagepera 1993; Lieven 1993; on the general impact of communist rule, cf. Chapters 2 and 12 of the present volume) contributed towards the transformation of the LKP and its successor party, the *Lietuvos demokratinė darbo partija* (LDDP, Lithuanian Democratic Labour Party), into a left-wing parliamentary party, albeit with a certain *nomenklatura* aroma. In contrast to the other two Baltic states of Latvia and Estonia, Lithuania quickly acquired a party system structured along a main bipolar dimension which remains in place even today.

The rather simple structure of the Lithuanian party system may be attributed to several factors. The Lithuanian communists and post-communists had a stronger organizational network than their counterparts in Estonia and Latvia; and they were ready to compete in free elections. Moreover, in contrast to Estonia and Latvia, ethnic issues were easily subsumed into this quasi left-right divide and did not go towards fragmenting the party system (Pettai 1997; on the interaction between party system format and ethnic issues in the other two Baltic states, see Lagerspetz' and Vogt's chapter on Estonia and Smith-Sivertsen's chapter on Latvia). Ethnic minorities in Lithuania tend to vote for left-wing parties, but ethnicity has never been politicized.

Finally, the Lithuanian electoral system has been conducive to the maintenance of a two-bloc system; in 1992, the electoral system requiring absolute majority in single-mandate districts (SMD) was replaced by a system combining single-member districts and multi-member districts (MMD) with a national electoral threshold of 4 per cent (Appendix 5.3). The first elections in 1990 were fought over one issue only – the strategy for re-establishing independence. The party system was not quite in place by the 1992 elections, but the switch to an electoral system with a strong majoritarian bias nevertheless served an effective obstacle for new political entrepreneurs. In 1992, 17.1 per cent of the total vote in the multi-member districts went to parties which failed to surpass the threshold. Four years later, the proportion of 'wasted' votes amounted to 35.9 per cent. Between 1992 and 1996, the share of the 71 SMD seats going to parties successful in the multi-member districts increased from 53 to 61. The strength of the majoritarian features in the Lithuanian electoral system is comparable only to Hungary (cf. Chapter 8).

The persistent bipolarity of Lithuanian party politics serves to refute the so-called third force thesis, formulated in 1992 and resurfacing from time to time (Šliogeris, 1994, 33). Briefly, this theory postulates that the confrontation between the two dominant parties, the TS(LK) and the LDDP, is in fact a derivative of past lines of conflict. The image of modern Lithuania would therefore be well served by a 'third force' – a party or a coalition of parties not aligned with either of the currently dominant parties. So far, however, a third force has failed to materialize in the parliamentary arena. There was an attempt to capitalize on the concept of a 'third force' in the presidential campaign of 1997, but to no avail (Juozaitis 1998). As far as parliamentary elections are concerned, parties prefer to compete on separate tickets. In the 1996 elections, only one of 24 lists competing in the MMDs was a coalition, and it won no more than 2.1 per cent of the vote. In 1992, four coalitions ran, obtaining 38.1 per cent of the vote, but if the figure is corrected for the *Sąjūdis* coalition (soon to be institutionalized as the TS[LK] party), genuine coalitions won a total of only 17.5 per cent. Only the LKDP-led coalition overcame the electoral hurdle. Whatever normative arguments may be raised against bipolar party systems, the Lithuanian party system ties in neatly with an underlying electoral cleavage. The election results have sometimes been surprising – as in 1992, when the ex-communist LDDP staged a comeback, and to some extent in 1996, when the TS[LK] was returned to power by a landslide victory in elections with a low (52.9 per cent) turnout – but these upsets occurred within the bipolar format, not outside it. The mainstream parties have clashed frequently, but when it comes to the stability of the party system, they have demonstrated remarkable consensus and concern. This concern was nicely captured by a leading LDDP politician. When asked whether Lithuania needed clear-cut absolute majorities in the *Seimas* (parliament), he answered by saying that 'in the difficult transitional period, two blocs or even two parties guarantee a certain degree of stability in the country... Even if we do not win the elections [the next time around], they had better be won by the right wing [TS(LK) and LKDP]. That is better than chaos' (Bernatonis 1995, 5).

Pre-War Party Alternatives and Conflict Lines

In contrast to Latvia and Estonia, Lithuania displayed a propensity for bipolar party politics during the inter-war democratic interlude. Two blocs dominated: a right-wing Christian Democratic bloc encompassing the Christian Democratic Party *(Lietuvos krikščionių demokratų partija,* LKDP), the Farmers' Union *(Lietuvos ūkininkų sąjunga),* and the Federation of Labour *(Darbo federacija)*; and the left-wing Peasant People's Alliance, including the Peasant People's Party *(Lietuvos valstiečių liaudininkų partija,* LVLP) and the Social Democratic Party *(Lietuvos socialdemokratų partija,* LSDP). The main party of Antanas Smetona's authoritarian regime from December 1926 to June 1940, was the Nationalist Union *(Lietuvos tautininkų sąjunga,* LTS), a vehicle for conservative landowners and industrialists. The Union was not, however, influential in democratic parliamentary politics during the 1920–26 democratic period. Its predecessor, the National Progressive Party *(Tautos pažangos partija,* TPP), had, along with the LKDP, been instrumental in forming cabinets in 1918–19, but it nevertheless failed to attract any significant support among voters. It was to gain organizational strength only after the 1926 *coup d'état.*

The Christian Democratic Party had a mainly peasant electorate, but it drew support from other social classes as well as the Catholic clergy. The party was anti-communist and moderately democratic; it was instrumental in promoting the land reform of 1922, while defending private property rights and advocating compensation for expropriated landlords. Moreover, the LKDP saw itself as the custodian of Catholicism and was fiercely anti-Polish in foreign policy, particularly on the Vilnius issue. The Farmers' Union was a class-based off-shoot of the LKDP, as was the Federation of Labour, designed to represent the interests of non-socialist workers, small landowners and new settlers.

The Christian Democratic bloc dominated Lithuanian politics until 1926, when the Peasants People's Alliance came to dominate the *Seimas*, but only to be overthrown by the military *coup d'état* in December that same year. Yet the Peasant People's Party (LVLP) was the single largest party in all four democratically elected parliaments. With the exception of a pronounced preference for totally secular politics, the programmatic outlook of the LVLP closely resembled that of the LKDP. The other main pillar of the Peasant People's Alliance, the Social Democratic LSDP was affiliated with the Second International and sought to nationalize banking and industry. In the spring of 1926, the LVLP and the LSDP formed a left-of-centre cabinet. The coalition was successful in negotiating a treaty of neutrality and non-aggression with the USSR, but this achievement did not satisfy popular expectations that trade with Russia would increase and alleviate the economic depression. Moreover, there was popular resentment about the concessions which the coalition made towards communists and minority groups. The decisions by the leftist government to cut down the defence budget and purge the civil service of Christian Democratic officials provoked the coup which terminated this experiment in democracy.

By way of summary, all major parties of democratic inter-war Lithuania were more or less under the sway of nationalists, but deeply divided on other cleavages, particularly on clericalism and property.

The Nationalist Union (LTS), dominant during the years of the authoritarian regime, openly espoused the interests of industrialists and landlords, but it would nevertheless be incorrect to infer that democracy broke down solely because of an irreconcilable conflict between industry and agriculture, or between classes. Indeed, Lithuania remained a hegemonic multiparty system until 1936, although no parliamentary elections were held in the ten years subsequent to the coup. Left-wing parties were subject to persecution, while right-wing parties benefited from a more tolerant attitude on the part of the authoritarian regime. However, in 1931 the LKDP fell out with the LTS, and it was finally banned in 1935. The ban was subsequently extended to all political parties excepting the LTS, and Lithuania remained a one-party state until it was forcefully incorporated into the Soviet Union in 1940. The persecution of the opposition did ease somewhat in 1938, when Lithuania gave in to a Polish ultimatum to establish diplomatic relations, and though parties other than the LTS were never allowed to operate legally, several prominent former LKDP members and other non-LTS politicians served in various cabinets until 1940 (for an overview of pre-war Lithuanian party politics, see Dellenbrant 1994; Krupavičius 1996; *The Baltic States* 1938; Rauch 1970).

Table 5.1: Elections to the pre-war Lithuanian Seimas

	Members	Constituent Assembly, 1920		1st Seimas 1922–23		2nd Seimas 1923–26		3rd Seimas 1926–27		4th Seimas 1936–40 [†]
		%	Seats	%	Seats	%	Seats	%	Seats	Seats
Christian Democratic Bloc										
LKDP	28,000	35	24	17	15	14	14	13	14	–
LŪS	4,000	1	20	12	12	14	14	11	11	–
Darbo federacija	15,000	10	15	12	11	15	12	8	5	–
Peasant People's Alliance										
LSLDP *	~33.000	6	9	1	5	18	16	22	22	–
LVS *	n/a	17	20	17	14	-	–	-	–	–
LSDP	3,000	13	14	10	11	11	9	17	15	–
TPP **	13,000	0.7	–	3	–	2	–	4	3	46
EPŽS	n/a	0.4	–	–	–	–	–	2	2	–
Others		16	10	28	10	26	13	23	13	3
Communists	n/a		-		5		–		–	–
Minorities										
Jews	n/a		6		3		6		3	–
Poles	n/a		3		2		4		4	–
Russians	n/a		–		–		1		–	–
Germans	n/a		1		–		2		1	–
Grand Total:			112		78		78		85	49

LKDP: *Lietuvos krikščionių demokratų partija* (Lithuanian Christian Democratic Party); LŪS: *Lietuvos ūkininkų sąjunga* (Lithuanian Farmers' Union); *Darbo federacija* (Federation of Labour); LSLDP: *Lietuvos socialistų liaudininkų demokratų partija* (Lithuanian Socialist People's Democratic Party); LVS: *Lietuvos valstiečių sąjunga* (Lithuanian Peasants' Union); LSDP: *Lietuvos socialdemokratų partija* (Lithuanian Social Democratic Party); TPP: *Tautos pažangos partija* (National Progressive Party); EPŽS: *Ekonominė ir politinė žemdirbių sąjunga* (Economic and Political Agrarian Union)
Notes: * LSPDP and LPU merged into *Lietuvos valstiečių liaudininkų partija* (LVLP, Lithuanian Peasant People's Party, or – literally – the Party of Rural People) in 1922; ** from 1924, *Lietuvos tautininkų sąjunga* (LTS, Lithuanian Nationalist Union); [†] non-party parliament elected on a corporative basis; nomination of candidates was by the district and municipal councils (except Klaipeda); votes were cast for individual candidates, not party lists; turnout was 68 per cent. Membership data: LKDP, 1931; LŪS, 1920; LSLDP and LSDP, 1926; TPP (LTS), 1938.
Source: Krupavičius, 1996, 21, Table 2; *The Baltic States* 1938, 56, Table 10.

It is tempting to draw parallels between the inter-war and the current party systems, but there is in fact hardly any meaningful continuity between the two. The non-democratic interlude between 1926 and 1990 was too long and the social impact of Soviet rule – through urbanization and secularization – too tremendous for pre-war party historical profiles to have an impact on the electorate. Thus, the history of current party competition dates back only to the national rebirth in Lithuania in the 1980s.

A Left–Right Dimension?

Parties in new democracies are often said to have confusing and inconsistent profiles. Clearly, if no dominant dimension and meaningful simplification of political conflict can be found, political parties as well as the electorate face a high degree of uncertainty. It is therefore appropriate to ask how the left/right axis relates to the main competitive dimensions in Eastern Europe. In Western Europe, the left/right divide primarily represents the socioeconomic dimension. In Eastern Europe, the left/right divide consists of other elements as well, such as 'authoritarianism versus democracy', 'traditional versus new culture', and 'conservatism versus change' (Huber and Inglehart 1995, Tables 3 and 4). However, the salience of socioeconomic issues is bound to increase as market reforms progress. In the Czech Republic and in Slovakia, economic conflict is already seen as the most important salient divide (88 and 67 per cent, respectively, by panels of experts; Huber and Inglehart 1995, Table 4). 'Left' and 'right' may also be treated as empty boxes, to be filled and refilled with cognitive-informative content in a concrete historical situation facing the party system (Sartori 1976, 337). In this sense, 'left' and 'right' represent the aggregate ordering of a competitive space and there is no reason why these concepts could not be applied in Eastern Europe even if they denote slightly different things than in the West.

Nørgaard et al. (1996, 104, Figure 3.9) argue that the left/right divide in the Lithuanian party system as of 1992, can be fully tapped only if seven issue dimensions are taken into account:

- perception of the nation state;
- religion;
- land restitution;
- perception of the Soviet era;
- industrial policy;
- nationality dimension;
- international orientation.

According to Nørgaard and his collaborators, the Lithuanian left/right axis has only a political-economic dimension (that is all dimensions are mingled into one), whereas the Latvian and Estonian systems have one extra dimension: nationality. But how do they know this? The exact political-economic content of their ordering cannot be clearly deduced from their ordering as such, as they provide several relevant – to them, anyway – dimensions which could be regarded as economic.

Competitive Party Space: Empirical Evidence [3]

The empirical part of this chapter will attempt to establish to what extent the party system is structured. This is a complex problem, often marred by methodological difficulties, but of manageable proportions in the Lithuanian case. Data is plentiful, and at least on the surface the Lithuanian party system has a somewhat more straightforward format than the party systems of Estonia and Latvia.

In a structured party system, party members should display a high degree of substantive agreement on what the party of their choice, and its competitors, stand for. However, this statement has to be qualified. First, the statistical analysis should only include 'established', i.e. relevant parliamentary parties. These are likely to display a high degree of substantive agreement on the policy stances taken by themselves and their competitors, as they all have a more or less secure place and role in national politics. Established parties are also more likely to feature catch-all characteristics and thus address a wide range of political issues. As a result, members of established parties should be more sophisticated than members of other parties in their evaluations of what are the basic conflicts structuring the party system.

So-called 'new politics' or single-issue parties can successfully challenge the existing format in two ways: either as anti-system parties denying any possibility of arriving at a compromise, and thus stretch the party system to the extremes; or by redefining the competitive space through different interpretations of the left/right axis. Thus, we cannot expect members of minor parliamentary parties to apply the same perspective as members of the major parties. Similar comments apply to members of parties of limited appeal, such as the Women's Party (LMP) and Polish Electoral Action (LLRA).

The following analysis is by and large restricted to major parties in the survey of candidates to the *Seimas*. Simply put, the statistical analysis was performed only on the five main parties which have been represented in parliament as independent party factions since 1992: the Homeland Union/ Lithuanian Conservatives (TS[LK]), the Lithuanian Christian Democratic

Party (LKDP), the Lithuanian Centre Union (LCS), the Lithuanian Social Democratic Party (LSDP) and the Lithuanian Labour Democratic Party (LDDP). The Lithuanian Democratic Party (LDP) and the Lithuanian Nationalist Union (LTS) were disqualified, as they did not retain their status as party factions in the 1996 *Seimas*, although they managed to get one or two candidates elected in single-seat constituencies.

Left–right party placement

As might have been expected, the Social Democratic Party occupies the position closest to the leftist end of the spectrum, and the Homeland Union the position closest to the rightist pole. From left to right, the Labour Democrats, Centrists and Christian Democrats claimed the middle ground.

Yet the content of the left/right conflict may not be fully captured by one single abstract scale. When candidates place other parties than their own on the left–right scale, the general LSDP–LDDP–LCS–LKDP–TS(LK) pattern is upset. LSDP-affiliated respondents 'transfer' the LDDP two steps to the right, to a position next to the conservative TS(LK). It is easy to understand why. The LSDP questions the genuine social democratic character of former communists within the LDDP. Membership in the Socialist International is not the only issue. The two main left-wing parties are also divided on the issue of economic reform. By way of example, it may be noted that leading LDDP ideologue Gediminas Kirkilas (1996, 177) has announced that the party attempts to establish a more liberal profile. Certainly, sound macroeconomic policies and shady privatization deals in 1992–96 added little to the social-democratic profile of the LDDP. Consequently, it is hardly surprising that LSDP candidates perceive the Labour Democrats as representatives of big business interests. LDDP members nevertheless position themselves on the left-hand side – perhaps on ideological grounds.

Table 5.2: 'Left–right' placement of five relevant parties on a scale running from–10 ('extreme left') to 10 ('extreme right') (mean scores, standard deviations within parenthesis)

LSDP	LDDP	LCS	LKDP	TS(LK)
–4,18 (3,97)	–2,28 (6,70)	2,33 (3,59)	4,17 (4,77)	5,77 (5,04)

Note: 205 respondents, including respondents from smaller parties

The remaining deviation from the overall ordering (*Table 5.2*) is also easily interpreted. The Centre Union (LCS) ranks itself as the second most rightist party and swaps places with the Christian Democrats (LKDP). It is tempting to interpret this as a consequence of the economic programmes of two parties. The Christian Democrats are clearly more socially oriented than the Centre Union. Finally, the rank ordering of the Christian Democrats and the Homeland Union/Lithuanian Conservatives are almost identical with regard to self-perception and as perceived by all respondents in the candidate survey. The only difference is that the Christian Democrats perceive the LDDP as the most leftist party, probably with an eye to coalition-making.

It is obvious that issues outside the socioeconomic conflict dominate the left/right divide in Lithuanian politics. More importantly, these issues interact with socioeconomic issues, making the left–right axis more fluid, but not necessarily more difficult to interpret.

The contents of the left/right divide
The relevant dimensions, where substantive agreement does emerge among the *Seimas* candidates, are: private capital versus state capital, state regulation versus free market, and foreign policy orientation (East versus West). By way of example, respondents from all parties agree to some extent that support for private capital is characteristic of right-wing parties. The high negative numbers in every column on this item in Table 5.3 mean that respondents were very close to consensus, regardless of party affiliation. Moreover, there was no agreement on which parties represent agricultural interests. Respondents affiliated with the parties of the right – the TS(LK) and LKDP – feel that right-wing parties represent these interests; the other respondents on the whole feel that left-wing parties care most about agriculture.

All five parties agreed that preferences for private capital in the economy, economic deregulation, and an orientation towards the West, best describe right-wing political parties in Lithuania. Conversely, an Eastward-oriented foreign policy was, to a varying extent, said to be a characteristic of left-wing parties. This item, however, is rather indicative of the political tactics applied in the late 1980s and early 1990s to achieve international recognition of Lithuanian independence. It reflects differences between the alternative approaches at that stage: step-by-step negotiations versus a clean break with Moscow. In fact, Lithuanian foreign policy is characterized by an increasing consensus; all parties nowadays agree that Lithuania should maintain good neighbourly relations with all her immediate neighbours and integrate into European and trans-Atlantic economic and security structures as soon as possible. The remaining attitude items single out the Christian Democrats from the other parties, at times along with the TS(LK).

Table 5.3: The contents of the left/right divide in Lithuanian politics (consensual items are in bold)

Attitude item	All[†]	LSDP	LDDP	LCS	LKDP	TS(LK)	R[‡]
Represent the poorest strata of people in society	43.9	86.4	87.9	39.6	-38.1	-25.0	.38***
Represent the interests of Soviet-era *nomenklatura*	34.8	-46.1	-10.9	65.2	84.0	93.3	.26**
Support an increasing share of private capital in economy	**-79.6**	**-93.0**	**-43.7**	**-82.9**	**-95.7**	**-100.0**	.05
Represent pensioners' interests	23.5	81.4	79.6	19.6	-60.0	-59.0	.42***
Represent interests of Lithuanian national minorities	45.4	61.6	76.8	48.8	0	0	.24**
Oriented towards the East	**60.8**	**28.1**	**16.4**	**71.4**	**96.0**	**97.7**	.24***
Represent agricultural interests	21.2	55.0	81.2	31.3	-79.2	-55.2	.44***
Defend and represent working class interests	28.5	81.8	87.7	11.1	-54.1	-51.4	.34***
Represent interests of big business (capital)	-47.1	-90.6	-85.2	-37.5	38.1	-2.6	.28***
Support the idea that state regulation and economic redistribution curtail individual liberties and is inefficient	**-76.5**	**-78.9**	**-86.0**	**-73.1**	**-71.5**	**-64.3**	.34***
Support the idea that equal rights to all individuals are possible to maintain only if the state guarantees the provision of basic human needs	38.4	61.6	44.8	25.0	-5.3	32.3	.13
Represent middle-class interests	-12.0	73.0	40.8	-48.9	-95.5	-78.1	.28***
Oriented towards the West	**-72.5**	**-23.5**	**-57.2**	**-91.1**	**-91.7**	**-97.7**	.14

Notes: Representatives of five main parliamentary parties only. The question in the VU TSPMI survey read as follows: 'Please specify which parties – left or right – the following descriptions (statements) best fit' (Coding: 1: 'left wing'; 2: 'right wing'; 3: 'neither'; 4: 'don't know') Numbers are subtractions of percentages of party members saying that the statement fits left-wing parties ('1') and party members saying that the statement fits right-wing parties ('2'). Those answering 'neither' and 'don't know' are included in calculation of column percentages, but excluded from subtraction.

[†] not very meaningful for comparisons between a party group and all respondents, because of unweighted data. [‡] Pearson's R (absolute value); * sign. at .05; ** sign. at .01; *** sign. at <=.001.

The value attitudes

The VU TSPMI 1996 poll clearly indicates that two groups are pitted against one another. However, the composition of these groups varies from one attitude item to the other. It is mainly the Centre Union that accounts for the variation, by shifting allegiance between the LSDP–LDDP 'bloc' and the LKDP–TS(LK) 'bloc'. The Social Democrats (LSDP), as well as the Democratic Labour Party (LDDP), express preference for a strong state in public life and a state-regulated economy. The LDDP does not in fact really qualify as a statist party due to its general pro-market stance, but the gap separating it from the right-wing parties and the Centre Union on this particular issue is too wide for us to classify the LDDP as a genuine free-market advocate. The Centre Union moves to the right when it comes to the issue of national defence; only the TS(LK) and LKDP are in favour of higher military spending.

On the whole, the Christian Democrats are closer to social democratic views on urgent social problems and expenditure priorities, and is the most authoritarian in non-material value dimensions. Those questioning the compatibility of a TS(LK)–LKDP coalition may thus have good reason to do so.

Table 5.4: Five attitude items by party affiliation

Attitude item	All[†]	LSDP	LDDP	LCS	LKDP	TS(LK)	R[‡]
The state must express public interests in the first place / the state must protect individuals' interests first	3.6	60.5	23.3	-18.4	-25.0	-36.9	.09
The right to free speech must not be limited under any circumstances / society sometimes slides into such circumstances that censorship is a must	44.2	51.1	47.5	48.0	13.1	44.5	.08
A good law instructs me what to do / good law shows me how I can behave	-54.6	-51.1	-48.4	-56.0	-50.0	-67.4	.03
The best way to guarantee Lithuania's national security is to strengthen military power / Lithuania cannot guarantee her security by military means	-60.5	-84.5	-90.1	-76.0	0	-10.8	.33[*]
A free market economy is the only way to solve economic problems / a state-regulated economy is the best means to secure economic growth	37.9	-13.6	20.0	75.2	62.5	60.8	.01

Note: Candidates representing five main parliamentary parties only. Percentage differences. A positive sign (= no sign) indicates that on the whole the party candidates supported the first statement by the margin of the percentage represented in the cell. A negative sign (-) indicates the overall support of the second statement within a party. Thus, for example, the percentage differential of 48.0 for the Centre Party (LCS) on the second attitude item indicates that the absolute free speech proponents outnumbered circumstantial censure supporters by 48 percentage points.

[†] not very meaningful for comparisons between a party group and all respondents, because of unweighted data. [‡] Pearson's R (absolute value); [*] sign. at <=.001.

It is evident from Table 5.5 that the widest variation among parties and party blocs pertains to the attitude towards public morality and corruption, i.e. issues of 'moral politics'. The Christian Democrats (LKDP) and the Conservatives (TS[LK]) certainly played this card during the election campaign in 1996. As one leading TS(LK) ideologue put it: 'The main dividing line between the leftist and rightist blocs is cultural in the broadest sense of this word. I think that the human values can be interpreted by using categories of left and right, and described through the different concepts of justice and morality. [This division] is very pronounced in the *Seimas*. The second most important source of bloc-building is the distribution of voter preferences according to their experiences during [Soviet] occupation. This historically-based difference between the blocs will survive and continue to divide even our children' (Kubilius 1995).

Table 5.5: Most urgent problems to be solved, by party

Problem	All[†]	LSDP	LDDP	LCS	LKDP	TS(LK)
Decline in living standards	36.4	28.9	27.4	43.1	30.8	51.1
Social protection	19.0	31.1	27.4	9.8	26.9	2.1
Health care	16.5	22.2	14.5	17.6	11.5	14.9
Environmental pollution	1.3	4.4	0	2.0	0	0
Weakening of public morals and norms	6.9	6.7	4.8	3.9	19.2	6.4
Relations with foreign countries	2.2	2.2	1.6	5.9	0	0
Increasing influence of Western culture	1.3	2.2	0	0	0	4.3
Higher crime rate	45.9	26.7	58.1	51.0	42.3	44.7
Shortage of investments into industry	58.9	68.9	66.1	62.7	19.2	57.4
Corrupt officials	31.6	20.0	9.7	37.3	65.4	46.8
Political disagreements among various political forces	5.6	2.2	14.5	2.0	3.8	2.1
Banking crisis	3.0	2.2	1.6	2.0	7.7	4.3
Ethnic conflicts	.4	0	0	2.0	0	0
Inflation	2.2	0	3.2	2.0	3.8	2.1
Violations of human rights	3.9	2.2	3.2	2.0	11.5	4.3
Unemployment	37.7	46.7	41.9	37.3	42.3	21.3

Note: The VU TSPMI survey read as follows: 'Please specify up to three urgent problems that you would try to address first if you are elected to the *Seimas*' (Percentages of those who marked a problem in respective categories of respondents). [†] Not very meaningful for comparisons between a party group and all respondents, because of unweighted data.

Social bases of politics in Lithuania

The thesis of 'the primacy of politics' in post-communist countries departs from the assumption that the social bases of electoral behaviour are very weak or non-existent at the outset and develop gradually over time. Political commentators and scholars sometimes confuse two different issues: the high levels of volatility, as compared to Western averages, are often portrayed as an indication of a lack of social attachments to political parties. However, as neat a measurement of change as electoral volatility might be, it is in fact an aggregate measure of party fortunes and a rather poor predictor of long-term trends. Hence, the high volatility (36.4 per cent; Žeruolis 1997, 74) reflecting voter mobility between 1992 and 1996 tells very little about who shifted loyalties and why. Peter Mair (1993) maintains that volatility measurements are prone to overemphasize the effects of extraordinary elections on long-term trends within the party system.

The 1992 Lithuanian parliamentary election was a landslide election, comparable to the Danish elections of 1973 in terms of its unexpected outcome. Yet there was one crucial difference between the two: Denmark had a stable party system – at least prior to 1973 – while Lithuania in 1992 had a party system only in formation. Therefore it would be totally wrong to interpret the 1996 Lithuanian election simply as a swing of the electoral pendulum (Degutis 1997b, 143).

It is easier to define the right-wing parties than the left-wing parties in terms of social attributes. The Conservatives tend to attract the upper age brackets, the well-educated and city-dwellers. This party also stands out as more successful than the other parties in mobilizing voters.[4] The Christian Democratic Party is preferred by the less-educated, the elderly, women and rural residents. Neither of the two main right-wing parties enjoys popularity among non-ethnic Lithuanian voters. The Centre Union draws support from among the middle-aged, and among high-income and well-educated urban groups.

On the left of the political spectrum, the LDDP is especially well received by less-educated rural voters and by Polish and Russian minorities, while the LSDP has its stronghold among the 'intelligentsia' (Gaidys 1996, 102). The LDDP voters are best defined as those side-tracked by modernization; the party's electorate has no clear social characteristics (Degutis, 1997a). It is worth noting, however, that the three largest Lithuanian parties – the TS(LK), LKDP and LDDP – now have voters who cast their votes on the basis of socio-psychological attachments to their respective parties; a phenomenon known as the Michigan factor. Thus, Conservative voters are inclined to say not only that their party would best solve problems in society, but also that it has a strong moral backbone. They also say that they have developed a habit of voting for the party. LKDP voters emphasise the party's moral profile and capacity to solve societal problems. The LDDP also enjoys the support of stable voters. The LSDP and the LCS seem to have a following of disillusioned voters attracted by the programmatic profiles (*Table 5.6*).

Table 5.6: Most important motivation factors behind party preference

Party	LSDP	LDDP	LCS	LKDP	TS(LK)	All*
Like party's programme	53.8	–	27.4	28.8	–	36.3
Like party's leaders	21.5	35.4	60.3	16.4	–	31.3
The party would best solve social problems	–	–	26.0	34.2	39.1	29.8
The party will help solve respondent's problems	18.8	17.5	–	15.1	–	23.1
Vote because it is the only 'moral' party	7.7	3.8	–	37.0	25.3	18.8
Developed a habit of voting for the party	9.2	45.0	4.1	13.7	24.3	17.8
Disliked all former governing parties (voted for those who have not yet been in power)	26.2	3.8	21.9		–	13.4
Vote influenced by family members' party preference	3.1	–	4.1	16.4	–	11.8
Vote randomly	–	–	–	–	–	1.1

Notes: Column percentages. Each respondent could choose up to three answers from a total of 20, thus sum total may be higher than 100 per cent. * Average response of all voters, not just of supporters of the five largest parties; — = less than 3 per cent. Data from Degutis (1997b).

Bipolarity and Presidentialism

The ideological divide based on attitudes towards the Soviet Union is still of relevance, but the Lithuanian political parties are in the process of carving out socioeconomic niches for themselves. The party competitive space or the left/right divide is thus defined by a mixture of ideological and socioeconomic issues. The resulting bipolar structure has helped maintain the semi-presidential constitutional format introduced in 1992. It was a compromise between *Sajūdis*, which favoured presidentialism, and the proponents of parliamentarism within the LDDP, LSDP and some other smaller parties. However, since the 1998 inauguration of President Valdas Adamkus, the newly established Office of the President seems to be losing initiative and powers to the government and parliament (Appendix 5.4). We would, therefore, be inclined to advance the hypothesis that the semi-presidential format was not only a compromise between two constitutional perspectives, but was also devised as a safeguard against political instability resulting from hung parliaments. The semi-presidential formula was designed to overcome legislative and executive deadlocks of the type which occurred in the spring and summer of 1992.

There is a good case to be made for interpreting the 1997 presidential elections as a failure of the party system. Vytautas Landsbergis (TS[LK]) and Vytenis Andriukaitis (LSDP), leaders of two parties with quite developed organizational structures, were both defeated by two non-party candidates (Appendix 5.1). Valdas Adamkus, the winner in the run-off round was a relative newcomer to Lithuanian day-to-day politics while the runner-up, former Prosecutor General Artūras Paulauskas, had been in politics for only six months prior to the election campaign. Yet this setback for the established parties need not have grave consequences for them, as Lithuania seems to be heading in the direction of a near-parliamentary model of policy-making. The relationship between the *Seimas*, the Government and the Office of the President is changing in favour of the parliament and the cabinet, and the constitutional requirement that the president-elect must immediately suspend his party membership serves to elevate the office-holder from day-to-day politics. With the presidency turning more and more into a figurehead institution, it may even be argued that the political parties have less and less at stake in presidential elections.

Government and opposition

The bipolar party system in Lithuania has ensured a clear distinction between government and opposition. Four out of five major parliamentary parties – the TS(LK), LKDP, LCS and LDDP – have participated in government. The availability of viable coalition alternatives and the smooth transfer of power in 1992 have served to strengthen democracy and boost the legitimacy of the new political system. As is generally the case in post-communist societies, Lithuanian political parties experience a dearth of inputs from society. But with access to key decision-making positions, they have eventually been able to strengthen their organizational structures. Voter apathy, however, should not be construed as dissatisfaction with politics in general; rather, it represents an adjustment of voter expectations to the real capacity of political parties to have an impact on the policy agenda. However low their expectations might be, Lithuanian voters have no difficulty identifying who is in government and who is in opposition.

Table 5.7: Distinction between government and opposition in 1992–96 Seimas *(%)*

Ruling parties		*Opposition*	
LDDP	99.0	TS(LK)	92.5
TS(LK)	1.2	LKDP	25.7
LCS	0.9	LCS	6.7
LSDP	0.6	LSDP	3.9
No answer	10.3	No answer	17.8

Note: Question: 'In your opinion, which were the ruling and opposition parties until the recent parliamentary elections in Lithuania?' (November 1996, an open-ended question; the correct answer was that the LDDP was the ruling party). Percentage of all responses, thus the sum total exceeds 100 per cent.

Source: Žeruolis (1997, 77, Table 3); based on VU TSPMI 1996 post-election survey results.

Satisfaction with democracy and political stability

Given the scope and intensity of social, economic and political change, the Lithuanian party system has been remarkably stable. But civil society or the possible lack thereof may constitute a threat to the political system in general and to the party system in particular. The persistently low degree of satisfaction with democracy in Central and Eastern European countries, including Lithuania (*Table 5.8*), lends support to the 'transition valley' theory, according to which, satisfaction with system performance falls dramatically as the costs of transition begin to burden the voters.

Table 5.8: Satisfaction with democracy in Central and East European countries (percentages of completely or partially satisfied)

	1991	1992	1995	1996
Czech Republic	n/a	39	46	38
Slovakia	n/a	28	27	21
Hungary	n/a	22	20	21
Poland	n/a	19	50	43
Lithuania	52	55	25	28
Latvia	37	16	29	26
Estonia	31	27	38	40

Sources: Tóka (1995, Table 6.1), Central and Eastern Eurobarometers 2 (1991), 3 (1992), 6 (1995) and 7 (1996).

As the transition from communism to a consolidated democracy progressed in Lithuania, the drop in satisfaction with democracy levelled off. It is an open question how to interpret these results, but there is no denying that the level of satisfaction remains low in Lithuania and in all of Eastern Europe even compared to Southern Europe. This fall may be indicative of increased voter demands on system performance. There is only one way out of the transition valley: a reservoir of support has to be accumulated. Although certain social groups in Lithuania – the young, the well-educated and the better-off – are more satisfied with democracy than others, there are indications that the existing level of support is not exclusively determined by socioeconomic variables. This is, in fact, very important considering that support for democracy has to be pervasive.

The effects of the transition valley are offset by the negative appraisal of the Soviet past. Despite all criticism of the current administrative structures and democratic performance, voters in the Baltic states and, for that matter, in other Central and East European countries, assess the communist past even more negatively. Put differently, they do not see any realistic alternative to the democratic system of governance. Another equally important factor offsetting current dissatisfaction is the belief that democratic governance has a bright future. An absolute majority of Lithuanian voters predict that the performance of the political system will improve. Hence, the level of support for democracy does not depend so much on attitudes towards day-to-day political and economic performance.

Table 5.9: Attitudes towards the system of government at three points in time: before independence, at the time of the polls (1993), and in the future

Attitudes towards:	Latvians	Non-Latvians	Estonians	Non-Estonians	Lithu-anians	Lithuanian Russians	Lithuanian Poles
System of government before independence							
Positive	36	66	32	65	46	66	75
Neutral	14	12	13	14	10	10	6
Negative	50	22	55	21	44	24	19
Current system of government							
Positive	43	43	58	50	46	58	44
Neutral	19	18	15	14	13	15	14
Negative	38	39	26	37	40	27	43
System of government in five years time							
Positive	81	71	88	79	81	82	80
Neutral	8	13	6	10	10	11	8
Negative	11	16	5	11	10	7	11

Source: Rose and Maley (1994, 34–36)

Trust in political and public institutions
Trust in political and public institutions also appears to have been affected by the transition valley. The low level of trust, especially in political institutions, may be accounted for in terms similar to those above. A certain period of time must elapse before citizens learn how to use these institutions to the benefit of societal interests. It is still too early to say whether the increase in trust in public institutions after the October 1996 parliamentary elections is a temporary fluctuation or the beginning of a new trend. In post-communist societies, attitudes towards public institutions are determined by the holistic satisfaction with democracy and not the other way around. We would therefore be inclined to believe that public opinion polls underestimate the level of trust.

Table 5.10: Trust in political and societal institutions in Lithuania (% of respondents feeling trust)

	1992	Oct.1996	March 1997	Oct. 1997	Nov. 1997
Church	60	68	64	70	70
Defence structures	47	33	36	39	38
Mass media	39*	69	74	78	74
Police	31	24	23	32	27
Municipal governments	30	32	32	45	36
Central government	29	20	43	45	40
The Courts	23	24	23	27	26
President's Office	–	23	40	45	45
Parliament	n/a	15	34	33	24
Tax Inspectorate	n/a	12	16	24	23
Central Bank	n/a	23	30	42	37
Commercial banks	n/a	3	5	11	10

Sources: Steen (1994, 8, Table 1); *Lietuvos barometrai* Nos. 49 and 54 (*Baltijos tyrimai*, October 1996 and March 1997); *Respublika/Batijos tyrimai*, 31 October 1997 and 2 December 1997; * Newspapers

Conclusion

The Lithuanian party system is not characterized by the kind of fragmentation typical of Latvia and Estonia; the underlying structure of the Lithuanian party system is rather reminiscent of that of Poland. Party labels, at least those of mainstream parties, sound familiar to students of West European politics. In fact, Lithuanian political parties have a tendency to imitate West European, particularly Scandinavian, parties. This may result in programmatic and social profiles not conducive to converting existing divisions into lasting cleavages. Yet the simple structure of the Lithuanian party system has proven a major source of political stability. In the Lithuanian context of low-density civil society, political parties may be even serve as vehicles of political modernization.

Acronyms and Names of Parties, Movements and Coalitions

LCJ *Lietuvos centro judėjimas* (Lithuanian Centre Movement); relabelled LCS
LCS *Lietuvos centro sąjunga* (Lithuanian Centre Union)
LDDP *Lietuvos demokratinė darbo partija* (Lithuanian Democratic Labour Party)
LDP Lietuvos demokratų partija (Lithuanian Democratic Party)
LGLP *Lietuvos gyvenimo logikos partija* (Lithuanian Party of Life Logic)
Lietuvos judėjimas Černobylis (Lithuanian Chernobyl Movement)
Lietuvos patriotų sąjunga (Union of Lithuanian Patriots)
Lietuvos sandrauga (Lithuanian Concord)

LK   *Lietuvos komjaunimas* (Lithuanian Komsomol)

LKDP   *Lietuvos krikščionių demokratų partija* (Lithuanian Christian Democratic Party)

LKDP, LPKTS *ir* LDP *jungtinis sąrašas,* joint list of LKDP, LPKTS and LDP

LKDS   *Lietuvos krikščionių demokratų sąjunga* (Lithuanian Christian Democratic Union)

LKDS *ir Lietuvių tautinio jaunimo 'Jaunoji Lietuva' susivienijimas už vieningą Lietuvą*
            (For United Lithuania); a coalition of LKDS and LTJS *'Jaunoji Lietuva'*

LKP   *Lietuvos komunistų partija* (Lithuanian Communist Party), relabelled LDDP in 1990

LKP–TSKP   Lithuanian Communist Party on CPSU platform (pro-Moscow)

LLENS   *Lietuvos lenkų sąjunga* (Union of Lithuanian Poles); relabelled LLRA *(Lietuvos lenkų rinkimų akcija,* Party of Electoral Action of Lithuanian Poles)

LLL   *Lietuvos laisvės lyga* (Lithuanian Freedom League)

LLS   *Lietuvos laisvės sąjunga* (Social Political Movement Lithuanian Freedom Union); developed into the LLSA party

LLSA   *Lietuvos laisvės sąjunga* (Lithuanian Freedom Union)

LLP   *Lietuvos liaudies partija* (Lithuanian People's Party)

LMP   *Lietuvos moterų partija* (Lithuanian Women's Party)

LNJ   *Lietuvos nuosaikiųjų judėjimas* (Lithuanian Moderate Movement)

LNPJL   *Lietuvių nacionalinė partija 'Jaunoji Lietuva'*
            (Lithuanian National Party Young Lithuania)

LPA   *Lietuvos piliečių aljansas* (Lithuanian Citizens' Alliance)

LPKTS   *Lietuvos politinių kalinių ir tremtinių sąjunga*
            (Lithuanian Union of Political Prisoners and Deportees)

LRS   *Lietuvos rusų sąjunga* (Lithuanian Russian Union)

LSDP   *Lietuvos socialdemokratų partija* (Lithuanian Social Democratic Party)

LSP   *Lietuvos socialistų partija* (Lithuanian Socialist Party)

LSTP   *Lietuvos socialinio teisingumo partija* (Lithuanian Social Justice Party)

LTJS *'Jaunoji Lietuva'* (Lithuanian National Youth Union 'Young Lithuania')

LTMA   *Lietuvos tautinių mažumų aljansas*
            (Lithuanian Alliance of National Minorities); relabelled LPA in February 1997

LTS   *Lietuvos tautininkų sąjunga* (Lithuanian Nationalist Union)

LTS *ir* NP *sąrašas ;* joint list of LTS and NP

LŪP   *Lietuvos ūkio partija* (Lithuanian Party of Economy)

LVP   *Lietuvos valstiečių partija* (Lithuanian Peasants' Party)

LŽP   *Lietuvos žaliųjų partija* (Lithuanian Green Party)

NJ   *Nepartinių judėjimas Rinkimai 96* (Non-Party Movement Elections 96)

NP   *Nepriklausomybės partija* (Independence Party)

Piliečių chartija (Citizens' Charter)

RP   *Respublikonų partija* (Republican Party)

Sąjūdžio santara (*Sąjūdis* Concord); a coalition of *Sąjūdis,* LŽP and *Piliečių chartija*

TPJ   *Tautos pažangos judėjimas*   (National Progressive Movement); relabelled TPP

TPP   *Tautos pažangos partija*   (National Progressive Party)

TS(LK)   *Tėvynės sąjunga (Lietuvos konservatoriai)*
            (Homeland Union [Lithuanian Conservatives])

VPJ   *Visuomeninis politinis judėjimas už socialinį teisingumą*
            (Social Political Movement for Social Justice)

NOTES

1. The author would like to thank Gábor Tóka, Sten Berglund and Frank Aarebrot for their useful comments on the draft paper. The author would also like to thank his student Aurimas Andrulis as well as Alvidas Lukošaitis of the *Seimas* Department of Information Analysis for their assistance in collecting data for the appendices.

2. It is important to keep in mind that the *perestroika* process could commence in Lithuania only in 1988, partly due to the conservatism of the LKP leadership. The nature of the Lithuanian dissident movement goes a long way towards explaining the failure to seize the opportunity for change in 1985. The main leaders of *Sąjūdis* did not come from the dissident movement but were rather recruited from the intelligentsia, the Soviet middle classes. As opposed to the Central European countries, there were practically no representatives of the intelligentsia in the dissident movement in Lithuania. Very few dissidents participated in the main political parties at the time of their establishment and all virtually disappeared from politics soon after independence.

3. The following is an extract from my unpublished paper 'Problems of party system research in the Baltic States (Lithuania): on the trail of appropriate strategy', submitted for the international seminar *Development and Government of Nation States. The Baltic Case: Estonia, Latvia and Lithuania After the Declaration of Independence*, Project Balticum, Faculty of Social Sciences, Oslo, 12–14 December 1996. The empirical evidence in this chapter has been derived from the survey of candidates to the Lithuanian *Seimas*. The mail survey was jointly sponsored by Professor Thomas Remeikis (Chicago), the Polybius Foundation and the Institute of International Relations and Political Science, University of Vilnius. (The survey data is referred to as VU TSPMI 1996). The survey was carried out between 4 and 20 October 1996. 1,352 candidates to the *Seimas* were asked to answer 32 questions by mail. The return ratio was 44 per cent (593 questionnaires returned) which can be considered normal for a mail survey.

4. In 1992, the TS(LK) received 395,500 votes (15.4 per cent of total registered voters, 20.5 per cent of the vote). In 1996, the respective numbers were 409,500, 15.8 per cent and 29.8 per cent (Lukošaitis 1996, 2).

REFERENCES

Agh, Attila (1995), 'The "Early Freezing" of East Central European parties: The case of the Hungarian Socialist Party', paper presented at the conference *Party Politics in the Year 2000*, Manchester University.

[The] *Baltic States: A Survey of the Political and Economic Structure and the Foreign Relations* (1938), The Information Department of the Royal Institute of International Affairs, Oxford, Oxford University Press.

Bernatonis, Juozas (1995), 'Šiandien LDDP aukso amžius', *Lietuvos aidas*, 25 July, 5.

Commission of the European Communities 1991–, *Central and Eastern Eurobarometer*, Brussels, European Commission.

Commission Opinion on Lithuania's Application for Membership of the European Union (1997), European Commission, http://europa.eu.int/comm/dg1a/agenda2000/en/opinions/lithuania/b1.htm.

Degutis, Mindaugas (1997a), 'Lietuvos rinkėjų partinių preferencijų kitimas nuo 1996 m. Seimo iki 1997 m. savivaldybių tarybų rinkimų', presentation at the seminar *Savivaldybių tarybų rinkimai '97 ir vietos savivaldos perspektyvos Lietuvoje*. Vilniaus universitetas, TSPMI and Konrad Adenauer Stiftung.

—— (1997b), Lietuvos rinkėjai: partijų pasirinkimo motyvai', *Politologija*, 1(9): 142–57.

Dellenbrant, Jan Åke (1994), 'The Re-Emergence of Multi-Partyism in the Baltic States', in Sten Berglund and Jan Åke Dellenbrant, eds., *The New Democracies in Eastern Europe: Party Systems and Political Cleavages*, Aldershot, Edward Elgar, 74–116.

Gaidys, Vladas (1996), 'Partijų populiarumas viešosios nuomonės apklausose 1989–1996 m.', in Algis Krupavičius, ed., *Politinės partijos Lietuvoje: Atgimimas ir veikla,* Kaunas, Litterae Universitatis, 93–114.

Helsinki Commission Staff Delegation to Vilnius, Lithuania (1990), 'A report on the Lithuanian Supreme Soviet Elections', in *Elections in the Baltic states and Soviet Republics: A Compendium of Reports on Parliamentary Elections Held in 1990,* Washington, DC.

Huber, John and Ronald Inglehart (1995), 'Expert Interpretations of Party Space and Party Locations', *Party Politics,* 1(1), 73–112.

Juozaitis, Arvydas (1998), 'Prezidentas: trečioji jėga', in *Gairės,* 1(46), 8–9.

Kirkilas, Gediminas (1996), 'Lietuvos demokratinė darbo partija', in Algis Krupavičius, ed., *Politinės partijos Lietuvoje. Atgimimas ir veikla,* Kaunas, Litterae Universitatis, 169–82.

Krupavičius, Algis (1996), 'Pokomunistinė transformacija ir Lietuvos partijos', in Algis Krupavičius, ed., *Politinės partijos Lietuvoje. Atgimimas ir veikla,* Kaunas, Litterae Universitatis, 1–92.

Kubilius, Andrius (1995), 'Partijos Lietuvoje: sistema, ideologijos, bendradarbiavimo galimybė' *Lietuvos aidas,* 11–13 July, 141–3.

—— (1997), 'Seimo veto kandidatų svajonėms', *Lietuvos aidas,* 18 December, 12–13.

Lieven, Anatol (1993), *The Baltic Revolution: Estonia, Latvia, Lithuania and the Path to Independence,* New Haven, Yale University Press.

Lukošaitis, Alvidas (1996), *Rinkimų rezultatai: politinės partijos ir partinė sistema,* Vilnius, Lietuvos Respublikos Seimas.

—— (1997), *Parlamentas ir parlementarizmas nepriklausomoje Lietuvoje. 1918–1940 ir 1990 1997 metai,* Vilnius, LR Seimo Informacijos analizės skyrius.

Mair, Peter (1993), 'Myths of Electoral Change and the Survival of Traditional Parties', *European Journal of Political Research,* 24, 121–33.

Misiūnas, Romuald and Rein Taagepera (1993), *The Baltic States: Years of Dependence 1940–1990,* 2nd ed., London, Hurst & Company.

Nekrašas, Evaldas (1994), *Legislature and the Executive in Foreign Policy Making,* Vilnius, Bitas.

Nørgaard, Ole et al. (1996), *The Baltic States After Independence,* Aldershot, Edward Elgar.

Tóka, Gábor (1995), 'Being Represented–Being Satisfied? Political Support in East-Central Europe', in Hans-Dieter Klingemann and Dieter Fuchs, eds., *Citizens and the State,* Oxford, Oxford University Press, 354–82.

Pettai, Vello (1997), 'Political Stability Through Disenfranchisement', *Transition,* 3(6), 21–3.

Rauch, Georg von (1970), *The Baltic States: The Years of Independence, 1917–1940.* London, C.Hurst & Company.

Rose, Richard and William Maley (1994), *Nationalities in the Baltic States: A Survey Study,* Studies in Public Policy, No. 222, Centre for the Study of Public Policy, Glasgow, University of Strathclyde.

Sartori, Giovanni (1976), *Parties and Party Systems,* Cambridge, Cambridge University Press.

Shugart, Matthew S. and John M. Carey (1992), *Presidents and Assemblies: Constitutional Design and Electoral Dynamics,* Cambridge, Cambridge University Press.

Steen, Anton (1996), 'Confidence in institutions in post-communist societies: the case of the Baltic States', *Scandinavian Political Studies,* 19(3), 205–25 (Draft version with complete set of data tables in Anton Steen (1994), 'Confidence in institutions in post-communist societies: the case of the Baltic States', *Working Paper* 12/94, University of Oslo, Department of Political Science).

Šliogeris, Arvydas (1994), 'Nepriklausomybės šokas ir liberaliosios demokratijos perspektyvos Lietuvoje', *Lietuvos rytas,* 6–7 December.

Žeruolis, Darius (1996), 'Rytai tampa Vakarais? Vakarų Europos konceptualinių instrumentų taikymas pokomunistinių partinių sistemų stabilizacijos bei kaitos analizei', *Politologija,* 1(6).

—— (1997), 'Politinis stabilumas ir demokratija Lietuvoje', in Klaudijus Maniokas and Gediminas Vitkus, eds., *Lietuvos integracija į Europos Sąjungą: būklės, perspektyvø ir pasekmių studija,* 65–89.

APPENDIX 5.1: ELECTION RESULTS

PARLIAMENTARY ELECTIONS

1990 elections to Aukščiausioji Taryba
First round
Date: 24 February
Turnout: 71.7%

	MPs elected	of which Sąjūdis MPs
No party affiliation	48	46
LKP	22	13
LKP–TSKP	7	0
LSDP	9	9
LZP	2	2
LKDP	2	2
Total	90	72

Second round
Date: 4, 7, 8 and 10 March;
      new elections to vacant seats after two rounds on 7 and 21 April
Turnout: 66.4%

	MPs elected	of which Sąjūdis MPs
No party affiliation	25	21
LKP	19	6
LKP–TSKP	2	0
LDP	3	2
Total	49	29

Candidate affiliation based on the number of names printed on the final ballots

	Total candidates	Sąjūdis endorsed
No party affiliation	142	94
LKP	205	30
LKP-TSKP	78	0
LSDP	23	11
LDP	16	3
LŽP	4	?
LKDP	2	2
LK	2	0
Total	472	142

Factions in Aukščiausioji Taryba (AT) 1990–92

	Registered in AT	Membership 8 May 1991	Membership October 1992
Sąjūdžio Centro frakcija (Sąjūdis Centre Faction)	21.06.1990	21	20
Kairiųjų frakcija (The Leftist Faction)	25.09.1992	14	9
Lenkų frakcija (Polish Faction)	23.10.1990	8	8
Jungtinė Sąjūdžio frakcija (Joint Sąjūdis Faction)	19.12.1990	34	14
Tautininkų frakcija (Faction of the Nationalists)	09.01.1991	12	9
Septintoji frakcija (The Seventh Faction)	23.04.1991	14	18
Liberalų frakcija (Faction of the Liberals)	08.05.1991	10	9
Sąjūdžio Santaros frakcija (Sąjūdis Concord Faction)	30.01.1992	–	11
Tautos pažangos frakcija (Faction of National Progress)	14.01.1992	–	9
Non-faction MPs		28*	31

Notes: On 11 February 1992, Kairiųjų frakcija was renamed LDDP frakcija (Faction of Lithuanian Labour Democratic Party); Septintoji frakcija was later renamed Nuosaikiųjų frakcija (Faction of the Moderates); Tautos pažangos frakcija was established by MPs who defected from Tautininkų frakcija; Sąjūdžio Santaros frakcija consisted of defectors from Jungtinė Sąjūdžio frakcija, * Highest estimate, exact data not available.

Sources: Helsinki Commission Staff Delegation to Vilnius, Lithuania (1990), 'A report on the Lithuanian Supreme Soviet Elections', in Elections in the Baltic states and Soviet Republics: A Compendium of Reports on Parliamentary Elections Held in 1990, Washington, DC; Lukošaitis, Alvidas (1997), Parlamentas ir parlementarizmas nepriklausomoje Lietuvoje. 1918–1940 ir 1990–1997 metai, Vilnius, LR Seimo Informacijos analizės skyrius; Žeruolis, Darius (1996), 'Rytai tampa Vakarais? Vakarų Europos konceptualinių instrumentų taikymas pokomunistinių partinių sistemų stabilizacijos bei kaitos analizei', Politologija, 1(6), 3–49, Table 5; Valstybės žinios, 16, 23 March 1990 and 11 April 1990; Report of Aloyzas Sakalas, Chairman of the Mandates Commission to the Supreme Council of Lithuania, Tiesa, 12 March 1990.

1992 elections to 2nd Seimas
Date: 25 October and 15 November
Turnout: 75.3% (average of two rounds)

	%	Seats in MMD	Seats in SMD
LDDP	42.6	36	37
Sąjūdžio santara	20.5	17	11
LKDP, LPKTS *ir* LDP *jungtinis sąrašas*	12.2		
LKDP		3	6
LPKTS		3	2
LDP		4	-
LSDP	5.5	5	3
LKDS *ir Lietuvių tautinio jaunimo Jaunoji*	3.4		
Lietuva susivienijimas už vieningą Lietuvą			
LKDS		–	1
LTJS *'Jaunoji Lietuva'*		–	–
LCJ	2.4	-	2
LLENS	2.1	2	2
LTS *ir* NP *sąrašas*	1.9		
LTS		–	3
NP		–	1
LLS	1.5	–	–
LLL	1.2	–	–
TPJ	1.0	–	–
LNJ	0.7	–	–
VPJ *už socialinį teisingumą*	0.5	–	–
VPJ *Lietuvos laisvės sąjunga*	0.4	–	–
Lietuvos judėjimas Černobylis	0.2	–	
Lietuvos sandrauga	0.2	–	–
Lietuvos patriotų sąjunga	0.1	–	–
Independent candidates	–	–	1
Total		70	71

Factions in Seimas 1992–1996

	31 Dec 1992		18 Nov 1993	Oct 1996
	Seats	%	Seats	Seats
LDDP *frakcija*	74	54.4	73	60
Sąjūdžio *frakcija*	14	10.0	14	–
LPKTS *'Laisvės' frakcija*	12	8.5	–	4
LKDP *frakcija*	10	7.1	10	12
Piliečių *chartija*	9	6.4	–	–
LSDP *frakcija*	7	5.0	7	7
Lenkų *frakcija*	4	2.8	4	3
LDP *frakcija*	4	2.8	–	3
TS(LK) *frakcija*	–		–	24
Mišri Seimo narių grupė	–		–	8
Independent MPs	7	5.0	32	8
Total	141		140	141

Notes: Piliečių chartija – Citizens' Charter; Lenkų frakcija (LF) – Polish Faction; *Mišri Seimo narių grupė* (MSNG) – Mixed Group of MPs.

Sources: Lietuvos Seimas (1996), Vilnius, Kultūra; Lukošaitis, Alvidas (1997) *Parlamentas ir parlementarizmas nepriklausomoje Lietuvoje. 1918–1940 ir 1990–1997 metai*, Vilnius, LR Seimo Informacijos analizės skyrius; Žeruolis, Darius (1996), 'Rytai tampa Vakarais? Vakarų Europos konceptualinių instrumentų taikymas pokomunistinių partinių sistemų stabilizacijos bei kaitos analizei', *Politologija*, 1(6):3–49, Table 5; Nørgaard, Ole et al. (1996), *The Baltic States After Independence*, Cheltenham, Edward Elgar, 95, Table 3.4.

1996 elections to 3rd Seimas
Date: 20 October (first round) and 10 November (second round)
Turnout: 52.9% (first round), 38.2% (second round)

Party/coalition	%	*Mandates* Total	in MMD	in SMD
TS(LK)	29.8	70	33	37
LKDP	9.9	16	11	5
LDDP	9.5	12	10	2
LCS	8.2	13	9	4
LSDP	6.6	12	7	5
LNPJL	3.8	1	–	1
LMP	3.7	1	–	1
LKDS	3.1	1	–	1
LLRA	3.0	1	–	1
LTMA	2.4	–	–	–
LTS and LDP coalition	2.1		–	
LTS		1	–	1
LDP		2	–	2
LLS	1.8	1	–	1
LVP	1.7	1	–	1
LRS	1.6	–	–	–
LPKTS	1.5	1	–	1
LLSA	1.5	–		–
LŪP	1.2	–	–	–
LLL	0.9	–	–	–
LSTS	0.9	–	–	–
LSP	0.7	–	–	–
RP	0.4	–	–	–
TPP	0.3	–	–	–
LGLP	0.2	–	–	–
LLP	0.2	–	–	–
NJ *Rinkimai '96*	–	–	–	–
NP		–	–	–
Independent candidates	–	4	–	4
Total		137	70	67
Total number of seats		141		

Factions in Seimas 1996–

	Number of MPs	*Participating parties*
TS(LK)	66	TS(LK)
LKDP	16	LKDP
LCS	14	LCS
LDDP	12	LDDP
LSDP	12	LSDP
Nepriklausoma frakcija	4	LMP, LVP, LLRA, LKDS
Demokratų frakcija	3	LDP, LPKTS
Jungtinė frakcija	3	LTS, LNPJL, independents
Liberalių reformų frakcija	3	LLS, independent

PRESIDENTIAL ELECTIONS

1993 Elections
Date: 14 February
Turnout: 78.6%

Candidate	Votes	%	Party affiliation
Algirdas Mykolas Brazauskas	1,212,075	60.0	LDDP
Stasys Lozoraitis	772,922	38.3	Non-affiliated, supported by *Sąjūdis*, LKDP, LCJ, LSDP and small non-left-wing parties
Invalid ballots	34,016	1.7	

Source: *Prezidento rinkimų komisijos protokolas* (Protocol of the Presidential Election Commission), 17 February 1993.

1997–98 Elections
First round
Date: 21 December 1997 (first round), 4 January 1998 (second round)
Turnout: 71.4% 73.6% (second round)

Candidate	Votes	%	Party affiliation
Artūras Paulauskas	838,819	44.7	Non-party, supported by LLS, LDDP, LMP, LLRA, LVP, LŪP
Valdas Adamkus	516,798	27.6	Non-party, supported by LCS, LTS, LDP
Vytautas Landsbergis	294,881	15.7	TS(LK), endorsed by LKDP
Vytenis Povilas Andriukaitis	105,916	5.6	LSDP
Kazys Bobelis	73,287	3.9	LKDS
Rolandas Pavilionis	16,070	0.9	Independent
Rimantas Smetona	6,697	0.4	*Nacionaldemokratis judėjimas Už nepriklausomą Lietuvą* (Lithuanian Eurosceptics)
Invalid ballots	22,680	1.2	

Second round
Date: 4 January 1998
Turnout: 73.6%

Candidate	Votes	%
Valdas Adamkus	968,031	50.0
Artūras Paulauskas	953,775	49.2
Invalid ballots	15,980	0.8

Source: *Vyriausioji rinkimų komisija* (High Electoral Commission); http://www.lrs.lt/pr97.

APPENDIX 5.2: GOVERNMENT COMPOSITION

Prime Minister (party)	Kazimiera Danutė Prunskienė *(Sąjūdis)*
Date	17 March 1990–8 January 1991
Cabinet composition (parties and number of governmental posts)	*Sąjūdis*, LKP and non-party ministers. *Sąjūdis* had the initiative in forming the Government but lacked professionals to fill all posts; it invited non-party and LKP professionals to participate in the government. 17 ministers and two Deputy Prime Ministers.
Political orientation (relation to the majority in the Parliament)	Majority government in the sense that it had the support of the Supreme Council (at the beginning of the term, *Sąjūdis* controlled 101 seats in the *Aukščiausioji Taryba*), but in essence it was a coalition government between *Sąjūdis* and LKP.
Reason for change of government	The government's resolution to liberalize prices was not supported by a majority in the *Aukščiausioji Taryba*, as it feared social tensions in the wake of the Soviet military crackdown of 13 January 1991.

Prime Minister (party)	Albertas Šimėnas (*Sąjūdžio Centro frakcija*)
Date	10–13 January 1991
Cabinet composition (parties and number of governmental posts)	11 ministers inherited from the Prunskienė government, no new appointments due to short life-span of the government.
Political orientation (relation to the majority in parliament)	Majority government based on the compromise of several *Sąjūdis* parliamentary factions.
Reason for change of government	Šimėnas went missing on the night of Soviet invasion on 13 January 1991. In his absence the parliament voted to dismiss him and install Gediminas Vagnorius as Prime Minister. Minister of Foreign Affairs Algirdas Saudargas, who was in Warsaw at the time, was appointed Prime Minister-in-exile, should the incumbent government be paralyzed by Soviet intervention.

Prime Minister (party)	Gediminas Vagnorius *(Jungtinė Sąjūdžio frakcija)*
Date	13 January 1991–15 July 1992
Cabinet composition (parties and the number of governmental posts)	*Sąjūdis* government. 19 ministers, two of which Deputy Prime Ministers and one without portfolio.
Political orientation (relation to the majority in Parliament)	Right-wing government supported by *Sąjūdis* majority in parliament.
Reason for change of government	*Sąjūdis* parliamentary majority disintegrated in April 1992. On 14 July 1992, Gediminas Vagnorius lost a vote of confidence.

Prime Minister (party)	Aleksandras Abišala (Minister without portfolio in Vagnorius' government, non-faction MP)
Date	21 July–26 November 1992
Cabinet composition (parties and the number of governmental posts)	*Sajūdis* government, 17 ministers, two of whom were without portfolio; one Deputy Prime Minister. 11 ministers inherited from the Vagnorius government.
Political orientation (relation to the majority in parliament)	Caretaker government until pre-term parliamentary elections of October 1992. Supported by *ad hoc* majorities.
Reason for the change of government	Pre-term parliamentary elections.

Prime Minister (party)	Bronislovas Lubys (Deputy PM in Abišala's government)
Date	2 December 1992–10 March 1993
Cabinet composition (parties and the number of governmental posts)	LDDP one-party government but with some non-party ministers. 15 ministerial posts, most filled by LDDP members. Five ministers continued from the Abišala government.
Political orientation (relation to the majority in the Parliament)	Caretaker left-wing government, supported by an absolute LDDP majority in the *Seimas*.
Reason for the change of government	Lubys declined to participate in the cabinet after the first direct presidential elections on 14 February 1993.

Prime Minister (party)	Adolfas Šleževičius (LDDP)
Date	10 March 1993–23 February 1996
Cabinet composition (parties and the number of governmental posts)	LDDP government with a majority of LDDP ministers. 16 ministerial posts at the beginning of the term, 18 at the time of resignation.
Political orientation (relation to the majority in parliament)	Left-wing government, supported by an absolute LDDP majority in the *Seimas*.
Reason for the change of government	*Seimas* vote of no confidence against Šleževičius, who had retrieved his deposits from a bankrupt bank in December 1995.

Prime Minister (party)	Laurynas Mindaugas Stankevičius (LDDP)
Date	23 February 1996–4 December 1996
Cabinet composition (parties and the number of governmental posts)	LDDP government. 12 ministers (out of 18) continued from the previous government.
Political orientation (relation to the majority in parliament)	Left-wing government, supported by absolute LDDP majority in the *Seimas*.
Reason for the change of government	Parliamentary elections of November 1996.

Prime Minister (party)	Gediminas Vagnorius (TS[LK])
Date	4 December 1996–
Cabinet composition (parties and the number of governmental posts)	Coalition government. Twelve cabinet posts for the TS(LK), of which ten where filled by ministers affiliated with the party; three posts for the LKDP. LCS is *de facto* a coalition member and holds two portfolios.
Political orientation (relation to the majority in parliament)	Centre-right coalition government, supported by a TS(LK) and LKDP majority in the *Seimas*.

APPENDIX 5.3: THE ELECTORAL SYSTEM

In the 1990 elections to the Supreme Council of Lithuania (*Lietuvos Aukščiausioji Taryba* or *Aukščiausioji Taryba*, AT), the 141 representatives were elected in single-mandate constituencies. For the elections to be valid, a turnout of 50 per cent was required. If the turnout in individual constituencies was lower, new elections had to be called. For a candidate to be elected, he or she had to receive an absolute majority for a straight win. If no straight winner emerged in the first round, the two top candidates advanced to the second round where the winner was determined by a simple majority.

The electoral system was changed ahead of the 1992 elections to the *Lietuvos Respublikos Seimas*. 71 of the 141 mandates were to be contested in single-member constituencies, while the remaining 70 were elected in multi-member constituencies. The deputies are elected for a four-year term. The *Seimas* is considered to have been elected when at least three-fifths of MPs have been elected. Any citizen of the Republic of Lithuania who, on election day, has reached the age of 25 and is a permanent resident in Lithuania, may be elected MP.

In the single-mandate constituencies, a turnout of at least 40 per cent plus one vote is required for the elections to be valid. In the first round, a candidate who obtains 50 per cent plus one of the votes is declared winner. If no winner emerges, the two front-runners have to contest a second round. If only two candidates participate in the first round and both fail to obtain 50 per cent plus one vote, new elections have to be held. In the second round, a simple majority is sufficient.

In the multi-member constituencies, a turnout of at least 25 per cent plus one vote is required for the elections to be valid. In order to qualify for the distribution of seats, parties and political movements have to overcome the national electoral threshold, which was 4 per cent in 1992 and raised to 5 per cent for individual parties and 7 per cent for electoral coalitions in 1996; in 1992, no threshold was applied to lists of national minorities, but they had to obtain enough votes for one quota. Seats are distributed according to a formula where all votes of the parties above the threshold are pooled. The pool is divided by 70, equivalent to the total number of seats allocated in multiple-member constituencies. The votes of the individual parties are divided by the divisor. Remaining unallocated mandates are allocated to parties whose remainder is closest to the divisor.

In 1996, provisions in the electoral law excepting ethnic minority parties from the 5 per cent threshold for parties and 7 per cent threshold for electoral coalitions was abolished. Moreover, voters were given the option of rating party lists. When voting for a particular party in multi-member constituencies, voters can express their approval (+) or disapproval (-) of as many candidates on the list as he/she wishes. All votes 'for' and 'against' a candidate on the list are counted, and the rating of candidates is calculated according to the formula $R=Re * Rp$, where R is the rating in the final list; Re (electoral rating) is the number of votes for the whole party list plus votes 'for' a particular candidate minus votes 'against' the candidate; Rp (party rating) is the number of candidates on the list plus one, minus the number of the candidates.

Regular elections to the *Seimas* are held no earlier than two, and no later than one month prior to the expiry of the term. Early elections to the *Seimas* may be held on the decision by a three-fifths majority of MPs or by decision of the President, if the *Seimas* fails to take a decision on the new programme of the Government within 30 days of its presentation, or if the *Seimas* twice in succession disapproves of the Government programme within 60 days of its initial presentation; or upon the proposal of the Government, if the *Seimas* expresses direct non-confidence in the Government. The President may not announce early elections to the *Seimas,* if his own term expires within less than six months or if six months have not passed since the early elections to the *Seimas*. The election to the new *Seimas* must be held within three months from the adoption of the decision on the early elections.

The President is elected in direct elections. In the first round, a candidate who obtains 50 per cent plus one of the votes is considered elected, provided that at least half of the eligible voters participate in the elections. If no winner is thus determined, a second round between the two front-runners is to be held in two weeks time. If voter turnout in the first round is less than 50 per cent, a candidate who obtains a majority of the votes cast, equivalent to at least one-third of the votes of all registered voters, is considered elected. If no winner can be declared, a second round between the top two candidates will be held in two weeks' time. If only two candidates run in the first round, none of them winning an absolute majority or, if turnout is below 50 per cent, a number of votes equivalent to one-third of the electorate, a new election is called. In the second round, the candidate who obtains the majority of all votes cast is considered elected, regardless of the turnout.

The President is elected for a five-year fixed term and may be elected for a maximum of two terms. A President-elect must immediately suspend his party membership until the beginning of the next political campaign.

APPENDIX 5.4: THE CONSTITUTIONAL FRAMEWORK

Lithuania became a semi-presidential republic when a new Constitution was passed by a referendum on 25 October 1992. For two and a half years after Lithuania regained her independence on 11 March 1990, the political system was regulated by the *Laikinasis Pagrindinis Įstatymas* (Basic Provisional Law), passed by the *Aukščiausioji Taryba* on 11 March 1990. It was in fact a revised version of the Constitution of the Lithuanian Socialist Soviet Republic, purged only of references to the Soviet system. In 1990–92, Lithuania was formally a parliamentary republic, but due to the extraordinary political circumstances of this period, the central figure in Lithuanian political life was not the Prime Minister but the Chairman of the Supreme Council (who was Speaker of Parliament *de jure* but Head of State *de facto*). Lithuania introduced a system of partial separation of powers as a consequence of political compromises in the summer and autumn of 1992. *Sąjūdis* had by then lost its clear parliamentary majority, and provisions for a directly elected President were introduced into the new Constitution – partly because of personal ambitions on the part of the key political actors at the time, partly as a safeguard against hung parliaments.

According to Article 68 of the Constitution, legislative initiative is vested in the *Seimas*, the Government, the President and in groups of at least 50,000 citizens.

The President proclaims laws passed by the *Seimas* and has a veto. He can return laws to the *Seimas*, which in turn may override the presidential veto by simple majority; constitutional laws require a three-fifths majority. The President is involved in the formation of the cabinet. He names the Prime Minister, who upon investiture by the *Seimas* forms the Government. The Ministers are appointed and dismissed by presidential decree upon the request of the Prime Minister. Only the *Seimas* can effectively censure or dismiss Ministers and the Government. The President may dissolve the *Seimas* if the Government is defeated in a vote of no confidence in the *Seimas*, but only if the Government asks the President to call early elections. The President may also call early parliamentary elections if the *Seimas* fails to make a decision on the Government's programme within 30 days or if it rejects the Government's programme twice within 60 days from the day the programme was first submitted to the *Seimas* floor. The *Seimas* may also dissolve itself if three-fifths of all *Seimas* members vote in favour of such a motion.

The President has significant powers in foreign and defence policy-making. However, when the President has to cohabit with a hostile parliament, there is no mechanism for the President to fulfil these duties and the initiative has recently been taken by the Chairman of the *Seimas*, the Minister of Foreign Affairs or even the Minister of European Affairs. The President is empowered to nominate the Chairman and justices of the Supreme Court; justices of the Appeals Court and the Chairman of the Appeals Court; lower-level judges; three (out of 9) justices of the Constitutional Court and the Chairman of the Constitutional Court; the Chairman of the State Control Office; and the Chairman of the Board of the National Bank. All these appointments are subject to investiture by the *Seimas*. The President also appoints and dismisses the Commander of the Armed Forces and the head of security services, both upon the approval of *Seimas*.

The constitutional set-up and political practice suggest that Lithuania is what Shugart and Carey (1992) would classify as a premier–presidential state leaning towards parliamentarism. All presidential powers are matched by countervailing powers vested in the *Seimas*. In the areas where the separation of powers is not clear enough, presidential supremacy is assumed (e.g. the President decides upon main foreign policy questions and, in tandem with the Government, implements foreign policy), but the constitution allows the presidency, as well as the parliament, to take the initiative. In such cases, the personality of the President becomes a decisive factor. President Brazauskas chose to be a weak president and to stay out of conflict even when his former party held a majority in the *Seimas*. He was initially reluctant to make major moves in the 'exclusive' domain allocated to him, that is foreign policy (Nekrašas 1994), and did so only in 1996–97, towards the end of his presidential term.

While in office, the President can be removed only through impeachment proceedings. Under normal circumstances, early presidential elections can be called when the President dissolves the *Seimas* and at least three-fifths of the membership of a newly-elected parliament calls for early presidential elections.

The Government consists of the Prime Minister and Ministers. The Prime Minister is appointed or dismissed by the President of the Republic with the approval of the *Seimas*. The Ministers are appointed by the President upon the nomination of the Prime Minister. The Prime Minister presents the members of the Government and the programme to the *Seimas* within 15 days of his or her appointment. A new Government is installed when the *Seimas* approves its programme by a majority vote. The Government returns its mandate to the President of the Republic after parliamentary and presidential elections. When more than half of the Ministers are replaced, the Government must be re-invested with authority by the *Seimas*. Otherwise, the Government must resign. The Government must also resign if the majority of all MPs express no confidence in the Government or in the Prime Minister in a secret ballot or if the Prime Minister resigns or dies. A Minister must resign if more than half of all MPs express no confidence in him or her in a secret ballot. Resignations are accepted by the President of the Republic. Upon the request of the *Seimas*, the Government or individual Ministers must account for their activities.

The Government of the Republic of Lithuania: (1) runs the affairs of the country, protects the inviolability of the territory of the Republic, and safeguards national security and public order; (2) implements laws and resolutions of the *Seimas* concerning the implementation of laws and the decrees of the President; (3) co-ordinates the activities of the ministries and other governmental institutions; (4) prepares the draft budget of the State and submits it to the *Seimas*; implements the state budget and reports the *Seimas* on this implementation to the *Seimas*; (5) drafts bills and submits them to the *Seimas* for consideration; (6) establishes diplomatic relations and maintains relations with foreign countries and international organizations; and (7) discharges other duties prescribed by the Constitution and other laws.

The Government resolves the affairs of state administration in session by issuing directives which must be passed by a majority vote of all members of the Government. The State Controller may also participate in the Government sessions. Government directives are signed by the Prime Minister and the responsible Minister. The Government is collectively responsible to the *Seimas* for the general activities of the Government. The Ministers are responsible to the *Seimas* and the President of the Republic, and are directly subordinated to the Prime Minister within their sphere of competence.

A member of the *Seimas* may be appointed Prime Minister or Minister but may not take up other posts, whether private or public. An MP may not receive any remuneration other than the parliamentary salary, except for honorariums for publications or related activities. Members of the *Seimas* have the right to submit inquiries to the Prime Minister, individual Ministers, and the heads of other state institutions formed or elected by the *Seimas*. These persons or bodies must respond orally or in writing at a *Seimas* session in the manner prescribed by the *Seimas*. A group of no less than one-fifth of the *Seimas* deputies may ask for a vote of no confidence in the Prime Minister or in a Minister. After having considered the response of the Prime Minister or the Minister to such a motion, the *Seimas* may, by an absolute majority vote of all MPs, express non confidence in the Prime Minister or a Minister.

The *Seimas*: (1) debates and passes amendments to the Constitution; (2) legislates; (3) decides on holding referenda; (4) announces presidential elections; (5) establishes state institutions as provided by law, and appoints and dismisses their chief officers; (6) approves or rejects a candidacy for Prime Minister proposed by the President of the Republic; (7) considers the programme of the Government submitted by the Prime Minister, and decides on its approval; (8) upon the recommendation of the Government, establishes or abolishes ministries of the Republic of Lithuania; (9) supervises the activities of the Government, and may express no confidence in the Prime Minister or in individual Ministers; (10) appoints justices to, and Chairs of, the Constitutional Court as well as the Supreme Court; (11) appoints to, and dismisses from, the Office of State Controllers as well as the Chair of the Board of the Bank of Lithuania; (12) announces elections to the councils of local government; (13) forms the Central Electoral

Committee and changes its composition; (14) approves the State budget and supervises the implementation thereof; (15) introduces taxes and other obligatory payments; (16) ratifies or rejects international treaties to which the Republic of Lithuania is a party, and considers other issues of foreign policy; (17) establishes administrative divisions of the Republic; (18) establishes state awards; (19) grants amnesty; and (20) imposes direct administration and martial law, declares a state of emergency, announces mobilization, and decides on the use of the Armed Forces.

For gross violation of the Constitution, breach of oath, or upon the disclosure of a felony crime, the *Seimas* may remove from office the President of the Republic, the Chair and justices of the Constitutional Court, the Supreme Court and the Court of Appeals, as well as *Seimas* members by a three-fifths majority vote of all MPs. Such actions are carried out in accordance with impeachment proceedings laid down by the Statute of the *Seimas*. The *Seimas* may also dismiss other appointed or elected officers by a majority vote of all MPs, or express no confidence in the officer in question.

The *Seimas* passes laws by majority vote. Constitutional laws of the Republic of Lithuania require an absolute majority of affirmative votes of all MPs. Constitutional amendments require an extraordinary majority of at least three-fifths of all *Seimas* members. The *Seimas* establishes a list of constitutional laws by a three-fifth majority vote of all MPs. Provisions of the laws may also be adopted by referendum. The laws passed by the *Seimas* come into force after they have been signed and officially promulgated by the President of the Republic, unless the laws themselves specify that they become applicable at a later date. Other acts passed by the *Seimas* as well as the Statute of the *Seimas* are signed by the Speaker of the *Seimas*. All these acts shall become effective the day following the promulgation, unless the acts themselves specify that they become applicable at a later date. Within ten days of receiving a law passed by the *Seimas*, the President of the Republic has to sign and promulgate it, or to refer it back to the *Seimas* with a specified request for reconsideration. If the President does not take any action, the law becomes effective when signed and promulgated by the Speaker of the *Seimas*. Within five days, the President must sign and promulgate laws and other acts approved by referendum; otherwise they become effective when signed and promulgated by the Speaker of the *Seimas*. A law vetoed by the President is passed if the presidential amendments and supplements are accepted by the *Seimas*. A presidential veto is overridden if more than a half of all *Seimas* members (three-fifths in the case of a constitutional law) vote in favour of the original reading of the law already passed by the *Seimas*. The President must sign and forthwith promulgate laws re-passed by the *Seimas* within three days.

The Constitutional Court decides whether the laws and other legal acts passed by the *Seimas* conform with the Constitution, and whether legal acts adopted by the President and the Government violate the Constitution or laws. The Constitutional Court also decides: (1) on the legality of presidential elections or elections to the *Seimas*; (2) whether the health of the President of the Republic is limits his or her capacity to continue in office; (3) Whether international agreements conform with the Constitution; and (4) on the compliance with the Constitution of specific actions of *Seimas* members or other state officers against whom impeachment proceedings have been instituted. The Constitutional Court consists of nine justices appointed for a single non-renewable term of nine years. Every three years, one-third of the Constitutional Court membership shall be renewed. The *Seimas* appoints all members of the Constitutional Court; the President of the Republic, the Speaker of the *Seimas*, and the President of the Supreme Court may each nominate three candidates. The *Seimas* appoints the Chair of the Constitutional Court from the justices of the Court and on the nomination of the President of the Republic. Only lawyers of impeccable reputation with no less than ten years of experience qualify to be candidates for nomination.

6. Poland

Marian Grzybowski

Stein Rokkan's concept of six phases of transmission of social cleavages into party systems (Rokkan 1970, 90–7) does not quite do justice to the divisions and the party relations in the new democracies of Central and Eastern Europe, nor does Rokkan's and Lipset's general theory of interplay between the cleavages and the party system (Lipset and Rokkan 1967). With the benefit of hindsight, it is obvious that the typology of cleavages ought to be modified (Rae and Taylor 1970, 23–5; Flanagan 1973, 47–76). In two recent articles (1995, 154–179; 1996, 43–5, 47–51), Georgi Kara-simeonov identifies at least four types of socio-political divisions: (1) historical or residual cleavages, (2) transitional cleavages, (3) current ('actual') political divisions, and (4) prospective or potential division.

The general acceptance of Karasimeonov's typology should not be construed as an acceptance without reservations. The first, historical (residual) group of cleavages seems to play a particularly important role in Poland. The social divisions, both ideological and strictly political, inherited from the pre-communist society are still of obvious significance in post-communist reality. A deeply rooted religious cleavage, a traditionally defined urban/rural cleavage and a nationalist cleavage with profound roots in Polish history, still make themselves felt in the views of numerous social groups in post-1989 Poland (Taras 1993, 23–4; Olson 1993, 416–41).

The transitional divisions appeared at the stage of system transition. They have accompanied the bulk of the economic and social changes of 1989–90 and continue to exist in modified forms in the next stages of transition. Some of them are related to the content of changes, others seem to be of a procedural variety; they are all interrelated.

The divisions determined by current politics are more elusive. It is difficult to say which of the present social divisions and differentiations are of crucial importance for the shaping of party lines and party formations. The current debates and political infighting may easily give way to new issues and rivalry. In this sense the structure of conflict in Poland does indeed remain fluid. Similar comments apply to the potential or expected divisions. On-going economic and political reform processes do contribute towards shaping the emerging new cleavage structure, but it is anybody's guess which of the potential cleavages, including the increasingly modern left/right, will have a lasting impact on the conflict structure in Poland.

The political parties are the crucial actors in all four cleavage categories. They exploit the existing cleavages for the purpose of mobilization and consolidation of their respective rank and file. In the process, they may contribute significantly towards the institutionalization of the existing cleavages and towards the emergence of new ones.

With one major exception, there is no evidence that the new cleavages have gained ground to the detriment of the historical in Poland after 1989. The tension between those interested in bringing down the pre-1989 communist regime and those committed to more or less limited reform within the framework of the communist regime, has had a special impact on and importance for the entire period, particularly for the first three or four years of the system transformation.

At least three of the historical cleavages have preserved their importance in the current stage of social and political development. First of all it may be noted that the paternalistic and traditional, and frequently religiously-inspired way of life of village and countryside (small-town) strata and, to some extent, the life-style of first-generation urban dwellers, remain at a distance from and in contradiction with the slightly opened, modernized and absorptive way of life of the lion's share of the intelligentsia, the students and the young and well-educated urban strata.[1] Second, the gap between those earning their livelihood as proprietors and salaried employees and workers seems to retain its significance, even to grow in importance. This social division, which was quite visible – even overestimated – in the formative years of the Solidarity movement, lost ground in the early 1990s, only to reappear with a vengeance in the advanced stage of transition of the late 1990s. Third, the legacy of the communist past has carried over into the present in the form of a division between, on the one hand, those opposed to secular socialism and highly critical of the practices of the old regime and of Soviet political domination, and, on the other, those more favourably disposed to or profiting from 'real socialism'. The careful 'thick line' policy adopted by the first non-communist government of Tadeusz Mazowiecki – with all its omissions and inconsistencies – did not contribute towards eliminating or reducing the tension (Jasiewicz 1993, 91–117). This division remains in place, interfering with other conflict dimensions structuring the interplay between the post-Solidarity camp and its rivals.

The 1989–91 Political Fragmentation

After the parliamentary elections of 4 and 18 June 1989 (first and second rounds, respectively), the Polish United Workers' Party (PUWP) lost political power (Małkiewicz 1994, 20–21). With hindsight, the well-known journalist and former secretary of the PUWP Mieczysław Rakowski has identified the most important causes of the breakdown of communism in Poland (Rakowski 1991, 227–30). The PUWP had exhausted all its political possibilities and, under a barrage of criticism, found itself forced to change its organizational and programmatic formula. The party members and even the party apparatus embarked on a search for a new party line (Jaruzelski and Orechowski 1991). On 27–29 January 1989, during the Eleventh Party Congress, the communist party was taken over by the majority Social Democracy of the Republic of Poland under the leadership of Aleksander Kwaśniewski, while the minority Polish Social Democratic Union (PUS) led by Tadeusz Fiszbach broke away. PUS had little electoral success and was dissolved in 1991. Most of its members subsequently defected to the Union of Labour and the Social Democratic Movement, a co-founder of the Democratic Union.

The political transformation also affected the remaining party segments of the pre-1989 political order. At its Eleventh Extraordinary Congress on 26–27 November 1989, the United Peasant Party replaced most of its leaders, revised the party programme and renamed itself the Polish Peasant Party 'Revival' (Dehnel-Szyc 1991, 101–3; Paluch 1995, 29–33). Almost simultaneously, two other peasant parties were established: one based on the pre-war independent peasant movement, the other on Rural Solidarity. In May 1990, the PPP 'Revival' merged with the moderates of the pre-war peasant party, while the rest of that party and the Polish Peasant Party 'Solidarity' decided to continue their independent activities (Sokół and Żmigrodzki 1994, 41–3).

The efforts by the Democratic Party (DP) – a former ally of the PUWP in the pre-1989 hegemonic multi-party system – to adapt to the new political situation were less successful. The party changed its leadership and programme and joined Mazowiecki's Solidarity cabinet (together with the UPP), but to no avail. The DP's reputation as a loyal and quiet ally of the PUWP before 1989 did not serve as the very best letter of recommendation for the non-communist future and it was hard for the DP to carve out a niche for itself within the space recently captured by the newly formed post-Solidarity centre and other liberal political formations and parties (Dudek 1995a, 80–115; 1995b, 35–8).

At the same time, the newly re-established massive Solidarity movement, and in addition a large number of new non-communist groups with a history of organized underground activities, started to function openly as political parties. Among them were the anti-communist and populist Confederation for an Independent Poland (*Konfederacja Polski Niepodległej*, KPN) of Leszek Moczulski, the conservative Liberal Union of Real Politics (*Unia Polityki Realnej*, UPR) of Janusz Korwin-Mikke, the Polish Socialist Party (*Polska Partia Socjalistyczna*, PPS) of Jan Józef Lipski, the Polish Socialist Party–Democratic Revolution (PPS–RD) of Piotr Ikonowicz and the radical Fighting Solidarity of Kornel Morawiecki. Most of these parties were small and played but a marginal role in Polish party politics, but two of them constituted exceptions to this rule.

The secular (even laic) and pro-European Liberal–Democratic Congress (*Kongres Liberalno–Demokratyczny*, KLD), initially formed in Gdańsk in November–December 1989 and then officially established in Warsaw on 29–30 June 1990, was to have a major impact on Polish political life. Among the founders of this party were the young political activists Janusz Lewandowski, Donald Tusk and Jan Krzysztof Bielecki, of whom the latter went on to serve as Prime Minister in 1990–91. The KLD articulates the interests of secular and liberally-oriented groups of younger, educated, urban and entrepreneurial strata, open to modernization and committed to European integration, economically as well as culturally.

Another newly formed party, namely the Christian National Alliance (*Zjednoczenie Chrześcijańsko–Narodowe*, ZChN), was also to be of major significance. With its close links to Polish Catholicism, the Alliance lands squarely on the opposite pole of the religious/secular cleavage. It is strongly sceptical of European integration and any kind of liberalization, especially within the fields of religion, education and morality. Officially established on 28 October 1989, the Alliance has become a rallying-point for numerous Catholic, Christian Democratic and national-democratic organizations, such as 'Order and Freedom', 'Freedom and Solidarity', and various Catholic academic clubs and associations. The organization known as 'National Revival of Poland' joined the Christian National Alliance for a short while, but left it in February 1990 (Dudek 1997, 110).

The appearance of new political parties resulted in parliamentary re-alignments. The partly freely elected ('Contract') Polish *Sejm* of 1989–1991 went through a series of splits and secessions (*Table 6.1*).

The autumn of 1989 and the first months of 1990 were marked by elite-level infighting and the gradual disintegration of the Solidarity camp. The personal rivalry between Lech Wałęsa and Tadeusz Mazowiecki, who both ran for the office of president, added fuel to the controversy within Solidarity. But the internal conflicts were not confined to the very top (Paszkiewicz 1996).

Table 6.1: Composition of the Sejm *in 1989–91*

Party	July 1989 seats	%	Dec 1990 seats	%	Feb 1991 seats	%	Oct 1991 seats	%
United Workers' Party (PZPR)	173	37.6	–	–	–	–	–	–
Democratic Left (PKLD)	–	–	104	22.7	104	22.7	102	22.3
Pol. Soc. Dem. Union (PUS)	–	–	41	8.9	40	8.7	–	–
Confed. for Indep. Pol. (KPN)	–	–	10	2.2	9	2.8	7	1.5
KPW	–	–	7	1.5	7	1.5	7	1.5
PKP	–	–	–	–	–	–	39	8.5
Citizens' Parl. Club (OKP)	161	35.0	155	33.7	111	24.1	105	23.0
Democratic Union (UD)	–	–	–	–	46	10.0	49	10.7
Solidarity of Labour (SP)	–		–	–	–	–	5	1.1
Solidarity camp total	161	35.0	155	33.7	157	34.1	159	34.8
UPP (ZSL)	76	16.5	–	–	–	–	–	–
Polish Peasant Party (PSL)	–	–	73	15.9	73	15.9	65	14.2
PPP Mikołajczyk	–	–	4	0.9	4	0.9	4	0.9
Peasant parties total	76	16.5	77	16.8	77	16.8	69	15.1
Democratic Party (SD)	27	5.9	22	4.8	22	4.8	21	4.6
Others (PAX, UChS, PZKS)	23	5.0	22	4.8	22	4.8	22	5.0
Independents, new groups	–	–	21	4.6	21	4.6	30	6.8
Grand Total	460	100	459	100	459	100	156	100

Source: Wasilewski and Wesołowski (1992), 82.

Immediately after Solidarity's landslide victory in the June 1989 elections, the trade union wing of the Solidarity movement found itself engaged in a power struggle with the so-called citizens' committees, which had fulfilled a remarkable role in mobilizing voters during the election campaign. On 17 June 1989, the trade-unionist core of the National Committee of Solidarity had decided to dissolve the regional citizens' committees, as they were felt to be superfluous after the elections and even potentially disruptive. As a result, the political role of Solidarity's numerous advisors was curtailed, a development which met with protests from intellectuals like Adam Michnik and Bronisław Geremek. The efforts of converting the citizens' committees into a social movement, linking the open-minded and pro-European bid for democracy with modernized national traditions, did not meet with success. Instead of institutional integration, the personal factor became dominant. Lech Wałęsa started to play the role of integrator for most of the movement (Grzybowski 1996, 54; Wojtaszczyk 1995, 243–4).

The competition between the evolutionist concepts of transition, supported by Mazowiecki, Geremek, Kuroń, Michnik and their followers, and the radical demand for 'acceleration' represented by Wałęsa himself and his sympathizers, began to overlap with the 1990 presidential race. A group of small centrist parties and political groupings formed the Alliance Centrum coalition – led by Jarosław Kaczyński, at that time one of Wałęsa's closest associates – which officially announced its support for Wałęsa's candidacy. Together with Solidarity itself, the Alliance became one of the two major engines of Wałęsa's presidential campaign. The political polarization instigated by the Alliance and by Solidarity leaders met with suspicion among left-oriented, laic Solidarity activists; a left-wing group of former Solidarity activists decided to form the Citizens' Movement–Democratic Action (ROAD). The growing gap between those who advocated an evolutionary and open concept of transition, and those in the nationalist- and religious-flavoured integrationist movement was to be significant for the cleavage structure. By the end of June 1990, the association of citizens' committees had broken up, with the majority of them rallying behind Wałęsa.

The Solidarity movement was split along the lines of one of the most distinct cleavages in transitional Poland. The split separated those clusters of Polish society which tend to support the concept of a modernized, open, primarily laic state and society, with pro-European sympathies, from those who are keen on national traditions and values. The latter have remained favourably disposed to the values and norms of traditional Catholicism and harbour some suspicion of European integration and rapid modernization. De-communization was an issue of importance for the advocates of modernization, mainly up to the liquidation of the PUWP and the abolition of its political hegemony. The traditionalists, on the other hand, only regarded the dissolution of the communist party as a small step in a long-term fight against communism and against all the remnants of the old regime.

At this juncture, the efforts towards preserving the unity of the Solidarity movement were bound to fail. But the split, once it had had occurred, did not separate the chaff from the wheat with anything even approaching accuracy. Within the Wałęsa camp, fervent Catholics allied with liberals, just as nationalists coexisted with moderate supporters of European integration, and determined supporters of 'acceleration' co-operated with cool pragmatists. On the other hand, the supporters of Mazowiecki's candidacy included moderate Catholics with liberal socialists as their next-door neighbours; social democrats like Zbigniew Bujak in coalition with progressive conservatives like Alexander Hall, and former PUWP members in co-operation with communist-era political prisoners (Wiatr 1993, 2–16). This kind of realignment did not promote the stabilization of the party system, but it was instrumental in paving the way for a further restructuring of the political preferences.

The results of the 1990 presidential elections (Appendix 6.1), confirmed the existence of deep cleavages cutting across the main Polish social strata. The rivalry between Mazowiecki and Wałęsa testifies to the resilience of the liberal–secular versus traditional–Catholic division among the voters. Wałęsa drew his electoral support mainly from among the elderly, less well-educated, villagers and industrial workers in urban environments. He had his electoral strongholds mainly in Eastern and South Eastern Poland as well as in the Gdańsk area. Mazowiecki, on the other hand, did particularly well among well-educated city dwellers of Western Poland, particularly in Cracow, Warsaw and Szczecin, while he performed poorly particularly in the villages (with only 7.4 per cent of the vote there), and generally in Central and Eastern Poland. The same electoral results brought out the politically and personally weak position of the Peasant Party candidate Roman Bartoszcze – he won only 7.2 per cent of the vote in a country with roughly 38 per cent of its inhabitants somehow linked to farming. Similarly, the electoral results highlighted the limited chances of the militant anti-communist and populist option, represented by the Confederation leader Leszek Moczulski. The fact that the candidate supported by the Alliance of the Democratic Left came in fourth was a tribute not only to the personal skills of Włodzimierz Cimoszewicz, but also led to the renaissance of the post-communist–socialist option. The unexpected success of self-styled populist leader Stanisław Tymiński was interpreted as a by-product of the nagging suspicion by many voters that the political establishment was neither willing nor capable of alleviating the widespread social misery in the immediate aftermath of the rapid transition from plan to market of the early 1990s.

The 1990 presidential elections had an additional impact on the Polish party system. In December 1990, just after the second round, Mazowiecki called upon his sympathizers to form a new party, the Democratic Union (*Unia Demokratyczna*, UD), based on the election committees supporting his candidacy. In May 1991, after some hesitation, two other organizations supporting Mazowiecki's candidacy joined the Democratic Union: the Citizens' Movement–Democratic Action (ROAD) and the Forum of Democratic Right with Alexander Hall (Żukowski 1992, 45–7). The ROAD subsequently disintegrated, with some of the ROAD activists joining forces with Zbigniew Bujak to establish the Social Democratic Movement (*Ruch Demo-kratyczno–Społeczny*, RDS), which subsequently merged with Solidarity of Labour and launched itself as the Union of Labour (*Unia Pracy*, UP) in June 1992. The UP obtained additional support from a faction within the disbanded Polish Social Union (PUS) and became, under the leadership of Ryszard Bugaj, the second leading non-communist party of the Polish left (Michta 1992, 49–52, 145–8).

Inspired by Cimoszewicz's promising results in the presidential race, the Social Democracy of the Republic of Poland set out to broaden its social and political base before the upcoming parliamentary elections. In February

1991, Kwaśniewski and Cimoszewicz called upon left-wing organizations and groups all over the country to form a broad electoral alliance. Some twenty organizations, including the trade union federation OPZZ, the post-communist youth organization and the Democratic Union of Women, responded favourably to the appeal and by July 1991 they had joined Kwaśniewski and Cimoszewicz in forming the Alliance of the Democratic Left (Gebethner 1992). The newly formed Alliance concentrated its efforts on the short-term goal of maximizing the socialist vote in the forthcoming parliamentary elections. Fierce criticism of governmental policies – most notably its 'dogmatic' monetarism, the impact of Catholicism on public life and the marginalization of the left – served as a unifying platform in the struggle against the post-Solidarity parties (Antoszewski and Jednaka 1993, 49–53).

At this juncture, the Polish Peasant Party elected a new leader. Roman Bartoszcze was replaced by 31-year-old Waldemar Pawlak. The new party leader broke the electoral co-operation pact with the Polish Peasant Party 'Solidarity' and the rural Solidarity trade union. This was not acceptable to Bartoszcze, who responded by forming a new peasant party, the Polish Peasant Party 'Homeland' (*Ojcowizna*).

Lech Wałęsa, sworn in as President of the Republic in December 1990, had embarked on a course which led to political isolation. Instead of forming a strong presidential party, he lashed out against the Alliance Centrum of the Kaczyński twins, who were running a well-organized political machine with some 30,000 paying members and with a recent record as staunch Wałęsa supporters (Żukowski 1992, 177–84).

The parliamentary elections of 27 October 1991 were notable for the low turnout. Out of 27.5 million eligible voters, only 11.9 million (43.2 per cent) showed up at the polling stations (Appendix 6.1). The young, the poor, the less well-educated and those living in rural areas tended to be over-repre-sented among those who opted out of the political process. Abstention was far more common in backward Eastern Poland than in the more prosperous Western parts of the country; and there is, in fact, a case to be made for the notion that the losers of the transition process were more likely to express their discontent by opting out of the political process altogether than by voting for the opposition.

The results of the 1991 parliamentary elections testify to the complex underlying conflict structure. The level of fragmentation in the *Sejm*, elected in 1991, actually exceeds the levels scored in the inter-war era, when one-third of the population belonged to various ethnic minorities and electoral thresholds were unheard of.

Formally, victory belonged to the Democratic Union, but polling 12.3 per cent of the votes cast, it was a limited triumph. The Union failed dismally in its attempts to mobilize the 1990 Mazowiecki presidential vote (Appendix 6.1). No less than 20 per cent of Mazowiecki's voters opted for the Liberal Democratic Congress, while some 15 per cent of them chose the Alliance of the Democratic Left. The Democratic Union remained the party of the intelligentsia; as many as 28 per cent of the votes for this party came from people with academic education, as opposed to a meagre 9 per cent from those with primary education. The party's electorate was concentrated to the bigger cities and remained particularly weak in the eastern parts of the country.

The Alliance of the Democratic Left came in second, defending its post-communist constituency. In addition, it benefited from a substantial influx – almost 20 per cent – from the Tymiński camp and a trickle of votes from the Mazowiecki camp. The Alliance stood particularly strong among the elderly and among middle-aged voters with secondary education and professional degrees, in small and medium-sized urban agglomerations. It performed particularly well in Northern Poland excluding the Gdańsk and Szczecin *voievodships*, in Western Poland, in Łódź and in Sosnowiec.

Somewhat surprisingly, the Confederation for an Independent Poland came out as one of the five strongest party formations in the *Sejm*. The party did well among workers (who constituted 11.6 per cent of its electorate), among the retired and among young men without the benefit of secondary education. Voters with higher education, farmers and women rarely counted among the party's supporters. The party did rather well in Southern and South Eastern Poland and less well in the Western and Northern voievodships (Januszewski et al. 1993, 91–3).

The Polish Peasant Party (PPP) consolidated its position as the main party of the rural electorate. The party could count on the loyalty of the majority of those who had supported Roman Bartoszcze's bid for the presidency, and in addition it gained a remarkable portion of Wałęsa's presidential electorate.

The Polish Peasant Party (PPP) and its main competitor for the rural vote, the Peasant Alliance, remained distinctly rural organizations, 75 per cent of their voters lived in the countryside. The peasant parties dominated in Central and Eastern Poland. With its ties to the inter-war agrarian movement and to the United Peasant Party of the communist-dominated multi-party system, the PPP received more votes than the pro-Solidarity Peasant Alliance in the Central and South Eastern voievodships.

The Catholic Election Action alliance could also claim victory. With its national, Christian (read: Catholic) appeal, the alliance enjoyed the support of the clergy. It was strongest among the older generations, particularly among elderly women. Among voters above the age of 60, the Catholic Election Action polled 15.6 per cent, as opposed to a meagre 5.4 per cent among those under 25 years of age. It had its strongholds in rural areas and its weak spots in industrial upper Silesia and in the voievodships of Northern Poland.

The Citizens' Alliance Centrum came out of the elections seriously weakened. The coalition gained its votes mostly in small towns, among pensioners, and less-educated white- and blue-collar workers. The results were more encouraging in Warsaw and, for that matter, in South Eastern and Eastern Poland.

The Liberal Democratic Congress did well among the young, the well-educated and the entrepreneurial strata, in some of the bigger cities (in those with over a hundred thousand inhabitants, the Liberals collected an average of 13.2 per cent of the votes), in its heartland of Gdańsk, in Warsaw and in some other towns. The party had almost no support in the rural East.

The defection of most Solidarity leaders to other political formation reduced the electoral prospects of Solidarity. In the elections, Solidarity was only the third most popular list among blue-collar workers, overtaken by the Democratic Union as well as by the Confederation for an Independent Poland. As of 1991, the typical Solidarity voters were recruited from among the less well-educated, among pensioners of working-class backgrounds and among the lower-middle-class. The Gdańsk and Bydgoszcz regions provided Solidarity with a solid base which compensated for the uphill battle in the rural and Western voievodships.

Only one-third of voters below 25 participated in the elections, and the young evidently felt sceptical towards most of the major parties (*Gazeta Wyborcza*, 6–13 July 1992). With the exception of the Democratic Union and the Liberal Democratic Congress, the major parties did not mobilize the young; close to 10 per cent of the young vote went to the cabaret-style Party of Friends of Beer.

In general terms, the 1991 elections marked the end of the transition from People's Poland to democratic Poland. The election results highlighted the disintegration of the former Solidarity movement. Most of the Solidarity sympathizers continued to support parties of the centre or the centre-right, a rather remarkable fact considering that Solidarity had started out as a trade-union movement. In a similar vein, it may be noted that the Solidarity veterans, white- and blue-collar alike, divided their sympathies across a wide range of political parties – from the Democratic Union with its intellectual appeal, to the Confederation for an Independent Poland with its distinctly populist image. Most of the parties of the right and of the left remained city-based. The rural electorate became dominated by the two peasant ('class-type' or 'sectoral') political formations: the dominant Polish Peasant Party (centre-left-oriented) and its competitor, the Peasant Alliance (PL).

The Democratic Union and the Liberal Democratic Congress had become visible exponents of young, successful and educated city-dwellers. They campaigned on similar platforms, and the rational choice for them was amalgamation rather than mutual competition. Indeed, the two parties soon decided to merge into the Union of Freedom (*Unia Wolności*, UW).

The centre and Christian Democratic cluster remained fragmented. The Citizens' Alliance Centrum came out greatly weakened by the bitter and fierce quarrel between party leader Jarosław Kaczyński and state President Lech Wałęsa. The Catholic Election Action is the only openly Christian party to have risen to a position of relative influence, no doubt due to its commitment to the Catholic Church hierarchy and the religious devotion of its supporters (mostly women in the upper age-brackets).

The 1991 elections to the *Sejm* spelled a modest revival for the political left. The post-communist Alliance of the Democratic Left moved from the level of 9.2 per cent of the voters (Cimoszewicz's result in the presidential first round in 1990) up to slightly less than 12 (11.99) per cent.

With the possible exception of the two major peasant formations, no party was able to dominate any social group or cluster. Party programmes and policies did not coincide neatly with well defined socioeconomic cleavages. Yet there were indeed linkages between the changing cleavage structure on the one hand and the emerging party system on the other. The peasant parties, the populist and radical Confederation for an Independent Poland, and, to some extent, the Alliance Centrum and the Catholic Election Action, did represent the small-town, less well-educated, traditionally-minded Catholic groups of society. The Democratic Union and the Liberal–Democratic Congress represented the young, urban, entrepreneurial strata which tend to be liberal-minded and favourably disposed towards market reform and European integration. The increasingly stable political geography of Poland also strongly suggests that there is a pattern to the political fluctuations. The parties of the right and of the centre, including the Catholic parties, seem to have found a particularly hospitable environment in Eastern and South Eastern Poland, while Northern Poland (excluding the city of Gdańsk) and the Western territories appear to provide fertile ground for the parties of the left and of the centre-left. The relative alienation of young Poles from party politics does, however, serve as a reminder that the process of consolidation is far from complete.

The Consolidation of 1991–93

Cabinet formation after the 1991 elections was not an easy venture, since the fragmented *Sejm* did not contain any self-evident basis for a majority. President Wałęsa tried to exploit this situation in order to strengthen the influence of the executive. He saw himself as the main political player, as the maker of prime ministers and the shaper of government coalitions. The first presidential initiatives, concerning the candidacies of Jacek Kuroń (Democratic Union), Jan Krzysztof Bielecki (Liberal Democratic Congress) and Bronisław Geremek (Democratic Union), remained ineffective.

The creation of the new cabinet was preceded by long, drawn-out negotiations. Almost two months after the elections, on 21 December 1991, the coalition government of Jan Olszewski was formed and confirmed by a vote of confidence in the *Sejm*. The parliamentary base of the government was rather narrow: only 235 of the 460 representatives voted for confidence; 60 votes were cast against, mainly by the Alliance of the Democratic Left and by the conservative Union of Real Politics, while no fewer than 139 deputies abstained, predominantly representatives of the Democratic Union, the Democratic Congress and the Confederation for an Independent Poland (Dudek 1997, 265–9).

The newly formed government was openly anti-communist and, at the same time, quite sceptical towards a strict market approach to the economy. Many of the ministers tended to favour limited state interventionist policies with respect to internal as well as external economic activities. Within the field of foreign policy, the government seemed to prefer broad European co-operation, inspired by the Organization of Security and Co-operation in Europe, to the institutional kind of integration represented by full membership of the European Union. The majority of the ministers, including Prime Minister Olszewski himself, remained fiercely critical of the round-table agreement and of any form of participation by former communists in decision-making and public life.

The Olszewski cabinet always kept a certain distance from the presidential office and from Wałęsa himself. The efforts undertaken to widen the parliamentary basis of the cabinet, towards the Democratic Union and the Confederation for an Independent Poland as well as towards the Polish Peasant Party, were to no avail. The demise of the Olszewski cabinet was brought about by the unexpected resolution of the *Sejm* – upon the initiative of Janusz Korwin-Mikke, leader of the Union of Real Politics – to institute lustration of leading state and government officials and to publish, under the auspices of the Ministry of Interior, a list of 'collaborators' of the communist security services, featuring, among others, President Wałęsa. The cabinet faced a vote of no confidence on 4 June 1992. The motion obtained the backing of 273 deputies from the Democratic Union, the Liberal Democratic Congress, the Alliance of the Democratic Left, the Confederation for an Independent Poland and the Polish Peasant Party. Only 119 parliamentarians voted against the motion and for the government; these were mainly representatives of the Catholic Action, the Alliance Centrum and the Peasant Alliance and Solidarity (Grzybowski 1996, 49–54). Once again, the political right had appeared divided and politically inconsistent.

Waldemar Pawlak, the 32-year-old leader of the Polish Peasant Party designated by President Wałęsa to take over as Prime Minister, was unable to form a centre-based government. His potential coalition partners, the Democratic Union and the Confederation for an Independent Poland, were not ready to agree on a compromise programme. After 33 days as caretaker Prime Minister, Pawlak was forced to resign. The fact that Pawlak, and nobody else, was called upon to form a new government was nevertheless a remarkable phenomenon. For the first time since the transition, a non-Solidarity politician – and a leader of a party connected with the old regime – was promoted to such an office. According to Aleksander Kwaśniewski, it was a 'historical step' towards a 'normalization' of Polish political and party life (cf. *Polityka*, 18 July 1992).

Pawlak's failure paved the way for another political coalition. It was formed by the Democratic Union, the Liberal Democratic Congress, the Peasant Alliance (PL), the Christian National Alliance and the small Polish Christian Democratic Party. The new cabinet, formed by centrist Democratic Union politician Hanna Suchocka, obtained the support of 226 deputies. 124 deputies voted against, mainly representatives of Olszewski's Movement for the Republic, the PPP, and the conservative Union of Real Politics. 28 parliamentarians abstained, predominantly from within the Alliance Centrum and the Alliance of the Democratic Left (Gebethner 1995, 15–20). Seven (subsequently eight) parties formed the parliamentary base of the Suchocka cabinet, of which three – the Democratic Union, the Liberal Democratic Congress and the National Christian Alliance – served as the main pillars. In fact, the Suchocka government often found it extremely difficult to mobilize even a fragile majority for its proposals. A wave of strikes spread through the industrial centres of Upper Silesia, the Głogów copper mining district and the aviation industry centre of Mielec. The unrest increased in magnitude. In 1990, 116,000 workers struck; in 1991 the number had risen to 222,000; and in late 1992 no less than 753,000 workers had been taken out on strike. Unemployment was also on an upward trend: from 2.5 million in 1992 (14.3 per cent of the labour force) to 2.9 million at the end of 1993.

The good news was that the recession was coming to an end and the inflation rate was assuming more manageable proportions, down from 43 per cent annually in 1992 to 35 per cent in 1993. Even so, the man in the street remained adversely affected. In 1993, the average income fell by 1.8 per cent and the average pension by 2.7 per cent. The economic and social inequalities kept growing, as did the gap between the winners and losers of the economic reforms. The government was able to accelerate the pace of privatization, but the ambitious – and controversial – programme of self-government reform never left the drawing board.

The issues of constitutional reform, abortion and European integration dominated a political agenda played out against the background of the economic difficulties. The austerity budget of 1993 did not satisfy the Solidarity union's regional organizations. The four-day general strike in Łódź, the protests by public sector employers and the teachers' strike paralyzed important sectors of the economy and the society. The Minister of Agriculture, Gabriel Janowski, a member of the Peasant Alliance, handed in his resignation when he could no longer guarantee minimum prices for agricultural products. The Peasant Alliance's withdrawal of its support thrust Suchocka's government into a minority position. The negotiations between the government and Solidarity about public sector salaries broke down twice, on 10 and 18 May 1993. A vote of no confidence was clearly in the making, and in late May, a motion to this effect was introduced by Alojzy Pietrzyk of the Solidarity. On 26 May 1993, Hanna Suchocka found herself defeated by the narrowest of margins (223 out 445). Three days later President Wałęsa decided to dissolve the *Sejm* as well as the Senate and call new elections. The Suchocka cabinet served as a caretaker government until the new elections on 19 September 1993. On 28 July 1993 – i.e. well after the vote of no confidence – the government signed a concordat with the Holy See which put an end to negotiations that had been going on since late 1992. The concordat contained stipulations concerning marriage, religious cemeteries, and subsidies for Catholic schools, which made for fierce controversy and delayed its ratification.

The parliamentary situation was paradoxical in the sense that a post-Solidarity government had been ousted upon the initiative of a representative of the Solidarity trade union; but such was the position of strength then enjoyed by Solidarity and its numerous offspring parties. President Wałęsa, who called the pre-term elections, also failed to predict the 1993 victory of the post-communist Alliance of the Democratic Left.

The 1993 elections were held according to the new electoral law of 15 April 1993, approved by the President on 1 July 1993 with some modifications introduced by the Senate. It was designed to curtail political fragmentation and introduced a 5 per cent threshold for political parties and an 8 per cent threshold for political cartels. This spelled serious difficulties for more than half of the parties in the outgoing parliament. Some technical changes – including a switch from St Lagüe's to d'Hondt's method of distributing the parliamentary seats among parties under proportional representation, and a reduction of the size of the voting districts – also played into the hands of the Alliance of the Democratic Left and the Polish Peasant Party.

1993–97: The Era of Centre-Left Domination

In 1992–93, there was a pervasive swing to the left as the centre-right government grew more and more unpopular. In late 1991, 52 per cent of those polled had expressed dissatisfaction with the government and its policies. By early 1993, the rate of dissatisfaction had reached 64 per cent (Janicki 1993). In the opinion polls, the Alliance of the Democratic Left took over the leading position with a support of some 20 per cent of the electorate. It was well ahead of the Democratic Union with 16 per cent, and the Confederation of an Independent Poland and the Polish Peasant Party, both hovering around the 10 per cent mark (*Rzeczpospolita*, 2 October 1993).

For the 1993 elections, 34 election committees registered lists of candidates, but only 23 of them in more than one electoral district. Only three committees declared themselves electoral cartels, subjected to the requirement of having to poll at least 8 per cent of the votes to gain parliamentary representation.

The primary beneficiaries of the swing to the left were the Alliance of the Democratic Left and the Union of Labour. When the Alliance tried to broaden its appeal, the Union of Labour countered by emphasizing its non-communist roots, while articulating serious doubts about privatization and the impact of Catholicism. The Union of Labour also jockeyed for the position as main defender of the interests of ordinary working people. This differentiation continued after the elections, marking a kind of institutionalization of the division of the Polish left.

The appearence of the Non-Partisan Bloc for Supporting Reforms (*Bezpartyjny Blok Wspierania Reform*, BBWR), initiated by President Wałęsa in June 1993, was yet another new feature that made the 1993 parliamentary elections unique. The President optimistically counted on an overwhelming electoral victory of some 400 out of a total of 460 seats. But not a single one of the parties participating in Suchocka's coalition joined the newly formed organization. The Bloc launched former Minister of Foreign Affairs, Andrzej Olechowski for Prime Minister and introduced a group of hopeful post-Solidarity activists as advisors and support team. The rather populist economic proposals initially earned the Bloc popularity ratings of around 18 per cent – a quite remarkable level it could not defend for long (Wiatr 1993, 80–9).

The arrival of the new post-Solidarity formation threatened the existence of the established post-Solidarity parties. The pre-election campaign thus became marked by a fierce propaganda battle between the Bloc on the one hand and the Democratic Union and, to some extent, the Liberal Democratic Congress, the Alliance Centrum and Jan Olszewski's Movement for the

Republic (RdR) on the other. At the same time, the Movement and the Alliance Centrum continued their campaign against the post-communists and the Democratic Union. Janusz Korwin-Mikke of the Union of Real Politics put forward an ultra-liberal programme designed to minimize the role of the state in order to attract the young and frustrated; Andrzej Lepper of the nationalistic and anti-reform rural organization 'Self-Defence' (*Samoobrona*) tried to rally support by exploiting the increasing dissatisfaction of the peasantry (Gebethner 1992, 220–45).

Voter turnout in the 1993 elections to the *Sejm* and the Senate was 52.1 per cent, some 10 percentage points higher than in 1991. The seats in the Senate were distributed in the following way: the Alliance of the Democratic Left, 37; the Polish Peasant Party, 36; Solidarity, 9; Democratic Union, 4; the Non-Partisan Bloc, 2; Union of Labour, 2; the Liberal-Democratic Congress, 1; Alliance Centrum, 1; independents, 4; and small parties (election committees), 4.

The new electoral system contributed towards increasing the representation of the Alliance of the Democratic Left and the Polish Peasant Party; the post-communists obtained one-fifth of the votes but one-third of the seats in the *Sejm* and the Senate. The Polish Peasant Party obtained twice as many seats as it would have obtained under the old electoral law. The Confederation for an Independent Poland (KPN) and the Non-Partisan Bloc (BBWR) did not reach the seven per cent threshold required to benefit from the distribution of seats from the national list. No less than 4.8 million votes (34.6 per cent of all cast) were wasted in the sense that they did not go towards representation in the *Sejm* (*Polityka*, 24 October 1994).

The elections spelled defeat for the Solidarity camp and victory for the parties of the left. Together, the parties supporting Suchocka's outgoing cabinet gained 23.3 per cent of the votes, only a few percentage points more than the Alliance of the Democratic Left scored in its own right. The latter, in fact, almost doubled its share of the Polish electorate compared with the 1991 elections. The Alliance remained a party supported by small-town dwellers, but it had also made inroads into new constituencies including the academic and business communities. 17 per cent of the entrepreneurs voted for the Alliance lists, as opposed to 13 per cent for the lists of the Democratic Union and 9 per cent for those of the Liberal Democratic Congress. The Alliance won 134,000 voters from the Democratic Union and 72,000 from the Confederation of an Independent Poland (Dudek 1997, 332–3).

The core of the Polish Peasant Party's electorate was, as in 1991, formed by farmers and their families, but the party was also gaining ground in small towns. The PPP victory was accompanied by the political marginalization of the remaining peasant parties, particularly the Peasant Alliance and the 'Self-Defence' (*Samoobrona*).

The Democratic Union remained the party of urban, well-educated people. Academic centres, like Poznań and Cracow, provided the party with a badly needed electoral base, in the face of the losses it incurred in the small towns of Lower Silesia and in Eastern Poland. Almost a quarter of the voters with academic education supported the Union. The electoral support was strongest among those aged over 60 or under 25.

The Union of Labour tripled the share of votes obtained by its predecessors, the Social Democratic Movement, 'Solidarity of Labour' and the Great Poland Social Democratic Union. It stood out as the party of salaried workers and minor civil servants, mostly in Greater Poland and Mazovia, less so in eastern and south (Paszkiewicz 1996, 86–7, 202–3).

The victory of the non-Solidarity parties was brought about by a number of factors. In Poland, like most of the countries of Central and Eastern Europe, the difficulties of the economic transition produced a swing to the left. The post-Solidarity formations were busy running the country and vying for political influence and either overlooked the swing or underestimated its impact. As a result, the heirs to the parties of People's Poland came back with a vengeance, as they represented the only alternative to an increasingly unpopular government. Sociological surveys at hand suggest that well over 50 per cent of those who voted for the Alliance of the Democratic Left did so out of dissatisfaction with the post-Solidarity government. It may also be worth noting that only 43 per cent of the voters for the Alliance said that they considered the ex-communists better prepared to run the country (Planeta and Chrabąszcz 1996, 11–15).

After the 1993 elections, a ten-point coalition agreement was signed between the victorious Alliance and the Polish Peasant Party – The Union of Labour did participate in political negotiations preceding the cabinet formation but eventually declined to join the government. Waldemar Pawlak, the young and ambitious PPP leader, shouldered the role as Prime Minister, while the Alliance took over the crucial economy-related ministries and had one of its leaders, Józef Oleksy, elected Chairman of the *Sejm*. The Alliance was also prepared to go to great lengths to rid itself of the stigma attached to its communist past. The Alliance and the PPP held an absolute majority in the *Sejm* and enjoyed the informal support of the Union of Labour until June 1994. The President had a decisive impact on the nomination of three ministers, those of the Interior, Defence, and Foreign Affairs. The government was in fact loosely integrated from the very beginning. It remained marked by the efforts of the two coalition partners to widen their respective spheres of influence, and the three ministries indirectly controlled by President Wałęsa became something of a focal point in the tug-of-war between the Alliance and the PPP. In terms of issues, the government was, from the very outset, divided on decentralization and insurance reform.

The forthcoming presidential elections served as a constant reminder that unity was crucial to the success of the right and centre-right in Poland. Even the Catholic Church made an unofficial and unsuccessful attempt to bring the parties of the right and centre-right together under the auspices of the Convent of St Catherine. 1994–95 nevertheless witnessed several initiatives designed to bring the right-wing parties together. The national and the Catholic image, as well as the sceptical approach towards the idea of European integration cultivated by the ailing Alliance Centrum and the National Christian Alliance, made these two parties obvious partners, but only in an unstable political alliance. The smallish parties of the right and the centre-right also made efforts to set up loose alliances.

Some parties split. Two formations broke out of the Non-Partisan Bloc for Supporting Reforms (BBWR): a new political party, known as the Republicans; and a group of liberal activists who eventually co-founded Committee of the One Hundred (*Komitet Stu*). Within the Union of Freedom, the establishment of the moderately leftist faction Democratic Forum (*Forum Demokratyczne*), made the party less cohesive. In April 1995, Leszek Balczerowicz, the architect of the economic austerity programme of the early 1990s, replaced former Prime Minister Tadeusz Mazowiecki as leader of the Union of Freedom.

The ruling coalition tightened its grip on political control over economic and public life, including the major state-owned companies, the banking system and local administration. However, the Foreign Ministry, the security services and the military, and to some extent public television, remained immune to the attempts at political domination by the coalition of the Alliance of the Democratic left and the Polish Peasant Party.

In the presidential elections of 5 and 19 November 1996, the candidates were evidently miles apart. In the first round, the candidate of the left, Aleksander Kwaśniewski, polled 35.1 per cent of the valid votes as opposed to 33.1 per cent for incumbent President Lech Wałęsa. In the second round, Kwaśniewski defeated Wałęsa by a slim margin (Appendix 6.1). Kwaśniewski's victory in the presidential race was the last political success of the left-wing coalition. Shortly afterwards, Prime Minister Oleksy was accused of having contacts with Russian intelligence, which marked the beginning of a drawn-out crisis of confidence.

In late 1995, the leaders of Solidarity had embarked on a programme designed to bring the post-Solidarity parties together on a common platform, prior to the parliamentary elections set for the autumn of 1997. This initiative by Solidarity national chairman, Marian Krzaklewski, met with the reluctant approval of the parties concerned and a broad coalition was formed, covering almost all the post-Solidarity formations.

The Solidarity Comeback

The 1993 success of the Alliance of the Democratic Left and the post-communist–peasant coalition was, to a large extent, caused by the fragmentation of the post-Solidarity political forces. Neither the post-Solidarity parties nor President Wałęsa were in a position to act as effective links. Though marginalized on the national level, the post-Solidarity parties and political formations remained influential in the local arena, including local self-government, as well as on the factory floor. In its capacity as a politically active trade union federation, Solidarity preserved its mobilizing potential in most of the large and medium-sized enterprises. In a number of localities – particularly in South Eastern and Southern Poland, as well as in cities like Gdańsk, Poznań, Warsaw and Cracow – the Alliance of the Democratic Left remained overshadowed by post-Solidarity parties. The ideological cleavage between the pro-Solidarity forces and those of the left-wing coalition, with its roots People's Poland, kept shaping consciousness and political behaviour among large segments of the electorate.

Casting itself as an exponent of modern, pro-European social democracy in favour of a mixed economy and political pluralism, the Alliance of the Democratic Left (SLD), lost credibility and appeal among the losers of the transition from plan to market. This loss of support was difficult to compensate for, since the new bourgeoisie and middle strata, as well as most of the intelligentsia, were solidly sceptical about formations rooted in the communist past.

The 1993–97 leftist government coalition was programmatically and politically inconsistent. The Alliance (and its main constituent party, the Social Democracy of the Republic of Poland, SDRP) remained openly secular, liberal, pro-European and open to many aspects of economic, cultural and behavioural modernization. In contrast, the Polish Peasant Party underlined the necessity of cultivating national and Catholic traditions and norms of social life, in line with the outlook of its predominantly rural electorate. The Alliance had the bulk of its electorate among city dwellers and salaried employees, i.e. among net consumers of agricultural products. The Polish Peasant Party, on the other hand, remained an interest party for food producers. Tensions were in a sense built into the leftist–peasant coalition from the very beginning.

The Solidarity opposition, now chiefly consolidated within the framework of the Election Action 'Solidarity' (AWS), lashed out at the governing leftist coalition, which was portrayed as a government by the heirs to the very parties which had been removed from power in 1989–90. The AWS campaign called on all former Solidarity members and sympathizers to rekindle the spirit of 1989–90. The AWS also, quite skilfully, exploited the differences between the two government parties on sensitive topics like privatization, abortion, the role of Catholicism, the Concordat with the Holy See (firmly supported by the PPP, but not well received by the SLD), local self-governance and decentralization.

A number of factors contributed to the declining popularity of the governing parties, particularly the Polish Peasant Party: the poor performance of the authorities during the catastrophic floods in July 1997; the allegations that Prime Minister Oleksy had worked for Soviet intelligence; the postponement of health care reform; and the feeble agricultural policy. The PPP faced a classical paradox: the bulk of the urban voters perceived it as a party of narrow sectoral interests, and rural voters increasingly saw it as an inefficient exponent of rural interests, due to its weak position in the coalition. At the same time, Catholic-oriented media stepped up their pressure on the predominantly Catholic voters, portraying the Alliance-dominated government as anti-Catholic and libertarian. The entrepreneurial and business sectors shifted allegiance to the Union of Freedom, which was seen as liberal, pro-European and reform-oriented without having the stigma of a linkage to the defunct regime. The Union of Freedom has so far refused the option of a coalition with the post-communist Alliance of the Democratic Left, with which it does indeed share many issue positions. Instead, it has repeatedly emphasized its Solidarity roots.

The 1997 campaign revived the division between the heirs to Solidarity and to the old regime, and between traditionalists and modernists. But there were also traces of a re-emerging socioeconomically defined left/right cleavage. The Union of Freedom campaigned on an explicitly pro-European and pro-market platform, while the PPP, the Union of Labour and some union-affiliated groups within the Alliance of the Democratic left emphasized the social costs of the transition to market, the high unemployment rate, social inequalities, the bleak prospects of Polish agriculture, and growing economic dependence on the outside world. The trade union wing of the Solidarity Election Action (AWS), the National Christian Alliance, and elements of the Confederation for an Independent Poland and the Movement for Rebuilding Poland (ROP) also voiced scepticism towards the liberal vision of a market economy. In fact, only the Union of Freedom was unconditionally in favour of full liberalization.

The Alliance and the PPP chose to run on different agendas in 1997. The campaign of the Alliance of the Democratic Left was based on the party's track record in macroeconomic management – inflation and unemployment were falling and GDP growth for 1997 was estimated at 7 per cent. The Alliance steered clear of criticizing the liberal programme of the Union of Freedom, thereby attempting to set the stage for post-election political co-operation between the two reform-oriented, secular and pro-European parties. Even so, the leaders of the Alliance considered it more likely that any post-election government in which they would participate would include the Polish Peasant Party and possibly also the Union of Labour and the left-oriented Pensioners' Party (KPEiR). The PPP attempted to manœuvre itself into a pivotal position as an indispensable coalition partner for a post-Solidarity as well as for a left-wing coalition, but failed to build up a level of support commensurate with this strategy.

The AWS was united by a strong will to win the elections, and this helped the arguably loose coalition to patch up its substantial internal differences. Some AWS leaders counted on winning an absolute majority, but most anticipated a coalition together with other post-Solidarity formations. Two main concepts for such a coalition were mentioned during the campaign: a 'small coalition' of the AWS–UW (Union of Freedom); and a 'large' AWS–UW–ROP coalition. Nor did the AWS rule out co-operation with the PPP.

The outcome of the 1997 *Sejm* elections (Appendix 6.1) allowed the AWS to choose the first coalition scenario. After a series of inter-party consultations with representatives of the Union of Freedom, the Movement for Rebuilding the Republic (ROP) and, also, the Polish Peasant Party (PSL), the AWS signed a ten-point coalition programme with the Union of Freedom. Quite unexpectedly, the victorious AWS chairman Marian Krzaklewski proposed Jerzy Buzek for Prime Minister. Sixteen seats in the Council of Ministers were taken by the AWS coalition and six by the Union of Freedom.

Conclusions

The division between the post-Solidarity parties and those linked to People's Poland remains of major significance for Polish political life. It was crucial in 1989–90 and revived in the run-up to the 1997 elections. It currently serves as the glue holding together the AWS electoral cartel as well as the AWS–UW parliamentary and cabinet coalition. Even so, this division is likely to be transitional. For a growing number of voters, particularly those in their twenties and early thirties, the organizational history of parties and election coalitions are of little consequence. One interpretation of the electoral results of 1997 is that the post-Solidarity parties were granted the role as 'guarantors' of the systemic transition, while the Union of Freedom was given the role of 'guardian' of modernization. It remains an open question if these two roles may be played simultaneously and smoothly by the AWS–UW coalition.

Even so, the historical cleavages have not lost their significance. The controversy between those advocating a stronger role for Catholicism in public life and education, and those preferring public institutions to be neutral *vis-à-vis* religion and Christian values, is a case in point. This particular dimension cuts right through the post-Solidarity–post-communist divide, as evidenced by the strongly Catholic flavour of the Polish Peasant Party and a number of the AWS parties. As yet, there is no unified 'socialist' cluster of parties: the two parties claiming to be Social Democratic – the SDRP and the Union of Labour – more often oppose than support each other. Similarly, the government coalition formed after the Solidarity come-back in late 1997 can hardly be considered right-wing. Trade-unionist elements cultivate many typically leftist social arguments and visions, far removed from liberal concepts of market, state and society. But there are nevertheless strong intimations of a re-emerging left/right cleavage in the form of the divide between the winners and the losers in the social and economic transformation processes.

Indeed, as time goes by, the impact of the transition from communism to democracy is likely to lose salience. The 'de-communization' of SLD youth sympathizers, the gradual decrease of public sector employment, the fading out of basic, historically rooted, ideological controversies between parties linked to People's Poland, and those once in opposition to the communist regime, all lend support to this thesis. For the time being, the emerging cleavage structure is not clearly defined: post-communist Poland has not yet left the cleavage-forming stage of development. The parties and electoral coalitions cannot rely on stable constituencies defined in terms of stable social divides. It will take some time yet for the Polish party system to 'freeze'.

NOTE

1. Flanagan (1971) refers to these cleavages as segmental cleavages. Eckstein's approach to this concept is somewhat broader. By segmental cleavages he understands the 'lines of objective social differentiation' (Eckstein 1966).

REFERENCES

Almond, Gabriel A. et al. (1971), *Choice and Change: Historical Studies on Political Development*, Boston, Little, Brown and Company.
Antoszewski, Andrzej, Ryszard Herbut and Wiesława Jednaka (1993), *Partie i system partyjny w Polsce: Pierwsza faza przejścia ku demokracji*, Wrocław, Wrocław University Press.
Chruściak, Ryszard, Tadeusz Mołdawa et al. (1995), *Polski system polityczny w okresie transformacji*, Warsaw, Elipsa.
Dehnel-Szyc, Małgorzata and Jadwiga Stachura (1991), *Gry polityczne: Orientacje na dziś*, Warsaw, Volumen.
Dudek, Antoni (1997), *Pierwsze lata III Rzeczypospolitej*, Cracow, GEO.
Dudek, Beata (1995a), *Geneza i działalność postsolidarnościowych partii politycznych w latach 1989–1991*, Cracow, unpublished doctoral dissertation, Jagiellonian Library of Cracow.
—— (1995b), 'Dekompozycja "Solidarnosci"', *Ad Meritum*, No. 1, p. 35-37.

Eckstein, Harry (1966), *Division and Cohesion of Democracy: A Study of Norway*, Princeton, Princeton University Press.

Flanagan, Scott, C. (1971), 'Models and Methods of Analysis', in Gabriel A. Almond, ed.,*Choice and Change: Historical Studies on Development*, Boston, Little, Brown and Company.

Gebethner, Stanisław, ed. (1995), *Wybory parlamentarne 1991 i 1993*, Warsaw, Wydawnictwo Sejmowe.

—— and Jacek Raciborski, eds., (1992), *Wybory '91 a polska scena polityczna*, Warsaw, Fundacja Inicjatyw Społecznych.

—— and Krzysztof Jasiewicz, eds., (1993), *Dlaczego tak głosowano? Wybory prezydenckie '90*, Warsaw, ISP PAN & IPN UW.

Grzybowski, Marian (1996), *Electoral Systems of Central Europe*, Kielce and Cracow, A. Wisniewski.

Janicki, Mariusz (1993), *Polityka*, No. 22, September, 1993.

Januszewski, Stanisław *et al.* (1993), *Leksykow opozycy polityczay 1976-1989*, Warsaw, BIS.

Jaruzelski, Wojciech and Marian Orechowski (1991), *Koniec epoki*, Warsaw, BGW.

Jasiewicz, Krzysztof (1993), 'Polski wyborca w dziesięć lat po Sierpniu', in Stanisław Gebethner and Krzysztof Jasiewicz, eds., *Dlaczego tak głosowano? Wybory prezydenckie '90*, Warsaw, ISP PAN & INP UW.

—— (1996), 'Wybory prezydenckie 1995 r. a kształtowanie się polskiego systemu partyjnego', *Studia Polityczne*, 5.

Karasimeonov, Georgi (1995), 'Differentiation Postponed: Party Pluralism in Bulgaria', in Gordon Whightman, ed., *Party Formation in East Central Europe*, Aldershot–Brookfield, Edward Elgar.

—— (1996), 'The Legislatures in Post-Communist Bulgaria', in David M. Olson and Philip Norton, eds., *The New Parliaments of Central and Eastern Europe*, London, Frank Cass & Company.

Lipset, Seymour Martin and Stein Rokkan (1967), 'Cleavage Structures, Party Systems and Voter Alignments', in Seymour Martin Lipset and Stein Rokkan, eds., *Party Systems and Voter Alignments*, New York, The Free Press.

Małkiewicz, Andrzej (1994), *Wybory czerwcowe 1989*, Warsaw. ISP PAN.

Michta, Andrew. A. (1993), 'The Presidential Parliamentary Systems', in: R. F. Staar, ed., *Transition to Democracy in Poland*, New York, St. Martin's Press.

Olson, David M. (1993), 'Compartmentalized Competition: The Managed Transitional Elections Systems of Politics', *Journal of Politics*, May.

Paluch, Piotr (1995), *PSL w systemie partyjnym Rzeczypospolitej*, Toruń, Adam Marszałek.

Paszkiewicz, Krystyna A., ed. (1996), *Polskie partie polityczne. Charakterystyki, dokumenty*, Wrocław, Wrocław University Press.

Planeta, Piotr and Ryszard Chrabąszcz (1996), 'I tura wyborow prezydenckich w prosie polskiej', *Zerzsyły Praroxnawcze/Press Studies*, No.1-2, p.88.

Rae, Douglas W. and Michael Taylor (1970), *The Analysis of Political Cleavages*, New Haven, Yale University Press.

Rakowski, Mieczysław (1991), *Jak siz stalo*, Warsaw, BGW

Ramet, Pedro (1992), 'The New Poland: Democratic and Authoritarian Tendencies', *Global Affairs*, VII (Spring).

Rokkan, Stein, ed. (1970), *Citizens, Elections, Parties: Approaches to the Comparative Study on the Process of Development*, Oslo, Scandinavian University Press.

—— (1970), 'Nation Building, Cleavage Formation and the Structuring of Mass Politics', in Stein Rokkan, ed., *Citizens, Elections, Parties: Approaches to the Comparative Study on the Process of Development*, Oslo, Scandinavian University Press.

Sokół, Wojciech and Marek Żmigrodzki (1994), 'Functions of Political Parties in Poland at the Time of Systemic Transformation', *Polish Political Science*.

Staar, Richard F., ed., (1993) *Transition to Democracy in Poland*, New York, St. Martin's Press.

Taras, Raymond C. (1993), 'Voters, Parties and Leaders', in Richard F. Staar, ed., *Transition to Democracy in Poland*, New York, St. Martin's Press.

Wasilewski, Andrzej and Włodzimierz Wesołowski (1992), *Początki parlamentarnej elity. Posłowie kontraktowego Sejmu*, Warsaw.

Whightman, Gordon, ed. (1995), *Party Formation in East Central Europe*, Aldershot–Brookfield, Edward Elgar.

Wiatr, Jerzy J. (1993), *Sejm, wszystko o Parlamentarnym Klubie SLD*, Warsaw. BGW.

—— (1993), *Wybory parlamentarne 19 września 1993: Przyczyny i następstwa*, Warsaw, Agencja SCHOLAR.

Wojtaszczyk, Konstanty Adam (1995), 'Prawica i lewica ha polskiej scenie politycznej', *Wybory parlamentare 1991 i 1993*, Warsaw, Wydaunistiso Sejmcwe, p. 87-90.

Żukowski, Tomasz (1992), 'Wybory parlamentarne '91', in *Studia Polityczne*, 1992:1.

APPENDIX 6.1: ELECTION RESULTS

PARLIAMENTARY ELECTIONS

1991 Elections
Date: 27 October
Turnout: 43.2%

Party/coalition	Sejm %	Sejm Mandates	Senate %	Senate Mandates
Democratic Union	12.2	62	20.0	21
Alliance of the Democratic Left	12.0	60	12.3	4
Polish Peasants' Party	9.2	50	11.5	9
Catholic Action	9.0	50	12.2	9
Confed. for an Independent Poland	8.9	51	7.7	4
Alliance Centrum	8.7	44	13.2	9
Lib. Dem. Congress	7.5	37	10.4	6
Peasant's Alliance (PL)	5.5	28	13.2	7
Solidarity	5.0	27	14.2	11
Party of Friends of Beer	3.0	16	–	–
German Minority	1.2	7	1.1	1
Christian Democracy	2.2	5	2.1	1
'Solidarity of Labour'	2.1	4	–	–
Polish Christian Democracy	1.1	4	3.9	3
Union of Real Politics	2.2	3	2.6	–
Party X (Tymiński)	0.5	3	3.2	–
Movement for Silesian Autonomy	0.4	2	–	–
Democratic Party	1.4	1	–	–
Social Democratic Movement (RDS)	0.5	1	–	–
Mountaineers' League	0.2	1	–	–
Great-Poland Social Union	0.02	1	–	–
Social Christian Union	0.1	1	–	–
Solidarity '80'	0.1	1	–	–
Union of Great Poland	0.1	1	–	–
Other parties/coalitions	6.2	–	5.7	8
Independent Senators	–	–	3.4	7

Note: The simple majority system and the varying density of population of the voievodships, or Senate elections voting districts, makes the electoral swing more visible in the Senate than in the *Sejm* elections. Each voievodship, regardless of population, was granted two seats in the Senate, with the exception of the Warsaw and Silesian (Katowice) voievodships, which were granted three mandates

1993 Sejm elections
Date: 19 September
Turnout: 52.1%

Party/coalition	Votes	%	Mandates	(%)
Alliance of the Democratic Left	2,815,169	20.4	171	37.2
Polish Peasant Party	2,124,367	15.4	132	28.7
Democratic Union	1,460,957	10.6	74	16.1
Union of Labour	1,005,004	7.3	41	8.9
Confederation for an Independent Poland	795,487	5.8	22	4.8
Non-Partisan Bloc (BBWR)	746,653	5.4	16	3.5
German Minority	78,689	0.6	4	0.9
Homeland *(Ojczyzna)* coalition	878,445	6.4	–	–
Solidarity	676,334	4.9	–	–
Alliance Centrum (PC–ZP)	609,973	4.4	–	–
Liberal–Democratic Congress (KLD)	550,578	4.0	–	–
Union of Real Politics (UPR)	438,559	3.2	–	–
Self-Defence *(Samoobrona)*	383,967	2.8	–	–
Party X	377,480	2.7	–	–
Coalition for Republic (KdR)	371,923	2.7	–	–
Peasant Alliance	327,085	2.4	–	–
Others	155,557	1.1	–	–

Source: 'Proclamation of the State Electoral Commission, 23 September 1993', *Rzeczpospolita*, 27 September 1993.

1993 Senate elections
Date: 19 September
Turnout: 52.1%

Party/Coalition	%	Mandates
Alliance of Democratic Left	21.4	37
Polish Peasants' Party	18.7	36
Democratic Union	15.7	4
Union of Labour	7.5	2
Confederation for an Independent Poland	11.4	–
Non-Partisan Bloc (BBWR)	10.7	2
German Minority	1.2	1
Catholic Election Committee *Ojczyzna*	5.9	–
Solidarity	15.4	9
Alliance Centrum	3.8	1
Liberal Democratic Congress (KLD)	6.5	1
Union of Real Politics (UPR)	2.6	–
Self-Defence *(Samoobrona)*	3.0	–
Party X	0.2	–
Coalition for Republic (KdR)	1.8	–
Peasants' Alliance	1.6	–
Polish League	3.8	1
Polish Christian Democracy (PCHD)	0.6	–
Other parties	0.3	3
Independent senators	2.3	4

1997 Sejm and Senate elections
Date: 21 September
Turnout: 47.9%

Party/coalition	%	Sejm Mandates	Senate Mandates*
Election Action 'Solidarity'	33.8	201	51
Alliance of Democratic Left (SLD)	27.1	164	28
Union of Freedom (UW)	13.4	60	8
Polish Peasant Party (PSL)	7.3	27	3
Movement for Rebuilding Poland (ROP)	5.6	6	5
German Minority	0.4	2	–
Union of Labour	4.7	–	–
Bloc for Poland	1.4	–	–
National Alliance of Pensioners (KPEIR RP)	1.6	–	–
Union of Republic's Right	2.0	–	–
National Party of Pensioners (KPEIR)	2.2	–	–
Polish National Community–PSN	0.07	–	–
Self-Defence (Samoobrona)	0.08	–	–
German Social-Cultural Association of Czestochova	0.04	–	–
Orthodox Slavonic Minority of the Polish Republic	0.1	–	–
German Social-Cultural Association of Katowice	0.1	–	–
German Social Cultural Association of Elbląg	0.005	–	–
Non-partisans	0.007	–	–
German Committee 'Reconciliation'	0.03	–	–
Olsztyn German Minority	0.01	–	–
People's Alliance 'Poland-Labour'	0.005		
Independents			5

* Candidates to the Senate tended to run as individual candidates, though supported by political parties or coalitions. After the election most of the elected Senators joined the parliamentary caucuses of the parties or coalitions with which they had been affiliated.

PRESIDENTIAL ELECTIONS

1990 elections
First round
Date: 25 November
Turnout: 60.6%

Candidate	Number of votes	%
Lech Wałęsa	3,569,889	40.0
Stanisław Tymiński	3,397,605	23.1
Tadeusz Mazowiecki	2,973,264	18.0
Włodzimierz Cimoszewicz	1,514,025	9.2
Roman Bartoszcze	1,176,175	7.2
Leszek Moczulski	411,516	2.5

Second round
Date: 9 December
Turnout: 53.4%

Candidate	Number of votes	%
Lech Wałęsa	10,622,696	74.3
Stanisław Tymiński	3,683,098	25.7

Source: Dudek 1997, 126.

1995 election
First round
Date: 5 November
Turnout: 64.8%

Candidate	%
Aleksander Kwaśniewski	35.1
Lech Wałęsa	33.1
Jacek Kuroń	9.2
Jan Olszewski	6.9
Waldemar Pawlak	4.3
Tadeusz Zielinski	3.5
Hanna Gronkiewicz-Waltz	2.8
Janusz Korwin-Mikke	2.4
Andrzej Lepper	1.3
Jan Pietrzak	1.1
Tadeusz Koźluk	0.15
Kazimierz Piotrowicz	0.07
Leszek Bubel	0.04

Second round
Date: 19 November
Turnout: 68%

Candidate	%
Aleksander Kwaśniewski	51.7
Lech Wałęsa	48.3

APPENDIX 6.2: GOVERNMENT COMPOSITION

Mazowiecki's Cabinet
Date of investiture: 24 August 1989

Party/Coalition	Parliamentary seats		Cabinet posts	
	Number	%	Number	%
Solidarity	160	34.8	12	50.0
Polish United Workers' Party	171	37.2	4	16.7
United Peasant Party	76	16.5	4	16.7
Democratic Party	27	5.9	3	12.5
Association Pax	10	2.2	–	–
Christian–Social Union	8	1.7	–	–
Polish Catholic Social League	5	1.1	–	–
Independents	–	–	1	1.2

Bielecki's Cabinet
Date of investiture: 4 January 1991

Party/Coalition	Parliamentary seats		Cabinet posts	
	Number	%	Number	%
Solidarity–OKP	130	28.3		
Liberal Democratic Congress			4	20.0
Alliance Centrum			3	15.0
National Christian Alliance			1	5.0
Democratic Party	27	5.9	1	5.0
Democratic Union	30	6.5	1	5.0
Non-partisan	n/m	n/m	10	50.0

Olszewski's Cabinet
Date of investiture: 23 December 1991

Party/Coalition	Parliamentary seats		Cabinet posts	
	Number	%	Number	%
Alliance Centrum (POC)	44	9.6	4	20.0
National Christian All. (ZChN)	48*+2	10.9	3	15.0
Peasants' Alliance (PL)	28	6.1	2	10.0
Party of Chr. Dem. (PChD)	4	0.9	1	5.0
Non-partisans	n/m	n/m	10	50.0

* In the 1991 elections, the National Christian Alliance ran in the 'Catholic Election Action' electoral alliance, which won a total of 48 seats.

Suchocka's Cabinet
Date of investiture: 11 July 1992

Party/Coalition	Parliamentary seats		Cabinet posts	
	Number	*%*	*Number*	*%*
Democratic Union (UD)	62	13.5	5	20.8
National Christian All. (ZChN)	48+2	10.9	6	25.0
Liberal Democr. Congress (KLD)	37	8.0	4	16.7
Peasants' Alliance	28	6.1	4	16.7
Party of Chr. Dem. (PChD)	4	0.9	1	4.1
Peasant Christian Association	–	–	1	4.1
Polish Economic Programme *	12	2.6	1	4.1

* A splinter party from the Party of Friends of Beer.

Pawlak's Cabinet
Date of investiture: 26 October 1993

Party/Coalition	Parliamentary seats		Cabinet post s	
	Number	*%*	*Number*	*%*
All. of Dem. Left (SLD)	171	37.2	6	28.6
Polish Peasants' Party (PSL)	132	28.7	5	23.8
Non-partisans	–	–	10	47.6
of which				
endorsed by PSL			1	
former members of Union of Labour	41	8.9	1	

Oleksy's Cabinet
Date of investiture: 4 March 1995

Party/Coalition	Parliamentary seats		Cabinet posts	
	Number	*%*	*Number*	*%*
All. of Dem. Left (SLD)	171	37.2	8	
Non-partisans, SLD endorsed			3	52.4
Polish Peasants' Party (PSL)	132	28.7	6	
Non-partisan, PSL endorsed			1	33.3
Non-partisans	n/m	n/m	3	14.3

Cimoszewicz's Cabinet
Date of investiture: 7 February 1996

Party/Coalition	Parliamentary seats		Cabinet posts	
	number	*%*	*Number*	*%*
All. of Dem. Left (SLD)	171	37.2	8	
Non-partisan, SLD endorsed			1	45.0
Polish Peasants' Party (PSL)	132	28.7	7	35.0
Non-partisans	n/m	n/m	4	20.0

Buzek's Cabinet
Date of investiture: 17 October 1997

Party/Coalition	Parliamentary seats		Cabinet posts	
	Number	*%*	*Number*	*%*
Elect. Action 'Solidarity' (AWS)	201	43.7	15+1[*]	69.6
Union of Freedom (UW)	60	13.0	5+1[*]	26.1
Alliance Centrum indep. member	–	–	1	5.3

[*] Ministers formally non-partisan but supported by a party/coalition.

APPENDIX 6.3: THE ELECTORAL SYSTEM

The elections to the *Sejm* are regulated by the Election Act to the *Sejm* of 28 May 1993 (slightly amended in 1995),which replaced the Election Act of 28 June 1991. The elections to the Senate are regulated by the Election Act to the Senate of 10 May 1991, amended in 1994. (For the full text of the laws and the amendments, cf. *Dziennik Ustaw*, No.45, 1993, 205; No. 132, 1993, 640; and No. 54, 1994, 224.)

Every citizen who has reached the age of 18 on election day is eligible to vote. Every citizen of the Republic of Poland over 21 years of age is eligible to stand as a candidate. Citizens banned from public life are deprived of the right to vote and to run as a candidate.

Of the 460 seats of the *Sejm*, 391 are distributed in multi-member constituencies; the remaining 69 seats are allocated to lists competing for the nationally allocated mandates. Parties must surpass a 5 per cent threshold nationally in order to qualify for the allocation of seats; electoral cartels or coalitions must obtain 8 per cent of the valid votes cast nationwide. The mandates on the national lists are allocated among lists which gather a minimum of 7 per cent of the valid votes cast nationally. In 1991, the Hare–Niemeyer formula of seat allocation was applied on the constituency level and the St Lagüe formula on the national level. As of 1993, these formulas were replaced by the d'Hondt method.

Candidates may be nominated by political parties, coalitions of parties or by electoral committees, upon the request of at least 3,000 eligible voters in the given constituency. An electoral committee which has registered lists in at least half of the voting districts is exempted from collecting signatures. Parties or coalitions with at least 15 representatives in the outgoing *Sejm* are also exempted from collecting signatures. The Election Act of 1993 stipulates that parties must be registered in no less than half the constituencies in order to qualify for nationwide registration.

The one hundred Senators are elected according to the simple majority system, with the voievodships serving as constituencies. Each voievodship is entitled to two mandates, with the exception of the densely populated voievodships of Katowice and Warsaw, which are entitled to three mandates each. Candidates for the Senate may run on a party ticket or independently. The election committees may nominate as many candidates as there are seats in a given constituencies, i.e. two or three. Each candidacy must be endorsed by at least 3,000 eligible voters in the given voievodship. Each candidate may run in one voievodship only, and not simultaneously for the *Sejm*.

The elections are supervised by the State Electoral Commission, chaired by the Chairman of the Constitutional Tribunal. The Supreme Court has the final word on the validity of the elections to the *Sejm* as well as to the Senate.

The President is elected for a five-year term in general and direct elections, in one or two rounds. During the first round, a candidate must obtain an absolute majority of the valid votes to be considered elected. If no candidate obtains that level of support, a second round is held between the two front-runners from the first run. In the second run, the candidate who wins a simple majority is elected. The President may be elected for only two consecutive terms.

APPENDIX 6.4: THE CONSTITUTIONAL FRAMEWORK

Since 1989, the constitutional framework of Poland has undergone several changes. The Constitution of the People's Republic of Poland, enacted on 22 July 1952, was amended on 7 April and 29 December 1989, and again on 8 March and 27 September 1990. As a result of these amendments, the official name of the state was changed from 'People's Republic of Poland' to 'Republic of Poland', the principle of the rule of law was codified, as was the formula for the division of power.

A bi-cameral system of representation, with a lower house (the *Sejm*) and an upper house (the Senate), was introduced. A President, first elected by the National Assembly (a joint session of the *Sejm* and the Senate) and, since 1990, by popular vote, replaced the State Council as Head of State. The local 'people's councils', which had been integrated into the state apparatus, were replaced by directly elected municipal councils with broad autonomy *vis-à-vis* the state administration.

A so-called Short Constitution was enacted on 17 October 1992, pending agreement on a new and comprehensive constitution. In the form of a Constitutional Act, the Short Constitution summarized the constitutional changes of 1989–90 in a comprehensive form. It specified the powers of the President and the legal framework for government formation and government responsibilities. The role of the Prime Minister was strengthened and the autonomy of local self-government was enhanced.

On 2 April 1997, the National Assembly approved the new comprehensive constitution for the Republic of Poland. It was endorsed by the voters in a national referendum of 25 May 1997 with 53.4 per cent of the votes in favour. The Constitution defines Poland as a unitary democratic state, abiding by the rule of law and applying a parliamentary formula for the division of power. Legislative power is shared by the *Sejm* and the Senate. Executive power is divided between the President and the Council of Ministers.

The Council of Ministers, consisting of the Prime Minister, the Deputy Prime Ministers (optional), the Ministers and the Chairmen of Committees defined by law, is nominated by the President and subject to the approval of the *Sejm*. The Council of Ministers and its members remain responsible to the *Sejm*, but can be removed by the *Sejm* only through a constructive vote of no confidence. The President may dissolve the *Sejm* and the Senate only in the events that the Budget Bill submitted by the Government is not acted upon within the three months after its submission, or in case the *Sejm* and the Senate cannot agree on the formation of a new Government.

The President has a suspensive veto. He represents the state abroad; he ratifies international treaties (some of them subject to approval by the *Sejm* and the Senate in the form of a law); he nominates representatives of Poland to foreign countries and to international organizations. The President serves as Head of State and as Commander-in-Chief of the Armed Forces.

The constitutionality of statutes and legal acts is controlled by the Constitutional Tribunal upon the initiative of the President of the Republic, the Marshals of the *Sejm* or the Senate, the Prime Minister, the Presidents of the Supreme Court and of the Highest Administrative Court, the President of the Supreme Chamber of Control, the General Prosecutor and the Defender of Citizens' Rights, or at least 50 deputies of the *Sejm* or 30 Senators. The Constitutional Tribunal, composed of a President, a Vice President and 13 justices, is elected by the *Sejm* for a 9-year term.

The *Sejm* passes ordinary laws and budget laws. It elects the President of the National Bank of Poland (for six years, upon the initiative of the President of the Republic), the President of the Supreme Chamber of Control (for six years), and the Defender of Citizens' Rights (with the consent of the Senate, for five years). The Senate has the right to amend or oppose laws passed by the *Sejm*. The *Sejm* can reject the amendments or corrections made by the Senate, by an absolute majority. Laws can be passed upon initiative of the President, the Senate, the Council of Ministers and at least 15 deputies of the *Sejm*. In addition, legal acts (statutes) can be proposed through a popular initiative signed by at least 100,000 citizens. The *Sejm*, as well as the President (with the consent of the Senate), may call national referenda. A referendum may also be initiated by no fewer than 500,000 citizens.

A broad catalogue of civil rights and freedoms are protected by the Constitution and by statute. The list of freedoms includes: personal freedom, human dignity, the secrecy of communication as well as the freedom of thought and religion, of speech and of assembly. A number of political and social rights are also guaranteed by the Constitution: the right to vote and to be elected, the right to choose one's own profession and place of work, the right to safe working conditions, the right to rest, the right for social care and health care, the right to attend public schools free of charge, and the protection of maternity and childhood. Different kinds of ownership are equally protected by law. Public power shall be decentralized and the competencies of local self-governmental bodies protected by constitutional or statutory regulations.

7. The Czech and Slovak Republics

Zdenka Mansfeldová

Analyses made in the post-communist countries commonly utilize three concepts harking back to Rokkan's classic cleavages (Lipset and Rokkan 1967). The first derives from Rokkan's contrapositions and attempts to verify their existence by pointing out various social conflicts and differences, which do not however, always take on the character of actual cleavages. The second, in contrast, issues from particular social problems, differences and contradictions in the post-communist countries, which are interpreted as new cleavages, specific to the post-communist phase. 'Cleavages' formulated in this manner lose the characteristics of true conflict structures or cleavages. The third concept is less conspicuous: it interprets cleavages as a specific form of the universal social precepts, which determine and explain the evolution of society. Common to all these concepts is that they do not take into account the question of whether actual cleavages exist in the actual societies.

The analytical perspective employed in this study ties in with the classic concept, which, however, should not be interpreted as an attempt to prove the non-existence of the determinants and designs of interpretation in question, i.e. cleavages.[1] In this chapter, a cleavage is understood as a set of long-running structural lines of conflict, 'grounding in a relatively enduring social division and institutional organization' (Knutsen and Scarbrough 1995, 497).

As is commonly understood, in this chapter cleavage crystallization is considered as a process or processes through which various contradictory interests are articulated, and on the basis of which political institutions, capable of influencing political decisions and orientations, are formed. Cleavage crystallization mobilizes citizens, their value orientations and attitudes to social issues, and creates an effective linkage between citizens and the political system in which they live (cf. Martin 1980). In order to put the cleavage label on such contractions, they must be parallel and divide society politically and according to interests. If, on the other hand, the contradictions and conflicts are multi-dimensional and cut across society, they are linked politically.

THE CZECH REPUBLIC

An evaluation of the transformation and consolidation of democracy in the Czech Republic (Brokl 1997a, 1997b) makes it evident that constitutive indicators of cleavages are absent, i.e. a pattern related to long-term structural conflicts, rooted in relatively stable social differences and organized institutionally. In the Czech Republic, the social structure and the interest structure are still in a flux and, in comparison with developed democracies, the intermediary structures – excepting the political parties – are still in a process of continuous crystallization. The crystallization of the social differentiation and the interest structure is discernible in the intermediary processes, which is characterized by a relatively mature party system and a catch-all electoral system. However, in contrast to developed democracies, this mechanism is not marked by intermediary super-institutionalization, but rather by a lower degree of interest differentiation and inadequate institutionalization.

In their study, Knutsen and Scarbrough point out that '[w]hereas the cleavage model suggests a relatively robust structuring of mass politics, the "new politics" perspective points to the more fluid, volatile relationship between social groups, value orientations and party preferences which might be expected of a politics unanchored in cleavages. A more appropriate description for this kind of politics would seem to be "politics without cleavages" – or "post-cleavage conflicts"' (Knutsen and Scarbrough 1995, 497). For the purposes of the present study – and possibly also in analyses of other post-communist countries – we are probably well-advised to analyse the conflict structure in terms of 'pre-cleavage conflicts', rather than embark on a speculative search for 'real' cleavages.

In the Czech Republic, the processes of party formation and party spectrum crystallization are still in progress, but the most important changes appear to have taken place already. The analyses of the eight years of transformation and of the three elections held, raise the question: what determines party strategies and electoral behaviour? When looking for new cleavages and their effects, one must take into account that some contemporary problems and conflicts are rooted in the past. Within the framework of democratic values, the social and political transformation is also seen as a remedy for wrongs committed in the past. This interpretation opens a Pandora's box of different interests and cleavages which already appeared solved. There is a tendency to unlock ever deeper levels of contradictions, and to convert historical rights and wrongs into new interests and conflicts. Thus, many of the current political conflicts may be only of a temporary character. Actual cleavages, i.e. structurally rooted conflicts, as presented more or less distinctly by actors in the Czech political arena, are likely to emerge only during the processes of democratization and consolidation of democracy.

The Initial Phase of Transformation

The first post-transition elections in Czechoslovakia were held on 8–9 June 1990, following the so-called Velvet Revolution of November 1989. They were the first free elections since 1935, as the first post-war elections in May 1946 cannot be considered fully free (Broklová 1996). Four bodies were elected: two chambers of the Federal Parliament, and a Czech and a Slovak National Council.

Czechoslovakia lacked experiences of an extended process of liberalization and negotiations between the old and new elites. The communist regime was in full control almost until the very end and collapsed within a period of only ten days. Therefore the new political parties could emerge only after the transformation, albeit that some parties were grounded in certain embryonic structures existing beforehand. The 'historic parties' such as the Social Democrats, also experienced a renaissance, after 40 years of suppression. The space of time between the collapse of the communist regime and the first elections was too short for voters to gain a clear understanding of the differences between the parties. Equally, the parties did not have enough time to present the electorate with distinct profiles, they were busy with the process of formation. Only the revocation in January 1990 of Article 4 in the constitution – which asserted the leading role of the Communist Party in society – and the approval of the new party law in February 1990 led to a rapid and eruptive process of party and movement creation. Many of the new parties and movements were formed on the elite level and embarked on a quest for interests to represent. Their aspirations as concerned non-institutionalized interests were similar.

The electoral law provided for a single-round system with proportional representation. Voters cast their ballots for parties or lists, but there was the possibility of naming preferred candidates. A five per cent threshold for individual parties was introduced. This electoral system has remained in place during all three elections held in the Czech Republic.

The electoral period was set at four years, but the first period was exceptionally shortened to two years. One reason for that was the expectation that party formation would proceed and that a new constitution would be enacted within two years after the elections.

As mentioned earlier, many of the parties participating in the first elections had emerged from the elite level and anticipated either the existence of cleavages or – for instance, in the case of the Agrarian Party – the continuation of historical cleavages. But on the other hand, some historical cleavages which were mobilized failed to find political representation. One example was the civic versus nationalist cleavage, which manifested itself in the problematic relationship between the Czech lands and Slovakia (*Table 7.1*). It was mainly realized on the Slovak side, where it also found its political representation.

Table 7.1: Evaluations of the Czech–Slovak relationship

'The relationship between Czechs and Slovaks is:'	1983			11/89			3/90		
	Fed.	CR	SR	Fed.	CR	SR	Fed.	CR	SR
'Friendly', 'Rather friendly'	79	75	86	69	66	76	47	45	49
No opinion	15	17	10	23	24	20	21	20	24
'Rather averse', 'averse'	4	6	3	8	10	4	32	35	27
Don't know	2	2	1	–	–	–	–	–	–

Note: Fed.: Federation average; CR: Czech Republic; SR: Slovak Republic.
Source: IVVM (Institute for Public Opinion Research) 89–6/12, 1990.

Only four Czech parties gained parliamentary representation in 1990, which goes to show that the elections took on the form of a plebiscite about the future of the country. The deep-seated conflict lines cleaving the political arena in which the political parties operated was not at the time expressed through electoral behaviour. The rejection of communism highlights the value-driven character of electoral behaviour. Anti-communism was an expression of a value cleavage rather than of a real cleavage, and it did not split the electorate; practically the whole population, with the exception of some 300,000 members and hangers-on of the *nomenklatura*, was anti-communist. However, the historical civic versus national cleavage began to develop and manifest itself within this value cleavage, although it was not yet crystallized and institutionalized (Brokl and Mansfeldová 1997). In Slovakia, national sentiments were strongly articulated, while civic attitudes prevailed in the Czech lands. At the same time, other classical cleavages were recognizable within the framework of the general anti-communism, e.g. the centre versus periphery cleavage in the intricate relationships between the Czech lands and Slovakia, between Bohemia and Moravia, and between Prague and the rest of the Czech lands.

The 1990 elections were characterized by an extremely high voter turnout – 98.8 per cent of the electorate took part in the polls. Apart from the absolute victors, the Civic Forum (OF) in the Czech lands and its Slovak counterpart, the Public against Violence (VPN) – three other formations gained seats in Parliament.

The Civic Forum, formed in November 1989, was the largest newly formed political formation. It had the character of a movement; it provided a platform and served as an umbrella for a broad range of independent initiatives and anti-communist opposition forces. The Civic Forum manifesto advocated in broad terms the transition to a free society and a market economy. The Civic Forum had a substantially broader base of support in the Bohemia than in Moravia.

The second largest political force in both the federal and the national parliament, far behind the OF, was the Communist Party, isolated but with a stable electorate. Two additional parties managed to gain representation in the Czech parliament. The Movement for Self-Governing Democracy–Society for Moravia and Silesia (HSD–SMS) was one of the new-comers. It was a movement which presented itself as an advocate of Moravian and regional interests – which turned out to be more regional than national – and as an agent in the struggle between centre and periphery. Its electoral programme focused on the introduction of regional autonomy and the reinvigoration of the Moravian–Silesian lands with the Moravian metropolis Brno as capital. In some constituencies the HSD–SMS won more votes than the OF. The other party to enter parliament was the Christian Democratic Union–The Czech People's Party (KDU–ČSL), a bloc party gathering some historical parties from the Czech political scene. It had a traditional electorate among Czech and, mainly, Moravian Catholics.

The Process of Differentiation

From 1991 onwards, after the first phase of party formation, a process of differentiation commenced. The internal differentiation within the Civic Forum was the most important event in this process. Particularly in the Czech lands, this differentiation reflected diverging opinions about how the common goal of political democratization should be reached.

At the time, the reform process focused on the sphere of the economy: economic democracy, privatization and anti-statism. The emerging party system was not yet organically fully attached to social stratification and the structure of economic interests; party attachment was rather based on an identification with values. Early in 1991, the variegated orientation of representatives and members, and the conceptions of political and economic transformation, led to the disintegration of the Civic Forum into two new parties. The liberal-oriented Civic Movement (OH) claimed the political middle ground, while the liberal and market economy-oriented Civic

Democratic Party (ODS) captured the right-hand side of the left–right spectrum.

After the 1992 elections, the number of parties represented in parliament more than doubled from four to nine. This raises the question of whether cleavages had started crystallizing and found political representation. The ODS was not the only civic, right-oriented party to gain representation in parliament: so did the Civic Democratic Alliance *(Občanská demokratická aliance,* ODA). Also new in parliament were the Social Democrats (ČSSD), who have since been on an upward trend, and the Liberal Social Union *(Liberální sociální unie,* LSU), a party which represents agrarian and ecological interests and which was formed as a coalition between the Greens, the Agrarian Party and the Czechoslovak Socialist Party. The LSU had its widest base of support in the agrarian regions of the country.

Also represented in parliament after the 1992 elections was the Republican Party (SPR–RSČ), a vehicle for xenophobic and nationalist tendencies. The party had its largest base of support in the mining districts of Northern Bohemia, and conversely was weakest in Prague.

The Movement for Self-Governing Democracy–Society for Moravia and Silesia (HSD–SMS) remained represented in parliament, although the marked regional differentiation of its electoral support meant that a significant portion of its votes did not result in parliamentary representation.

In the 1992 elections, the ODS was the victor by a large margin (Appendix 7.1). The most important differentiating factor between the elections of 1990 and 1992 was the impact of economic reform. Satisfaction with the way reforms progressed showed a high correlation with support for the ODS; a party which identified itself with liberal democratic values and individualism *(Tables 7.2, 7.3 and 7.4).* The rump Civic Movement appealed to similar values, but did not manage to gain representation in the 1992 parliament. In the elections to the two chambers of the Federal Assembly, the Civic Movement won only 4.7 per cent of the votes for the House of Nations and 4.4 per cent for the House of People.

Table 7.2: Satisfaction with development: In general, do you feel things in the Czech Republic are going in the right or in the wrong direction? (%)

	1991	*1992*	*1993*	*1994*
Right	51.7	58.1	66.8	58.9
Wrong	30.5	33.8	33.2	30.0
Don't know	17.9	7.8	–	11.1

Source: CEEB 2; CEEB 3; CEEB 4; CEEB 5

Table 7.3: Evaluations of economic reforms: The economic reforms in the Czech Republic are going – (%)

	1991	1992	1993	1994
Too fast	16.8	19.6	19.2	24.9
Too slow	37.7	29.3	22.2	24.8
Right speed	35.3	42.3	56.7	34.6
Don't know, MS	10.2	1.8	1.5	13.5

Source: CEEB 2; CEEB 3; CEEB 4; CEEB 5

Table 7.4: Evaluation of the economic transformation in 1993–96 (%)

	1993				1994			1995				1996		
	03	06	09	12	03	06	09	02	06	08	10	01	03	10
Successful	26	24	26	24	28	32	33	31	26	25	31	28	28	23
Partly successful	42	44	42	45	47	44	41	44	47	44	46	46	43	42
Not successful	26	20	22	18	17	16	18	18	19	18	18	18	19	26

Source: IVVM (Institute for Public Opinion Research) 96–10, Prague 1996.

Criticism of the economic reforms was linked to support for left-oriented parties, particularly for the Communist Party, and partly to support for the right-wing Republican Party, which appealed to citizens with oppositional, radical or even extremist preferences. General support for economic reform and their long-term support for the political development (*Tables 7.5, 7.6*) showed a high degree of correlation with support for individual parties.

Table 7.5: Satisfaction with the development of democracy in the Czech Republic (%)

	1991	1992	1993	1994
Very satisfied	2.1	2.3	2.2	3.0
Fairly satisfied	31.3	35.9	47.6	41.1
Not very satisfied	48.9	47.5	38.7	40.1
Not at all satisfied	12.3	10.7	11.5	13.5

Source: CEEB 2; CEEB 3; CEEB 4; CEEB 5

Table 7.6: Evaluation of human rights situation: How much respect is there for individual human rights nowadays in the Czech Republic? (%)

	1991	1992	1993	1994
A lot of respect	12.7	5.8	7.1	5.3
Some respect	55.0	48.7	49.6	47.0
Not much respect	22.7	30.1	37.7	38.0
No respect at all	3.6	5.1	5.6	6.3
Don't know	6.0	10.3	–	3.4

Source: CEEB 2; CEEB 3; CEEB 4; CEEB 5

In contrast to Slovakia, attitudes towards the future of the federation did not have a major impact on electoral preferences in the Czech Republic, although parties certainly took different stands on this issue. But not a single party advocated the formation of an independent Czech state.

The common Czech–Slovak state, joining two nations with diverse historical experiences, forms a historical residual cleavage of the kind described by Georgi Karasimeonov in Chapter 11. This cleavage may be described as civic rather than national. The cleavage gained particular importance after the early 1930s, when the Slovaks emerged as a modern nation. During the Second World War, this cleavage manifested itself in the form of the Slovak state, but it was subsequently suppressed by the communist regime. In 1968, however, it returned to the forefront, resulting in the federative re-organization of the Czechoslovak state. In 1990, the cleavage again appeared in full strength in conjunction with the so-called hyphen war – the issue was whether the state should be called Czechoslovakia or Czecho-Slovakia. During 1990 and 1991, this resulted in a heated debate on federalism and the division of power between the two republics, as illustrated by the so-called Competence Law of December 1990.

This obviously influenced party formation within the Czechoslovak framework, though maybe not directly. From the very beginning, two separate and parallel party systems emerged, with their roots in the socialist federation. Nevertheless, in the elections of 1990 and 1992, several parties ran throughout the federation, and part of the new political élite was indeed concerned with mobilizing a federation-wide electorate. But in contrast to inter-war Czechoslovakia, such an electorate was no longer to be found (Brokl and Mansfeldová 1995).[2] The federation-wide parties were later dissolved through the emergence of a double structure with two independent, national parties – one Czech and one Slovak – with comparable agendas. This development was reinforced by the electoral legislation at the time, which provided representation in the federal parliament for parties which surpassed the five per cent threshold in either of the constituent republics. The emergence of two autonomous party systems was an important precursor for the later break-up of the Czechoslovak Federation.

Apart from the legal prerequisites, the two somewhat differentiated party systems were the result of divergent conditions in the two halves of the federation. In particular, this applied to economic conditions and the progress of economic reforms. During 1990–92, Czechoslovakia was marked by a serious fall in economic performance and an increasing economic divergence between the two republics, with the Slovak economy hit particularly hard (*Table 7.7*). In both parts of the federation, this led to the politicization of the transformation process and to conflicts pertaining to economic policy. Yet the national cleavage was, at the time, even more important in Slovakia.

Table 7.7: Preferred economic system (%)

	January 1991			November 1991		
	Fed.	*CR*	*SR*	*Fed.*	*CR*	*SR*
Market economy	48	52	39	45	52	33
Mixed economy	36	33	43	44	39	53
Socialist plan economy	4	3	6	6	5	8
Don't know	12	12	12	5	5	6

Source: AISA, November 1991

The collapse of the federation was one possible outcome of the 1992 elections, since the successful parties had widely diverging views on economic reform and on the federation, and manifested differences pertaining to democratic traditions and liberal values (*Table 7.8*). The polarization of the political scene in both republics manifested itself in parliament during the presidential elections in 1992. The complicated situation was exacerbated by the majority prohibition on major issues in the Federal Assembly; it led to deadlocks which *de facto* eliminated the Federal parliament from the decision-making process. For the Czech Republic, the national cleavage appears to have been solved through the dissolution of the federation.

Table 7.8: Preferred form of state: Which form of state do you prefer? (%)

	In Czech Republic			In Slovak Republic		
	5/92	*6/92*	*7/92*	*5/92*	*6/92*	*7/92*
Unitary state	34	29	38	12	11	14
Federation	28	28	19	33	26	27
Federal Republic	22	31	18	6	6	8
Confederation	6	5	3	31	31	30
Independent states	6	13	16	11	18	16

Source: IVVM (Institute for Public Opinion Research) 1992.

From Independence to the Third Elections

After the 1992 elections, attitudes towards economic reform became such a clear dividing line that the Czech political system was characterized as 'one-dimensional' (Kitschelt 1994, 36). This dimension was consistent with the lef/right axis. Opinion polls made between the second and third elections show that the positions on the left/right axis, on which the parties placed themselves, corresponded with their positions as perceived by the voters (Markowski 1995; Večerník 1996; Vlachová 1996). The conformity of the self-perception of the parties with that of the electorate was also reflected in inter-party interaction during the electoral campaign of 1996 and thereafter (Krause 1996, 428)

Several circumstances made the parliamentary elections of 1996 particularly important. They completed the formation of the Czech political system. They were the first elections held in the Czech Republic after the dissolution of the federation. They were also the first elections to the Senate, which commenced its work only three years after the constitution had provided for the establishment of the body, and after long discussions about the wisdom of having a second chamber.

In 1996, no new party managed to enter the lower chamber of the parliament of the Czech Republic, while three of the nine parties represented earlier lost out.[3] Of the six remaining, two were civic, right-oriented parties; one was Christian in character; one was social democratic; and one each on the extreme left and the extreme right of the political spectrum, the Communist Party and the Republican party, respectively– the term 'extreme' is here applied in a Sartorian sense (Sartori 1976).

The 1996 elections resulted in the emergence of a party of equal strength and a weighty rival to the previously dominant Civic Democratic Party: the Social Democrats (ČSSD). Brokl has pointed to the interesting effect created by the electoral formula: the first chamber was elected by proportional representation, while the second was elected through a majority system (Brokl 1996, 392–393). The larger parties were the beneficiaries of the majority effect, which resulted in a rather large portion of cast votes – some 10 per cent – being squandered. The five per cent hurdle also had an psychological effect, because voters were reluctant to cast their ballot for parties that had little chance of gaining parliamentary representation (Novák 1996, 411). For the election results, the psychological effect of the electoral formula can indeed be compared to the influence of cleavages. The electoral system had a psychological impact on the voters and a reductionist effect on the parties (Sartori 1994).

What can be inferred from the election results? Brokl sums up three main explanations for the electoral success of the Social Democrats (Brokl 1996)

1   Domestic observers tended to interpret it as a result of the renewal of the social class structure, which also provided for the renewal of the classical role of the social democratic party, creating a marked linkage between political party and social class.

2   Foreign observers, in many cases, saw the success of the Czech Social Democrats as a parallel to the successes of leftist political parties in other post-communist countries, and feared that it would led to a setback for the

transformation process. This interpretation, however, ignores the fact that the ČSSD is dissimilar to other post-communist leftist parties in the sense that it is not a renamed or transformed Communist Party. Instead, it harks back to historical social democracy, thus differentiating itself from the political right as well as from the Communist Party. In fact, the existence of the more left-wing Communist party (KSČM) enabled the Czech Social Democracy to present itself as a social democratic party rather than as a crypto-communist successor party. The survey data show that the evaluation of the current situation and the pre-1989 regime did not change rapidly (*Tables 7.9 and 7.10*) and that a shift to the left did not occur (*Table 7.11*). The KSČM won fewer votes than in the 1992 elections and the support for the KSČM was not a sign of nostalgia about communism.

Table 7.9: Evaluation of the current situation and the pre 1989 regime (%)

The current regime is	1991	96/03	97/06	97/10
Better	37	34	26	29
About the same	46	41	40	37
The regime before 1989 was better	14	18	25	24
Don't know	3	7	9	10

Source: IVVM (Institute for Public Opinion Research) 97–10 (October), Prague 1997.

Table 7.10: Evaluation of the current situation and the pre-1989 regime based on voters' party preferences (%)

The current regime is	ODS	ODA	KDU-ČSL	ČSSD	KSČM	SPR-RSČ	Don't know	Total
Better	74	72	36	14	1	5	29	29
About the same	21	17	46	47	23	25	46	37
The regime before 1989 was better	2	6	17	34	71	57	16	24

Source: IVVM (Institute for Public Opinion Research) 97–10 (October), Prague 1997.

Table 7.11: Left–right self-placement of Czech voters 1991–97 (%)

	6/90	6/91	6/92	6/93	6/94	5/95	12/95	7/96	12/97 [*]
Left-wing	19	20	16	20	21	23	22	22	21
Centre	51	43	33	40	41	41	41	41	36
Right-wing	30	37	51	40	38	36	37	37	32

Source: STEM, Trendy 1993–1996 and *Vývoj spolecensko-politické situace v letech 1990–1992*; [*] IVVM 92–12, 1998.

3 The third interpretation sees the electoral success of the Social Democrats as a manifestation of the emergence of a standard political spectrum, and as a result of the electoral formula with its five per cent hurdle for

parliamentary representation. Analyses of the flow of votes suggest that the ČSSD had been successful among voters who had previously supported parties likely to fail the five per cent threshold, and who were not prepared to vote for the parties in government, or for the Communists, or the extreme right wing. A comparison of electoral preferences over time shows that a large portion of electoral support for the Social Democrats did not emanate from its core constituency, but from voters who made up their minds very late in the campaign. Sympathies also played a role. According to the centre for Empirical Social Studies, STEM, 14.7 per cent of 'non-decided' voters mentioned the ČSSD as the most attractive party.

Opinion polls show that the right-oriented ODS and the left-oriented ČSSD were seen as alternative political parties. Yet in the 1996 elections, voting behaviour did not quite follow social stratification; in fact, it cut right through the political spectrum, which leads to centripetal rather that centrifugal tendencies. This was clearly a case of cross-cutting cleavages. 39 per cent of the 'poor', i.e. groups with lowest levels of income, voted for the right-wing parties. 56 per cent of the 'poor' voted for the left. Conversely, 25 per cent of the 'rich' – citizens in the highest income brackets – and 30 per cent of entrepreneurs voted for the left. Czech society is thus still in a flux as comes to voting behaviour. The voting behaviour of social groups nevertheless offers some observations. Of the two main parties, the ODS represents the upper part of the social hierarchy, while the ČSSD may be seen as a representative of dependent persons. Even so, at the same time both parties present themselves as broad all-national parties attractive to the members of most social groups.

A positive development in parliamentary politics in recent years has been the emergence of a new political élite with a degree of political experience. Of 200 members in the 1996 lower chamber, 74 had held seats in the previous parliament.

The 1996 elections, and developments thereafter, also demonstrated that the earlier dominant socioeconomic dimension is receding in importance. As privatization is almost completed, the question of the role of the state, and the juxtaposition of economic populism with market principles constitute the main political issues. This is closely connected to the question of social security, where the idea of redistribution through a paternalistic state is juxtaposed with the vision of social policy guided by market-oriented principles.

The cosmopolitan–nationalist antagonism is made concrete in attitudes towards the European Union and NATO (*see Table 7.12*), in attitudes towards neighbouring countries – particularly Germany – and towards foreign influences and foreign capital. Associated with this conflict dimension are attitudes towards ethnic minorities, in particular the Roma, and to asylum policy. The political parties have formulated clear opinions on this issue, as has the public. This conflict dimension is above all exploited by the populist Republican Party, and can not be accounted for by socio-political variables. The Republican Party opposes all supranational institutions, and advocates that contention with an extreme nationalist posture.

Table 7.12: Attitudes in the Czech Republic towards EU and NATO membership applications, by party preference

	ODS	ODA	KDU-ČSL	ČSSD	KSČM	LB	SPR-RSČ
Approval	75	54	52	36	6	16	15
Disapproval	14	13	18	28	71	43	43

Source: IVVM (Institute for Public Opinion Research) 96–03.

The government formed after the 1996 elections included the same three parties as the outgoing government: the right-wing ODS and ODA and the centre-right KDU–ČSL. The other three main parties – the ČSSD, the KSČM and the SPR–RSČ – remained opposition parties, but the communists and republicans lacked 'coalition potential'. The new government was a minority government with only 99 MPs out of 200. After two Social Democrats had to leave the party, the fate of the government depended on the vote of only one independent deputy, as demonstrated when a vote of no confidence was called in June 1997. Growing economic problems and decreasing confidence in constitutional institutions (*Table 7.13*) made for growing tensions among the coalition and within the ODS. The predictions that the government would be weak and unstable were fulfilled in December 1997, when the Václav Klaus cabinet resigned after a public scandal about ODS party finances.

Table 7.13: Confidence of Czech citizens in constitutional institutions (%)

	1994		1995				1996				1997			
Confidence in	09	12	03	06	09	12	03	06	09	12	01	03	06	10
President	72	74	75	78	71	73	77	77	82	84	87	68	68	62
Government	58	54	52	53	53	56	55	53	53	51	50	43	22	33
Parliament	29	24	27	29	24	31	31	27	35	33	34	25	19	22
Senate	-	-	-	-	-				-	-	21	23	20	17

Source: IVVM (Institute for Public Opinion Research) 95–09; 96–10; 97–4; 97–10.

The resignation of the ODS government did not automatically imply a change in political orientation, but Václav Klaus, who had been re-elected as party leader, nevertheless decided that the ODS would not participate in the new government.

On 2 January 1998, President Václav Havel appointed the new govern-ment headed by Josef Tošovský, a former Governor of the Czech National Bank. The Prime Minister was independent, as were of seven of the sixteen cabinet ministers. Four 'rebels' from the ODS were appointed to the cabinet. The ODS, KSČM and SPR–RSČ did not support the new government, but parliament gave it a vote of confidence on 28 January 1998, on the understanding that early elections would be called for June or November 1998. Before the vote of confidence, 28 deputies defected from the ODS parliamentary club to form a new caucus and later a new party, the Freedom Union, but such a split on the right of the political spectrum cannot be interpreted as a sign of essential programmatic differentiation.

Cleavages and Conflicts in Post-Communist Consolidation

Cleavage crystallization can be defined as a process through which the cleavage of interests and identity are crystallized and articulated in a political formation which is able to influence decision-making. One can observe distinct phases of cleavage crystallization in the three elections in the Czech Republic. The first elections were rather a plebiscite on the future orientation of the country than about deep-rooted conflicts. But by the second elections, the latent effect of the civic/national and centre/periphery cleavages were already apparent, as is shown by the election results.

The historical civic/national cleavage, manifested in conflicting attitudes towards the common, federal state and towards political and economic transformation, led to the dissolution of the Czechoslovak federation, and (in the Czech Republic) to a left–right polarization of the political spectrum with a weakened centre. During this period, social democracy grew in strength; election by election, it increased its share of the vote.

For twenty years the inter-war the Czechoslovak republic attempted – without success – to form a political nation. Then came 50 years of non-democratic government, first under the Nazis and then under the Commu-nists. During those years, an asymmetric federation emerged, characterized by disparate conditions in the two halves of the state. The Slovak nation matured, and in contrast to the officially-stated goal, two nations with different political cultures developed (Brokl 1994).

The third elections, in 1996, demonstrated that the socioeconomic dimension appeared to have become dominant in the Czech Republic. With increasing economic problems – or rather, through the effects these prob-lems have on the population (*cf. Tables 7.14 and 7.15*) – trades unions have become more active. Even if a closer union collaboration with their 'natural' political partners is to be expected, trade unions are likely to remain independent of the political parties.

Table 7.14: Satisfaction with the current political situation (%)

	97/01	97/02	97/03	97/04	97/05	97/06	97/07	97/09	97/10
'Satisfied', 'Rather satisfied'	38	38	34	24	24	16	18	27	25
'Not very satisfied', 'Not at all satisfied'	58	59	61	72	72	81	79	67	71

Source: IVVM (Institute for Public Opinion Research) 97–10, Prague 1997.

Table 7.15: Satisfaction with the standard of living in the Czech Republic (%)

	92/07	93/07	94/07	95/07	96/07	96/11	97/01	97/03	97/06
Very good	2	3	4	5	4	4	4	5	3
Rather good	51	56	53	60	56	56	60	54	50
Rather bad	42	34	35	30	34	34	30	34	39
Very bad	5	5	6	3	4	4	4	5	6

Source: IVVM (Institute for Public Opinion Research) 97–06, Prague 1997.

Social and political polarization in Czech society has continued to develop and found political representation. The number of parliamentary parties has fallen and no new actors have emerged. The main representative of the centre/periphery cleavage, the Movement for Autonomous Democracy–Society for Moravia and Silesia (HSD–SMS), later the ČMSS, has disappeared.[1] This cleavage is not yet mature; as the relatively large contrasts between Prague and the rest of the country – also as regards unemployment – have been resolvable within the framework social and economic transformation. Traditional conflict structures, such as state versus church, rural versus urban or ethnic antagonism, are not articulated in Czech politics, or at least not in electoral behaviour. The cleavage structure of state versus Church has all but disappeared due to the secularization of the land.

THE SLOVAK REPUBLIC

In the eight years following the political transformation, Slovakia has experienced three elections, the most recent of which were held ahead of schedule as the first elections of the independent state. During these eight years, five governments have been in power, of which two have been since the 1992 break-up of the federation. Vladimír Mečiar has headed three governments; twice he had to resign as premier after losing the majority in parliament, but the party he leads has remained the most popular among voters. The relatively stable voter preferences raises the question on what social processes and cleavages this alignment is founded.

When comparing the Czech and Slovak political scenes, both before and after the dismantling of the federation, one can point at the building-up and maturing of parallel institutions and political structures; first Czech and Slovak, subsequently Slovak and Magyar. This process may be seen as an articulation, unfolding and institutionalization of the national cleavage, which has proved dominant in the formation of the political arena.

The 1990 Founding Elections

The founding elections in 1990 marked the end of the first phase of the transition to democracy in Slovakia. As in other post-communist countries, the elections took on an emotional and euphoric character. Almost all participating parties had emerged after November 1989, and only a few of them could either claim historical roots or count upon support based on a natural identification arising from class, nationality or religion.

Five parties cleared the 5 per cent threshold for representation in the federal parliament – the VPN (Public Against Violence); the KDH (Christian-Democratic Movement); the KSS (Communist Party of Slovakia); the SNS (Slovak National Party); and *Együttélés* (Co-Existence). The first of the three were not active on the federal level but had ideological partners in the Czech political system, while the SNS represented 'Slovak' and *Együttélés* 'Magyar' interests. The formation of the two latter parties signalled the latent cleavage that was subsequently to dominate political life in Slovakia. They were also more successful in the elections to the national parliament – the Slovak National Council – than in the federation-wide polls.

Seven parties cleared the 3 per cent threshold for the Slovak National Council.[5] The broad citizens' movement, the VPN, which had entered into an electoral alliance with the MNI (Magyar Independent Initiative), won the largest share of votes. The second-largest force in parliament was the KDH, reflecting the Christian, particularly Catholic, tradition of Slovakia. The SNS, which presented itself as a representative of the national interest and national emancipation, came in third, while the KSS was the fourth largest party, registering about the same level of electoral support as the Communists. *Együttélés* (Co-Existence), the Democratic Party (DS) and the Greens were the remaining three.

The VPN/MNI alliance, the victor in Slovakia, won 29.34 per cent of the votes, far less than the 49.55 per cent its Czech counterpart, the Civic Forum, received in the Czech half of the federation. The distance to the second-greatest force was also far smaller than was the case in the Czech republic. With the benefit of hindsight, the diffusion of electoral support serves as an indication of the cleavages which had shaped the Slovak political landscape from the very outset. In Czechoslovakia as in other post-communist countries, the founding elections were about an alternative to communism. Nevertheless, in Slovakia one may already, at this point in time, discern the emergence of historical national cleavages relevant to the attitude towards the common Czechoslovak state and the Magyar minority.

The coalition government formed by the VPN/MNI, the KDH and the DS, was reform-oriented in terms of its economic programme (which was comparable to the federal programme of economic reform) and in terms of its support for the common state. The dividing line between the government coalition and the opposition was defined not only by the different approaches to democratic and economic reforms, but also by the conflict over the future of the common Czechoslovak state and the status of the Magyar minority. The ethnic division of the electorate was promoted by nationalist-oriented parties and movements, and it resulted in the formation of two parallel party systems, one Slovak and one Magyar (Malová 1995, 2–3). This made the Magyar parties choose their political partners not on political, economic or ideological grounds, but with reference to ethnicity.

In the early part of the electoral period 1990–92, the profiles of the political formations were mainly influenced by the following factors: the initiation of the economic reforms, the slowly commencing change in social structure, the attempts at finding a solution to the constitutional problems, and the articulation of national minority demands. Regional differences also played a particular role. At the time, attempts at solving the problems of the national minorities did not yet impede co-operation within the governing coalition. The agenda was dominated by a common interest in concluding legislation on transformation, and implementing it. In April 1991, the government of Vladimír Mečiar of the VPN (later the HZDS) lost its parliamentary majority and was replaced by one led by Ján Čarnogurský from the coalition partner, the KDH. The first Mečiar government was voted out of office by the presidium of the parliament,[6] and not in a plenary session of the full chambers. In the plenary session, Mečiar could actually command a majority, but not so in the presidium where the parliamentary parties were not proportionately represented.

The initial Czech–Slovak consensus started falling apart after the 1990 elections, due to the emerging cleavages. The electoral term, shortened to only two years, was characterized by long-running constitutional conflicts concerning the division of powers and competence between the federation and the republics. These conflicts also showed in the relationships between the Czech and Slovak elites, and within the Slovak elite. The Slovak elite stressed the national principle and greater autonomy of the republics, while the Czech elite put stronger emphasis on the federation.

In 1991, the broad-based VPN movement split into two clearly defined political formations: the Movement for a Democratic Slovakia (HZDS) and the Civic Democratic Union (ODÚ–VPN). The former won over the majority of the VPN rank and file, and was more nationalist and leftist than the latter. In 1994, the Alliance of Democrats broke off from the HZDS and formed the liberal Democratic Union together with some other political forces.

The differences between Czech and Slovak attitudes to the federation were determined not only by incongruous considerations pertaining to the transformation, but also by the deviating dispositions towards the present and the past. The reasons for this were to be found in the two republics' disparate historical development, in Slovakia's new position in the common state after the 1968 establishment of the Czechoslovak federation, and in the two countries' dissimilar political cultures. In the Czech Republic, citizens were aware of certain problems in the transformation process, but still perceived a change for the better. In Slovakia, however, the transformation process was evaluated differently (*Tables 7.16, 7.17, 7.18 and 7.19*).

Table 7.16: General political satisfaction: In general, do you feel things in the Slovak Republic are going in the right or in the wrong direction? (%)

	1991	1992	1993	1994
Right	24.9	47.0	31.0	24.7
Wrong	52.5	45.8	69.0	64.6
Don't know	22.6	6.5	–	10.7

Source: CEEB 2; CEEB 3; CEEB 4; CEEB 5

Table 7.17: Satisfaction with economic reforms: The economic reforms in the Slovak Republic are going – (%)

	1991	1992	1993	1994
Too fast	31.6	16.3	14.0	13.2
Too slow	27.1	32.6	55.1	63.2
Right way	26.6	37.2	27.5	9.5
n/a, Don't know	14.7	5.6	3.5	10.7

Source: CEEB 2; CEEB 3; CEEB 4; CEEB 5

Table 7.18: Satisfaction with the development of democracy(%)

	1991	1992	1993	1994
Very satisfied	0.6	1.5	1.7	1.5
Fairly satisfied	15.5	21.9	19.0	15.3
Not very satisfied	56.8	57.2	57.3	55.1
Not at all satisfied	20.6	16.6	22.0	25.2

Source: CEEB 2; CEEB 3; CEEB 4; CEEB 5

Table 7.19: Evaluation of human rights situation: How much respect is there for individual human rights nowadays in the Slovak Republic? (%)

	1991	1992	1993	1994
A lot of respect	17.5	26.6	19.8	21.4
Some respect	45.8	37.1	44.4	44.3
Not much respect	22.0	21.1	23.0	19.9
No respect at all	8.5	6.7	12.8	9.1
Don't know	6.2	8.5	–	5.2

Source: CEEB 2; CEEB 3; CEEB 4; CEEB 5

The more left-oriented stance of the Slovak citizens, as compared to the Czechs, is often explained by a more positive attitude towards the previous regime. Krivý (1996, 41) argues that traditional Slovak society did not turn to socialism immediately after the Second World War, but later was attracted to it due to its statist paternalism, collectivism, closed character, egalitarianism and anti-intellectual attitude. Indeed, it is better to compare the two countries on the liberalism–parternalism axis than on the left–right axis (Tymowski and Petrusek 1992). The more positive attitude of Slovak citizens towards the past should, however, not be understood as an expression of particular socialist sentiments, but rather as a preference for the paternalistic mission of the state, as a manifestation of economic thought, and as an evaluation of the economic reforms and their anticipated costs. Important were also the different attitudes towards political leadership, the methods of conflict resolution, and towards the boundaries of democratic behaviour (Krivý 1993).

The different orientations of Czech and Slovak citizens, as represented by the political parties, are best described in terms of a two-dimensional space with two reference axes: paternalism–liberalism and civic–national; or statist paternalism–liberal market economy and libertarian–authoritarian (Kitschelt 1992, Brokl 1994). The party positions on these two axes go a long way towards accounting for the different structuring of the Czech and Slovak party systems.

The two countries also differed in their attitudes towards religion. In Slovakia, the proportion of devout believers is considerably higher than in the Czech Republic. This difference did not, however, lead to a conflict between the countries, as it was sublimated into the civic-national cleavage. The national-oriented Slovak parties found greater support in the Catholic constituency than among secular, Greek Catholic and Orthodox voters (Krivý 1996).

The developments of the early 1990s lead up to the resolution of the historic Czechoslovak civic/national cleavage in 1992. In the elections of that year, Slovak voters preferred formations that supported the national principle, while the Czech electorate embraced parties which represented the civic principle.

The 1992 Elections and Their Effects

The victors in the 1992 elections in the Czech and Slovak republics were political parties of different hues. The Democratic Citizens' Party in the Czech Republic presented a liberal, market-oriented and libertarian profile, while the HZDS in Slovakia was paternalist-oriented, authoritarian-tinged and emphasized the national principle. In its electoral programme, the HZDS stressed the necessity of continuing the transformation process and supported the voucher privatization strategy, but at the same time voiced concern about the sale of state property to foreign investors and emphasized the need for a strong social policy. Before the 1992 elections, the HZDS influenced voters through a suggestive, emancipatory rhetoric, while at the same time obscuring the constitutional problems with a social argumentation containing elements of social demagoguery (Bútorová 1993, 95). Due to the terminological haze enveloping the constitutional revision process, it is possible that the electorate actually voted for social security and a range of personal perceptions, rather than for an independent national state.

The number of parties in the Slovak National Council fell from eight to five. The second strongest party, though far behind the HZDS, was the post-communist SDL, while the KDH came in third this time. The fourth party gaining representation was the Slovak National Party, and the fifth a coalition of ethnic-Magyar parties. Among these parties one could discern a stronger territorial differentiation, reflecting the irregular pattern of habitation. In general, one may speak of a differentiation both along the East–West axis (Western, Central and Eastern Slovakia), and between the North and the South.

Sentiments before the 1992 elections were vastly different from the euphoria in 1990. There was a general scepticism over the new political elite dominated by the VPN and the KDH, and a fatigue with the drawn-out, puzzling negotiations about the future of the common Czech-Slovak state. The strongest Slovak advocate of the idea of a common state, the Civic Democratic Union (ODÚ), did not overcome the threshold for parliamentary representation;[7] voters felt that it did not stand up for Slovak interests and that it lacked concern for the plight of the common man. The distrust in the dominant political elite, and its ability to emancipate Slovakia, was combined with fears that the reform process would lead to the subjugation of Slovak national interests to the more economically advanced Czech parts of the federation. Hence, the Slovak electorate rallied to a political force which symbolized national emancipation and held out the promise of maintaining the socialist welfare state.

Table 7.20: Attitudes towards the collapse of the Czechoslovak federation (%)

		6/92	7/92	9/92	10/92	11/92
Czech Republic	*For*	35.5	43.7	46	51	50
	Against	64.5	56.3	45	38	43
	Don't know	–	–	9	11	7
Slovak Republic	*For*	34.9	36.8	41	37	40
	Against	65.1	63.2	46	52	49
	Don't know	–	–	13	11	11

Source: IVVM (Institute for Public Opinion Research) 1992.

The dismantling of the Czechoslovak federation might seem puzzling considering the fairly strong mass-level preferences for a common state (*Table 7.20*), but it may be attributed to long-term trends within the Slovak polity. In pre-war democratic Czechoslovakia, the Slovaks emerged as a genuine nation with a corresponding tendency towards the attainment of national sovereignty in the form of an individual state. Then, this sovereignty could be realized either by reference to the democratic civic principle of the Czech-Slovak political nation, or to the national principle – as was indeed the case when an 'independent' Slovak state was formed after the fascist occupation of Czechoslovakia. The historically-based tendency to democratic conflict resolution was later suppressed by the communist regime, which, however, did not open up for a national solution. It was obviously the Slovak political elite that articulated the need for national decision-making autonomy. From this followed the concept of another type of federation, strongly resembling a confederation. It should also be pointed out that the decision to break up the common Czech–Slovak state was taken at the elite level.

The electoral success enabled the HZDS to form what was nearly a one-party government. Vladimír Mečiar was again appointed Prime Minister. Before the elections, the SDL, which emerged as the second strongest party, had advocated the formation of a grand coalition, but victory at the polls provided the means for Mečiar to govern without the support of such a broad-based combination. Soon after the government presented its manifesto, on 17 June 1992 the Slovak National Council declared the sovereignty of the Slovak Republic. The declaration began with the following words: 'We, the democratically elected Slovak National Council, solemnly declare that the Slovak people's thousand-year long effort to reach independence has been successful'.

The negotiations to form a federal coalition government between the ODS and the HZDS – respectively the Czech and Slovak victors in the 1992 elections – revealed fundamental disagreements pertaining to the constitutional order. The ODS had set out to save the federation, which was not the case for the HZDS. The political negotiations continued for several rounds, the fifth of which resulted in a political agreement which in practice necessitated the transformation of Czechoslovakia into two independent entities. This called for either the formation of a new working federation or for the division of the then federation into two truly independent states; of these two alternatives, the latter was the eventual outcome. The KDH opposed the break-up of the federation, as did, with some reservation, the ambivalent and tactically manoeuvring SDL. Nevertheless, the SDL eventually voted for the Slovak declaration of sovereignty.

Independent Slovakia

Newly independent Slovakia was one of the smallest states in Central Europe, encompassing a considerable Magyar minority – 14 per cent of the population are not ethnic Slovaks. The resolution of the Czech-Slovak constitutional strife and the realization of the national cleavage provided for the stronger articulation of the national Slovak/Magyar cleavage and its resolution. The Slovak representative system did not, however, manage to harmonize the national principle with civil society. After the 1992 elections, the proponents of Slovak independence did not have a positive programme for the formation of a civic state; instead of a democratic principle of inclusion, they went for exclusion (Szomolányi 1997, 21).

In the newly independent state, the conflict between the governing coalition and the opposition to the continuation of democratization and the market reforms – in particular privatization – led to the gradual re-composition of the Slovak parliament, as several MPs left the HZDS. This resulted in the fall of the Mečiar minority government and the decision to hold early elections. The new government, with Jozef Moravčík as Prime Minister, was a broad-based 'right–center–left' coalition which included not only Slovak oppositional groups but also parties representing the Magyar minority. Moravčík's coalition was composed of the KDH, the SDL, the Alternative of Political Realism (APR), the Alliance of Democrats (AD), the New Alternative (NA) as well as the ethnic-Magyar parties *Együttélés* (Co-existence) and the Magyar Christian Democratic Movement. The Moravčík government was in power for six months, and despite its political heterogeneity, it supported the transition towards a liberal market economy. The fact that it was oriented towards the EU and NATO structures did not, however, win unequivocal public support.

The 1994 Early Elections

The results of the 1994 pre-term elections did not return Moravčík's liberal, market and civic-oriented government to power. In fact, the elections confirmed the stable orientation of the electorate towards political forces representing state paternalism, authoritarian and populist tendencies, and a nationalist stance. Voters' positions in the social structure did not determine electoral behaviour, and the socioeconomic cleavage proved to be of minor importance; the correspondence of voters' personal value orientation with that of the parties' character was decisive for party choice. From a programmatic and ideological point of view, the elections did not result in a clearer outline of the Slovak political scene.

In 1994, seven formations gained representation in parliament. With three electoral coalitions involved, no fewer than sixteen parties actually gained representation. The government formed after the elections was again led by the ideologically ambiguous HZDS, this time supported by the nationalist, or rather right-oriented SNS and by the populist, left-oriented ZRS. The ZRS's base of support is mainly among workers and the unemployed. The coalition therefore included parties which preferred the national and collectivist principle to the civic and national one, and this showed in its position on integration into the EU and NATO. With the creation of an independent Slovakia, the SNS lost its major *raison d'être* and had to find a new identity. It gradually evolved into a extreme nationalist party, looking for partners among other European republican parties.

Table 7.21 Attitudes towards EU and NATO membership: 'Imagine that a referendum is to be held on the next weekend. How would you answer the following questions: Do you agree with Slovakia's integration into the EU? Do you agree with Slovakia's joining NATO?' (%)

| | EU | | NATO | |
	1995	*1997*	*1995*	*1997*
I would answer 'yes'	59	56	43	39
I would answer 'no'	13	12	22	21
I would not participate	15	17	18	23
Don't know	13	16	18	18
Positive answers, %	82	82	66	65

Sources: FOCUS, December 1995 and January 1997.

The opposition, too, was heterogeneous. The KDH was, and remains, a right-oriented, traditional conservative party with a mono-confessional base, and oriented towards European integration.[8] The Common Choice (SV) – an electoral coalition formed by the SDL, the SDSS, the Green Party of Slovakia and the Movement of Peasants – supported the paternalistic role of the state in economic policy, rejected liberal individualism, but nevertheless championed integration into European structures. The Democratic Union, also in opposition, profiled itself as a liberal, market-oriented party supporting integration into the EU and NATO (*Table 7.21*). The coalition of Magyar parties was supported by ethnic Magyar voters, not purely on the basis of its programmatic orientation, but also as a champion and defender of the interests of the Magyar minority in Slovakia. The Magyar alliance included liberal, market-oriented parties as well as paternalistic-oriented ones.

Table 7.22: Development of party preferences in Slovakia in 1995–97 (percentage of respondents declaring that they would vote for:)

Party	7/94	2/96	4/96	6/96	9/96	11/96	1/97
HZDS	29.4	30.8	32.4	28.0	28.3	24.4	24.5
KDH	10.3	11.9	10.8	12.8	10.8	13.2	12.7
DÚ	11.9	9.7	8.2	9.4	10.9	11.4	12.2
SDL	7.6	10.6	10.0	9.1	9.9	8.8	11.0
MKDH	3.9	6.9	7.4	7.5	6.2	7.5	7.3
SNS	6.3	5.6	6.4	6.4	5.6	7.1	5.3
ZRS	6.9	5.0	4.3	5.1	3.8	3.7	4.6
DS	3.6	4.0	4.8	5.1	5.0	6.2	5.3
SZS	1.3	3.8	4.3	5.4	5.6	4.5	2.6
KSS	3.4	2.9	2.9	3.7	3.9	4.5	4.4
SDSS	2.9	2.2	2.9	3.2	3.8	5.0	4.3
Együttélés	3.9	3.4	3.1	2.7	3.4	1.5	2.7
MOS	2.1	2.1	1.7	1.1	2.4	1.5	2.0

Source: Bútora 1997, 347

After the 1994 elections, the Slovak political arena developed through a process which followed two dimensions. The first was the democratic versus authoritarian cleavage, which was represented with an ever-growing differentiation between 'standard' and non-standard' political parties – a classification often used by Slovak political scientists – and which corresponded with the traditional left–right axis. 'Standard' parties are the ones with counterparts in the European 'party families' – i.e. all the opposition parties: the KDH, DÚ, DS, SDL, SDSS, MKDH, MOS and *Együttélés*. Currently, the strength of support for these parties is growing (*Table 7.22*) and they have built up a 'democratic coalition'. 'Non-standard' parties are those which cannot be classified as: this group includes all the post-1994 Slovak government parties, the HZDS, SNS and ZRS. With reference to Herbert Kitschelt's typology of parties according to their organization (1995, 449), Szomolányi (1997) has categorized the 'non-standard' parties as charismatic and clientelistic, whereas the 'standard' parties are programmatic. The second dimension along which Slovak politics developed was the natural ideological differentiation of the 'standard' parties (Mesežnikov 1994, 101–4). This stabilization of the party system may be seen as a reflection of the structural development of the civic/national and the East/West cleavages – although the Movement for a Democratic Slovakia (HZDS) attempts to present itself as a force outside and above the latter cleavage, as a bridge between East and West.

The Present Political Scene

As a result of the existing national/cosmopolitan, democratic/authoritarian, and socioeconomic conflict structures, the Slovak political scene is segmented into distinct political sub-cultures represented by two parliamentary groupings. One is formed by the national-populist government parties – the HZDS, the ZRS and the SNS – and the other by the opposition parties KDH, DÚ, DS, SDL, SDSS and SZ. The opposition includes the whole political spectrum from the right-oriented, conservative KDH to the post-communist SDL, which is oriented towards the Socialist International. The credibility of top political institutions is still high in Slovakia in comparison with the Czech Republic (*Table 7.23*, compare with *Table 7.13*).

The developments in the Slovak party structure shows that a classical Rokkan-type cleavage is coming to the forefront. One may discern both an ethnic (Slovak/Magyar) cleavage and a regionally differentiated cleavage between East and West or between centre and periphery. The existence of a 'broad-spectrum' government coalition and a left/right opposition serves as a clear indication of this.

It is obvious that the main political base of the governing coalition is found in the socially conservative rural areas, not in the culturally more modern urban or metropolitan milieu. Krivý (1997, 39) stresses the importance of Slovakia's rural past, as the rapid and delayed industrialization process did not really start until the 1950s. In a way, the rural/urban cleavage supersedes national/civil society cleavage.

Table 7.23 Credibility of top political institutions in Slovakia (%)

	12/94	3/95	6/95	10/95	12/95	2/96	9/96	1/97
Constitutional Court	61	61	58	–	65	61	59	66
President	67	66	55	48	59	52	56	56
National Council	57	51	41	41	53	48	44	44
Government	52	45	39	40	42	40	36	40

Source: FOCUS 1994, 1995, 1996 and 1997

The culmination of the historical Czech/Slovak cleavage in the form of the resolution of the constitutional argument through the establishment of two independent states, opened up vistas for a stronger articulation of the national Slovak/Magyar cleavage and its resolution. Subsequently, this had a major influence on the formation and operation of the Slovak political system. Other historically-determined conflicts operate within the framework of this cleavage, although not institutionalized to the same extent. One should, however, not underestimate their importance. Among these conflicts is the issue of a Western versus an Eastern orientation, reflected in another cleavage dividing the Slovak political spectrum – that of a national or a cosmopolitan orientation, manifested in the diverging attitudes towards the integration into the European structures of the EU and NATO.

From the civic or national point of view, the collectivist/individualist conflict dimension permeates the whole political scene. A majority of the electorate prefers the nationalist–populist parties, which reject individualism and advocate collective solutions of problems. The socioeconomic cleavage has so far not had a decisive influence on electoral behaviour, due to the fact that the transformation of the social structure is not yet completed. Voters do not make decisions according to their personal social position, but according to other criteria.

Acronyms of Parties, Movements and Coalitions

THE CZECH REPUBLIC

ČMUS	Bohemian and Moravian Union of the Centre *(Českomoravská unie středu)*
ČSSD	Czech Social Democratic Party *(Česká strana sociálně demokratická)*
DEU	Democratic Union *(Demokratická unie)*
HSD-SMS	Self-Governing Democracy Movement–Association for Moravia and Silesia *(Hnutí za samosprávnou demokracii–sdružení pro Moravu a Slezsko)*
KDU-ČSL	Christian Democratic Union/Czechoslovak Peoples' Party *(Křesťansko demokratická unie/Československá strana lidová)*
KDS	Christian Democratic Party *(Křesťansko demokratická strana)*
KSČM	Communist Party of Bohemia and Moravia *(Komunistická strana Čech a Moravy)*
LB	Left Block *(Levý blok)*, consisted of the Left Bloc and the Communist Party of Bohemia and Moravia
LSNS	National Socialist Liberal Party *(Liberální strana národně sociální)*
LSU	Liberal Social Union *(Liberálně sociální unie)*, a formation with three collective members: the Czechoslovak Socialist Party, Green Party and Agrarian Party
ODA	Civic Democratic Alliance *(Občanská demokratická aliance)*
ODS	Civic Democratic Party *(Občanská demokratická strana)*
OF	Civic Forum *(Občanské hnutí)*
OH/SD	Free Democrats/Civic Movement *(Občanské hnutí/Svobodní demokraté)*
SPR-RSČ	Association for the Republic–Republican Party of Czechoslovakia *(Sdružení pro republiku–Republikánská strana Československa)*
SZ	Green Party *(Strana zelených)*
US	Freedom Union *(Unie svobody)*
ZS	Agrarian Party *(Zemědělská strana)*

SLOVAKIA

AD	Alliance of Democrats *(Aliancia demokratov)*. Later merged with AD to form the Democratic Union *(Demokratická únia)*
APR	Alternative of Political Realism *(Alternatíva politického realismu)*
DS	Democratic Party *(Demokratická strana)*
DÚ	Democratic Union of Slovakia *(Demokratická únia Slovenska)*
Együttélés	Spolužitie, Coexistentia, Co-Existence
HP	Movement of Peasants *(Hnutie polnohospodárov)*
HZDS	Movement for a Democratic Slovakia *(Hnutie za demokratické Slovensko)*
HZPČS	Movement for a Prosperous Czechia and Slovakia *(Hnutie za prosperujúce Česko a Slovensko)*
KDH	Christian-Democratic Movement *(Kresťansko-demokratické hnutie)*
KSS	Communist Party of Slovakia *(Komunistická strana Slovenska)*
KSU	Christian Social Union *(Kresťansko-sociálna únia)*
MK	Magyar Coalition *(Magyar Koalicio, Maďarská koalícia)*
MKDH	Magyar Christian Democratic Movement *(Maďarské krestiansko demokratické hnutie)*
MNI	Magyar Independent Initiative *(Maďarská nezávislá iniciativa)*
MOS	Magyar Civic Party *(Maďarská občianska strana)*
NA	New Alternative *(Nová alternatíva)*
NS	Movement New Slovakia *(Hnutie Nové Slovensko)*
ODÚ	Civic Democratic Union *(Občianská demokratická únia)*
ROI	Roma Civic Initiative *(Rómska občianska iniciativa)*
RSDS	Real Social Democracy of Slovaks *(Reálna sociálna demokracia Slovakov)*
RSS	Peasant Party of Slovakia *(Rolnická strana Slovenska)*
SDC	Party of the Democratic Centre *(Strana demokratického centra)*
SDL	Party of the Democratic Left *(Strana demokratickej lavice)*
SDSS	Social Democratic Party of Slovakia *(Socialno-demokratická strana Slovenska)*
SNS	Slovak National Party *(Slovenská národná strana)*
SOS	Party of Civic Concord *(Strana občianskej svornosti)*
SPK	Party Against Corruption–For Order, Work and Money for Decent People *(Strana proti korupcii–za poriadok, prácu a peniaze pre slušných ľudí)*
SSL	Freedom Party *(Strana slobody)*
SV	Common Choice *(Spoločná volba)*; 1994 electoral coalition between SDL, SDSS, SZS and HP
SZA	Slovak Green Alternative *(Slovenská zelená alternatíva)*
SZS	Green Party of Slovakia *(Strana zelených na Slovensku)*
VPN	Public Against Violence *(Verejnosť proti násiliu)*
ZZR	Association for the Republic–Republicans *(Združenie za republiku – Republikáni)*
ZRS	Association of Workers of Slovakia *(Združenie robotníkov Slovenska)*

NOTES

1. The opinions presented here are the products of many years of discussions and a unpublished paper of the Project Group 'Change in Political Systems' at the Institute of Sociology at the Czech Academy of Sciences, of which the author is a member.
2. The 1918–38 Czechoslovak Republic was a multi-national state, incorporating some of the most backward regions of the Austro–Hungarian monarchy, with their particular contradictions and newly crystallising cleavages. For twenty years (1918–38), the Czechs and Slovaks attempted to build a common political system; Czechoslovak politicians strove to solve the cleavage on a civic basis. During the communist era, the split was in fact cemented by the asymmetrical constitutional arrangement.
3. In the spring of 1996, the Christian Democratic Party merged with the Civic Democratic Party.

4. In January 1993, the HSD–SMS changed its name into HSDMS (The Movement for Self-Governing Democracy of Moravia and Silesia). The same month some deputies from the HSD–SMS left the parliamentary club to form the HSD-SMS II club in order to better protect the interests of Moravia. In January 1994 the HSDMS again changed its name to ČMSS (Czech Moravian Party of the Centre); in December 1994 it fused with a faction of the of LSU club and was renamed the ČMSS (Czech Moravian Union of the Centre).

5. The Slovak National Council reduced the threshold to 3 per cent (although it raised it back to 5 per cent for the 1992 elections). Otherwise, the same electoral law applied for the federal parliament as well as for the two national parliaments, the Czech and Slovak National Councils.

6. According to Article 122 (1) of the Constitutional Act on Czechoslovak Federation.

7. The attempt to create a Civic Democratic Party also in Slovakia early in 1992 possibly took some votes away from the ODÚ.

8. Although the Roman Catholic Church plays a prominent role in Slovak society, the issue of religion has not emerged into the public realm with enough force to shape Slovak politics (Krause 1996, 173).

REFERENCES

Aktuálne problémy slovenskej spoločnosti–máj 1991. Bratislava, Ústav pre sociálnu analýzu UKo.

Brokl, Lubomír (1996), 'Parlamentní volby 1996', *Sociologický časopis*, Vol. 32, No. 4, 389–406.

——, ed., (1997a), *Reprezentace zájmů v politickém systému ČR. Pluralitní demokracie nebo neokorporativismus?* Prague, SLON.

—— (1997b), Past and present cleavages in the Czech Republic, MS, Prague, Institute of Sociology, Academy of Science of the Czech Republic.

—— and Zdenka Mansfeldová, (1993), 'Die letzten Wahlen der ČSFR 1992 und die Lage danach', *Berichte des Bundesinstituts für ostwissenschaftliche und internationale Studien*, No. 2.

—— et al. (1994), 'Politický prostor České republiky'. *Lidové noviny,* 11 November, 8.

—— and Zdenka, Mansfeldová (1995) 'Zerfall der Tschechoslowakei: strukturelle Ursachen und Parteihandeln', in Dieter Segert and Csilla Machos, eds., *Parteien in Osteuropa*, Opladen, Westdeutscher Verlag, 133–147.

—— and Zdenka Mansfeldová (1997) 'Czech and Slovak Political and Parliamentary Elites', in John Higley, Jan Pakulski and Wlodzimierz Weselowski, eds., *Postcommunist Elites and Democracy in Eastern Europe,* London, Macmillan.

Broklová, Eva, (1996) 'Historical Roots for the Restoration of Democracy in Czechoslovakia', in Ivan Gabal, ed., *The 1990 Election to the Czechoslovakian Federal Assembly: Analyses, Dokuments and Data*, Berlin, Edition Sigma, 25–50.

Bútora, Martin, ed. (1997), *Slovensko 1996*, Bratislava, Inštitút pre verejné otázky.

Bútorová, Zora (1993), 'Premyslené "áno" zániku ČSFR?', *Sociologický časopis*, Vol. 29, No.1, 88–104.

Commission of the European Communities 1991–, *Central and Eastern Eurobarometer,* Brussels, European Commission.

Dostál, Ondrej (1997), 'Minorities', in: Martin Bútora and Hunčík Pavol, eds., *Global Report of Slovakia,* Bratislava, Sándor Márai Foundation, 63–74.

Kitschelt, Herbert (1992), 'The Formation of Party Systems in East Central Europe', *Politics & Society*, Vol. 20, No. 1.

—— (1994), 'Party Systems in East Central Europe: Consolidation or Fluidity', Paper presented at the *Annual Meeting of the American Political Science Association*, New York, 1–4 September.

—— (1995), 'Formation of Party Cleavages in Post-Communist Democracies, *Party Politics*, Vol. 1, No. 4, 447–72.

Knutsen, Oddbjørn and Scarbrough, Elinor (1995). 'Cleavage Politics', in Jan W. van Deth, ed., *The Impact of Values,* Oxford, Oxford University Press, 493–523.

Krause, Kevin (1996), 'Systém politických stran v České republice, demokracie a volby roku 1996', *Sociologický časopis*, Vol. 32, No. 4, 423–38.

Krivý, Vladimír (1993), 'Slovenská a česká definícia situácie. Čas: 1992, január', *Sociologický časopis*, Vol. 29, No. 1, 73–87.

—— (1997), 'Regionálne súvislosti formovania režimu', in Soňa Szomolányi, ed., *Slovensko: problémy konsolidácie demokracie*, Bratislava, Friedrich Ebert Stiftung, 101–14.

——, Viera Feglová, and Daniel Balko (1996), *Slovensko a jeho regióny. Sociokultúrne súvislosti volebného správania*. Bratislava, Nadácia Médiá.

Lipset, Seymour Martin. and Stein Rokkan (1967), 'Cleavage Structures, Party Systems and Voters Alignments: An Introduction', in Seymour Martin Lipset and Stein Rokkan, eds., *Party Systems and Voter Alignments: Cross-National Perspectives*, New York, The Free Press.

Malová, Darina (1995), 'The institutionalization of parliamentary parties and political representation in Slovakia', paper prepared for the *Third Annual Conference of the Individual vs. The State Political Representation: Parties and Parliamentary Democracy*, Central European University, Budapest, 16–17 June.

Markowski, Radoslaw, (1995), *Political Competition and Ideological Dimensions in Central Eastern Europe*, Studies in Public Policy No. 257, Glasgow, University of Strathclyde.

Martin, William C. and Hopkins Karen (1980), 'Cleavage Crystallization and Party Linkages in Finland, 1900–1918', in Kay Lawson, ed., *Political Parties & Linkage*, New Haven and London, Yale University Press, 183–203.

Mesežnikov, Grigorij (1994), 'Parlamentné volby 1994: potvrdenije "rozdvojenosti" politickej scény na Slovensku', in Soňa Szomolányi and Grigorij Mesežnikov, eds., *Slovensko Volby 1994: Príčiny–dosledky–perspektívy*, Bratislava, Slovenské združenie pre politické vedy a Nadácia Friedricha Eberta, 101–11.

Novák, Miroslav (1996), 'Volby do poslanecké sněmovny, vládní nestabilita a perspektivy demokracie v ČR' *Sociologický časopis*, Vol. 32, No. 4, 407–22.

Sartori, Giovanni (1976), *Parties and Party Systems*, Cambridge, Cambridge University Press.

—— (1994) *Comparative Constitutional Engineering*, London, Macmillan Press.

Szomolányi, Soňa (1997), 'Aký režim sa vynára na Slovensku', in Soňa Szomolányi, ed., *Slovensko: problémy konsolidácie demokracie*, Bratislava, Friedrich Ebert Stiftung, 7–26.

Šanderová, Jadwiga (1993), 'Vnímání důsledků transformace českou a slovenskou populací', *Sociologický časopis*, Vol. 29, No. 1, 57–72.

Šimoník, Pavel (1996), 'Politické spektrum v České republice. Český volič mezi pravicí a levicí', *Sociologický časopis*, No. 4, 457–70.

Tymowski, Andrzej and Miroslav Petrusek (1992), 'Grafika politické scény: Československo a Polsko', *S-Obzor*, No.1, 31–5.

Večerník, Jiří (1996), 'Levice a pravice jisté, střed nejistý', *Lidové noviny*, 16 September, 8.

Vlachová, Klára (1996), 'Několik poznámek k matení pojmů', *Lidové noviny*, 6 September, 9.

Volby do Poslanecké sněmovny Parlamentu ČR 1996 z pohledu sociologie, *Sociologický časopis* 32, 471–92.

APPENDIX 7.1:   ELECTION RESULTS

Czech Republic

PARLIAMENTARY ELECTIONS

1990 Elections
Date: 8 and 9 June
Turnout: 96.8%

Party	Federal Assembly Chamber of People		Czech Republic Chamber of Nations	
	%	Seats	%	Seats
OF	49.9	50	53.1	68
KSČ	13.8	12	13.1	15
HSD–SMS	9.1	7	7.9	9
KDU	8.8	6	8.7	9
Others	18.4	–	16.8	–
Total	100.0	75	100.0	101

Czech National Assembly

Party	%	Seats
OF	49.5	127
KSČ	13.2	32
HSD–SMS	10.0	22
KDU–ČSL	8.4	19
Others	18.8	–
Total	100.0	200

1992 Elections
Date: 5 and 6 June
Turnout: 85.1%

Party	Federal Assembly Chamber of People		Czech Republic Chamber of Nations	
	%	Seats	%	Seats
ODS-KDS	33.4	37	33.9	48
LB	14.5	15	14.3	19
ČSSD	6.8	6	7.7	10
SPR-RSČ	6.8	6	6.5	8
KDU-ČSL	6.1	6	6.0	7
LSU	6.1	5	5.8	7
Others	26.8	–	25.8	–
Total	100.0	75	100.0	99

Czech National Assembly

Party	%	Seats
ODS-KDS	29.7	76
LB	14.0	35
ČSSD	6.5	16
LSU	6.5	16
KDU–ČSL	6.9	15
SPR–RSČ	6.0	14
ODA	5.9	14
HSD–SMS	5.9	14
Others	19.1	–
Total	100.0	200

1996 Elections to the Lower House of Parliament
Date: 31 May and 1 June
Turnout: 76.4%

Party	%	Seats
ODS	29.6	68
KDU–ČSL	8.1	18
ODA	6.4	13
ČSSD	26.4	61
KSČM	10.3	22
SPR-RSČ	8.0	18
Others	11.1	–
Total	100.0	200

1996 Elections to the Upper House of Parliament (Senát)
Date: 15–16 November (first round), 22–23 November (second round)
Turnout: 35.0% (first round), 30.6% (second round)

Party	%	Seats	Members elected for 2 years	4 years	6 years
ODS	39.5	32	13	13	6
ČSSD	30.9	25	5	9	11
KDU–ČSL	16.1	13	4	3	6
ODA	8.6	7	4	–	3
KSČM	2.5	2	–	1	1
DEU	1.2	1	–	1	–
Independent	1.2	1	1	–	–
Total	100.0	81	27	27	27

*1990, 1992 parliamentary elections for the Czech National Council and 1996 elections for the
Lower House of Parliament of the Czech Republic (parties winning more than 5 per cent of votes)*

Party	1990 %	1990 Seats	1992 %	1992 Seats	1996 %	1996 Seats
OF	49.5	127	–	–	–	–
ODS/KDS *	–	–	29.7	76	29.6	68
KDU/ČSL	8.4	19	6.3	15	8.1	18
ODA	–	–	5.9	14	6.7	13
HSD–SMS	10.0	22	5.9	14	–	–
LSU	–	–	6.5	16	–	–
ČSSD	–	–	6.5	16	26.4	61
KSČM	13.2	32	–	–	10.3	22
LB	–	–	14.1	35	–	–
SPR–RSČ	–	–	6.0	14	8.0	18
Others	18.8	200	19.1	200	11.1	150

* The Christian Democratic Party merged with the Democratic Party in 1996.

Slovakia

PARLIAMENTARY ELECTIONS

1990 Elections
Date: 8 and 9 June
Turnout: 98.9%

Party	Federal Assembly Chamber of People %	Seats	Slovak Republic Chamber of Nations %	Seats
VPN	32.5	19	37.3	33
KDH	19.0	11	16.7	14
KSS	13.8	8	13.4	12
SNS	11.0	6	11.4	9
Együttélés	8.6	5	8.5	7
Total		49		75

Slovak National Council

Party	%	Seats
VPN/MNI	29.3	48
KDH	19.2	31
SNS	13.9	22
KSS/	13.3	22
MKDH-*Együttélés*	8.7	14
DS	4.4	7
SZ	3.5	6
Others	7.7	
Total	100.0	150

1992 Elections
Date: 5 and 6 June
Turnout: 84.2%

Party	Federal Assembly Chamber of People		Slovak Republic Chamber of Nations	
	%	Seats	%	Seats
HZDS	33.5	24	33.8	33
SDL	14.4	10	14.0	13
SNS	9.4	6	9.4	8
KDH	9.0	6	8.8	9
Együttélés	7.4	5	7.4	7
SDSS	–	–	6.1	5
Others	26.3	–	20.5	–
Total	100.0	51	100.0	75

Slovak National Council

Party	%	Seats
HZDS	37.3	74
SDL	14.7	29
KDH	8.9	18
SNS	7.9	15
Együ.–MKDH	7.4	14 (9+5)
Others	23.8	–
Total	100.0	150

1994 Elections to the Slovak National Council
Date: 30 September–1 October 1994
Turnout: 75.7%

Party	%	Seats
HZDS	35.0	61
SV	10.4	18
KDH	10.1	17
Mag. Coalition	10.2	17
DÚ	8.6	15
ZRS	7.3	13
SNS	5.4	9
Others	13.0	–
Total	100.0	150

Note: The HZDS formed an electoral alliance with the Peasant Party of Slova-kia *(Roľnícka strana Slovenska);* the list also included some candidates of the Slovak Green Alternative *(Slovenská zelená alternatíva).* The Magyar Coalition joined the *Együttélés*–Magyar Christian Democratic Movement *(Maďarské kresťansko-demokratické hnutie)* and the Magyar Civic Party *(Maďarská občianská strana).*

APPENDIX 7.2: GOVERNMENT COMPOSITION

Federal Government

The Federal Čalfa Government after the 1990 Elections
Date of investiture: 27 June 1990

	Cabinet posts	
Party	Number	(%)
OF	9	(56)
VPN	4	(25)
KDH	2	(12)
Independent	1	(6)

The Federal Stráský Government after the 1992 Elections
Date of investiture: 3 July 1992

	Parliamentary seats		Cabinet posts	
Party	Number	(%)	Number	(%)
ODS	48	(32)	4	(40)
HZDS	24	(16)	4	(40)
KDU–ČSL	7	(5)	1	(10)
Independent	–	–	1	(10)

Czech Governments

Pithart Cabinet
Date of investiture: 30 June 1990

	Parliamentary seats		Cabinet posts	
Party	Number	(%)	Number	(%)
OF	127	(49)	10	(48)
KDU–ČSL	19	(8)	2	(9)
HSD–SMS	22	(10)	1	(5)
Independent	–	–	8	(38)

Klaus I Cabinet
Date of investiture: 3 July 1992

	Parliamentary seats		Cabinet posts	
Party	Number	(%)	Number	(%)
ODS	66	(33)	11	(58)
KDU–ČSL	15	(7)	4	(21)
ODA	14	(7)	2	(10)
KDS	10	(5)	2	(10)

Note: The table depicts the situation as of 4 January 1993. After the Czech Republic became independent, the government added two ministries, those of defence and transportation, which had previously existed only at the federal level.

Klaus II Cabinet
Date of investiture: 1 July 1996

Party	Parliamentary seats		Cabinet posts	
	Number	(%)	Number	(%)
ODS	68	(34)	8	(50)
KDU–ČSL	18	(9)	4	(22)
ODA	13	(6)	4	(22)
Total	99	(50)	16	

Tošovský Cabinet
Appointed by the President : 2 January 1998
Approved by parliament: 28 January 1998

Party	Parliamentary seats		Cabinet posts	
	Number	(%)	Number	(%)
ODS *	41	(34)	4	(24)
US	28			
KDU–ČSL	18	(9)	3	(18)
ODA	13	(6)	3	(18)
Independent	–	–	7	(41)
Total	–	–	17	

* ODS cabinet members were not nominated by their party. The parliamentary club split into an ODS caucus and the Freedom Union (US) club before the vote of confidence. Three former ODS ministers became members of the US.

Slovak Governments

Mečiar cabinet
Date of nomination: 27 June 1990

Party	Parliamentary seats		Cabinet posts	
	Number	(%)	Number	(%)
VPN	29.3	(48)	12	(52)
KDH	19.2	(31)	8	(35)
DS	4.4	(7)	3	(13)

Čarnogurský cabinet
Date of nomination: 23 April 1991

Party	Cabinet seats	
	Number	(%)
VPN *	12	(52)
KDH	9	(39)
DS	2	(9)

* The VPN split into HZDS and ODÚ–VPN only at the end of April. When Mečiar and some other ministers resigned and Ján Čarnogurský was appointed Prime Minister, the parliamentary situation became unclear and even some MPs were not sure of which party they belonged to.

Mečiar I Cabinet
Date of nomination: 24.June 1992

Party	Parliamentary seats		Cabinet posts	
	Number	(%)	Number	(%)
HZDS	74	(49)	13	(81)
SNS	15	(10)	1	(6)
Independent	–	–	2	(13)

Note: 14 ministries were nominated after the elections: 12 by HZDS, one by SNS and one independent. After the break-up of the federation, the Slovak government added two ministries which had previously only existed at the federal level.

Mečiar II Cabinet
Date of nomination: 10 November 1993

Party	Parliamentary seats		Cabinet posts	
	Number	(%)	Number	(%)
HZDS	66	(44)	13	(67)
SNS	8	(5)	3	(17)
Independent	–	–	3	(17)

Moravčík I Cabinet
Date of nomination: 16 March 1994

Party	Parliamentary seats		Cabinet posts	
	Number	(%)	Number	(%)
SDL	28	(19)	7	(39)
KDH	18	(12)	5	(28)
APR	10	(7)	4	(22)
AD	8	(5)	1	(6)
NDK	5	(3)	1	(6)

Mečiar III Cabinet
Date of nomination: 12 December 1994

Party	Parliamentary seats		Cabinet posts	
	Number	(%)	Number	(%)
HZDS	61	(41)	12	(67)
SNS	9	(6)	2	(11
ZRS	1	(9)	4	(22)

APPENDIX 7.3: THE ELECTORAL SYSTEM

The Czech Republic

An electoral system based on proportional representation was adopted before the June 1990 elections. The system was almost identical for all three parliaments in the Federation (the Federal Assembly, the Czech National Council, and the Slovak National Council).

The original Election Act was slightly amended before the elections in 1992. In 1995 a new Act on the Elections to the Parliament of the Czech Republic (No. 247/1995) was adopted, which included amendments of the elections to the Chamber of Deputies as well as new elections to the Senate, which was elected for the first time in 1996. The principles of the election system to the Chamber of Deputies are identical to the system adopted in 1990. The members of the Senate are elected in direct, majority elections.

The election system to the Chamber of Deputies is characterized by the following traits: multi-mandate constituencies (8); the number of deputies (mandates) for one constituency is calculated proportionately according to the number of valid votes in the constituency, competition among party lists; possibility of preference voting for the selection of candidates within the list; a 5 per cent threshold for individual parties and a higher one for coalitions (from 7 to 11 per cent); covering of the mandates within the constituency according to the Haggenbach–Bischoff formula.

The Senate is permanently active, the term of election is six years and every two years one third of 81 senators is elected. The elections take place in one-mandate constituencies. In the first round, candidates who win an absolute majority are elected. If no one gets an absolute majority, the two candidates with the greatest number of votes proceed to a second round.

A citizen who has reached the age of 21 and is a permanent resident in the territory of the Czech Republic, has the right to vote and can be elected to the Chamber of Deputies. For the Senate, the age limit is 40 years. The 1995 electoral law introduced a deposit of 200,000 Kč for each constituency a party is contesting. The deposit is returned to parties that pass the electoral threshold. In the elections to the Senate, the deposit is 20,000 Kč for each candidate; it is returned to candidates who obtain at least 6 per cent of the votes in their constituencies.

Slovakia

The National Council of the Slovak Republic has 150 deputies who are elected for a four-year period. Deputies are elected by secret ballot in general, equal, and direct elections. A citizen who has the right to vote, has reached the age of 21, and is permanently resident in the territory of the Slovak Republic, can be elected deputy. The office of parliamentary deputy is incompatible with holding offices as President, judge, prosecutor, member of the Police Corps, member of the Prison Guard Corps, and professional soldier. If a deputy is appointed member of the Government of the Slovak Republic, the mandate is not terminated; it is simply suspended.

The election system to the National Council of the Slovak Republic is characterized by the following traits: four multi-mandate constituencies; competition among party lists; a five per cent threshold for the individual parties and a 7 to 10 per cent threshold for electoral coalitions. In the 1990 elections, the threshold for the Slovak National Council was 3 per cent for a single party; mandates are allocated with the help of a divisor: the total number of valid votes is divided by the number of mandates for the election district, plus one.

APPENDIX 7.4: THE CONSTITUTIONAL FRAMEWORK

The Czech Republic

The Government is the supreme body of executive power. It consists of the Prime Minister, Deputy Prime Ministers and Ministers. The Government co-ordinates the activities of ministries and central bodies of State administration. It holds the right of legislative initiative and the right to express its opinion on any and all bills.

The Government makes decisions collectively. The adoption of a resolution of the Government requires the consent of more than one-half of all its members. The Government is authorized to issue Government decrees, signed by the Prime Minister and the appropriate member of the Government, and to implement Acts.

The Government is accountable to the Chamber of Deputies for the fulfilment of the State budget and it disposes of the Government budget reserve and controls the management of the funds of the State budget and the State Funds of the Republic.

The Prime Minister is appointed by the President of the Republic, who appoints other members of the Government upon his proposal and entrusts them with the control of ministries or other authorities. Within 30 days of its appointment, the Government shall appear before the Chamber of Deputies and request its vote of confidence. Should the newly appointed Government not receive the confidence of the Chamber of Deputies, a new Government is appointed. Should such an appointed Government not receive the confidence of the Chamber of Deputies, the President appoints the Prime Minister upon the proposal of the Chairman of the Chamber of Deputies.

The Government may request the vote of confidence of the Chamber of Deputies at any time. It may combine the question of confidence with the request that the Chamber of Deputies should resolve upon a Government Bill within three months. The Chamber of Deputies may express to the Government its no confidence at any time. However, a motion for a vote of no confidence will be discussed by the Chamber of Deputies only if submitted in writing by at least fifty deputies. The Government must resign after the constituent meeting of the newly elected Chamber of Deputies. Otherwise, the Government resigns if the Chamber of Deputies has refused it a requested vote of confidence or expressed its non-confidence.

The President of the Republic is elected for a term of five years at a joint session of both houses of Parliament. He may not be elected for more than two terms in a row. Any citizen qualified to stand for elections to the Senate is qualified to stand for election to the office of President. The presidency is non-partisan.

The President of the Republic cannot be held accountable as a result of the performance of his office. The President has the following powers: (1) He names and recalls the Prime Minister and members of the government, as well as accepts their resignations; (2) convenes sessions of the Assembly of Deputies; (3) dissolves the Assembly of Deputies; (4) empowers the government whose resignation he has accepted or which he has recalled with the temporary execution of its office until the naming of a new government; (5) appoints judges to the Constitutional Court and its chairman and vice- chairman with the approval of the Senate; (6) appoints the Chairman and Vice-Chairman of the Supreme Court; declares amnesties and grants pardons; (7) has the right to send laws, except for constitutional laws, back to Parliament; (8) signs laws; (9) appoints a President and Vice President of the Auditor General's Office; (10) appoints members of the Board of Governors of the Czech National Bank.

The Constitutional Court consists of 15 judges, appointed by the President for a period of 10 years with the agreement of the Senate.

Slovakia

The Government of the Slovak Republic is the supreme body of executive power. The Prime Minister is appointed and recalled by the President. The Government is accountable for the execution of its duties to the National Council of the Slovak Republic, which can pass a vote of non-confidence in it at any time.

Laws passed by the National Council of the Slovak Republic are signed by the Chairman of the National Council, the President and the Prime Minister. Bills can be tabled by committees of the National Council, individual deputies and the Government.

The President of the Slovak Republic is elected by the National Council of the Slovak Republic by secret ballot. A majority vote of three-fifths of all deputies is required for a candidate to be elected President. Any citizen of the Slovak Republic who is eligible to vote and has reached the age of 35, can be elected President. The same person can be elected President for a maximum of two consecutive five-year terms. The presidency is non-partisan. If a President-elect is a member of a political party, he has to rescind his membership for the duration of the term in office.

The President has the following tasks: He (1) represents the Slovak Republic outwardly and concludes and ratifies international treaties. He may delegate to the Government of the Slovak Republic or, with the Government's consent, to individual members of the Slovak Republic, the conclusion of international treaties that do not require approval by the National Council of the Slovak Republic; (2) receives and accredits ambassadors; (3) calls the constituent meeting of the National Council of the Slovak Republic; (4) may dissolve the National Council of the Slovak Republic if the policy statement of the Government of the Slovak Republic is not approved three times within six months after the elections; (5) signs laws; (6) appoints and recalls the Prime Minister and other members of the government, and higher-level state officials in cases specified by law; (7) appoints university professors and rectors, appoints and promotes generals; (8) awards distinctions; (9) grants amnesty and pardon; (10) acts as Supreme Commander of the Armed Forces; (11) declares martial law at the recommendation of the Government of the Slovak Republic and declares war on the basis of a decision of the National Council of the Slovak Republic; if the Slovak Republic is attacked or as a result of commitments arising from international treaties on common defence against aggression; (12) declares a state of emergency on the basis of a constitutional law; (13) calls referenda; (14) can return to the National Council of the Slovak Republic constitutional and other laws with comments; (15) presents to the National Council of the Slovak Republic reports on the state of the Slovak Republic and on important political issues, submits to it draft laws and proposals for other measures.

The National Council of the Slovak Republic can recall the President from his post if the President is engaged in activity directed against the sovereignty and territorial integrity of the Slovak Republic or in activity aimed at eliminating the Slovak Republic's democratic constitutional system. In such cases, the motion to recall the President may be tabled by more than one-half of all deputies. The consent of at least a three-fifths majority of all deputies is required for the President to be recalled.

The Constitutional Court consists of 10 justices elected for a period of seven years. They are appointed by the President of the Slovak Republic from a list of 20 candidates proposed to him by the National Council of the Slovak Republic.

8. Hungary

Gábor Tóka

Students of mass electoral behaviour have often argued that the bulk of the voters do not seem to respond strongly to the topical issues of the day, but continue voting according to long-established patterns. 'Critical elections' – marked by particularly intense contestation, a jump in turnout, and a sudden change in what kind of opinions and group identities will go together with a preference for one or the other party alternative – occur rarely, if at all. Electoral change is glacially slow.

This often-noted dominance of persistent divisions over short-term effects elevated the notion of cleavages to a central place in the study of electoral behaviour. This chapter will discuss how Hungarian political parties after 1989 mobilized or downplayed potential cleavage lines, and how the voters responded. It will also offer some thoughts on why this happened and how all this influenced the way the political system works. In this chapter, the cleavage concept will be used in a colloquial way, so as to avoid the theoretical issue of whether all persistent political divisions can be called cleavages. Thus, cleavage is 'a tendency in rocks or crystals to divide or split in certain directions' and 'the process of division of a fertilized ovum by which the original single cell becomes a mass of smaller cells' (*The New International Webster's Comprehensive Dictionary of the English Language* 1995, 246). In other words, cleavages are assumed to divide a society politically only if that division is triggered by political events, but the way they divide camps is determined by factors that predate the triggering event.

General propositions

It has become part of conventional wisdom that Eastern European cleavage structures are doomed to be weak. Strong cleavage mobilization presumes organizational carriers and collective identities, over and above the political parties themselves. After decades of systematic destruction and officially encouraged erosion of social pluralism, the post-communist countries may have very little of cleavage politics. Ethnicity may at times be an exception, as ethno-linguistic identities were occasionally promoted by the Soviet-type regimes, but in all other respects East European party politics is likely to be even more fluid than is common in new democracies. Established parties will split and decline, and new ones will emerge out of the blue with an astonishing regularity, as politicians will – quite rightly – expect that voters have only the shallowest of loyalties to the parties they supported previously (Mair 1996). Indeed, aggregate volatility (i.e. the percentage of the vote changing hands between different parties from one election to another)[1] seems to be much higher all over East Central Europe than in Italy and Germany after the Second World War, or in Spain, Portugal and Greece in the 1970s and early 1980s (Tóka 1997).[2] The 28.3 per cent net volatility between the 1990 and 1994 Hungarian elections is three-and-a-half times higher than the West European average between 1885 and 1985, and comparable to the very highest West European figures registered in that period, such as the 32 and 27 per cent figures produced by the first elections in Weimar Germany.[3]

The excessive fragmentation of the party system, and the consequent difficulty of sustaining for long a legislative majority behind any govern-ment or coherent policy, may be a scary but not necessarily inevitable result of volatile elite and mass behaviour. The stalemate in the fractionalized legislature will then provide ample justification for the expansion of presidential powers and rule by decree. While this scenario of curtailing democracy is familiar from some member states of the Commonwealth of Independent States (CIS), it is certainly not what has been happening in Hungary in the 1990s. Quite to the contrary, Hungarian politicians and political analysts alike commonly emphasize how much political stability their country has had since 1989, compared to other post-communist countries.

While the vigour of their reasoning may be taken as an indication that they themselves see something unexpected or unnatural in this somewhat overstated tranquillity, they seem to have a point. No significant consti-tutional change has occurred since May 1990; the election law has remained almost unchanged since October 1989;[4] political violence remained unheard of and political freedom is well preserved (cf. Karatnycky 1997; US State Dept. 1997 and previous editions of the same two reports). The number of working days lost because of industrial disputes has been among the lowest in Europe, and not a single no-confidence motion was tabled in the parliament. Elections have taken place strictly on schedule in March–April 1990 and in May 1994, and were, as this volume went to press, set to be held on schedule in May 1998.

It may be unwarranted to present all these as obvious signs of political maturity and success, but the appearance of stability is conspicuous enough to call for explanation. It is not that Hungarians have been particularly happy with their political system or their governments. In 1990 as well as in 1994, the incumbent government suffered a humiliating defeat, with the opposition winning, respectively, over 90 and over 80 per cent of the seats in the incoming parliament (Appendix 8.1). Comparative surveys like the Central and Eastern Eurobarometer, the New Democracies Barometer, and the International Social Justice Survey have always found Hungarians among the (economically and politically) most dissatisfied nations in Europe – if not as wary of the transformation process as the people of Belarus, Bulgaria, Russia and Ukraine (Commission 1991–; Rose and Haerpfer 1996, 25, 81; Alwin 1992). Table 8.1 demonstrates the dramatic depth of the persistent popular disenchantment in Hungary.

Table 8.1: Satisfaction with the development of democracy: On the whole, are you satisfied, fairly satisfied, not very satisfied or not at all satisfied with the way democracy is developing in our country? Combined proportion of 'satisfied' and 'fairly satisfied' respondents from the autumn of 1991 to November 1995 (%) [5]

	1991	1992	1993	1994	1995
Albania	44	45	42	33	59
Armenia	n/a	11	8	9	18
Belarus	n/a	12	15	14	17
Bulgaria	46	40	23	4	14
Croatia	n/a	n/a	n/a	n/a	55
Czechoslovakia	29	n/a	n/a	n/a	n/a
Czech Republic	n/a	40	50	45	48
Estonia	36	31	41	36	39
Georgia	n/a	48	n/a	20	48
Hungary	34	23	21	25	20
Kazakhstan	n/a	n/a	n/a	14	23
Latvia	42	19	32	28	30
Lithuania	62	53	38	33	28
Macedonia	n/a	49	47	36	40
Poland	35	37	41	27	57
Romania	43	30	34	32	39
Russia	18	12	17	8	6
Slovakia	n/a	23.	21	18	29
Slovenia	n/a	48	38	35	37
Ukraine	n/a	18	18	19	17

Neither do Hungarians show much deference to their political leaders. On the one hand, the transition to democracy did not involve revolutionary catharsis or the birth of a new state – which probably makes the absence of hugely popular political leaders and movements more understandable. On the other hand, non-elites appear to be perfectly able to organize on their own, if not to sustain these efforts. In late October 1990, just a few hours after the announcement of an unexpected petrol price rise, non-unionized taxi and lorry drivers organized a three-day-long, nation-wide road blockade, which eventually forced the government to agree to compromise. In the Winter of 1992/93, a group of lower class citizens established the 'Society of Those Living Under the Subsistence Level' (LÉT) and swiftly collected vastly more than the required number of signatures to initiate a referendum (their proposed referendum question was whether the current parliament should be dissolved and early elections called; the Constitutional Court did not allow these issues to become the subjects of a referendum).

Why, then, did the Hungarian political system prove so stable – or rigid? There are reasons to doubt that the stability and legitimacy of the constitutional framework was a product of developments in the party political arena, and thus in the cleavage structure (Tóka 1997). Rather, the stability of governments – given the considerable number of policy U-turns and cabinet reshuffles, one should rather talk of the endurance of prime ministers and, to a lesser extent, of coalitions – was probably more a result of the institution of the constructive vote of no-confidence than anything else (Szoboszlai 1996). In a similar vein, the dearth of protest and populism stemming from economic plight might be explained by a number of socio-structural features without much reference to party politics (Greskovits 1993, 1995).

In addition, the Hungarian transition to democracy was somewhat peculiar in that it allowed the negotiation of a comprehensive deal on constitutional reform before the first free elections (Munck and Leff 1997). The resulting document (formally an amended version of the 1949 Stalinist constitution, even though one constitutional lawyer figured that the only rule left unchanged was that the capital of Hungary is Budapest) removed the compelling need for a new constitution. No one is fully satisfied with the institutional framework that evolved, and there are a number of pro-posals for further reforms of the electoral system and of judicial review; for the introduction of direct presidential elections; for bi-cameralism; or for the introduction of references to social rights and corporatist intermediation in the constitution. Yet the lack of an adequate consensus blocked any major institutional changes after 1990. As the fate of a number of legislative issues requiring a two-thirds majority and a degree of co-operation between government and opposition made clear, Hungary seems to experience more of a stalemate than tranquil stability. For instance, the parliament could not pass a law on the electronic media until December 1995; it struggled to fill vacancies in the Constitutional Court long after the constitutionally pre-scribed deadline; and spectacularly failed to get any results, after years of negotiations, on drafting a genuinely new constitution.

True, elite consensus almost certainly played a residual role in demo-cratic consolidation. All parties kept endorsing and supporting democracy, even though they were not entirely certain that the other parties would comply with the democratic rules of the game.[6] A broad commitment to market, military and legal reforms, with an eye to integration into the European Union and NATO was also shared by the six main parties and the business, media and academic establishments.[7] This consensus made the major parties extremely wary of political instability and mass mobilization on socioeconomic issues, and allowed for very effective sanctions against any deviants. Several major parties did, at one point or another, violate this gentleman's agreement, but they backed down very quickly after the invariably unfavourable reception of their initiatives in the press and among the other parties.

This consensus was not perfect, but the minor disagreements over the importance of joining the EU and NATO, and the considerably wider, but ideologically not much more articulate, inter-party dissent on economic policies did not serve as major building blocks of party identities. Previous studies of party elites by Herbert Kitschelt (1995) and Radoslaw Markowski (1995) show that party positions on economic issues in Hungary are less polarized than, more diffuse than, and not so critical for the definition of inter-party ideological distances as in the Czech Republic and Poland. In congruence with this, analyses of mass electoral behaviour found that social status and class are less important determinants of party preferences in Hungary than in most other East Central European, and several Western, democracies (Evans and Whitefield 1996; Tóka 1996). Table 8.2 presents bi-variate statistics on the impact of various attitudes on party preferences in some East European countries in late 1995. The important finding for the present chapter is that attitudes on foreign and economic policy issues apparently did not become such important determinants of party preferences in Hungary as in most other East European countries.

Because party preference (i.e. which party the respondent would support if there were an election) is not a metric scale but a nominal variable, we have to use the so-called 'uncertainty coefficient' to measure how well we can predict party choice, on the basis of responses to other questions. This coefficient tends to have very small numerical values even in the case of relatively strong relationships. For instance, using this measure we find that the impact of a social-class variable (coded 1 for blue-collar workers and 0 otherwise) on party preference was just 0.04 in Great Britain in 1990 (see Tóka 1996, 116).

The data in Table 8.2 come from the Eastern and Central Eurobarometer No. 6, in which the respondents in the Eastern countries aspiring for EU and NATO membership were asked how they would vote in a referendum on the entry of their country into these organizations. The responses to these two questions are much better predictors of party preference in Bulgaria and the Czech Republic than elsewhere. In other words, these are much more divisive partisan issues for these two party systems than for others. The explanation seems to be simple: these are the two countries among the nine in the analysis, where the (former) communist parties were the least reformed and remained relatively orthodox during and after the transition to democracy. Poland, Estonia and Hungary, with their thoroughly trans-formed post-communist parties are at the other extreme. There, the issues of NATO and EU membership hardly differentiates between the supporters of the different parties.

Table 8.2: Impact of attitudes towards the market, the EU and NATO on party preferences in November 1995 (uncertainty coefficient) [8]

| | Uncertainty coefficient | | |
	Market	EU	NATO
Albania	.071		
Armenia	.052		
Belarus	.044		
Bulgaria	.081	.057	.075
Croatia	.009		
Czech Republic	.059	.053	.079
Slovakia	.030	.019	.015
Estonia	.027	.017	.019
Hungary	.017	.015	.012
Latvia	.012	.011	.025
Lithuania	.031	.017	.032
Macedonia	.055		
Poland	.032	.013	.015
Romania	.025	.022	.021
Russia	.040		
Slovenia	.015	.022	.013
Ukraine	.053		
Georgia	.021		
Kazakhstan	.031		

A more complicated picture emerges when we move to the approval of a free market economy. This issue predicts voting behaviour much better in the unlikely group of Albania, Armenia, Bulgaria, the Czech Republic and Macedonia than elsewhere. The cross-national differences are now less easily explained than those on foreign policy issues. It is true that the attitude in question seems to have the least to do with voting behaviour in Croatia, Latvia, Slovenia, and Hungary, none of which has significant orthodox communist parties. But the Russian and Ukrainian successor parties of the CPSU give the impression of being ideologically more orthodox formations than the Macedonian, Armenian, and Albanian post-communist parties. Yet attitudes towards the market do not appear to have had greater impact on party preferences in 1995 in Russia and Ukraine than south of the Balkan and Caucasus mountains. At first sight, the same comparison seems to defy Peter Katzenstein's ingenious proposal that small countries, because of their greater openness to trade, are more constrained in their economic policy choices than big countries. Thus, adversarial party competition on economic issues is more likely to appear in big, and corpo-ratist institutions in small countries (Katzenstein 1985). Obviously, Albania, Macedonia, and Armenia are small, even in comparison with Hungary. Note, however, that their openness to trade may well have been lower in critical periods of their recent political development than that of Hungary, Slovenia and the Baltic states – indeed lower than that of Russia and Ukraine. The reasons are Albania's protracted policy of autarky under Enver Hoxha, and the trade blockade against Macedonia and Armenia by some of their neighbours, coupled with ongoing warfare in neighbouring territories.

Formal testing of the hypothesis is not easy given the difficulties when it comes to evaluating the amount of unregistered foreign trade (read: smugg-ling) across some borders in Eastern Europe. But it seems clear enough that Hungarian party competition in the 1990s had little use for many a traditional left-right issue related to foreign and economic policy. This, in turn, can probably be explained by two interrelated factors: the reformist attitude of the former communist party and the high level of trade openness of the country, especially towards Western Europe.

Overall, political stability in Hungary probably benefited from the fact that the major issues of economic transformation became a matter of partisan controversy only to a limited extent. Nevertheless, this factor cannot explain why the Hungarian party system remained relatively stable. On the contrary, as an analysis of Polish, Czech, Slovak and Hungarian data shows, the less strongly related party preference is to attitudes on persistent and salient issues (such as market reforms), the easier it is for voters to move from one party to another (Tóka, forthcoming); hence, the dearth of party competition on divisive economic issues should provide for more, rather than less instability in the party arena.

Yet, the same six parties which won parliamentary representation in the 1990 and 1994 Hungarian elections came out as front-runners in the opinion polls prior to the 1998 elections. Indeed, since the demise – before the 1990 elections – of the reformed communists now running as socialists (MSZDP), these six parties have alone surpassed the legal threshold for parliamentary representation in public opinion polls. Furthermore, the 28.3 per cent electoral volatility in Hungary between 1990 and 1994 was clearly less than the 34 per cent scored in Poland between 1991 and 1993, the 54 per cent net volatility between 1992 and 1995 in Estonia, the 31.4 per cent 1992–96 volatility in the Czech Republic, and the volatility of more than 40 per cent estimated for Lithuania.[9]

The absence of disruption and upheaval in other elements of the political system presumably helped the stabilization of the party system. But this cannot be a total explanation, as the absence of disruption was far less unusual in the post-communist world than party-political stability. Rather, the following factors can be emphasized.

First, the Opposition Roundtable (EKA) had dissolved itself by 1990 instead of remaining a heterogeneous and oversized electoral alliance, contesting the first elections on its own and doomed to break up like all the umbrella organizations in the other countries covered in this volume (cf. Chapters 3–7, 9–11). Hungary was thus spared at least one phase of organizational transformation, which nearly all other East European countries went through when their popular fronts gradually disintegrated.

Second, the parties of the Opposition Roundtable gained real influence through the national round-table talks with the communist establishment, and a monopoly of representing the anti-regime opinion in the process of transition. Thus, they attracted the best human, organizational and material resources available for competitive party politics in Hungary in 1989–90. This gave them a considerable advantage over other parties which were founded after the Spring of 1989.

But this was not enough to safeguard the electoral viability of all the parties of the EKA,[10] nor was it enough to prevent the entry of newcomers into the party arena. In the 1994 election campaign, two outsiders – the Agrarian Alliance (ASZ) and the Republic Party (KP) – showed evidence of having electorally attractive leaders, financial resources and grass-root organizations that should have been sufficient for gaining parliamentary representation – provided that their message to the voters was right. Yet they failed, probably because they lacked a truly unique ideological position within the party system. This was due not to their lack of imagination or talent, but rather to the almost one-dimensional simplicity of the emerging cleavage structure, in which their position was difficult to distinguish from those of the triumphant Socialists (MSZP) and the Free Democrats (SZDSZ). In other words, given the already high number of parliamentary parties, Hungary's relatively simple cleavage structure acted as a gatekeeper against the entry of new parties.

Fourth, Hungary does have a politically mobilized cleavage line that exerts some hold over the electorate and the party elites. This cleavage divides society into two camps: a socially conservative, religious, somewhat nationalist, and anti-communist camp; and a secular, morally permissive and generally less nationalist camp. The former wishes to see undone the historical injustices that occurred under communism. The latter — at the core of which are supporters of former communist regime and those who at least appreciate the modernizing and secularizing thrust thereof – would prefer to draw a heavy line between past and present. This divide is cemented by being related to a large number of different issues. Another major reason for the persistence of this division is that it was reinforced by organizational carriers and collective identities throughout the entire communist era: active membership in churches (i.e. attendance at religious services) on the one hand, and (pre-1989) communist party membership on the other.[11] The religious cleavage is fairly well politicized in all predominantly Catholic countries of Eastern Europe (on the impact of church attendance on party choice in different countries, cf. Tóka 1996). The fact that it divides partisan camps more strongly in Hungary than in Poland may go some way towards explaining why Hungary has lower electoral volatility, despite the weaker mobilization of socioeconomic cleavages.

Finally, there is less to be explained about the stability of the Hungarian party system than sometimes appears to observers. As pointed out earlier, voters are not particularly loyal to their parties. Also, some of the parties changed their identity significantly over time. Occasionally, several of them became endangered species, and at the time of writing, the chances are that the number of relevant parties will significantly decrease in the 1998 elections. Just as the simplicity of the cleavage structure may have served as a gatekeeper against the entry of new parties, it may yet be unable to sustain the six-party system as it existed between 1990 and 1997. At the very least, the one-dimensional party system had something to do with the fact that for a long time it seemed very difficult to distinguish in ideological terms between the Young Democrats (FIDESZ) and the Free Democrats (SZDSZ), and between the Christian Democrats (KDNP) and the Hungarian Democratic Forum (MDF). The ideological reorientation of FIDESZ in 1993–94, and of the KDNP in 1995–96, was directly linked to their failure to carve out unique and distinct ideological niches for themselves. This ideological shift contributed – at least indirectly and through its impact on opinion-makers – to the free-fall of these two parties in the public opinion polls of the respective periods. Thus, the tendency of some parties to engage in extremely risky, almost suicidal, ideological manœuvres seems to derive from the fact that it is rather hard to define distinctive and electorally viable ideological positions, for as many as six parties, in the largely one-dimensional ideological space of the Hungarian party system. If so, then the dearth of party polarization on economic issues does indeed undermine the six-party regime as it existed between 1990 and 1997.

Several of the above propositions do not lend themselves easily to formal testing. Consequently, what follows is merely a short history of the Hungarian party system that, at most, can demonstrate the plausibility of the above explanations of political stability and instability under Hungary's (first) post-communist party system.

The Evolution of the Hungarian Party System

After the Iron Curtain came down, all non-communist parties ceased to exist in Hungary. They began to re-emerge on the political scene in the autumn of 1987, to support the progress towards more political freedom and various other reforms. The historical parties were reorganized six to ten months after the breakthrough conference of the Hungarian Socialist Workers' Party (MSZMP) in May 1988, when the most stubborn opponents of political liberalization were removed from the Politburo. Another forty or so non-communist parties emerged in the year following the official recognition of the multi-party system on the MSZMP's Central Committee meeting in February 1989. Only one of these newcomers, the Christian Democratic People's Party (KDNP), was invited to participate in the Opposition Roundtable (EKA). The EKA was founded in March 1989 by eight existing opposition organizations, and became the representative of the united opposition in the National Roundtable talks which took place in June–September 1989. Admission to the EKA in itself entailed a recognition of a party's potential strength and respectability, and the round-table talks further increased the gap between outsiders and insiders. In the most crucial period of party formation, the Roundtable drew the attention of the media and potential party cadres to seven opposition parties, and accelerated these parties' professionalization. Not one of the opposition parties excluded from the Roundtable was to win more than 2 per cent of the votes in 1990.

On the other side of the Roundtable sat representatives of the Hungarian Socialist Workers' Party (MSZMP), a party soon to disappear. The October 1989 congress of the MSZMP announced the party's break with Marxism–Leninism and established a new party named the Hungarian Socialist Party (MSZP). The losing Marxist-Leninist faction rejected the new programme and helped organize a relatively orthodox communist party under the old MSZMP label. The reformist wing inherited the government positions and party assets, but not the ideological positions, or the members of the troubled old party – former MSZMP members were not automatically registered as MSZP members. In the 1990 election campaign, the party emphasized pragmatism, statesmanship, the need for economic reforms, its commitment to democracy and European integration, the party's role in maintaining political stability and the combination of social democratic, patriotic, moderately liberal and technocratic elements in the party's programme and leadership.

The voters presumably had little difficulty guessing what social groups and issue concerns the reorganized historical parties intended to speak for. From the autumn of 1989, the Independent Smallholders Party (FKGP) – before 1948 a moderately nationalist and religious agrarian centre party – had came out strongly in favour of the restoration of ex-farmers' pre-1948 property rights, a proposition emphatically rejected by all the other parties. The Social Democratic Party of Hungary (MSZDP), as well as the fiercely anti-communist FKGP, usually joined the more radical wing of the opposition in the political conflicts of 1989. The greatest concern, apparently, of the party leaders was to dissociate themselves from the incumbent reform socialists who were also contesting the social democratic field. The Christian Democratic KDNP stressed the traditional religious issues and emphasized its moral commitment to protect the poor. In the 1989 referendum, it supported the same option as the Socialist Party; in other respects it usually shared the views of the moderate opposition. All parties with some historical roots attempted to develop organizations following the traditional mass party model (Enyedi 1996).

The dominant actors in the Opposition Roundtable were not, however, the historical parties, but three newly created umbrella organizations of anti-communist mobilization, which represented a much broader ideological spectrum. In addition, the overarching issue promoted by these umbrella organizations – the transition to democracy – represented more transient concerns. But the high internal cohesion within the pre-existing social networks of intellectuals upon which these three organizations – the MDF, SZDSZ and FIDESZ – were based, made them the most successful non-communist actors in mobilizing human and material resources for politics. In Hungary's negotiated revolution, the media constituted the main channel of communication from parties to voters. This kind of technique was mastered by the otherwise discredited reform socialists within the MSZP, as well as by the MDF, SZDSZ and FIDESZ politicians, who all proved themselves masters compared to other teams, who became the sources of most political initiatives, and were able to react promptly to any event. Unlike the historical parties and the reform socialists, the MDF, SZDSZ and FIDESZ did not have pre-determined fixed positions on any issue: they were free and – due to their evident skill and internal cohesion – able to adapt their policies to events and experiences as they saw fit. For several years to come, these three organizations had the character of a professional electoral organization rather than that of a mass party.

The transferability of the initial advantages into electoral superiority over less broadly based parties may seem less mysterious than the mere survival of these umbrella organizations in the ordinary business of party politics. Maybe they were 'organized along tribal lines' (as an insider put it), and – as the late MDF leader József Antall claimed – 'nobody beyond the Grand Boulevard [the dividing line between downtown and midtown Budapest] was interested in' their ideological debates, which reflected only the traditional micro-cleavage dividing the Hungarian intelligentsia (Körösényi 1991). But their founding fathers would never have acquired their un-deniable charisma had they been unable to deduce, from their ideological heritage, a distinctive position on every single newly arising issue, thus maintaining the ideological cohesion of their parties. The mere fact that there were three of them forced these parties into a competition, which, in turn, provided sufficient incentive to keep each party united.

Before being formally established in the autumn of 1988, the Hungarian Democratic Forum (MDF) and the Alliance of Free Democrats (SZDSZ) both had at least a decade-long pre-history. The SZDSZ was more or less the direct successor to the informal network of the dissent movement, dating back to the late seventies. For the general public, the only visible difference between the SZDSZ and the MDF, until late 1989, was tactical. The founding fathers of the MDF, aiming at a moral reorganization of the nation, advocated *Realpolitik* and tried to co-operate with the reformers in the communist party.

In terms of leadership, the MDF initially relied on a group of intellectuals under the guardianship of the reformist Politburo member Imre Pozsgay. Many of the most influential founding fathers shared with Pozsgay a left-wing version of the pre-war *népi-nemzeti* (literally populist–national or *völkisch*–national) orientation. The *népi* ideology rejected both cosmo-politan capitalism and internationalist communism, and sought a third way based on participatory democracy, a new national elite originating from lower-class (preferably rural) families, and to some extent on collective ownership mixed with small- and medium-size private enterprises. The network of dissenters, reform-economists and sympathizers that rallied around SZDSZ tended to despise the *népi* ideology, and missed no oppor-tunity to point out its historical links with anti-Semitic and authoritarian tendencies.

Of all opposition groups, the MDF was the most swift and efficient in building up a nation-wide party organization. By the summer of 1989 it became recognized as the most likely non-communist contender for electoral victory in the next elections, which were due no later than in June

1990. Its relative moderation may have been a key asset in 1988 and early 1989, but it soon turned into a liability as the breakdown of communist rule accelerated throughout the Soviet bloc in late 1989. Through a number of bold political initiatives, the SZDSZ turned from a small party, apparently unable to obtain more than 5–8 per cent of votes, into a formidable electoral machine matching the MDF both in terms of membership and popularity. The MDF responded to this challenge in two ways. It started presenting itself as a centre-right, strongly patriotic Christian party facing a cosmopolitan, radical and agnostic SZDSZ. On the other hand, the MDF claimed it was pursuing a more cautious approach than its liberal rival to the introduction of market economy and to economic recovery. Conventional wisdom has it that the SZDSZ was trapped by its previously successful strategy of radical opposition to the regime, and that its radical postures had turned into an electoral liability by the 1990 elections.

The Federation of Young Democrats (FIDESZ) was established by a network of university students and young professionals that crystallized in the second half of the 1980s. Initially, the FIDESZ became known mainly for its protest actions. Seeing its electoral niche eroded by the SZDSZ, its increasingly popular ideological twin, the Young Democrats fought for survival during the 1990 election campaign. The campaign strategy was based on maximizing the party's generational appeal so as to differentiate the party from the Free Democrats. In early 1990, the electoral strength of the Young Democrats was fairly limited; after the elections, however, the FIDESZ was the only party able to capitalize on the decreasing popularity of the MDF as well as of the SZDSZ.

Quite apart from the information overflow resulting from the exceptional circumstances of regime change, there was a significant reason why the 1990 distribution of electoral preferences could not have been expected to reflect very closely the distribution of the population along some underlying cleavage dimensions. The point is not, as journalistic accounts often suggested, that the parties had no 'clear programmes' apart from some vague anti-communism. Had the parties not already had a considerable ideological cohesion when they entered the legislature, party discipline within the ranks of the backbenchers would hardly have been as high as it actually was in 1990–91.[12]

The numerous allegations about the absence of clear programmes may be attributed to the lack of a relevant record against which to evaluate the credibility of the new parties. The parties clearly and consistently propagated differences in priorities and policies, but the many issue conflicts between them were not yet incorporated into one all-embracing ideological super-dimension, where the incumbent socialists were pitted against their anti-communist challengers. The future importance of the several partly cross-cutting divisions was unclear, since the communism versus Western-style democracy dimension was rightly believed to lose its relevance after the first elections. Thus, the post-election period was to determine the dominant divide of the future, as well as how the political parties were to unfold on the dominant dimensions.

Issue dimensions in 1989 and early 1990

The anti-communism factor, or, in other words, the radicalism versus gradual change divide, pitted the small party of orthodox communists (MSZMP) against the liberals (SZDSZ, FIDESZ), the Smallholders (FKGP), and some smaller right-wing parties. From this perspective, the Socialists (MSZP) were somewhere near the communists (MSZMP), while the Democratic Forum and the Social Democrats were close to the centre but still on the radical side. The Christian Democrats (KNDP) and the People's Party (MNP) – the two opposition parties which, in the 1989 referendum, sided with the socialists to support direct presidential elections – were probably in the centre. The divide between the pro-market and the social protectionist parties ran mostly, but not entirely, parallel to this first dimension. Here again, the SZDSZ and the FIDESZ were at the one pole and the Communists at the other, but the exact ordering of the Socialists (MSZP), the Democratic Forum (MDF), the Social Democrats and the Smallholders (all being on the pro-market side) was somewhat uncertain. The Social Democrats and the Smallholders were more in favour of pro-market policies and full-scale privatization than the other two, but the first had an ambiguous attitude towards declining industries, and the second obviously had an affinity for agrarian protectionism. The People's Party and the Christian Democrats seemed to be somewhere on the social protectionist side.

The parties' attitudes towards class interests could not be easily inferred from their respective positions on the pro-market versus social protectionism axis. With the economy in recession and an inflation rate in the range of 25 to 30 per cent at the time of the elections, the parties were not inclined to commit themselves to substantial increases in welfare outlays, save for education and what was necessitated by the growing rate of unemployment. Under state socialism, the actual flow of cash transfers and benefits in kind favoured middle and high status groups (Ferge 1991). Thus, one could easily pledge – as did pro-market Free Democrats – to divert more public spending to the poor without increasing the overall level of welfare spending. The Smallholders and the MDF also tended to hold out the prospect of a broad national bourgeoisie as a remedy to social problems, a position which might intimate that they were advocating the interests of would-be proprietors. The Free and Young Democrats, however, saw private property as an economic necessity only, not as a moral goal in its own right (Körösényi 1991, 10). The rhetoric of the Free Democrats came very close to that of the Social Democrats and the Socialists, who called for strong trade unions in order to protect the interests of wage-earners against what they believed was bound to become a small, propertied minority. As if to make things even more obscure, the MDF publicly pledged itself to restrict unemployment and pauperization. The Socialists, who took pride in speaking for the interests of wage-earners, were inevitably associated with the former *nomenklatura,* and not quite credible on welfare issues after the austerity measures of the late 1980s. The Democratic People's Party and the Christian Democrats also committed themselves to the non-propertied poor, but their main issue concerns laid elsewhere.

Most parties seemed to agree that a nationalist/cosmopolitan divide was present and fairly important in 1990: in fact, the campaign apparently convinced some, like BBC correspondent Misha Glenny (1990), that this represented the dominant conflict dimension between the main contenders. On this dimension, the Hungarian Democratic Forum, the Democratic People's Party and probably the Smallholders as well, constituted the 'national' *(nemzeti)* pole, while the pro-Soviet Communists in the MSZMP along with the pro-Western Free and Young Democrats occupied the anti-nationalist end of the spectrum. Although the parties themselves rarely referred to it, commentators took the Christian Democrats' moderately nationalist and the Social Democrats' moderately anti-nationalist stands for granted. The Socialist Party was in a difficult position. As an heir to János Kádár's Hungarian Socialist Workers' Party, it was open to the dual charge of having betrayed national sovereignty in and after 1956, and for not having made sufficient efforts to protect the large Magyar minority in Ceauşescu's Romania. But the presence of Imre Pozsgay in the leadership secured a certain *népi* and 'national' credibility for the Socialists. As a matter of fact, practically no controversial or salient policy issues were associated with the nationalist/cosmopolitan dimension. The protection of the Magyar minorities living in neighbouring countries, the break with the Warsaw Pact and with the Comecon fitted the liberal just as well as the national agenda, and both sides seemed credible and outspoken on these issues.

The political alignments on the rural/urban, religious/secular, and moral libertarianism/authoritarianism dimensions largely coincided with the national/cosmopolitan divide. The Democratic Forum and the liberal parties seemed to have distinct, but not extreme, positions on these three dimensions. The MDF had its strongholds in provincial cities; it was moderately religious, slightly conservative on moral issues, and demanded a measure of respect for authority. The Free Democrats was a distinctly urban or even metropolitan phenomenon; along with the other liberal party, the FIDESZ, it was secular but outspoken on freedom of religion; mostly libertarian and always suspicious of authority. In 1990, however, only the urban-rural dimension had salience. The agrarian-rural parties, particularly the People's Party and the Agrarian Alliance (ASZ), were trying to mobilize against the privileges which Budapest and other urban centres were perceived to enjoy at the expense of the countryside.

The coalition formula chosen after the 1990 elections strongly affected the future importance and combination of the potential ideological divides. The 'reformist/anti-reformist' conflict and the class cleavage were rated the most important by the citizens; analyses of party manifestos, to some extent corroborated by mass survey data, suggest that these two cleavages pitted the liberal parties against the 'Left'. (Tóka 1993).

With the socialist government out of power, 'democratic anti-communism' was likely to lose its importance for the structuring of the political field, but there were good reasons to believe that the social protectionist versus pro-market divide was to dominate the party system. Thus, the liberal and socialist camps were to remain poles apart even after the 1990 elections. Indeed, pre-election commentaries suggested the following coalition formulas to be the most likely: MDF and MSZP with some smaller parties; SZDSZ–FIDESZ–FKGP (probably with the MSZDP); MDF–SZDSZ (probably joined by FIDESZ). This last formula was supposed to have the best chance of winning.[13]

However, all these pre-election speculations failed to grasp the full impact of the newly created electoral system. In the elections, the MDF won more than 42 per cent of the mandates with somewhat less than a quarter of the (first round) votes. Altogether, the Hungarian Democratic Forum (MDF), the Independent Smallholders (FKGP) and the Christian Democrats (KDNP) had close to 60 per cent of the seats, and the trio soon reached an agreement on the composition and programme of the new government. The FIDESZ also participated in the talks leading up to the formation of the new government, but it is a moot point whether it was included in these talks as a potential coalition partner or as a device to keep FKGP demands at bay.

The impact of the 1990 elections
The coalition formula replaced the previous political divides with a new one, that of Ins versus Outs, between a Christian-National coalition government and its liberal and socialist opposition. The main emotional divide in early 1990 was between the Socialists and the radical opposition (SZDSZ, FIDESZ, FKGP), with the Democratic Forum close to the centre (Tóka 1993). By May 1991, the main divide became the one pitting the government parties against the two liberal parties (Free and Young Democrats) and the

Socialist Party: by way of example, the more sympathy one had for the Free Democrats, the more likely one was to like the Socialists and the Young Democrats and to dislike the Smallholders and the Democratic Forum.

Unfortunately, no systematically collected data are available on shifts in the parties' policy proposals and rhetoric after the 1990 election. Referring to external constraints, until 1992 the MDF leadership opted for monetary and privatization policies along the lines suggested by the liberal parties during the campaign, and it suspended its plans to increase the money supply and invest in education. Some rhetorical and tangible differences certainly remained between the government and the liberal opposition: the latter called for a smaller budget deficit, curtailed spending on bureaucracy, a little more spending on welfare, lower taxes and a quicker pace of privatization. Even so, fiscal policy and privatization were not very controversial areas in 1990–91. The constraints which the MDF had imposed upon government also made themselves felt on the Christian Democrats and the Smallholders: The KDNP Minister of Welfare could not live up to his party's promises of social protectionism, and the FKGP Minister of Agriculture faced a similar problem. The opposition parties, including the Socialists, bent over backwards not to align themselves with any kind of social protectionism. Thus, the differences between the parties' attitudes on most socioeconomic issues either diminished or lost their relevance altogether.

Some of the major controversial issues in 1990–91 were related to the sectoral interests represented by the two smaller coalition partners. In exchange for FKGP support, the Democratic Forum and the Christian Democrats had to give up much of their opposition to the Smallholders' restitution policies. Fearing that the government might score points among former owners of collectivized and nationalized property, the SZDSZ also shifted its position, but the Young Democrats and the Socialists all but rejected the idea of compensating pre-1949 owners. On the issue of financial compensation to the churches, one of the pet projects of the KDNP, polarization was moderate, but a few details divided the parties into two distinctive and united blocs, with the government parties advocating a somewhat greater role of organized religion in social life than the opposition parties did.

The extent of central government power was a recurrent issue. Referring to the need for rational government, the MDF advocated a greater degree of central control over local government, but also over education, national media and state-owned companies. On this dimension, the liberal and socialist opposition was unified, and the Socialists and the Free Democrats frequently claimed that the MDF wanted to create large clientelistic networks and subject ever more spheres of life to political control.

Finally, a major controversy surrounded issues of retroactive justice, on which the government parties repeatedly showed anti-communist zeal and determination to undo past injustices, while the liberals and the socialists insisted that retroactive justice violated the rule of law.

Overall, the government parties managed to act in concert, even on such a matter as restitution, which had caused very pronounced disagreements between them before the 1990 elections. The Socialist Party, which sought to affirm its position as a relevant player on the political scene, readily found issues where it could appear as an ally of the liberal parties. The liberal parties, on the other hand, mostly abandoned their anti-communist rhetoric, partly because the content of the practical issues related to it had changed since the Socialists lost power, but possibly also because they found a ready and willing ally in the Socialist Party. The difference between the Socialists and the once-united opposition did not disappear entirely; a small number of bills (particularly trade union law) were passed against the Socialists only. But on the main controversial issues discussed below, it had no relevance anymore. Moreover, the anti-communist pole – previously the domain of the liberal parties and the FKGP – was gradually occupied by the three government parties.

Towards the break-up of the liberal bloc

The last three years of MDF-dominated government did little to reshape the issue agenda of Hungarian politics. True, the – more apparent than real – consensus on economic issues was weakened by increasing criticism by the MSZP, KDNP and SZDSZ of the allegedly corrupt and clientelistic practices in the privatization process; by the KDNP's and the MSZP's calls for greater social justice, and a more equal sharing of the burdens of economic trans-formation by rich and poor; and by the SZDSZ and the FIDESZ talking more and more about cutting corporate taxes. But if anything, the battles on non-economic issues became ever more bitter as Hungary's media war escalated (Oltay 1993a; Patáki 1994a) and the emergence of the extreme right generated considerable anxiety (Patáki 1992; Oltay 1993b, 1994a) – even making a few pundits publicly panic in late 1993 over the possibility of a right-wing coup.

Most of the parties embarked on a course of organizational development and important changes in electoral strategy, even though the issue agenda remained essentially unchanged. The Christian-National bloc fragmented and lost its cohesion. At the same time, small but steady steps paved the way for a future socialist-liberal coalition through the establishment of the 'Democratic Charter' – a loose framework for protest action, organized by leaders from within the SZDSZ and MSZP, along with other intellectuals who were wary of what they saw as the authoritarian propensity of the MDF government (Bozóki 1996). But probably the most important steps were taken by the FIDESZ.

In the September–October 1990 municipal elections, the electoral coalition of FIDESZ and SZDSZ had defeated the government parties by a great margin in virtually all major cities. Beginning in early 1991, parliamentary and local by-elections were more increasingly won by Socialist candidates, but the FIDESZ maintained a huge lead in the opinion polls, with the MDF and SZDSZ each falling back to a 10–15 per cent level of support by late 1991. The levels of support for the other mainstream parties were even lower and fluctuated within a rather narrow range. One popular theory has it that the heavy losses by the MDF in 1990–91 was a case of policy-blind 'pocketbook' voting. But the newly acquired Christian-radical image must have something to do with the fact that the MDF lost considerably more among secular than among anti-market voters (Tóka 1992; 1995).

Premier József Antall's strategy of maintaining the cohesion of the Christian-national bloc by policy compromises, and his discrete manipulation of leadership elections in the KDNP and the FKGP, worked out with the KDNP but almost completely failed with the FKGP. József Torgyán, the former FKGP caucus leader, proved an absolutely unacceptable partner for Antall, and the Premier encouraged and aided those trying to remove Torgyán from all party offices. Torgyán managed to rally most of the FKGP organizations behind him in the conflict with the FKGP MPs who remained loyal to Antall and the government coalition. Once Torgyán had won the battle for leadership, he expelled his critics (i.e. the majority of the parliamentary club) from the party and took the party into opposition. For most of 1992–94, the parliamentary deputies of Torgyán's FKGP were one or two members short to form a separate caucus. The expelled MPs remained on the government benches as 'the Smallholder 35' caucus and eventually founded a party of their own, known as the United Smallholders Party or EKGP (Patáki 1994b). However, the EKGP had very little appeal among the Smallholders rank and file and lost out miserably in the 1994 elections.

A second series of defection from the government benches affected the MDF directly. By mid-1991, some sections of the MDF had lost patience with the failure of the MDF government to purge the economic and cultural elites of what they perceived as a hostile mix of the former *nomenklatura* and secular-cosmopolitan liberals. This growing dissatisfaction within the ranks of the MDF found its most radical expression in the views of the notorious editor of the MDF weekly, party vice-president István Csurka. The tolerance or even encouragement supposedly shown by the government and the MDF towards various extremists – from Csurka to skinhead gangs masquerading in fascists uniforms – became the most hotly debated issue in Hungarian politics. In a major embarrassment to the government, several MDF deputies questioned the legitimacy and permanence of the current state borders of Hungary, and at least one even called for a peaceful reunification of the entire Carpathian Basin (read: historical, pre-Trianon Hungary). In the year following the publication of a notorious Csurka essay in the MDF weekly in August 1992, the Foreign Ministry counted approximately one thousand articles in the mainstream world press (approximately one-half of all the entries it found on Hungary) discussing Csurka's views, which were labelled fascist even by some fellow party members (Patáki 1992). The MDF was apparently paralyzed: the leadership sensed that Csurka's views faithfully reflected the frustration of many rank-and-file members, yet it could not agree with him, either on policy objectives or on pre-election tactics. By way of example, Csurka argued that the 1994 elections were already lost; what remained at stake was the preservation of the ideological integrity of the party and a decisive increase in the social influence of the *népi-nemzeti* forces, requiring radical steps to promote faithful cadres in the media, the privatization agency, the civil service, and on the boards of state-owned companies.

Csurka did not even refrain from making comments on the Premier's health. Antall had been known to be terminally ill since November 1990, and Csurka publicly called upon him to nominate a successor. Coming on top of his public criticism of the beleaguered government, this *faux pas* alienated the bulk of the party from Csurka. Even so, the party leadership suspected that a left-liberal alliance aiming at the total delegitimation of the Christian-National bloc was emerging under the guise of the public outrage over Csurka's views. Thus, the MDF leaders were reluctant to turn against Csurka in a concession to the voices of anti-fascism.

In June 1993, Csurka and his followers were eventually expelled from the MDF; in August, they went on to found the Party of Hungarian Justice and Life (MIÉP). As an illustration of the delicate balance of forces within the MDF, the most vocal critics of Csurka were expelled at the same time (Oltay 1993b; 1993c). Even more important than the public image was the fact that Csurka had became a serious threat to the organizational unity of the MDF. First, he had developed an organization parallel to the MDF called the Movement of the Hungarian Path; then he organized a strong faction within the MDF caucus, which defied the government in the vote on the Basic Treaty signed with Ukraine.[14] After Csurka had been expelled, the conservative and Christian Democratic elements regained control of the MDF, but the party was unable to change its image accordingly in the run-up to the elections. The period of national mourning following Prime Minister Antall's death induced a surge of support for the MDF in the public opinion polls, but this effect proved short-lived and did not translate into increased electoral support. There was no consolidation of the party's position in the centre-right, nor any of the somewhat lax fiscal policies of the last 16 months before the elections, or the 7 per cent real wage increase in the last 6 months before the elections (cf. Okolicsányi 1994).

In late 1992, a group of FIDESZ leaders engaged in a reorientation of the party. They were anxious to prepare voters for the economic policy measures that a liberal government would implement after the 1994 elections. As anybody familiar with the mechanics of the Hungarian electoral system was to discover, the 1992 opinion poll figures would spell a victory of a two-thirds majority in the incoming parliament for the SZDSZ–FIDESZ coalition. It was therefore clear that the FIDESZ could easily afford to lose quite a few 'pocketbook'-oriented and protest voters. Moreover, the strong showing of the Socialists in the by-elections alerted the FIDESZ leaders to the fact that the MSZP was the most serious contender in the electoral arena. Thus, the attractive prospect of a FIDESZ–SZDSZ government made it important for the FIDESZ to prevent the SZDSZ from co-operating with the socialists, but most FIDESZ leaders envisaged the FIDESZ as the future leading force of the Hungarian right, rather than of the centre. This objective seemed better served by courting the Democratic Forum rather than the Socialists. As a defector from the MDF to the FIDESZ succinctly put it, in an article before the 1994 elections – in a FIDESZ–SZDSZ–MSZP coalition, the SZDSZ would be the pivotal party, while the FIDESZ would hold that position in a MDF–FIDESZ–SZDSZ coalition.

Thus, early in 1993, the FIDESZ stopped espousing left-liberal views on religious and 'national' issues, voted against a routine adjustment of state pensions to the increase in nominal wages, and implicitly called for a boy-cott of the elections of union representatives to the social security council. They lashed out against the Democratic Charter and the SZDSZ for their supposedly exaggerated anxiety about the nationalist as opposed to the Red menace, thus laying the track for the 'Warsaw express' (or infecting Hungary with the 'Lithuanian disease') – i.e. the return of the MSZP to power.[15]

The 1993–94 period proved electorally disastrous for FIDESZ. First, the Christian-National constituency was reluctant to switch to the FIDESZ immediately after receiving the news of the party's reorientation. The expulsion of Csurka from the MDF put an end to what ever hopes the FIDESZ might have entertained to the effect that at least the more conservative elements of the Christian-National camp might turn towards it. The image of the party was also tainted by two scandals related to party finances, which triggered an accelerating slide in the opinion polls. Moreover, as the FIDESZ lost and the MSZP gained ground in the polls, the rejection of any coalition with the MSZP implied a post-election coalition with the MDF – a prospect unattractive to large sections of the FIDESZ constituency. Within just one year, support in the public opinion polls for the FIDESZ dropped from some 40 to less than 10 per cent. The new FIDESZ strategy certainly renewed the party's image and gave it an electorate in which the anti-market voters were not as over-represented as in some 1992–93 private polls taken by the party. Even so, the decimated constituency remained distinctive in terms of age and oppositional attitude, rather than being identifiable through its pro-market attitudes (Tóka 1995).

With first the MDF and the SZDSZ and then the FIDESZ falling out of grace with the voters, the MSZP went on to win an overall majority of seats in the 1994 elections, without having had any new items on the electoral platform, save the inclusion of a populist twist to its economic policy rhetoric and a more confident posture on non-economic issues (Oltay 1994b). The MSZP promised much the same as the liberals: more competent and pragmatic leadership; greater economic prosperity; a continuation of the economic reforms and privatization instead of government-promoted re-socialization of society in the name of systemic change; no retroactive revision of past privatization deals but tightened control of privatization by parliament; the implementation of all the restitution laws enacted during MDF rule; and probably some improvements in the relations with Slovakia and Romania.

The SZDSZ went through a brief leadership crisis in 1991–92. After the resignation of its founding father, Péter Tölgyessy was elected party leader against strong resistance from veteran dissenters of the 1970s and 1980s. For about a year, the combination of influential factions and a weak executive paralyzed the party. When Tölgyessy came up for re-election in 1992, the old establishment had launched a better-known candidate than in the year before, and Tölgyessy suffered a crushing defeat. In the following years, the SZDSZ tried to adapt to electoral considerations in every respect save on some issues concerning economic policy, civic liberties and the constitutional framework. The nomination of a relatively unknown new-comer, instead of the party leader, for Prime Minister in the 1994 campaign, testifies to the new style. By 1993–94, the SZDSZ emerged as the most united and probably most well-heeled Hungarian party. The 1994 campaign of the Free Democrats steered clear of divisive issues and controversial policy pledges, emphasizing the personal qualities and appeal of the party's leading candidates.

Bits and pieces of evidence suggest that the SZDSZ did particularly well among pro-market voters in early 1994. In 1992–93, the supporters of the SZDSZ had not differed much from the national average in terms of their economic policy attitudes, but at the time of the 1994 elections the Free Democrats featured the most pro-market electorate of any party, just as it had in 1990 (cf. the impact of the PROMARKET variable on SZDSZ support in *Table 8.5*). As mentioned earlier, the SZDSZ had done precious little to attract voters with pro-market attitudes and had turned into a catch-all party.

This presumably made the Free Democrats attractive as an alternative to the triumphant Socialists, who were equally non-nationalist and secular, but somewhat anti-market.[16]

The New Party Space

Party positions

Clearly, the issue dimensions that defined the ideological identity of the Hungarian parties changed considerably between 1990 and 1994. The most comprehensive data set currently available about the issue positions of the Hungarian parties serves as the point of departure for an evaluation. These data derive from an international survey conducted by Herbert Kitschelt and his associates just before the 1994 elections in Hungary (Kitschelt 1995; Kitschelt et al., forthcoming). In Hungary, 129 mid-level party activists – among them, heads of regional or municipal party organizations – were interviewed. They were recruited in almost equal numbers from each of the six main parties. Among other things, they had to locate seven Hungarian parties on 16 twenty-point issue scales.

The original answers were recoded, so that the resulting scores show how much closer to point 1 or point 20 the party in question was placed by the respondents, compared to their average placement of all seven parties on the given question. Minus scores indicate a placement deviating from the average towards the first of the two response alternatives offered to the respondents, and positive scores the opposite. By way of example, the alternative positions on the first issue were 'Social policy cannot protect citizens from all risks, they also have to rely on themselves. For instance, all costs of medical treatment should be paid either directly by everybody from his or her own pocket, or by joining voluntary health insurance schemes individually'; and 'The social policy of the state must protect citizens from every sort of social risk. For instance, all medical expenses should be financed from the social security fund'.

Table 8.3 shows the mean issue placement of the seven parties by the cross-party jury. With the exception of the question on environmental protection, the respondents apparently saw sizeable differences between the positions of the different parties on virtually every issue. On economic issues, the FIDESZ and the SZDSZ were attributed the most, and the MSZP the least pro-market position. Foreign direct investments and the third issue item – which was essentially about the restitution of property rights, originally promoted by the Smallholders – are slightly deviant cases. The Socialists and the liberals were seen to be more in favour of foreign direct investment than the average, while the Christian-National parties were believed to favour property restitution, and the defence of supposed national interests from the intrusion of foreign capital.

Table 8.3: Mean position of seven parties vis-à-vis other parties as perceived by a panel of party activists [17]

Variable					Rated party			
No.	Content domain	MSZP	FKGP	KDNP	SZDSZ	FIDESZ	MIÉP	MDF
1	social security	3.2	.1	1.6	-2.1	-2.8	.6	-.7
2	market versus state	4.2	.4	1.3	-3.3	-3.6	1.8	-.8
3	mode of privatization	-.3	3.5	2.3	-4.5	-4.4	4.2	-.9
4	inflation–unemployment	3.5	.9	.8	-2.3	-2.2	1.7	-2.4
5	foreign investment	.9	-5.2	-1.2	5.4	4.7	-6.0	1.3
6	income taxation	.0	-1.6	-.9	2.5	2.3	-2.3	.1
7	immigration	2.9	-4.0	-.9	3.7	3.1	-4.7	-.1
8	women at work	-5.5	4.2	3.1	-3.1	-3.3	3.8	.8
9	abortion	5.9	-5.3	-6.4	6.8	6.6	-6.3	-1.2
10	churches and education	7.9	-5.6	-6.7	7.1	6.7	-5.8	-3.6
11	urban–rural	.7	-5.6	-.6	3.3	2.9	-2.5	1.8
12	authority–autonomy	3.6	-5.1	-4.6	7.1	7.1	-5.5	-2.7
13	environment	-1.3	-.1	.5	.6	1.8	-.8	-.7
14	censorship	-3.6	4.1	4.5	-6.3	-6.1	4.9	2.5
15	former communists	8.7	-6.2	-2.8	5.1	2.7	-7.0	-.5
16	basic treaties with neighbours	-6.5	6.6	2.0	-5.6	-4.6	7.9	.2

Table 8.4: Principal component analysis of the issue variables in Table 8.3 (N=903). Matrix of factor loadings (after varimax rotation) [18]

Variable		% of variance		
		47.6	13.3	7.5
No.	Content domain			
1	social security	-.01	.77	.09
2	market versus state	-.12	.82	-.20
3	mode of privatization	-.53	.60	.01
4	inflation–unemployment	-.02	.74	.03
5	foreign investments	.67	-.25	.34
6	income taxation	.37	-.42	-.13
7	immigration	.77	-.15	.03
8	women at work	-.80	.03	.18
9	abortion	.88	-.14	.13
10	churches and education	.91	-.06	.09
11	urban–rural	.55	-.46	-.28
12	authority–autonomy	.87	-.22	.20
13	environment	.08	.07	.92
14	censorship	-.82	.23	-.09
15	former communists	.87	-.02	-.15
16	basic treaties with neighbours	-.86	.10	-.01

Factor scores of rated parties

	% of variance		
	47.6	13.3	7.5
MSZP	1.24	1.21	-.64
FKGP	-1.04	.16	.21
KDNP	-.63	.23	.05
SZDSZ	.96	-.69	.24
FIDESZ	.81	-.78	.55
MIÉP	-1.07	.31	-.17
MDF	-.27	-.45	-.24

For all intents and purposes, the underlying structure of the party space is stable, but the overall polarization of party positions seems to be much larger on non-economic than on economic issues. Comparing the Hungarian results to Bulgarian, Czech and Polish figures, Kitschelt (1995) found that the Hungarian party system was characterized by a high degree of ideological polarization on non-economic, particularly religious, issues, while polarization on issues of economic policy was unusually low.

The next relevant finding emerges in Table 8.4, which derives from a factor analysis of the items in Table 8.3. For each issue, one variable was created. For every respondent there are seven observations, one for each party. The question is whether we can predict the perceived position of a given party on one issue from the position attributed to the same party on some other issues. If a small number of factors emerges, and all the original variables have high positive or negative factor loading on at least one of the factors, we have identified a relatively simple party space, where party positions on practically any relevant issue can be neatly predicted, once we know the position of the party on certain other issues.

In the given Hungarian data, the issue variables define essentially two dimensions. There are intimations of a third dimension or factor with an *Eigenvalue* higher than one, but this factor is almost exclusively defined by the deviant item on environmental protection. No less than 48 per cent of the variations in party positions, across the 16 issues and seven parties, can be explained by party positions on the first of the three factors. All non-economic issues, except for environmental protection, have very high loadings on this factor. Thus, preferences regarding any one of them are good predictors of preferences regarding any other. In other words, inter-party conflict on national, religious and other non-economic issues tends to be structured along a similar pattern; such issue dimensions or cleavages are not cross-cutting but overlapping.

Most economic policy items have a high loading on the second, but not on the first factor. This factor explains a mere 13.3 per cent of the variance in party positions across issues, and it does not correlate with party positions on non-economic issues. This is clearly an economically defined left/right cleavage, pitting the socialist MSZP against the two liberal parties (SZDSZ and FIDESZ) and the MDF. On the first and primary dimension, the Christian-National, anti-communist and slightly agrarian FKGP, the MIÉP, the KDNP and the MDF are differentiated from the secular, cosmopolitan, and urban MSZP, FIDESZ and SZDSZ. Thus, the analysis of the elite perceptions of party space lends support to the notion of a fairly simple cleavage structure. It is dominated by a strongly polarizing cultural dimension, cut across by a much less important and less polarizing economic left/right cleavage. This sets Hungary apart from the Czech Republic and Poland, where economic issues play a much greater role in defining the major lines of conflict in the party system and where the number of cross-cutting issue dimensions tends to be higher (Markowski 1995).

The era of the socialist–liberal coalition
In the 1994 elections, the MSZP won 54 percent of the seats with just one-third of the popular vote. On the one hand, they needed no coalition partners and on the other, they did not have to be afraid of having some. All factions of the party agreed that some coalition partners would be desirable, to avoid being locked into an unfavourable position on the (ex) communist–democrat axis, and in order to broaden the base of support for new government, which was bound to have to tackle the mounting budget and trade deficits. The Socialists rejected the FKGP and MDF as potential coalition partners because of their radical nationalist leanings and anti-communism. For their part, the FIDESZ and the KDNP plainly refused to co-operate in any way with the MSZP. This left the SZDSZ as the only alternative coalition partner. The Free Democrats, with their credentials of anti-communist dissent and monetarist and pro-Western stance, seemed to be ideal for boosting the incoming government's legitimacy at home and its credibility among investors, creditors and Western governments. A coalition partner might also provide a handy scapegoat, in the event of the Socialist government failing to live up to the expectations of Socialist voters.

When joining the coalition, the SZDSZ entertained high hopes of being able to ally themselves with the right wing of the Socialist Party in side-lining the union leaders doubling as socialist MPs. But the Free Democrats also felt that they might lose electoral support if they were to reject an offer of governmental responsibility; in any case, they felt closer affinity with the Socialists than with the Christian–Nationals on the opposition benches.[19]

Conventional wisdom has it that the economic policies of the Socialist–liberal coalition were liberal rather than socialist, but this did not prevent the liberals from losing ground in the opinion polls over the next four years. Support for the Socialists also fluctuated, but by the end of 1997 it was slightly over the May 1994 level.

In stark contrast to the period of MDF rule, the political agenda in 1994–98 was dominated by economic, social welfare and foreign policy issues. Foreign ownership of land, the Basic Treaties with Slovakia and Romania, the sale of electricity and gas companies to foreign investors, and the 1995 austerity programme were among the most divisive issues. All parties of the opposition unequivocally accused the government of betraying strategic national interests, the impoverished middle class, as well as the Magyar minorities in neighbouring countries. The MSZP and the SZDSZ cast themselves as advocates of the market, bent on rolling back a spendthrift welfare state, and as champions of European integration and foreign investment. The issue agenda had changed, but the major divisions remained related to conflicting ideas about statehood and nationhood.

With the government coalition firmly in control, the opposition struggled to form a potentially winning electoral alliance for the forthcoming elections. The elections of 1990 and 1994 had taught Hungarian party strategists that the single-member districts were crucial for the success of the political parties. *Ad hoc* alliances formed after the first round are unlikely to influence the voters of the eliminated candidates. In this light, the FIDESZ, MDF and KDNP leaders concluded that they were well advised to form a stable electoral alliance well in advance of the 1998 elections. However, bringing the FIDESZ and the FKGP into an alliance proved all but impossible, and the MDF and KDNP had held a grudge against the FKGP leader ever since he had taken his party out of the Antall government. In the final analysis, this issue of electoral coalition-building turned out to be extremely divisive within the parties of the right. In March 1996, a new party – the Hungarian Democratic People's Party (MDNP) – was formed by MDF deputies who defected on this very issue.

Mass Electoral Alignments

Table 8.5 presents data on the determinants of mass electoral behaviour (CEU 1992–). For each of the six major parties, there is a separate dependent variable coded 1 if the respondent preferred that party, and 0 if he or she preferred another party. The predictor variables were identical in all five surveys; they tap socio-demographic traits, religiosity, former communist party membership, and political attitudes. The regression coefficients measure the relative impact of each independent variable at each point in time on the preferences for each of the six parties; the statistical significance of this impact is also reported.

There is evidence of overwhelming voting stability throughout the entire period of 1992–97. The electoral base has changed significantly in only a few instances. In the case of FKGP preference, rural residence, and possibly also low education, decreased in importance over time, while the impact of anti-communism increased. On top of this, the moderately (but not the very) religious were apparently more, and former communist party members less, likely to be FKGP supporters than others in 1992–94;[21] by 1995–97, however, these relationships have lost momentum. None of the remaining predictor variables have ever been significantly related to a preference for the FKGP.

Table 8.5: Logistic regression analyses of the determinants of party preferences in five CEU surveys: B-coefficients (standard errors in parentheses) [20]

Dependent variable: FIDESZ

Date	Sept 1992	Dec 1993	Apr 1994	June 1995	Jan 1997
N of cases	740	740	740	740	740
	B S.E	B S.E	B S.E	B S.E	B S.E
YBIRTH	**.04** (.01)	**.05** (.01)	**.06** (.01)	**.04** (.01)	**.02** (.01)
EDUC	-.07 (.14)	.03 (.19)	.08 (.24)	.23 (.21)	.29 (.20)
RURAL	.06 (.18)	-.22 (.23)	-.12 (.29)	**-.50** (.24)	-.15 (.25)
PROFMANA	.01 (.34)	-.23 (.43)	**-.91** (.52)	.51 (.46)	-.27 (.49)
WHITECOL	.46 (.35)	-.17 (.40)	**-1.00** (.50)	.55 (.43)	.11 (.41)
FARM	-.36 (.41)	-.25 (.53)	-.78 (.69)	-.04 (.71)	.38 (.58)
BLUECOL	.11 (.29)	-.19 (.33)	-.49 (.35)	.53 (.37)	.00 (.34)
NOTCPMEMBER	.08 (.24)	**.76** (.35)	.08 (.43)	**1.10** (.43)	**.98** (.46)
DEVOUT	-.08 (.34)	-.40 (.45)	-.85 (.70)	-.65 (.41)	.41 (.41)
NOCHURCH	**.40** (.22)	.21 (.28)	.18 (.37)	-.37 (.27)	.27 (.32)
PROMARKET	-.06 (.08)	**.15** (.09)	-.07 (.12)	.09 (.10)	.10 (.11)
NATIONAL	**-.27** (.15)	.30 (.19)	-.04 (.23)	.29 (.20)	.28 (.20)
PROCHURCH	**-.30** (.13)	-.16 (.15)	**.34** (.20)	.16 (.15)	.06 (.15)
ANTICOMM	-.04 (.27)	-.25 (.33)	.30 (.42)	.17 (.35)	.30 (.39)

Dependent variable: FKGP

Date	Sept 1992	Dec 1993	Apr 1994	June 1995	Jan 1997
N of cases	740	740	740	740	740
	B S.E	B S.E	B S.E	B S.E	B S.E
YBIRTH	-.01 (.01)	-.01 (.01)	**-.02** (.01)	**.01** (.01)	-.00 (.01)
EDUC	**-.62** (.27)	**-.81** (.31)	**-.45** (.27)	**-.62** (.19)	-.27 (.17)
RURAL	**.94** (.32)	**1.04** (.35)	.27 (.31)	.25 (.20)	.08 (.21)
PROFMANA	-.66 (.81)	.89 (.78)	-.44 (.77)	**-.95** (.49)	-.71 (.49)
WHITECOL	-.38 (.78)	-.17 (.80)	.61 (.58)	-.58 (.41)	-.29 (.39)
FARM	.48 (.55)	.29 (.64)	.68 (.59)	-.37 (.43)	-.55 (.57)
BLUECOL	.07 (.49)	.29 (.51)	.28 (.47)	-.32 (.29)	.11 (.30)
NOTCPMEMBER	.86 (.76)	1.18 (.76)	**1.46** (.76)	.54 (.36)	.20 (.33)
DEVOUT	-.53 (.47)	-.38 (.51)	-.70 (.43)	.14 (.35)	**-.63** (.36)
NOCHURCH	-.51 (.36)	-.37 (.38) -	**1.17** (.34)	.22 (.27)	.06 (.26)
PROMARKET	-.07 (.16)	.04 (.15)	.11 (.14)	.09 (.09)	-.07 (.10)
NATIONAL	.26 (.29)	.14 (.31)	.41 (.25)	.13 (.19)	.17 (.18)
PROCHURCH	.25 (.21)	.12 (.21)	-.06 (.20)	-.04 (.13)	**.35** (.14)
ANTICOMM	.72 (.48)	**1.56** (.58)	**1.25** (.49)	**1.29** (.32)	**1.86** (.35)

Dependent variable: KDNP

Date	Sept 1992	Dec 1993	Apr 1994	June 1995	Jan 1997
N of cases	740	740	740	740	740
	B S.E	B S.E	B S.E	B S.E	B S.E
YBIRTH	-.01 (.01)	-.03 (.01)	.00 (.01)	-.03 (.01)	.01 (.01)
EDUC	-.10 (.30)	.08 (.28)	-.69 (.35)	.03 (.26)	-.48 (.33)
RURAL	-.09 (.42)	-.59 (.40)	-.42 (.46)	.03 (.33)	.09 (.43)
PROFMANA	-.96 (.79)	-.80 (.66)	1.30 (.89)	.05 (.72)	2.44 (.93)
WHITECOL	-.06 (.74)	.29 (.58)	-.11 (.92)	-.22 (.67)	1.02 (.85)
FARM	-.51 (.73)	.47 (.65)	.08 (.87)	-.19 (.68)	.78 (1.3)
BLUECOL	-.86 (.60)	-.48 (.51)	.47 (.65)	.36 (.53)	.74 (.70)
NOTCPMEMBER	6.40 (13.7)	.69 (.66)	-.29 (.66)	1.24 (.66)	-.78 (.62)
DEVOUT	.96 (.46)	1.14 (.42)	2.45 (.66)	.43 (.38)	.95 (.52)
NOCHURCH	-1.36 (.53)	-.81 (.44)	.10 (.70)	-1.44 (.41)	-1.04 (.53)
PROMARKET	.08 (.20)	.14 (.15)	.33 (.18)	-.05 (.14)	-.26 (.19)
NATIONAL	.88 (.37)	-.06 (.31)	-.15 (.35)	.45 (.31)	-.18 (.37)
PROCHURCH	1.08 (.27)	.61 (.21)	1.02 (.26)	.62 (.19)	.67 (.25)
ANTICOMM	-1.60 (.63)	.89 (.57)	-.44 (.64)	.34 (.49)	.64 (.67)

Dependent variable: MDF

Date	Sept 1992	Dec 1993	Apr 1994	June 1995	Jan 1997
N of cases	740	740	740	740	740
	B S.E	B S.E	B S.E	B S.E	B S.E
YBIRTH	-.02 (.01)	-.01 (.01)	-.02 (.01)	-.01 (.01)	.02 (.02)
EDUC	.04 (.18)	-.07 (.24)	.27 (.22)	.06 (.23)	-.23 (.39)
RURAL	.12 (.24)	.21 (.31)	.20 (.28)	-.47 (.28)	-.83 (.53)
PROFMANA	.51 (.46)	1.00 (.58)	-.73 (.55)	.43 (.58)	1.14 (1.4)
WHITECOL	-.27 (.50)	-.53 (.70)	-.10 (.48)	.31 (.57)	2.17 (1.2)
FARM	.07 (.49)	1.09 (.60)	-.18 (.56)	.44 (.68)	1.83 (1.5)
BLUECOL	-.01 (.39)	.52 (.48)	-.07 (.39)	.46 (.49)	1.61 (1.1)
NOTCPMEMBER	.79 (.40)	-.15 (.41)	.11 (.39)	.36 (.41)	.01 (.82)
DEVOUT	.03 (.36)	-.44 (.41)	-.04 (.42)	.24 (.41)	.13 (.63)
NOCHURCH	-.17 (.28)	-.62 (.32)	.09 (.35)	.15 (.34)	-1.29 (.54)
PROMARKET	.20 (.11)	.43 (.12)	.24 (.12)	.29 (.11)	-.13 (.21)
NATIONAL	.36 (.20)	.49 (.25)	.50 (.22)	.24 (.24)	-.06 (.42)
PROCHURCH	.24 (.15)	.44 (.17)	.58 (.18)	.28 (.17)	.27 (.29)
ANTICOMM	.68 (.36)	1.27 (.46)	.85 (.41)	2.35 (.47)	1.17 (.80)

Dependent variable: MSZP

Date	Sept 1992	Dec 1993	Apr 1994	June 1995	Jan 1997
N of cases	740	740	740	740	740
	B S.E	B S.E	B S.E	B S.E	B S.E
YBIRTH	-.03 (.01)	-.02 (.01)	-.00 (.01)	-.04 (.01)	-.02 (.01)
EDUC	.43 (.20)	-.02 (.16)	-.29 (.17)	-.11 (.18)	-.04 (.19)
RURAL	-.37 (.28)	.05 (.20)	.01 (.20)	.34 (.21)	.46 (.25)
PROFMANA	-.30 (.47)	.55 (.41)	.91 (.40)	.55 (.45)	-.37 (.47)
WHITECOL	-.43 (.51)	.78 (.39)	1.11 (.36)	.65 (.42)	-.83 (.43)
FARM	.77 (.58)	.34 (.46)	.56 (.43)	.43 (.49)	-.80 (.76)
BLUECOL	.33 (.44)	.45 (.34)	.29 (.31)	.36 (.36)	-.67 (.34)
NOTCPMEMBER	-.95 (.27)	-.91 (.23)	-.71 (.25)	-.99 (.24)	-.81 (.30)
DEVOUT	-1.42 (.59)	.09 (.35)	-.87 (.44)	-.55 (.40)	.50 (.46)
NOCHURCH	-.40 (.29)	.49 (.25)	.46 (.26)	.38 (.27)	.60 (.33)
PROMARKET	-.13 (.11)	-.36 (.08)	-.44 (.09)	-.07 (.08)	.00 (.11)
NATIONAL	-.28 (.21)	-.45 (.16)	-.02 (.16)	-.44 (.18)	-.03 (.20)
PROCHURCH	-.30 (.19)	-.41 (.13)	-.52 (.14)	-.30 (.14)	-.69 (.17)
ANTICOMM	-.94 (.37)	-.94 (.29)	-1.45 (.28)	-2.00 (.30)	-2.74 (.38)

Dependent variable: SZDSZP

Date	Sept 1992		Dec 1993		Apr 1994		June 1995		Jan 1997	
N of cases	740		740		740		740		740	
	B	S.E	B	S.E	B	S.E	B	S.E	B	S.E
YBIRTH	.01 (.01)		.01 (.01)		**.01** (.01)		**.03** (.01)		.02 (.01)	
EDUC	-.23 (.22)		.22 (.20)		.19 (.19)		.26 (.19)		.21 (.25)	
RURAL	**-.85** (.32)		-.34 (.27)		**-.46** (.26)		.18 (.21)		-.23 (.35)	
PROFMANA	.49 (.56)		.30 (.51)		.53 (.43)		-.05 (.40)		.44 (.59)	
WHITECOL	.50 (.55)		.41 (.49)		.07 (.42)		.24 (.36)		.53 (.52)	
FARM	.25 (.67)		.38 (.63)		-.17 (.63)		-.07 (.54)		-.56 (1.1)	
BLUECOL	.17 (.47)		.25 (.42)		.21 (.36)		-.07 (.31)		.10 (.47)	
NOTCPMEMBER	**.87** (.46)		**1.21** (.40)		**.80** (.34)		.41 (.31)		**2.74** (1.1)	
DEVOUT	-.62 (.57)		**-1.10** (.54)		-.33 (.47)		-.21 (.40)		-.46 (.59)	
NOCHURCH	.20 (.34)		.05 (.29)		.10 (.30)		-.00 (.26)		-.23 (.39)	
PROMARKET	-.05 (.13)		.10 (.10)		**.30** (.10)		.05 (.09)		**.41** (.14)	
NATIONAL	.14 (.22)		**-.42** (.21)		**-.69** (.19)		**-.33** (.18)		**-.45** (.27)	
PROCHURCH	-.01 (.19)		.04 (.16)		-.19 (.17)		**-.28** (.14)		-.23 (.22)	
ANTICOMM	.44 (.41)		.02 (.37)		**.65** (.34)		-.07 (.31)		-.68 (.51)	

In the case of the FIDESZ, only two of our independent variables seem to have had a persistent effect on the basis of support. FIDESZ voters have always been younger, and – even after controlling for their age – less likely than others to have been communist party members before 1989. There are some indications in the data to the effect that the role of age has been declining since 1994. It may also be noted that the FIDESZ scrapped the 35-year age limit for party members in the spring of 1993. The changing sign of three variables – NATIONAL, PROCHURCH and ANTICOMM – is striking and too consistent to be random, even though they are all statistically insignificant. In 1992, the FIDESZ apparently had a constituency of mildly anti-communist, mildly non-nationalist, and fewer pro-church voters, while the opposite held true after 1993–94. This is consistent with the political reorientation of the party since early 1993.

The determinants of KDNP support have been strikingly stable. The most consistent determinants are clerical attitudes, as captured by the PRO-CHURCH variable, and church attendance, as captured by the DEVOUT and NOCHURCH variables.

SZDSZ support has usually been stronger than average among those whose attitudes are less nationalist, who were not former communist party members, and the young. The evaporation in 1994 of the party's urban and anti-communist constituency, as captured by the RURAL and ANTICOMM variables, constitutes the only noteworthy change over time. Pro-market attitudes have also been directly related to support for the SZDSZ since 1994, but also in 1990 (Tóka 1995a).

With the exception of the 1997 data set (which may well prove exceptional), MDF support is invariably linked to pro-market, nationalist, pro-church and anti-communist attitudes. The socio-demographic characteristics of the voters seem to make little or no difference. The determinants of MSZP support are an almost exact mirror-image: the typical MSZP supporter was usually less pro-market, less nationalist, less pro-church, and less anti-communist than the national average. In addition, the typical MSZP voter is recruited from among the upper age brackets, the former communist party rank and file, and those who never attend church services. The data would seem to suggest that a change occurred either in, or shortly before, 1995: until then, pro-market attitudes were negatively related, but subsequently absolutely unrelated to MSZP support.

Conclusions

All in all, the determinants of party preferences vary by party, a lot more than the all-but-one-dimensional structure of party positions would seem to suggest. This is probably why the six-party system has been viable for so long. It has been possible for the political parties to carve out socio-cultural niches for themselves, more or less independently of the day-to-day political agenda. The FIDESZ, KNDP and FKGP, with their special appeal among the young, the religious, and the rural population, respectively, are cases in point. Yet economic policy issues and social class play but a minor role in party competition, on the elite as well as on the mass level. Party positions, inter-party distances and electoral behaviour are rather defined by non-economic issues. Economic conditions do have an impact on the popularity of government parties, but as long as performance evaluations remain unrelated to preferences with respect to divisive policy issues and social group identities, they cannot translate into a stable socioeconomically defined left/right cleavage.

After 1994, this effect was reinforced in one critical respect. As Table 8.5 and previous studies (cf. Markowski and Tóka 1995; Tóka 1995) suggest, MSZP support in 1993–94 was to some extent dependent on economic policy attitudes. The more bitter a voter was about market reforms, the more likely he or she was to support the Socialist Party. Yet after winning the 1994 elections, the MSZP decided to form a coalition government with the Free Democrats, the most pro-market formation of all Hungarian parties at the time, but admittedly close to the MSZP on non-economic issues. Along with the introduction of a harsh austerity programme, this move served to reinforce the dominance of cultural issues in the determination of partisan attitudes in Hungary. This development restored the largely one-dimensional nature of programmatic party competition, but the content of the dimension was fluid and redefined between-party distances from one election to another. In early 1990, inter-party relations were determined by attitudes towards the change of regime; in 1991–92 cultural and particularly religious issues became dominant. By 1996, nationalism and anti-communism were the primary determinants of coalition preferences.

The logic of the electoral system contributed towards a simplification of the party scene. Having seen and experienced the electoral system at work in 1990 and 1994, many party leaders drew the conclusion that declared coalition preferences were at least as important as the policy platforms. In 1994–97, this was to cause dramatic factional fights over the alternative 1998 electoral alliances within the MDF and KDNP. The SZDSZ found itself in a similar dilemma concerning the prospective electoral pact with the MSZP. The incentives stemming from the majoritarian features of the institutional framework – e.g. the electoral system; the strong position of the Prime Minister *vis-à-vis* the cabinet; the constructive vote of no confidence; and the relative absence of checks and balances – make parties strongly dependent on their coalition preferences and force them to declare them well in advance of an election. The majoritarian features also make it difficult to reconcile six unique ideological niches with a variety of coalition set-ups. It seems likely that a relatively simple cleavage structure, with little rooting in the class structure or other non-cultural variables, will continue to characterize Hungary for some time to come.

Acronyms used in the text and the tables

ASZ	Agrarian Alliance
EKA	Opposition Roundtable
FIDESZ	Federation of Young Democrats
FKGP	Independent Smallholders Party
KDNP	Christian Democratic People's Party
KP	Republic Party
MDF	Hungarian Democratic Forum
MDNP	Hungarian Democratic People's Party
MIÉP	Party of Hungarian Justice and Life
MNP	Hungarian People's Party
MSZDP	Social Democratic Party of Hungary
MSZMP	Hungarian Socialist Workers' Party
MSZP	Hungarian Socialist Party
SZDSZ	Alliance of Free Democrats

NOTES

1. More precisely, aggregate level or net volatility means half the sum of the absolute percentage differences between the votes received by each party in two consecutive elections. Suppose that there are three parties contesting the first of two elections, each receiving 33.3 per cent of the vote; if one of them goes out of business by the time of the next election, and the remaining two receive 60 and 40 per cent of the vote, respectively, then the total volatility between the two elections was $(33.3+|33.3–60|+|33.3–40|)/2=(33.3+26.7+6.7)/2= 33.3$ per cent.

2. Only a few – though certainly not all – elections in Albania, Bulgaria, Croatia, and Romania might be exceptions, but the lack of sufficiently detailed data on the small parties in these countries precludes a firm conclusion.

3. On the West European figures for 1885–1985, cf. Bartolini and Mair (1990).

4. For parliamentary elections, the legal threshold for party lists winning mandates was raised from 4 to 5 per cent of the list votes. Otherwise, even the constituency boundaries have remained unchanged since 1990. The local election law, however, was altered in October 1994 despite a walk out of the entire parliamentary opposition from the final vote. Yet the controversy over the substance of this reform must not be exaggerated. The preferred strategy of the opposition – i.e. implicit electoral alliances in run-off elections between parties that were not ready to enter a formal electoral pact – had to be abandoned because of the shift to a single-round electoral system. The main features of the reform enjoyed all-party consensus.

5. *Source:* Central and Eastern Eurobarometer 6, Machine readable data file. Cologne, Zentralarchiv.

6. Searching for the roots and motivation of this consensus is well beyond the scope of this chapter.

7. The orthodox communist MSZMP and the radical nationalist MIÉP, which had a small parliamentary representation in 1993–94, were exceptions to this.

8. The wording of the questions and the coding of the responses for this analysis were as follows: *Market:* 'Do you personally feel that the creation of a free market economy, that is one largely free from state control, is right or wrong for [OUR COUNTRY'S] future?' (1=right, 2=wrong, 3=do not know, no answer). *EU:* 'If there were to be a referendum tomorrow on the question of [OUR COUNTRY'S] membership in the European Union, would you personally vote for or against membership?' (1=for, 2=against, 3=do not know, no answer) *NATO:* 'If there were to be a referendum tomorrow on the question of [OUR COUNTRY'S] membership in NATO, would you personally vote for or against membership?' (1=for, 2=against, 3=do not know, no answer) All coefficients are significant at least on the .01 level. Respondents who were not entitled to vote in their country of residence are excluded from the computation of the percentages. *Source:* Eastern and Central Eurobarometer 6. Machine readable data file. Cologne, Zentralarchiv.

9. On Czech, Hungarian, Polish and Slovak volatility estimates, cf. Tóka (1997). Note that the Czech and Polish volatility figures were corrected for mere changes of party labels. On volatility in Estonia, cf. Taagepera (1995). The Lithuanian figure was calculated from partial election returns and is a lower bound estimate due to the lack of data on some very small parties.

10. The Bajcsy–Zsilinszky Society (BZSBT) did not even contest any election on its own, and two other member organizations, the Hungarian People's Party (MNP) and the Social Democratic Party (MSZDP) dismally failed to win parliamentary representation.

11. A similar, but much more detailed analysis is given by Körösényi (forthcoming).

12. For 1990 roll-call data, cf. Hanyecz and Perger (1991).

13. For pre-election analyses of election platforms, cf. Urbán (1990); Kovács and Tóth (1990).

14. The treaty was opposed by the far right because of a clause confirming that Hungary had no claims on Ukrainian territory. The treaty was nevertheless ratified with unanimous support from the opposition, but in order to avoid further defections the government had to pledge itself not to sign any such treaty with other neighbours for the duration of its term.

15. The dominant faction in the FIDESZ leadership anticipated that the more SZDSZ-leaning elements might leave the party as a result of the new strategy (indeed, former vice-president Fodor ended up as the number two candidate on the SZDSZ national list in 1994 and as one of the three SZDSZ ministers of Gyula Horn's first government). This, however, was a welcome rather than an unwanted by-product of the new strategy: e.g. Fodor was the only potentially serious challenger of party leader Viktor Orbán in the leadership races and could well have unseated the latter after the 1994 election fiasco if he had not already left the party.

16. See the Gallup reports in *Magyar Nemzet* (30 May 1994) and *Pesti Hírlap* (1 June 1994); also Tóka (1995a).

17. The responses were recoded as explained in the text. N=129. *Source:* Four-country survey of middle-level party elites by Herbert Kitschelt et al., Spring 1994, Durham, NC, Duke University.

18. The responses were recoded as explained in the text. N=129. Source: Four-country survey of mid-level party elites by Herbert Kitschelt et al., Spring 1994, Durham, NC, Duke University.
19. For a different and much more detailed assessment, cf. Körösényi (1995).
20. Parameters significant on the .10 level are printed in bold. The regression constants are not reproduced. The Bs are logistic regression coefficients, showing the net impact of each independent variable on party choice when all other variables in the equation are controlled for. Since they are non-standardized parameters, the effect of the various independent variables can only be compared in terms of their positive or negative sign and statistical significance level, but they do not, strictly speaking, tell whether FIDESZ support in 1992 was better explained by YBIRTH or by EDUC. However, the magnitude of the net impact of the given independent variable can be compared across equations, i.e. the table tells us whether support for FIDESZ in 1992 was more strongly influenced by YBIRTH than, e.g. MDF support in 1997. The column headed 'S.E.' shows the standard error of each B coefficient. Dependent variables are coded 1 if the respondent named the party in question as his or her preferred choice 'if there were an election next Sunday', and 0 if she or he named another party. Respondents without party preference are excluded from the analysis. Independent variables are:

YBIRTH: year of birth (last two digits)
EDUC: education (1=less than primary; 2=primary completed; 3=secondary completed; 4=university or college completed)
RURAL: place of residence (2=city; 3=village)
PROFMANA: current or last occupation (1=manager or professional; 0=all others)
WHITECOL: current or last occupation (1=white collar employee; 0=all others)
FARM: current or last occupation (1=farmer or agricultural worker; 0=all others)
BLUECOL: current or last occupation (1=blue collar employee; 0=all others)
NOTCPMEMBER: communist party membership before 1990 (2=never was a communist party member; 1=was a communist party member some time before 1990)
DEVOUT: how frequently the respondent attends religious services (1=at least once a week; 0=less frequently)
NOCHURCH: how frequently the respondent attends religious services (1=never; 0=more frequently)
PROMARKET, NATIONAL, PROCHURCH, and ANTICOMM are attitude indices constructed from responses to the following questions in the way described below:
'Please tell me how much you agree or disagree with the following statements: [Responses to all items were coded as 0=definitely agree; 0.33=rather agree; 0.67=rather disagree; 1=definitely disagree]
(Q16C:) It should be the government's responsibility to provide a job for everyone who wants one.
(Q16D:) It is harmful for the economy if the government tries to reduce income differences between rich and poor.
(Q16F:) Giving the former state-owned companies private property is going to help a lot in solving the economic problems of our country.
(Q16G:) Unprofitable factories and mines should be closed down immediately, even if this leads to unemployment.
(Q16H:) Politicians who do not believe in God should not perform public functions.
(Q16I:) Nationalism is (always) harmful for the development of our country.
(Q16N:) A woman should be allowed to have an abortion in the early weeks of pregnancy, if she decides so.
(Q16O:) In case of a politician, I prefer a strong (good) patriot to an expert.
(Q16P:) The Church has (the Churches have) too much influence in our country.
Political parties may pursue very different goals. Now I am going to read you some and I would like to ask your opinion about them. Please answer using this card: [The response card showed a nine point scale running from 'very strongly in favour of' – coded as 1 – through 'neither in favour, nor against' – coded as 0.5 – to 'very strongly against it' – coded as 0.]
(Q18B:) Help the development of private enterprises and a free market economy in Hungary.

(Q18K:) Strengthen national feelings.

(Q18L:) Increase pensions and social benefits.

(Q18E:) Guarantee that less economic burden is put on the shoulder of people during the transformation of our economy.

(Q18M:) Increase the influence of religion and the Churches.

(Q18N:) Speed up the privatization of state-owned companies.

(Q18Q:) Removing former communist party members from positions of influence.

Missing values were replaced with the sample mean on all attitude variables used in constructing the PROMARKET, NATIONAL, PROCHURCH, and ANTICOMM indices.

PROMARKET: index of economic policy attitudes. High values indicate pro-, low values indicate anti-market attitudes. The index was computed as: PROMARKET=Q16C–Q16D–Q16F–Q16G+Q18B–Q18L–Q18E+Q18N.

NATIONAL: index of nationalist attitudes. High values indicate more, low values indicate less nationalist attitudes. The index was computed as: NATIONAL=Q16I–Q16O+Q18K.

PROCHURCH: index of pro- versus anti-religious attitudes. High values indicate pro-, low values indicate anti-clerical attitudes. The index was computed as: PROCHURCH=Q16N–Q16H+Q16P+Q18M.

ANTICOMM: attitudes towards communists. High values indicate pro-, low values indicate anti-communist attitudes. The index was computed as: ANTICOMM=Q18Q.

Source: CEU (1992–).

21. Note that in Table 8.5 the negative effects of DEVOUT (frequent church attendance) and NOCHURCH (no church attendance), and the positive effect of NOTCPMEMBER on FKGP support show up very consistently in the 1992–94 surveys, even though they are not always statistically significant.

REFERENCES

Alwin, Duane F. (1992), *The International Social Justice Survey, Codebook*, Ann Arbor, MI, Institute of Social Research.

Angelusz, Róbert and Róbert Tardos (1996), 'Választási részvétel Magyarországon 1990–1994', *Politikatudományi Szemle* 5 (4).

Bartolini, Stefano and Peter Mair (1990), *Identity, Competition, and Electoral Availability: The Stabilisation of the European Electorates 1885–1985*, Cambridge, Cambridge University Press.

Benoit, Kenneth (1996), 'Hungary's two-ballot electoral system', *Representation* 33 (4), 162–70.

Bozóki, András (1996), 'Intellectuals in a new democracy, the democratic charter in Hungary', *East European Politics and Societies* 10 (Spring 1996), 173–213.

——, András Körösényi and George Schöpflin, eds. (1992), *Post-Communist Transition: Emerging Pluralism in Hungary*, London, Frances Pinter.

Bruszt, László (1990), 'The negotiated revolution in Hungary', *Social Forces* 57, 365–87.

CEU (Central European University) 1992–, *The Development of Party Systems and Electoral Alignments in East Central Europe*, Machine readable data files, Budapest, Department of Political Science, Central European University.

Chronicle of Parliamentary Elections and Developments, Geneva, Interparliamentary Union, International Centre for Parliamentary Documentation, annual edition.

Commission of the European Communities 1991–, *Central and Eastern Eurobarometer*, Brussels, European Commission.

Dohnalik, Jacek, Jan Hartl, Krzysztof Jasiewicz, Radoslaw Markowski, Petr Mateju, Lubos Rezler, Gábor Tóka and Milan Tucek, (1991), *Dismantling of the Social Safety Net and Its Political Consequences in East Central Europe: An International Comparative Study Initiated and Sponsored by the Institute of East-West Studies, N.Y. and Prague*, Machine readable data file, Distributors: IEWS, New York and TÁRKI, Budapest.

Enyedi, Zsolt (1996), 'Organizing a subcultural party in Eastern Europe', *Party Politics* 2, 377–97.

Evans, Geoffrey and Stephen Whitefield (1996), 'The social bases of electoral competition in

Eastern Europe', Paper prepared for presentation at the European Science Foundation conference on *Transition and Political Power Structures* in Cambridge, UK, 19–21 April.

Ferge, Zsuzsa (1991), 'Social Security Systems in the New Democracies of Central and Eastern Europe: Past Legacies and Possible Futures', in Giovanni Andrea Cornia and Sándor Sipos, eds., *Children and the Transition to the Market Economy: Safety Nets and Social Policies in Central and Eastern Europe*, Aldershot, Avebury, 69–90.

Glenny, Misha (1990), *The Rebirth of History: Eastern Europe in the Age of Democracy*, London, Penguin Books, 72–95.

Greskovits, Béla (1993), 'Dominant economy, subordinated politics: the absence of economic populism in the transition of East-Central Europe', *Political Science Department Working Paper* Series No.1, Budapest, Central European University.

—— (1995), 'Demagogic populism in Eastern Europe?' *Telos,* 102 (1995), 91–106.

Hanyecz, Imre and János Perger 1992, 'A Parlament munkája számokban', in Sándor Kurtán, Péter Sándor and László Vass, eds., *Political Yearbook of Hungary 1992*, Budapest, DKMKA – Economix, 92–122.

ISSP 1990, The Role of Government, Machine readable data file, Distributor, Köln, Zentralarchiv.

Karatnycky, Adrian, Alexander Motyl and Boris Shor, eds. (1997), *Nations in Transit,* Washington, DC, Freedom House.

Katzenstein, Peter (1985), *Small States in World Markets,* Ithaca, NY, Cornell University Press.

Kitschelt, Herbert (1995), 'Patterns of competition in East Central European party systems', Paper prepared for presentation at the 1995 Annual Meeting of the *American Political Science Association*, Chicago, 31 August–3 September.

——, Zdenka Mansfeldová, Radoslaw Markowski and Gábor Tóka (forthcoming), *Post-Communist Party Systems: Competition, Representation, and Inter-Party Cooperation.*

Körösényi, András (1991), 'Revival of the past or a new beginning? The nature of post-communist politics', *Political Quarterly,* 62 (1), 1–23.

—— (1995), 'Forced Coalition or Natural Alliance? The Socialist-Liberal Democrat Coalition 1994', in Csaba Gombár, Elemér Hankiss, László Lengyel and Györgyi Várnai, eds.,*Question Marks: The Hungarian Government 1994–1995*, Budapest: Korridor, 256–77.

—— (forthcoming), 'Cleavages and Party System in Hungary', chapter prepared for Gábor Tóka and Zsolt Enyedi, eds., *The 1994 Elections to the Hungarian National Assembly*, Berlin, Sigma.

Kovács, Éva and István J. Tóth (1990), 'Pártok és pártprogrammok 1990', Budapest University of Economics, manuscript.

Kurtán, Sándor (1997), 'Tények és adatok az Országgyűlés tevékenységéről', in Sándor Kurtán, Péter Sándor and László Vass, eds., *Magyarország politikai évkönyve – Political Yearbook of Hungary 1997*, Budapest, DKMKA.

Mair, Peter (1996), 'What is different about post-communist party systems?', *Studies in Public Policy* 259, Glasgow, University of Strathclyde, Centre for the Study of Public Policy.

Markowski, Radoslaw (1995), 'Political competition and ideological dimensions in Central Eastern Europe', *Studies in Public Policy* 257, Glasgow, University of Strathclyde, Centre for the Study of Public Policy.

Munck, Gerardo L. and Carol Skalnik Leff (1997), 'Models of transition and democratization, South America and Eastern Europe in comparative perspective', *Comparative Politics,* 30 (April 1997), 343–61.

Okolicsányi, Károly (1994), 'Hungary's budget deficit worsens', *RFE/RL Research Report*, 14 January, 36–8.

Oltay, Edith (1993a), 'Hungarian radio and television under fire', *RFE/RL Research Report*, 24 September, 40–4.

—— (1993b), 'Hungary: Csurka launches 'National Movement'' *RFE/RL Research Report*, 26 March, 25–31.

—— (1993c), 'Hungarian Democratic Forum expels radical leader', *RFE/RL Research Report,* 30 July, 24–9.

—— (1994a), 'Hungary', *RFE/RL Research Report*, 22 April, 55–61.

—— (1994b), 'Hungarian socialists prepare for come-back', *RFE/RL Research Report,* 4 March, 21–6.

Patáki, Judith (1992), 'István Csurka's tract: summary and reactions',*RFE/RL Research Report*, 9

October, 15–22.

—— (1994a), 'Hungarian radio staff cuts cause uproar', *RFE/RL Research Report*, 13 May, 38–40.

—— (1994b), 'Hungary's smallholders fail to unite before national elections', *RFE/RL Research Report*, 11 March, 15–9.

Rose, Richard and Christian Haerpfer (1996), 'Change and stability in the new democracies barometer: a trend analysis', *Studies in Public Policy* 270, Glasgow, University of Strathclyde, Centre for the Study of Public Policy.

Szoboszlai, György (1996), 'Parliamentarism in the Making: Crisis and Political Transformation in Hungary', in Arend Lijphart and Carlos H. Waisman, eds., *Institutional Design in New Democracies*, Boulder, CO, Westview Press, 117–36.

Taagepera, Rein (1995), 'Estonian parliamentary elections, March 1995', *Electoral Studies* 14, 328–31.

Tóth, István János (1992), 'Képviselők és pártok a Parlamentben', in Sándor Kurtán, Péter Sándor, and László Vass, eds., *Political Yearbook of Hungary 1992*, Budapest, DKMKA–Economix, 81–91.

Tóka, Gábor (1992), 'A kakukk fészke: Pártrendszer és törésvonalak Magyarországon' *Politikatudományi Szemle*, 1 (2), 123–59

—— (1993), 'Changing Dimensions of Party Competition, Hungary 1990–1991', in Gerd Meyer, ed., *The Political Cultures of Eastern Central Europe in Transition*, Tübingen and Basel, Francke Verlag, 165–228.

—— (1995a), 'Parties and Elections in Hungary in 1990 and 1994', in Béla K. Király and András Bozóki, eds., *Lawful Revolution in Hungary, 1989–94*, Highland Lakes, NJ, Atlantic Research and Publications, Inc., 131–58.

—— (1995b), 'The Working and Political Background of the Hungarian Election Law', in Gábor Tóka, ed., *The 1990 Hungarian Elections to the National Assembly*, Berlin, Sigma, 41–66.

—— (1996), 'Parties and Electoral Choices in East Central Europe,' in Paul Lewis and Geoffrey Pridham, eds., *Stabilising Fragile Democracies*, London, Routledge, 100–25.

—— (1997), 'Political Parties in East Central Europe', in Larry Diamond, Marc F. Plattner, Yunhan Chu and Hung-mao Tien, eds., *Consolidating the Third Wave Democracies, Themes and Perspectives*, Baltimore, MD, Johns Hopkins University Press, 93–134.

Tóka, Gábor (forthcoming). 'The Effect of Various Modes of Party Appeals, Evidence from New Democracies', in Richard I. Hofferbert, ed., *Political Studies*, special issue of *Party Performance*, Oxford, Blackwell.

Tóka, Gábor and Zsolt Enyedi, eds., (forthcoming), *The 1994 Elections to the Hungarian National Assembly*, Berlin, Sigma

Urbán, László (1990), 'Gazdasági programjavaslatok, koalíciós esélyek,' *Magyar Narancs* 2 (4), 1–5.

US State Department 1997. *1996 Country Reports on Human Rights Practices,* Washington, DC, US State Department, also at: http://www.state.gov/www/global/human_rights/index.html.

Voter Turnout from 1945 to 1997: A Global Report on Political Participation, Stockholm, International Institute for Democracy and Electoral Assistance, 1997.

APPENDIX 8.1: ELECTORAL RESULTS

Distribution of list votes in the 1990 and 1994 parliamentary elections

	1990, %	*1994, %*
Workers' Party (MP, ex-MSZMP)	3.7	3.2
Hungarian Socialist Party (MSZP)	10.9	33.0
Social Democratic Party of Hungary (MSZDP)	3.6	0.9
Green Party of Hungary (MZP)	0.4	0.2
Agrarian Alliance (ASZ)	3.1	2.1
Alliance of Free Democrats (SZDSZ)	21.4	19.7
Federation of Young Democrats (FIDESZ)	9.0	7.0
Party of Entrepreneurs (VP)	1.9	0.6
Hungarian Democratic Forum (MDF)	24.7	11.7
Christian Democratic People's Party (KDNP)	6.5	7.0
Independent Smallholders' Party (FKGP)	11.7	8.8
Others	3.2	5.6

Note: Parties in the 'other' category only contested one of the two elections and none won any seats.

Sources: 'Az Országos Választási Bizottság jelentése' (Report of the National Election Committee), *Magyar Közlöny,* 13 May 1990, and 'Az Országos Választási Bizottság jelentése' (Report of the National Election Committee), *Magyar Közlöny,* 24 June 1994.

Distribution of seats in the 1990 and 1994 parliamentary elections

	1990				1994			
	SMD	*Regional list*	*National list*	*Total*	*SMD*	*Regional list*	*National list*	*Total*
ASZ	1	0	0	1	1	0	0	1
FIDESZ	1	8	12	21	0	7	13	20
FKGP	11	16	17	44	1	14	11	26
KDNP	3	8	10	21	3	5	14	22
MDF	114	40	10	164	5	18	15	38
MSZP	1	14	18	33	149	53	7	209
SZDSZ	35	34	23	92	16	28	25	69
Joint candidates	4	0	0	4	1	0	0	1
Independents	6	0	0	6	0	0	0	0
Total	176	120	90	386	176	125	85	386

Sources: 'Az Országos Választási Bizottság jelentése (Report of the National Election Committee)', *Magyar Közlöny,* 13 May 1990; 'Az Országos Választási Bizottság jelentése (Report of the National Election Committee)', *Magyar Közlöny,* 24 June 1994.

Turnout in the 1990 and 1994 parliamentary elections (including invalid and blank votes)

1990			1994		
Party lists	Single-member districts		Party lists	Single-member districts	
	1st round	2nd round		1st round	2nd round
65.1	65.0	45.5	68.9	68.9	55.1

Note: Turnout in the voting for party lists is higher than in the single-member districts, because voters casting their ballot outside their home constituency can only vote for regional party lists, and not for the candidates standing in the single-member districts.

Sources: On the turnout in the list voting see 'Az Országos Választási Bizottság jelentése (Report of the National Election Committee)', *Magyar Közlöny,* 13 May 1990, and 'Az Országos Választási Bizottság jelentése (Report of the National Election Committee)', *Magyar Közlöny,* 24 June 1994. On turnout in the single-member districts see Tóka (1995b); Róbert Angelusz and Róbert Tardos (1996), 'Választási részvétel Magyarországon 1990–1994', *Politikatudományi Szemle* 5 (4). An edited English version is forthcoming as 'Electoral participation in Hungary, 1990–1994', in Gábor Tóka and Zsolt Enyedi, eds., *The 1994 Elections to the Hungarian National Assembly,* Berlin, Sigma. Note that slightly different figures regarding 1990 and 1994, respectively, are reported by the widely used *Chronicle of Parliamentary Elections and Developments,* Geneva, Interparliamentary Union, International Centre for Parliamentary Documentation, annual edition, and *Voter Turnout from 1945 to 1997: A Global Report on Political Participation,* Stockholm, International Institute for Democracy and Electoral Assistance, 1997.

Distribution of seats in the 1990–94 parliament at its first session on 2 May 1990 and immediately before its dissolution on 7 April 1994

	May 1990		April 1994	
	N	(%)	N	(%)
Formally recognized party caucuses:				
FIDESZ	22	(6)	26	(7)
FKGP	44	(11)		
'Smallholder 35s'	-		36	(9)
KDNP	21	(5)	23	6
MDF	165	(43)	136	(35)
MIÉP	—		12	(3)
MSZP	33	(9)	33	(9)
SZDSZ	94	(24)	83	(22)
Party affiliation of deputies not belonging to party caucus:				
ASZ	1	(0)	2	(1)
FKGP	-		9	(2)
Any one of 8 other parties	-		15	(4)
None	6	(2)	11	(3)
Grand Total	386		386	

Note: Percentages may not add up to 100 due to rounding errors. The distribution of seats at the first session of the parliament is not identical to the election results, because some deputies elected as independents or joint candidates joined various party caucuses.

Source: Magyar Hírlap, 8 April 1994, 11.

Distribution of seats in the 1994–98 parliament at its first session on 28 June 1994 and on 31 December 1996

	June 1994		December 1996	
	N	(%)	N	(%)
Formally recognized party caucuses:				
FIDESZ	20	(5)	21	(5)
FKGP	26	(7)	24	(6)
KDNP *	22	(6)	23	(6)
MDF	38	(10)	19	(5)
MDNP	-		15	(4)
MSZP	209	(54)	209	(54)
SZDSZ	70	(18)	68	(18)
Party affiliation of deputies not belonging to party caucuses				
LPSZ–VP	1	(0)	1	(0)
MDF	-		1	(0)
None	-		4	(1)
Grand Total	386		385	

Notes: Percentages may not add up to 100 due to rounding errors. The distribution of the seats at the first session of the parliament is not identical to the election results, because an ASZ deputy joined the SZDSZ caucus, and an elected joint candidate of the LPSZ-VP-ASZ-FIDESZ-SZDSZ electoral alliance decided to sit as an independent. * During the summer recess of 1997, most of the KDNP deputies were expelled from the party or left it voluntarily. The remaining KDNP members of the parliament were not numerous enough to have a parliamentary caucus of their own. Most of the expelled MPs formed the Christian Democratic Alliance and joined the parliamentary caucus of the FIDESZ.

Source: Kurtán, Sándor (1997), 'Tények és adatok az Országgyűlés tevékenységéről', in Sándor Kurtán, Péter Sándor and László Vass, eds., *Magyarország politikai évkönyve – Political Yearbook of Hungary 1997*, Budapest, DKMKA, 413–4.

APPENDIX 8.2: GOVERNMENT COMPOSITION

Partisan composition of governments and the cause of their termination, 1989–1998

December 1988 – 23 May 1990

Premier: Miklós Németh

Government parties: MSZMP until October 1989, thereafter MSZP. Overwhelming but not entirely quantifiable legislative support from virtually all deputies elected in the 1985 non-competitive elections.

Cause of termination: March–April 1990 general elections.

23 May 1990 – 21 February 1992

Premier: József Antall

Government parties: MDF, KDNP, FKGP

Cause of termination: the FKGP left the coalition, though 35 FKGP deputies (eventually expelled from the party) continued to support the government. Since the Premier did not resign and no no-confidence motion was passed by the Parliament, from the point of view of Hungarian constitutional law, no change of government occurred.

21 February 1992 – 21 December 1993

Premier: József Antall

Government parties: MDF, KDNP, and various splinter groups from FKGP; in June 1993 the Hungarian Justice National Politics Group and from July 1993 the MIÉP also supported the government in the legislature.

Cause of termination: József Antall died on 12 December 1993, and a new Prime Minister had to be elected.

21 December 1993 – 15 July 1994

Premier: Péter Boross

Government parties: MDF, KDNP, EKGP; legislative support from the MIÉP caucus.

Cause of termination: May 1994 general elections.

15 July 1994 –

Premier: Gyula Horn

Government parties: MSZP, SZDSZ

Cause of termination: May 1998 general elections.

APPENDIX 8.3: THE ELECTORAL SYSTEM

The rules pertaining to parliamentary elections are laid down in Act. No. XXXIV of 1989, slightly amended in 1994 and 1997, as indicated below. All Hungarian citizens over 18 years of age are eligible to stand as candidates and vote in parliamentary elections, with the exception of citizens who have no domicile in Hungary, are abroad on the day of the given election, are under guardianship, have been banned from public affairs, or are serving a sentence of imprisonment or under forced medical treatment ordered in the course of a criminal procedure. Further rules regarding the campaign and so on, are formulated by the National Election Committee, which also supervises the elections and announces the election results. The composition of the National Election Committee is based on parity among the parties. The secretary and two members of the local returning boards are elected by the local council, and one member can be delegated by each party and each independent candidate running in the district.

Every voter may cast two votes: for a candidate in a single-member district (henceforth SMD); and for a regional party list in a multi-member constituency. If the turnout remains below 50 per cent either in a regional district (henceforth RD) or in an SMD, the result is invalid and the election has to be repeated on the day set by the National Election Committee for the second round of the general elections.

Candidates running in the SMDs are considered elected if they receive an absolute majority of the valid votes in the first round. Barring this, a run-off round takes place between those candidates who received more than 15 percent of the valid votes or were among the top three vote-winners. If the turnout in the first round is below 50 per cent, all candidates can contest the run-off. In either case, the candidate with the largest number of votes in the run-off round is elected, provided that the turnout was over 25 percent.

The average RD has 7 seats which are filled from party lists according to a quota system. The quota equals the number of valid votes divided by one plus the number of seats. If unallocated seats remain after one seat has been awarded to each full quota, the party lists win these remaining seats in the order of their number of remainder votes, provided that their remainder votes are equal to at least two-thirds of the quota. The difference between the full quota and the remainder votes that earned a mandate is subtracted from the party's cumulated remainder votes on the national level. Due to the above mentioned two-thirds rule, about one-fifth or more of RD seats remain unallocated on the regional level and are added to the national pool of compensatory mandates. The relatively small multi-member constituencies and the allocation rules significantly favour those parties that obtain at least 10–15 per cent of the vote locally. Apart from this, no party can gain any list mandates if it obtains less than 4 per cent (since January 1994, 5 per cent) of the list votes nationally (henceforth legal threshold). Voters cannot express preferences regarding the ranking of the candidates on the party lists.

Candidates can also win seats on the national lists of the parties. The voters do not vote directly for these lists. Rather, the remainder votes – i.e. votes which, after the completion of the above steps, did not yet go towards obtaining a mandate either in the multi-member or in the single-member constituencies are cumulated on the national level by party. Fifty-eight compensatory mandates plus the unallocated RD seats are distributed according to their cumulated number of remainder votes among the national lists of those parties which surpassed the legal threshold according to the d'Hondt highest average method.

The country is divided into 176 SMDs and 20 RDs. Candidates standing for parliament in a single-member district must collect at least 750 supporting signatures in the district to appear on the ballot. Every party which has nominated candidates in one quarter, but at least in two of all SMDs within an RD, have the right to set up a regional list. Parties which have lists in more than six RDs are allowed to have a national list.

Source: Tóka (1995b) and Benoit (1996).

APPENDIX 8.4: THE CONSTITUTIONAL FRAMEWORK

The constitutional framework of post-communist Hungary was laid down in the amendments passed in October 1989 and in the summer of 1990 following the agreements in the National Roundtable Talks in 1989, and the 30 April 1990 MDF–SZDSZ agreement, respectively.

Hungary is a parliamentary republic without any trace of federalism. There are nineteen regional assemblies, and since 1994 they have been directly elected, but their prerogatives and political significance are such that they practically never appear in the news. The Parliament is uni-cameral and is elected for four years, and nearly all executive power is held by a Government responsible to this assembly. The Parliament has a specialized committee system and access to generous public funds for party caucuses. Individual members have the right to initiate legislation and propose amendments; they enjoy legal immunity that can only be waived by the assembly; they are entitled to submit interpellations to the Prime Minister and other Ministers. The Parliament can dissolve itself at any time, but failing that, it is likely to serve its full term since the President of the Republic can dissolve it only under highly unusual circumstances.

The major checks on the power of the Parliament are provided by referenda and especially by the Constitutional Court. Members of the Court are elected by a super-majority in parliament from among a relatively broadly defined pool of legal professionals. Anyone can ask the Court to declare a law, decree or rule unconstitutional, even before it comes into effect. The Court has considerable leverage in extending its investigation to related rules not mentioned by the appeal on the table, and it routinely interprets the supposed spirit or implications rather than the letter of the constitution. Referenda can only be called by the legislature, which, however, is bound to call a referendum if a referendum has been proposed by at least 100,000 (from 1997: 200,000) citizens. However, no referendum may be called on constitutional and budgetary issues or questions that might lead to the revocal of international agreements.

The President can single-handedly dissolve parliament if, following an election or the death or resignation of the Prime Minister, no candidate for Prime Minister candidate wins a vote of investiture within 40 days of the first nomination, or if four different governments are brought down by the parliament within a year. The deputies can bring down a Prime Minister either through a constructive vote of no confidence (which can be initiated by one-fifth of the deputies), or by defeating a simple vote of confidence initiated by the Prime Minister. The constructive vote of no confidence, if passed, automatically installs as new Prime Minister the alternative candidate named in the motion. Otherwise, it is the President's exclusive right to nominate a Prime Minister – who can be any Hungarian citizen. In practice, President Göncz always consulted the parliamentary parties and followed their unanimous advice, i.e. that the candidate named by the strongest parliamentary caucus must be given the first opportunity. A nominee for Prime Minister has to present a programme to the assembly, which then votes on the candidate and the programme. An investiture or constructive no-confidence vote needs the support of an absolute majority of all members of the parliament. Cabinet ministers are nominated by the Prime Minister and appointed by the President. The constitution refers to the responsibility of individual Ministers to the assembly, but gives the latter no power to remove the former. Obviously, in actual practice the prospective coalition partners agree on the composition of the cabinet prior to the election of a Prime Minister.

The head of state is elected by the parliament for a five-year term. One re-election is allowed. If no candidate receives a two-thirds majority in the first two rounds, a candidate can be elected by a simple majority in a third round within three days. The current President, Árpád Göncz, was a little known opposition (SZDSZ) backbencher when he was unanimously elected in May 1990 as part of a comprehensive MDF–SZDSZ deal. In June 1995, he was re-elected for a second term by the two government parties, against a candidate of the opposition, when his party of origin was a junior coalition partner of the MSZP, which had an overall majority on its own right. These facts probably explain why it is not widely appreciated that the Hungarian President is – formally – among the most powerful presidents in East Central Europe. Before signing a law, the President can send it back to Parliament once, with comments urging reconsideration, or refer it for judicial review to the Constitutional Court. The President's right to refuse appointments or dismissals proposed by the Prime Minister is severely limited, but there is no legal remedy against his or her decision. The President has the right to address the Parliament, and to initiate legislation and referenda. According to Article 29 of the constitution, the President 'shall express the unity of the nation and safeguard the democratic functioning of the state', and acts as the (nominal) Commander-in-Chief of the army.

The Prime Minister dominates the executive since he or she is the sole focus of parliamentary accountability. The Prime Minister's office has a staff of several hundred. In addition to the 13 (since July 1994: only 12) ordinary cabinet Ministers, there is an ever-changing number of ministers without portfolio, who are responsible for specific jurisdictions and work out of the Prime Minister's Office.

9. Slovenia

Drago Zajc

The countries in East Central Europe are characterized by an intensive process of pluralization of political, economic, social and cultural life. New cleavage lines and conflicts are emerging; handling these conflicts is even more demanding and challenging in the new democracies than in the more established ones. It is also closely related to the consolidation of democracy.

The new democracies are faced with the problem of managing a variety of new conflicts, through a viable conflict-regulating system capable of producing stable consensus. This chapter attempts to identify, at least in a rudimentary form, the old and new cleavage lines appearing in the transitory phase; which of them are relevant for party-political conflicts; and what are the principles for the management of these conflicts. We will also attempt to describe the extent to which the new party systems correspond to the main social cleavages, and the role of the political parties within the context of conflicts, particularly in transmitting the conflicts into the parliamentary arena. Finally, we will try to evaluate the ability of the new parliamentary institutions to handle the transitional conflicts.

Cleavage Structures in Modern Democracies

Lipset's and Rokkan's historical and comparative reconstruction of conflicts is one of the most influential approaches to the study of political cleavages and cleavage structures. According to these two authors, the main course of political development has been determined chiefly by the national and industrial revolutions (Lipset and Rokkan 1967), which have created four major cleavage lines. The cleavage between central nation-building forces and the resisting ethnically, linguistically or religiously distinct subject nations, is one product of the national revolution; the cleavage between the centralising modern nation-state and the privileges of the church is the other. The two remaining cleavages are products of the industrial revolu-

275

tion: the cleavage between rural and urban interests; and that between capital and labour (Lipset and Rokkan 1967).

The dissolution of the Austrian, Russian and Ottoman empires at the end of the First World War deeply influenced nation-building and state-building in Central Eastern and South Eastern Europe, particularly in the 'buffer' area from the Baltic Sea to the Adriatic, where Western and Eastern cultural and political influences mix. The breakdown of the empires solved many tensions in this region, but it also led to the creation of a number of culturally and economically very heterogeneous states, such as Yugoslavia, Czechoslovakia and Italy (Lipset and Rokkan 1967), where tensions between less and more advanced areas persisted. Thus, the changes which occurred in the late 1980s are by no means unique. They can be understood as new junctures in the territorial consolidation and administrative reorganization of the region.

Though drawing mainly on historical data from Western Europe, the Lipset–Rokkan model certainly helps us understand the cleavages which are emerging and re-emerging in Central and Eastern Europe, some of which are strongly related to state-building and nation-building processes. But the countries of contemporary Eastern Europe are also looking beyond the nation state and towards new forms of integration with the centres of gravity of Central and Western Europe (Márkus 1996). These contradictory processes make for a cleavage between intensive modernization and deeply rooted traditionalism.

It might also be worthwhile to combine Lipset's and Rokkan's approach with that of Herbert Kitschelt (1992), who sets out to explain the initial configuration of cleavages in the new democracies of Eastern Europe. He identifies three dimensions along which modern political cleavages are organized: the rules specifying who are admitted as players (citizens); the rules of the game (the collective decision-making procedure); and the assets with which the players must be endowed in order to be qualified as participants.

In a modern democratic country, the choice of players involves the question of citizenship linked to human rights. Political conflicts about ethnicity combined with migration processes are founded on two alternative ideas of citizenship: inclusive or exclusive. An inclusive definition of citizenship calls for the acceptance of individuals as members of the polity, regardless of ascriptive economic, cultural or racial attributes. The exclusive definition has the cultural or racial homogeneity of the citizenry as its ideal. The rules of the game determine mainly the scope and mode of collective decision-making. The procedural dimension ranges from the hierarchical or authoritarian and centralized to the decentralized and participatory or libertarian. The third important dimension pertains to the distribution of the elementary resources and capabilities which make it possible for the citizens to participate in the daily life of the political system, within the framework of a given set of rules. Among these resources are: the standard of living; degree of education; child protection; and social security. Democracy cannot be built on abstract rights of participation alone; democracy presupposes that the citizens have what it takes to exercise their political rights in practice.

These dimensions are abstract, but nevertheless practical for analytical purposes. They make it possible to identify different types of cleavages in post-communist countries and to evaluate them in terms of their relative intensity. Nor are these three dimensions far removed from Lipset's and Rokkan's model; the urban/rural and centre/periphery cleavages identified by Lipset and Rokkan may, for instance, be translated into a conflict between modernizers and defenders of autonomy. The multi-dimensional space defined by Kitschelt's main cleavage dimensions – redistribution versus market and libertarian versus authoritarian – is helpful when it comes to classifying and interpreting continuous political controversies over 'basic' questions and matters of principle, as well as disagreements on specific issues (*Figure 9.1*).

A number of actual and potential conflicts strongly connected with the authoritarian–libertarian or procedural cleavage, can be identified in contemporary East Central Europe. These conflicts typically revolve around the organization of the democratic process, including the separation of powers; the electoral system; and local self-management. Conflicts regarding citizenship, protection of civil rights, the institutionalization of the *ombudsmen*, or the role of the constitutional courts, can also be related to the procedural dimension – as are conflicts linked to state–church relations, particularly within the fields of education and social welfare, as well as family and gender relationships. In East Central European countries where the Catholic Church exerts a high degree of influence, the Church tends to insist on decision-making prerogatives beyond the reach of democratic institutions, favouring authoritarian mechanisms and traditional forms of decision-making.

Along the distributive dimension, intense allocation conflicts may be discerned. State intervention in the economy is a matter of principle for those in favour of national solidarity or concerned about the prospects of the underprivileged strata, including wage-earners in non-competitive industries or in government agencies, made superfluous by the modernization of public administration.

The two dimensions – procedural and distributive – interact. Advocates of economic liberalism in the post-communist democracies are likely to favour an expanded scope for individual choice and increasing social mobility, as well as of membership in international political, military and economic organizations. On the other hand, those defending nationalist or conservative values are likely to reject the notion of the market as the main allocator of resources. It is, however, conceivable that communists-turned-socialists may be inclined to come out in favour of a market economy so as to demonstrate their commitment to the economic reform process. In a similar vein, it is possible for political formations, with their roots in the struggle against the communist regime but driven by authoritarian or paternalistic values, to be wary about marketization and to come out in favour of a strong state.

During periods of cataclysmic social and economic transformation, certain social groups are more likely than others to develop a disposition for authoritarian and anti-market parties. Some groups and individuals have resources and skills of limited value in a market economy, which they set out to curtail by turning to authoritarian, statist parties. Others have skills and positions which enable them to adapt easily to the need of a liberal market. This group includes many of the well-educated, and individuals with entrepreneurial skills; even many members of the former *nomenklatura* are in demand, since they posses managerial and networking know-how. These groups are all likely to support parties of a libertarian, pro-market flavour. In Slovenia, liberal-minded social groups prevailed in the early stage of the transition from communism, which was of importance for the formation of a party system with space for libertarian and pro-market forces.

The level of economic prosperity under and after communism also has a bearing on political preferences. In economically advanced countries like Slovenia, Hungary and the Czech Republic, where a large proportion of the citizenry expects benefits from the change from plan to market, the libertarian market option is likely to be much more attractive to the voters than it is in economically more backward countries like Romania, Serbia and Albania.

The Transformation of Basic Cleavages into Party Structures

Cleavages cannot necessarily be translated into party structures nor, for that matter, into party oppositions. Some cleavages have an obvious impact on party formation and development, others do not. Parties are not 'prisoners' of cleavages, but play an autonomous role in cleavage mediation and policy-making, as well as in the general structuring of the political space (Sartori 1968). New political parties are not only expressions of political cleavages but also agents for them. Whether conflictual or consensual, party strategies, ideologies and orientations may influence the way a particular cleavage is transmitted into the party system. When communism collapsed, the political elites in Hungary and Slovenia were divided on the issue of how political conflict was structured. Some leaders tried to force visions based on past cleavages on a profoundly changed electorate (Márkus 1996), thereby neglected the actual underlying cleavage structure.

The transformation of cleavages is determined by a variety of intermediary variables, such as the traditions of political participation, the openness of the political system, the transparency of political processes and the prevalence of democratic, as opposed to autocratic, procedures. A cost-benefit evaluation also comes into play – is it better to attempt to gain individual representation or to join an established political actor? The issue of majority versus proportional representation has strong implications: does electoral victory give a party a disproportionate share of the parliamentary seats, enabling it to bring about major structural changes? This electoral framework also affects the composition of institutions and government formation. Of importance also is the ability of political parties and individual politicians to introduce new alternatives. If they lose the elections, they will set out to formulate or politicize issues likely to attract a majority of voters (Riker 1986).

The socialist systems weakened the institutions of civil society, and political parties did not serve as intermediary organizations. After the transition from communism, new political parties were formed and shaped within an extremely short period of time, and it was only in parliament that they were tested (Olson 1994). The subsequent fragmentation of many of the pre-transition political organizations, and the emergence of completely new formations, testify to the tentative character of many of these parties. The post-communist leaders and cadres have limited experience of competitive party politics and often fail to evaluate correctly the gains and costs of alternative policy standpoints; at times they even act in contradiction of their declared goals.

It is well worth bearing in mind that political parties define the legal framework within which they operate, including electoral laws, laws on political parties and, for that matter, the entire constitutional framework. The transitional stage is marked by confrontations between the political establishment and dissident groups – a division which carries over into the emerging party system. Some even argue that the choice of institutional features provides the key to explaining political cleavage structures in the new democracies in East Central Europe (Kitschelt 1992).

The post-transition parties and party systems were, in many cases, created 'from above' by political elites. They were weakly defined and often unstable, and they only imperfectly reflected the divisions inherited from the socialist regime, and the socioeconomic and socio-political divisions resulting from the large-scale transformation processes. Even so, there are intimations that the party systems of East Central Europe are in the process of consolidating and adapting to a simplified cleavage structure; the number of parliamentary parties has declined and it is easier to mobilize clear majorities (Jackiewicz and Jackiewicz 1996). In Slovenia, the number of the parliamentary parties dropped from nine in 1990 to seven in 1996, and the share of votes wasted declined from 17 per cent in the 1992 elections to 12 per cent in 1996.

The political parties can now be classified in terms of major cleavage lines. The principal division in Poland, the Czech Republic, Hungary and most other East Central European countries has been that between right-wing and left-wing parties, of which the latter tend to be parties with a communist heritage. There is a manifest ideological confrontation between left-wing and right-wing parties in Slovenia, but so far it has been curtailed by the existence of a strong political centre. Indeed, electoral data testify to a relatively even strength of the three main party 'families': left, centre and right (*Table 9.1*). Given this pattern, Slovene political parties have been prepared to choose from a wide variety of coalition partners. All governments, including the 1996 coalition government, have been 'centre-oriented' or 'broad' since the break-down of the Demos coalition in late 1991.

Table 9.1: Share of votes of party families (%)

Year of election	Left-wing parties, reformed and new	Pro-liberal, centrist parties	Right-wing parties	Other parties
	ZSLD, SDSS	LS, DS, ZS, LDS	SKD, SLS	
1990	30.5	33.8	25.4	–
1992	19.7	32.4	23.1	10.5 (SNS)
1996	25.1	27.1	29.0	3.2 (SNS)
				4.3 (DeSUS)

The United List of Social Democrats (ZLSD) and the Social Democratic Party of Slovenia (SDSS) belong squarely on the statist side of the distributive dimension, which in a sense reflects the traditional capital/labour cleavage. An heir to the reformist wing of the Slovene Communist Party, the ZLSD can take credit for contributing towards Slovenia's independence, by defending national sovereignty against the centralist pressure of the communist leadership dominating the institutions of the former Yugoslav federation. Nevertheless, it remains a *nomenklatura* party; it has a heterogeneous core electorate, and it forfeited the chance to take positions on the most urgent transitional problems. The ZLSD developed into a buffer against further modernization, and as a result, its share of votes has been declining since 1990. The Social Democratic Party of Slovenia (SDSS) was formed as a socialist alternative without ties to the former regime of which it has remained critical. The SDSS has set out to establish close co-operation with the two main right-wing parties. In 1996, the SDSS was successful among voters who felt they could not bear the costs of the transition and were unable to adapt to the new economic framework. Though claiming to be ideologically detached, the two social democratic parties are both in favour of increased financial transfers to underprivileged social groups, and of subsidies to financially troubled large enterprises.

Liberal Democracy of Slovenia (LDS), is located somewhat on the market side of the distributive dimension and clearly on the libertarian side of the procedural dimension *(Figure 9.1)*. In the 1992 elections, the Liberal Democratic Party won the largest share of votes, and it repeated the feat in 1996, following a merger with the Democrats (DS) and the Greens (ZS) in 1994. The new LDS promotes individualistic and cosmopolitan values; it is clearly pro-European, and an advocate of sound economic and financial policies. Catering to the secular intelligentsia and young optimistic entre-preneurs and managers, the LDS rules out populism and adopts a pragmatic and unbiased approach towards the communist heritage.

Two parties reflect the modernization/traditionalism and state/church cleavages: the Slovene Christian Democrats (SKD) and the Slovene People's Party (SLS). The Christian Democrats support traditional values and defend the position of the Catholic Church in society, as well as urging the re-introduction of religious education in public schools. Though clearly pro-European in the sense that it supports Slovenia's membership in the EU, it has brought some of the unresolved issues from the pre-war and inter-war eras onto the political agenda. The People's Party, which is mainly a party of the rural defence, has been explicitly critical of European integration and has called for legislation barring foreigners from purchasing agricultural land and real estate in Slovenia. Its moderately traditionalist appeal helped boost its popularity in the 1996 elections. The SKD and the SLS adopt similar positions on the issue of privatization, but like the SDSS they have also been known to voice the opinion that the *nomenklatura* is in charge of the process of transition.

In the East European context, the Slovene political system is relatively open to political entrepreneurs, the electoral threshold for the National Assembly is equivalent to three out of ninety mandates. Two smaller parties in the Assembly reflect a mixture of new cleavages specific to Slovene society. The Slovene National Party, which was very successful in the 1992 elections, but suffered a defeat in 1996, has been promoting strongly nationalist views on the issues of citizenship, and on the relationships between Slovenia and her neighbours. It has called for rejection of the demands by the Catholic Church for restitution of nationalized Church property, and come out against Slovenia joining the European Union, NATO and other international organizations. The Party of Retired People (DeSUS), the most recent entry into the parliamentary arena, reflects the profound division between the oldest generation and the rest of the population. The pensions system, introduced some 30 years ago, was built on the assumption of an unchanging demographic structure and has proven inefficient under the new economic circumstances.

Figure 9.1: Political cleavages and party competition: party positions on the main axes of party competition

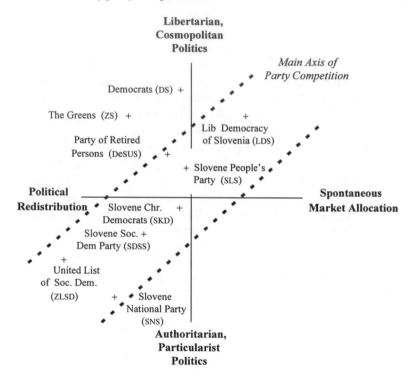

The positions attributed to the parties in the two-dimensional party space are admittedly approximations, but they nevertheless serve to highlight the somewhat fluid character of the Slovene party system, as of the late 1990s. There are intimations of a latent left/right cleavage along the distributive dimension, but there is preciously little by way of variation between the political parties. LDS, and LDS alone, lands squarely on the pro-market side of the distributive axis. The libertarian–authoritarian dimension provides for more by way of variation, but the internal logic of party positions is not always self-evident. Going beyond Figure 9.1, it is also well worth remembering that the linkages between parties and voters in Slovenia remain in an embryonic stage. The alignments in the parliamentary arena might give some clues as to how parties and voters may link up in the future.

Parliaments as Arenas for Conflict Regulation

Recent literature on legislatures has drawn attention to the role of parliaments as arenas for political parties (DiPalma 1990). The internal rules and procedures of the parliament help party elites rationalize their goals, economize their actions and accommodate their conflicts within and outside parliament. Political conflicts are thus channelled from society at large to parliament, where they are rationally articulated and 'parliamentarized'. Conflicts come into focus, get exposed in the process of parliamentary agenda-setting and are regulated by standard parliamentary rules and techniques (Schmitter 1988). The conflict-solution capacity of a parliament is dependent on a variety of factors and differs according to the stages of the decision-making process – deliberation, decision-making, adjudication and catharsis (Blondel 1973).

In well-established democratic systems, purely ideological approaches to problems are rare and conflicts are processed as a matter of course. If parties see prospects for gains without jeopardizing basic party commitments, they are likely to compromise on a number of practical issues. Even so, the conflict-resolution capacity of a parliament is limited. Philip Norton (1993) argues that parliamentary decision-making does have an impact, but only a marginal one. Parliaments can and do serve as arbiters or brokers between competing sides, but the potential is certainly greater than the reality.

The parliaments of the countries in early post-communist transition present a rather heterogeneous picture. They have all started with an authoritarian heritage and found themselves confronted with a large number of accumulated policy problems (Olson 1994). Following Lowi's classification of policy types, policies in the first period of transition are characterized by large-scale redistribution of social resources and political power, and they are highly conflictual (Lowi 1964). Regulative and distributive policies become less conflictual only in the period of consolidation, when standard operating procedures for allocating resources have acquired a degree of legitimacy. Parliaments in transitional societies must promote consensus-building in order to enact new policies, the outcomes of which are far from clear at a time when demands are building up rapidly. As if to make things even more complicated, there are parties which are bent on using their power in parliament to exclude other political forces from influencing the decision-making process (Agh 1994). Parliaments in post-communist societies are thus frequently turned into arenas of ideological confrontation and do not serve as instruments of democratic decision-making – the legacy of the communist heritage with all which that entails, reduces the capacity of parliaments to act pragmatically and efficiently. It sometimes seems as if the parliaments of East Central Europe assent to badly needed legislation only as a last resort. The legislative output of the Slovene National Assembly – the main legislative chamber, responsible for preparation and passing of legislature – testifies to the impact of an over-burdened agenda and a 'hectic' legislative activity.

Table 9.2: Legislative output of the Slovene National Assembly 1990–96

	1990	1991	1992	1993	1994	1995	1996
Constitutional Laws	1	4	–	–	2	–	–
New Laws	23	44	44	71	82	49	40
Amended Laws	20	35	13	38	26	35	32
Ratifications	–	–	–	47	73	41	39

Source: Slovenian National Assembly, Activity Reports 1992–96.

In modern parliaments, conflicts appear between main interest blocs, chiefly between the government majority and the opposition. Opposition is considered the most institutionalized form of political conflict (Ionescu and De Madariaga 1971). In post-communist societies, the vitality of the opposition and the capacity to form stable political coalitions depend on the pre-transition behaviour of the political elite, and on its capacity to co-operate in solving past and present problems of development. By now, the oppositions in the East Central European countries cannot be considered weak and fragmented; they are gradually demonstrating their capacity for government. The cleavage structure and the degree of national consensus on central social and political values are of crucial importance for the ability of the opposition to serve efficiently (Bibič 1993). The ability of the opposition to establish itself in a number of arenas – in parliament, through the media, and on the local and national levels – is also important. These factors go a long way towards accounting for the role of the opposition in East European countries, including Slovenia and other successor states of the former Yugoslav federation.

Slovenia has had four different kinds of coalitions since 1990 (Appendix 9.2). The first ruling coalition, Demos, was a broad popular front similar to Civic Forum in the Czech lands and Public Against Violence in Slovakia. Demos included most of the newly established democratic parties: the

Christian Democrats (SKD); the Slovene Peasants' Union (later relabelled the Slovene People's Party, SLS); the Social Democratic Union (later renamed the Social Democratic Party, SDSS); the Slovene Democratic Union (subsequently known as the Slovene Democrats, DS); the Liberal Party (LS); and the Greens (ZS). In opposition were the ZSMS–LDS (later renamed the Liberal Democratic Party, LDS), the United List of Social Democrats (ZLSD) and the Slovene Socialist Party (SSS).

With the 1992 elections approaching, the Demos coalition was replaced by a temporary 'Small Coalition' including the LDS, SDSS, ZS, SSS and DS. In 1992–96, Slovenia was ruled by a number of oversized 'Grand Coalitions', all led by the LDS. As a result, conflicts normally handled in parliament were transferred to negotiations between the coalition parties. The government ments found it politically expedient to avoid debate and decisions on important economic policy issues. The Grand Coalitions had little understanding for the role of the opposition; and the parties of the opposition turned out to be incapable of presenting a viable alternative, but tried to undermine the legitimacy of the governments by a series of counterproductive accusations. However, the 1996 elections provided for a more balanced and more pragmatic government coalition. It is a coalition of the LDS and SLS, both parties close to the political centre, with the small Party of Retired Persons (DeSUS) as junior partner.

Parliamentary committees are important arenas for conflict solution (Zajc 1996). Of particular importance are committees dealing with policy areas where social cleavages are pronounced and the impact of ideology accentuated. Parliamentary committees in East Central Europe have managed to carve out stable niches for themselves in the decision-making process, although the level of membership continuity tends to be low. In some countries, like Slovakia and the Czech Republic, parliamentary committees seem to be ruled by party logic – the opposition is excluded from several committees in the Slovak parliament (Reschova and Syllova 1996) – and in the Croatian House of Representatives, the committee Chairs, who as a rule are members of the dominant party, have what practically amounts to veto power (Jović 1996).

The new Standing Orders of the Slovene National Assembly have, to some extent, consolidated parliamentary working procedures, but not without leaving some gaps. The large number of committees seems to be one of the major remaining problems – 23 committees were established between 1992 and 1996, and at the beginning of 1997 the number was increased to 26. There are more than four committee seats to each deputy (*Table 9.3*). This work load of individual parliamentarians is in fact of such magnitude that the committees are tempted to opt for fast-track procedures which leave little scope for scrutiny and rational problem-solving.

Table 9.3: Number of parliamentary committees and committee membership

Parliament	Number of deputies	Number of Committees	Total number of committee seats
Hungary	386	19	389
Czech Republic	200	12	200
Croatia	127	19	254
Slovenia	90	26	382
Germany	662	21	785
Sweden	349	17	240

In the Slovene National Assembly, the legislative process is highly fragmented. Power is divided between: the floor; the party groups; the Speaker and the Speaker's Presidium; the parliamentary committees; and the individual deputies, who have an independent right to convene a session. In the Czech National Assembly, the Standing Orders differentiate between large and small parties, as well as between parties which do and do not belong to the current parliamentary majority.

A special feature in the Slovene parliamentary setting is the existence of a second, corporative chamber with limited powers, known as the National Council. The council may give opinions on legislative initiative by the National Assembly and has a suspensive veto as its final resort. However, in most cases when the suspensive veto has been used, it has been overruled by an absolute majority of the National Assembly – that is, by a minimum of 46 out of 90 deputies. Given the relatively small number of Council vetoes not eventually overruled by the Assembly, it is difficult not to draw the conclusion that the suspensive veto is of limited importance (Kristan 1997).

Table 9.4: Suspensive vetoes in the National Council

Year	Total number of vetoes	Number of vetoes overruled in NA	Number of efficient vetoes
1993	12	10	2
1994	8	6	2
1995	1	1	–
1996	6	3	2
1–9/1997	7	5	2
Total	34	25	8

Source: Kristan 1997, 310.

The Impact of Cleavages

Slovenia is currently characterized by an intensive social and economic transformation process, accompanied by material inequality and the concomitant socioeconomic deprivation of some segments of the society. One of key cleavages is defined by different concepts of authority. Two hostile groups have appeared along this value dimension. On the one hand, there are the traditionalists and conservative advocates of the value orientations which existed long before the communist take-over of power, who call for the defence of independence and sovereignty. On the other hand, there are the 'modernizers'; liberals, intellectuals and the well-educated, young and optimistic entrepreneurs as well as top-level officials, who are in favour of rejuvenating Slovene society. These two groups are not internally homogenous; some people may have a traditionalist outlook though being in favour of, say, European integration, and support joining international organizations; others may express libertarian values while supporting interventionist economic policies. The distributive dimension differentiating between those favouring state interventionism and those of a pro-market orientation, constitutes the second basic cleavage in Slovene politics. This cleavage dimension is brought out by the tensions between the winners and the losers in the economic transformation process. This dimension has a flavour of capital–labour to it.

The prominent role played by market allocation makes Slovenia different from most other countries in Eastern Europe. Slovenia's relative economic affluence, based on high levels of education, and her ability to maintain close economic and scientific relations with the West, have been decisive in shaping the political space. Long before the dissolution of the former Yugoslav federation, there was strong consensus in favour of market reform within the population at large, and especially among economists with expertise on competitive markets in Western Europe.

Even before independence, Slovenia went through several waves of economic liberalization. The first reform attempts in the early 1970s were terminated by political intervention; in the 1980s, reforms of a magnitude unparalleled in the communist world were introduced. After independence, even the ex-communists agreed with the other parties that privatization was necessary, in order to speed up economic development and strengthen democracy. Basic legislation providing for privatization was adopted in 1991–93, even though the method of ownership transformation remained a source of strong disagreement. In the special Slovene setting, where enterprises were collectively rather than state-owned, the basic conflict was about management relations. The parties of the right called for the state to take control of privatization to avoid obstruction by company managers in charge; other parties were in favour of a status quo concept. The conflict sharpened in the spring of 1991 when the first government after the 1990 elections resigned. Draft legislation was prepared, in the second half of 1992, by a special commission of politicians and experts; the commission covered the full range of views on this subject and managed to work out a compromise which parliament passed after lengthy debates in December 1992.

The Law on Ownership Transformation, which regulates privatization in trade and industry, provides for a combination of worker buy-outs, voucher-based mass privatization and direct sales. Parliament also enacted legislation on denationalization, which calls for the restitution of property confiscated by the previous regime. The basic principle for denationalization is restitution in kind and shares of confiscated enterprises.

Rational government, including local self-government, is generally seen as a prerequisite for political modernization. Reforming local self-government is difficult, time-consuming and expensive, even during a period of great political upheaval such as the post-communist transition. The Slovene attempts at reform in the 1990s seem to have been introduced at the right point in time; favourable internal political constellations in combination with a need to adapt to EU norms have broken the deadlock. The debate about local self-government in Slovenia reflects a deep underlying cleavage about the extent and scope of democratic decision-making, with centralists pitted against autonomists. The centralist lobby was initially able to block many of the crucial reform proposals, but after a period of extensive public debate and pressure from the constituency level, a number of centralist-oriented parliamentarians gave in, and the Law on Local Self-Government was passed by a solid majority of 42 votes for and 19 against. The bill was a product of compromise and drawn-out negotiations and turned out to be less than consistent (Igličar 1993); some provisions – see elsewhere the criteria for establishment of new counties – subsequently had to be settled by the Constitutional Court and by a second round of parliamentary decisions.

So far, political modernization in Slovenia has provided many new institutions and rules, but not necessarily the proper tools for handling conflicts, particularly cleavage-related conflicts. The political linkage between citizens and representative institutions remains weak, and the political parties have but vague perceptions of the cleavages existing in society. In fact, the case of Slovenia confirms Sartori's view that parties do not automatically translate cleavages into politics: so far, the parties are simply too preoccupied with electoral and day-to-day parliamentary politics to form solid and persistent links with specific social groups.

REFERENCES

Agh, Attila (1994), 'Policy Effectiveness and Agenda Concentration in the Hungarian Legislation (1990–1993)', in Agh, Attila, ed., *The Emergence of ECE Parliaments: The First Steps*, HCDS, Budapest.

Bibič, Adolf (1993), 'Racionalnost opozicije', in Drago Zajc, ed., *Slovenski parlament v procesu politične modernizacije*, Ljubljana, FDV.

Blondel, Jean (1973), *Comparative Legislatures*, Englewood Cliffs, N.J., Prentice-Hall.

DiPalma, Giuseppe (1990), 'Consolidation, Institutionalization: A Minimalist View', in Ulrike Liebert and Maurizio Cotta, eds., *Parliament and Democratic Consolidation in Southern Europe: Greece, Italy, Portugal, Spain and Turkey*, London, Pinter.

Igličar, Albin (1996), 'Problemi lokalne samouprave', paper presented at a *Conference on the Transformation of Slovene Public Administration*, Ljubljana.

Ionescu, Ghita and Isabel De Madariaga (1971), *Die Opposition: Ihre Funktion in Vergangenheit und Gegenwart*, Munich, C.H Beck Verlag.

Ilonszki, Gabriella (1996), Paper presented at the *International Conference on the Changing Roles of Parliamentary Committees*, Budapest, Hungary, 20–22 June.

Jović, Dejan (1996), 'Party System Developments from a Parliamentary Perspective in Croatia', in Attila Agh and Gabriella Ilonszki, eds., *Parliament and Organized Interests: The Second Steps*, Budapest, HCDS.

Jackiewicz, Irena and Zbigniew Jackiewicz (1996), 'The Polish Parliament in Transition: The Search for a Model', in Attila Agh and Gabriella Ilonszki, eds., *Parliaments and Organized Interests: Second Steps*, Budapest, HCDS.

Kitschelt, Herbert (1992), 'The formation of the party systems in East Central Europe': *Politics&Society*, No.1

Kristan, Ivan (1997), 'Specifics of the Slovene Bicameralism', in Samo Kropivnik, Igor Luksic and Drago Zajc, eds., *Conflicts and Consensus*, Ljubljana, Slovenian Political Science Association.

Lipset, Seymour Martin and Stein Rokkan (1967), 'Cleavage Structures, Party Systems and Voter Alignments: An Introduction', in Seymour Martin Lipset and Stein Rokkan, eds., *Party Systems and Voter Alignments: Cross-National Perspectives*, New York, The Free Press.

Lowi, Theodore (1964), 'American business, public policy, case studies and political theory', *World Politics*, Vol. 16.

Márkus, György G. (1996), 'Cleavage dynamics and party system in Hungary', paper presented at the *Third Regional Conference of the Central European Political Science Associations on Conflicts and Consensus*, Bled (Slovenia), 22–23 November.

Norton, Philip (1993), *Does Parliament Matter?* New York, Harvester & Wheatsheaf.

Olson, David M. (1994), 'The New Parliaments of New Democracies: The Experience of the Federal Assembly of the Czech and Slovak Federal Republic', in Attila Agh, ed., *The Emergence of East Central European Parliaments: The First Steps*, Budapest, HCDS.

Reschova, Jana and Jindriska Syllova (1996), 'The Legislature of the Czech Republic', in Attila Agh and Gabriella Ilonszki, eds., *Parliaments and Organized Interests: The Second Steps*, Budapest, HCDS.

Riker, William (1985), *The Art of Manipulation*, New Haven, CT, Yale University Press.

Sartori, Giovanni (1968), 'Political development and political engineering', *Public Policy*, No.17.

Schmitter, Philippe C. (1988), *The Consolidation of Political Democracy in Southern Europe*, Stanford University and Instituto Universitario Europeo.

Zajc, Drago (1996), 'Functions and powers of the committees in the new parliaments: comparison between the East-Central and West-Central European countries', paper presented at the *International Conference on The Changing Roles of Parliamentary Committees*, Budapest, 20–22 June.

APPENDIX 9.1: ELECTORAL RESULTS

NATIONAL ASSEMBLY ELECTIONS

Party/list	1990 * %	seats‹	1992 %	seats	1996 %	seats
Party of Democratic Renewal – United List of Soc. Dem. (ZLSD)	17.3	36	13.6	14	9.0	9
ZSMS–Liberal Democratic Party Lib. Dem. of Slovenia (LDS)	14.5	39	23.5	22	27.0	25
Slovene Democratic Union – The Democrats (DS)	9.5	30	5.1	6	2.7	–
Liberal Party (LS)	2.5	4	1.5	–	0.8	–
The Greens (ZS)	8.8	17	3.7	5	1.8	–
Christian Democratic Party (SKD)	13.0	23	14.5	15	9.6	10
Social Democratic Party (SDSS)	7.1	17	3.3	4	16.1	16
Slovene Peasants' Party – Slovene People's Party (SLS)	12.6	32	8.7	10	19.4	19
Slovene National Party (SNS)	–	–	10.2	12	3.2	4
Party of Retired Persons (DeSUS)	–	–	–	–	4.3	5
Nationalities **		6		2		2
Total		240		90		90
Date	April		10 December		10 November	
Turnout, %	83		86		73	

* The 1990 elections were to the three-chamber Assembly of Slovenia (as instituted by the 1974 Constitution of the Socialist Republic of Slovenia) with 80 deputies in each chamber. Only the deputies to the Socio-Political Chamber were elected on the basis of a proportional system. The elections in 1992 and 1996 were to the one-chamber, 90-member National Assembly (Constitution of the RS, adopted in 1991). ** Seats reserved for the Magyar and Italian minorities

PRESIDENTIAL ELECTIONS

Year	Victor	Votes, %	Name of office
1990	Milan Kučan	58	Chairman of the Presidency of the Republic of Slovenia
1992	Milan Kučan	64	President of the Republic of Slovenia
1997	Milan Kučan	56	President of the Republic of Slovenia

1997 elections

Candidate	Share of votes, %
Milan Kučan	55.6
Janez Podobnik	18.4
Jožef Bernik	9.4
Marjan Cerar	7.1
Marjan Poljšak	3.2
Anton Peršak	3.1
Bogomir Kovač	2.7
Franc Miklavčič	0.6

APPENDIX 9.2: GOVERMENT COMPOSITION

Duration	Type, Prime Minister	Parties participating	Seats in National Assembly (of total*)	Reason for resignation
16 May 1990–14 May 1992	Majority, 'Demos' Lojze Peterle	SKD, SKZ, ZS, SDSS, SDZ, LS	47/80	Constructive vote of no confidence
14 May 1992–12 Jan. 1993	Majority, 'Small Coalition' Janez Drnovšek	LDS, SDSS, ZS, SSS, DS	50/80	Elections of 10 Dec. 1992
12 Jan. 1993–12.Mar.1994	Majority, 'Grand Coalition' Janez Drnovšek	LDS, SKD, ZLSD, SDSS	55/90	LDS merger with oppositional DS and ZS
12 Mar. 1993–6 Apr. 1994	Majority, Janez Drnovšek	(NEW) LDS, SKD, ZLSD, SDSS	63/90	SDSS resigned
6 Apr. 1994–31 Jan. 1996	Majority, Janez Drnovšek	(New) LDS, SKD, ZSLD	59/90	ZLSD resigned
31 Jan. 1996–2 Feb. 1997	Minority, Janez Drnovšek	(New) LDS, SKD	42/90	Elections of 10 Nov.1996
2 Feb. 1997	Majority, 'Pragmatic Coalition', Janez Drnovšek	(New) LDS, SLS, DeSUS	49/90	

* In 1990–92, the National Assembly had a three-chamber structure, with each chamber consisting of 80 deputies. The parliamentary strength of the government side is calculated according to its number of seats in the Socio-Political Chamber. According to the 1991 Constitution, the National Assembly has only one chamber with 90 deputies.

APPENDIX 9.3: THE ELECTORAL SYSTEM

The National Assembly *(Državni zbor)*, the highest legislative authority endowed with the sole power to enact laws, has 90 deputies. Deputies are elected for a four-year term at equal, direct and secret elections. Every citizen of the Republic of Slovenia who has reached the age of 18 by election day is eligible to vote and stand as a candidate. The Italian and Magyar ethnic communities in Slovenia are entitled to one deputy each in the National Assembly, elected by a preferential voting system.

Slovenia is divided into 8 constituencies, each of which elect 11 deputies (altogether 88 deputies). Constituencies are defined so as to make sure that deputies represent an approximately equal number of inhabitants. Each constituency is divided into 11 geographically-defined electoral sub-districts. As a general rule, individual candidates stand in one constituency only, although in exceptional circumstances candidates may be allowed to stand in a maximum of two constituencies. Lists of candidates must contain a minimum of six and a maximum of eleven candidates for each constituency. A political party nominates candidates in accordance with its own internal rules. Under certain circumstances a party may put up a list in every constituency. The law also permits the formation of pre-electoral coalitions, so that two or more parties present a joint list of candidates. Such a list, however, must have a single label. Voters may also nominate candidates by collection of signatures. In an individual constituency, a voters' list is accepted if supported by at least one hundred voters with residence in the constituency. Such a list can consist of a number of independent candidates or of one alone, in which case the candidate stands in all eleven sub-districts.

The allocation of seats takes place in two stages: first in each of the eight constituencies, where the electoral commissions publish the number of directly elected mandates for a particular list. Each list gets as many seats as there are whole Hare quotas contained in its vote; i.e. at least 9.1 per cent of the total constituency vote must be obtained for every direct mandate. Independent candidates are associated with one (or two) of the geographically defined sub-districts. The candidates on each list are ranked in terms of the percentage of the total vote each has received in his or her sub-district. The top candidates on the list get the seats to which their list is entitled. In the second stage, seats unallocated in the constituencies are aggregated at the national level and distributed by d'Hondt method, on the basis of each electoral cartel's remainder vote (the sum of all remainders from associated constituency lists). Only those cartels which would win at least three seats, if all seats were allocated at the national level by the d'Hondt method on the basis of the total vote cast, are eligible to participate in the distribution of the remainder seats.

For the election of ethnic representatives, special constituencies are formed in regions where the indigenous Italian and Magyar communities live. These deputies are elected according to the majority principle.

The second chamber, the National Council *(Državni svet)*, has 40 members elected for a five-year term. The council is an advisory body with 22 representatives of local interests and a total of 18 representatives of social, economic and professional interests. National Councillors are elected not on the grounds of a general, but of a special, right to vote, specified in separate law for each interest group. The persons who are entitled to vote and to be elected as members of the National Council are representatives of the following functional interests: employers; employees; farmers; small businesses and independent professionals; and non-profit activities.

All citizens of the Republic of Slovenia who have reached the age of 18 by election day, and who are not legally barred from voting, have the right to vote and to be elected as a member of the National Council. Foreigners have the right to vote under the same conditions as citizens of Slovenia, i.e. if they are engaged in a relevant activity in Slovenia, but may not themselves be elected members of the National Council.

At the National Council elections of 10 December 1992, 18 representatives of functional interests were elected by electors who were themselves elected within the interest groups and constituted electoral colleges. Four represented the employers and were elected by the chambers of commerce and the employers' associations; four represented the employees and were elected by the unions and the associations or confederations of unions; two represented the farmers and were elected by professional farmers' organizations; one representative each of small businesses and independent professionals were elected by their respective professional organizations. The six representatives of non-profit organizations were elected as follows: one by the universities and colleges; one for the area of education by the professional teachers' organization; one for the area of research activity by the professional researchers' organization; one for the area of sport and culture by the professional organization of cultural and sport workers; one for the field of medicine by the professional organization of medical workers and associates; and one for the area of social care by the professional social workers' organization. Local communities elected 22 representatives, each in geographically, historically and interest-based constituencies. In 1992, local representative councillors were elected directly, but in 1997 they were elected by municipal or city councils, or by the elected representatives of these councils in electoral colleges.

The President of the Republic is elected in direct, general elections by secret ballot. The candidate who receives a majority of the valid votes cast is elected to office for a term of five years. The President may be elected for a maximum of two consecutive terms.

APPENDIX 9.4: THE CONSTITUTIONAL FRAMEWORK

The Slovene constitution of 1991 opts for a system of 'incomplete bi-cameralism'. Notwithstanding a certain terminological vagueness in the constitution, the Slovene parliament consists of two chambers. The National Assembly *(Državni zbor)* with its 90 deputies is the main chamber. The National Council *(Državni svet)*, with 40 members, is a second chamber with limited legislative competence.

The National Assembly convenes to regular sessions during the last week of each month during the spring and autumn terms, to enact laws and make other decisions. In addition, the National Assembly meets in extraordinary sessions. Bills may be proposed by the Government, individual deputies or by a minimum of 5,000 voters signing a petition. The National Council may propose legislation by the National Assembly. The National Assembly debates a bill in three readings. When required due to exceptional circumstances, a bill may be adopted according to a fast-track procedure.

The National Assembly only makes decisions when a majority of deputies are present, i. e. at least 46. Decisions are taken by a majority of votes of the deputies attending and voting. Individual decisions of exceptional importance (e.g. amendments to the Constitution, the election of a Prime Minister) require a qualified two-thirds majority of all the 90 deputies in the National Assembly. Laws are proclaimed by the President of the Republic of Slovenia no later than 8 days after their enactment.

The Prime Minister is chosen by a majority of the deputies of the National Assembly in a secret ballot. If a majority of at least 46 deputies is not found, the President shall dissolve the National Assembly and call new elections. Other Ministers are appointed and dismissed by the National Assembly upon the proposal of the Prime Minister. Ministers are collectively responsible for the work of the government and each Minister is responsible for his or her ministry. The government shall resign when a new National Assembly convenes after an election. The National Assembly may, upon the motion of no fewer than 10 deputies and by the vote of a majority of all elected deputies, elect a new Prime Minister. The Prime Minister may himself or herself call for a vote of confidence. If such a vote is not carried by a majority of all elected deputies, the National Assembly must, within thirty days, either elect a new Prime Minister or express its confidence in the incumbent Prime Minister in a fresh vote. If this requirement is not fulfilled, the President of the Republic shall dissolve the National Assembly and call new elections.

According to Article 97 of the Constitution of 1991, the National Council may propose the enactment of laws by the National Assembly (legislative initiative); communicate to the National Assembly opinions on all matters within its jurisdiction; require that the National Assembly reconsiders laws prior to their proclamation; require that a referendum be called on matters regulated by law; call for the establishment of a parliamentary inquiry into a matter of public importance; and address requests to the Constitutional Court. In a similar vein, the National Assembly may require the National Council to provide its opinion on a specific matter.

The President of the Republic is empowered to: (1) call elections for the National Assembly; (2) proclaim statutes; (3) to appoint State officers and functionaries in accordance with statute; (4) accredit Slovene ambassadors and consuls and accept the credentials of foreign diplomatic representatives; (5) Sign international treaties and agreements; (6) grant pardons; and (7) confer state honours, decorations and honorary titles. In the event of the National Assembly being unable to convene due to a state of war or a state of emergency, the President may, at the request of the Government, issue decrees which have the binding force and effect of statute.

10. Romania

William Crowther

Nearly all aspects of the post-communist political transition in Central Europe have been the subject of contention and alternative explanation. Analysts have raised fundamental questions concerning the applicability of models of political behaviour developed in other political contexts to post-communist conditions. This is notably true of the nature and impact of cleavages in post-communist societies. Lipset's and Rokkan's conceptualization of the role of abiding, socially-based ideological divisions has been a staple of political analysis of the developed democracies (Lipset and Rokkan 1967). Its applicability in the Central European context, however, has been sharply contested on a number of grounds, primarily relating either to the presumed lack of a social basis sufficient for ideological structuring, or to a presumed disjunction between elite competition and mass attitudes.[1]

Given its pre-communist and communist past, Romania is often taken as an arch-typical example of the post-communist countries' dearth of civil society. Given the absence of independent associations; a predominantly Orthodox rather than Protestant or Catholic religious tradition; for the most part Ottoman rather than Habsburg influences; lack of economic development; highly repressive rather than reformist trends during the late communist period; and a near total absence of market forces during communism; Romania would seem to provide the strongest possible case for anyone wishing to argue that the social bases for political cleavages do not pertain in the immediate post-communist context. Conversely, if cleavage politics does play a significant role in Romania – a country with an undisputed 'outlier' status – one would be hard pressed to argue that they do not play a role elsewhere in Central Europe.

Cleavages, as the term will be used here, are politically salient ideological divisions that are grounded in the social structure of a particular country. As such, they clearly comprise something more long lasting and deeply rooted than transitory policy disputes. Employing mass public opinion and elite survey data, this chapter argues that Romania has been characterized by a clear cleavage structure from a very early point in the transition.[2] Moreover, it will be shown that cleavages have played a crucial role in determining electoral competition and party political outcomes. First, the social and political background of the Romanian transition will be reviewed in order to better assess the source and nature of post-communist ideological divisions. The character of political cleavages in the society will then be examined, and the impact of cleavages on party competition during the post-communist transition will be assessed.

Precursors to Transition in Romania

Like neighbouring South Eastern European countries, Romania has confronted serious obstacles across the course of the 20th century. A late modernizer, it was marginalized in the international economy, and failed to establish stable democratic politics. In many ways, the already substantial problems of the Romanians were compounded by the incorporation of additional territory after the First World War, and with it a significantly increased minority population. During the inter-war years the country found itself in a state of turmoil, racked by internal divisions and beset by economic problems.[3] Romania's far-from-perfected democratic institutions were overwhelmed by the associated challenges of the depression and the resurgence of Germany. The dominant democratic parties, the National Peasant Party and the Liberals gave way before the advance of right-wing extremists.[4] Linked with resentment toward the failed democratic regime and its economic policies, xenophobia propelled a powerful indigenous fascist movement in the 1930s. Left-wing forces were, in contrast, notably weak. Identified by many in the largely peasant and Orthodox population as atheist as well as anti-nationalist, the socialist parties failed to attract a strong following.[5]

By the outbreak of the Second World War, the civil consensus had disintegrated almost entirely. In late 1938, members of the fascist Iron Guard movement unleashed a campaign of political terror against the increasingly isolated royalist government. Power passed briefly to the Iron Guard in 1940, after which General Ion Antonescu established a military government and led Romania through the Second World War in military alliance with Germany.

Rather than erasing its national peculiarities, Romania's communist experience acted to reinforce crucial aspects of the country's traditional political culture. While space does not permit a comprehensive exploration of the communist period, it is safe to brand what developed as 'national communism', characterized by a legitimization system and socio-political patterns that differed significantly from those found elsewhere in Central Europe (Crowther 1988; Verdery 1991).

Even prior to its public deviation from Soviet orthodoxy, the Romanian communist regime showed signs of singularity. The Communist Party's unresolved internal factionalism retarded efforts to restructure the country's economy and, in contrast to events in most other East European countries, enabled a national communist faction to survive the Stalinist period. Under Gheorghiu Gheorghiu-Dej, the Romanian leadership embarked on an independent 'Stalinist' strategy of industrialization, and took preliminary steps toward a 'national' legitimization strategy. The rise to power of Nicolae Ceauşescu in the second half of the 1960s was accompanied by further turmoil, as the new leader purged potential opponents and elevated supporters in order to consolidate his position. Betraying the potential for an independent and more moderate form of communism that many saw in his regime, within five years Ceauşescu was moving Romania in a more intensely nationalist and more authoritarian direction than his predecessor.

The Ceauşescu regime's failure to reach accommodation with – and indeed, its increasing isolation from – Romanian civil society, strengthened important continuities between the communist period and the inter-war political tradition. Sharp divisions between elites and the rest of the population; subject rather than participant attitudes with respect to civil–state relations; an abiding distrust of established authority; and intense nationalism were all conspicuous elements in the pre-communist political culture. These attitudes were reinforced, and in some cases exaggerated to the point of extreme distortion under Ceauşescu's national communist legitimization formula.

Transition, Proto-Politics and the Founding Elections

Excepting Albania, at the end of the 1980s Romania was arguably less prepared than any other country in Eastern Europe to undertake democratization. Up to the very end of the communist period, the Ceauşescu leadership systematically fostered political alienation and fractured society along class and ethnic lines. The consequences of this strategy for the postcommunist body politic were catastrophic. The level of political knowledge and the political culture suffered; institutionalized alternatives to the communist party simply did not exist; and reformist opposition within the Romanian Communist Party was limited at best. Immediately after the fall of the RCP dictatorship, elite-level politics resolved into a contest between forces associated with the previous regime and an initially ineffective liberal opposition. Despite these stark conditions, however, coherent societal level interests rapidly took shape and clearly influenced party competition.

As the edifice of communist political repression disintegrated, a diverse coalition formed with the intent of guiding the December 1989 popular revolt to a successful conclusion.[6] Its main components were the leaders of the spontaneous uprising, marginalized reform communists, and elements that abandoned the failing Ceauşescu regime. Organized as the National Salvation Front (FSN) and headed by former Politburo member Ion Iliescu, these forces announced their assumption of provisional control over the country on 22 December 1989.

Upon coming to power, the FSN immediately announced a programme of reform, including a call for elections to be held in April 1990.[7] FSN spokesmen asserted that the Front was as a non-political umbrella organization that would act in the interest of all those who fought to bring down the Ceauşescu dictatorship. It pledged to act in a caretaker role until the situation could be regularized and elections could be held to select a freely elected democratic successor regime.

Almost immediately, however, both the character of the FSN and its electoral intentions changed. In essence, the two best-positioned elements of the original makeshift coalition (reform communists and representatives of the military) banded together at the expense of the less politically experienced leaders of mass uprising. A dominant core formed within the ruling council of the FSN around Iliescu. While the RCP itself was abolished in early January 1990, significant elements of the party's administrative network remained intact and passed into the structure of the provisional government. This dynamic strengthened the hand of the former RCP cadre within the FSN Council, and at the same time alienated anti-communists.

Thus transformed, the leadership of the FSN reversed its position on running candidates for office in a successor government. The organization's initial competitive advantage was obvious. Among the general population, the FSN's reputation was on the whole quite positive. FSN leaders were able to associate their organization successfully with the December revolution, and garnered an immediate favourable response by abolishing several hated Ceauşescu policies. Furthermore, unlike other transition regimes, Romania entered the post-communist period with no foreign debt, due to the former dictator's draconian polices directed at repayment in the late 1980s. Hence the FSN was able to take immediate steps to improve public consumption.

Opposition forces were, however, not long in emerging. Already in December, the FSN's major rivals had begun to organize in Bucharest. The first of these were the so-called 'historic parties', the National Liberal Party (PNL), the National Peasant–Christian Democratic Party (PNT–CD), and the Social Democratic Party (SDP). By early January another major force, the Democratic Magyar Union of Romania (UDMR) had begun to function in Transylvania as well.[8] Other less formal organizations, like the student movement, while not explicitly aspiring to power, also brought substantial pressure on the government.

Within weeks – almost days – of Ceauşescu's overthrow, this nascent opposition launched public attacks on Iliescu and his colleagues as 'neo-communists'. Faced with growing criticism, the FSN's leaders decided to take advantage of their immediate broad support to consolidate control over the country through election. Thus on 23 January 1990, the FSN reversed its earlier commitment to neutrality, and announced its intention to participate in the forthcoming elections.

The decision to take part in national elections instantly destabilized an already volatile situation, touching off a series of anti-regime demonstrations by the student movement and anti-FSN political parties. Street demonstrations in Bucharest demanding resignation of the FSN were brought to an end only through the use of force. Unable to call on the military to contain the protesters, Iliescu mobilized supportive workers, who responded by rampaging in the capital and attacking presumed opponents of the new regime. Coupled with the extension of compromises to the opposition political parties, the threat of further violence by the workers served to pressure opponents into acceptance of the new political circumstances. After substantial discord and resistance from the opposition parties, an agreement was reached, setting 20 May 1990 as the date for elections.

The first round of national elections can only be understood adequately if they are evaluated within this polarized and highly fluid political context, in which the FSN enjoyed nearly unassailable advantages as a quasi-government. This remained the case, despite the fact that the Council of the National Salvation Front formally dissolved itself as a government in order to ease opposition from the non-governing parties. In its place, a new body, the Provisional Council of National Unity, was established to govern until elections could be held. The new body retained most of the membership of the old council (fully half of the positions on it were allocated to the FSN) while adding members from the other political parties. But the more experienced and firmly ensconced Front leaders were clearly able to retain control over the state.

As established by law, the legislature (the Assembly of Deputies) was elected with a mechanism combining multi-member districts and proportional representation. The Assembly consisted of 396 seats, of which 387 were determined by election, with the remaining posts reserved for representatives of ethnic minorities. Elections were also held for 119 positions in the Romanian upper house, the Senate. Voters chose among party lists in 41 multi-member districts.

The president was elected simultaneously with the legislature. The presidential elections were direct. If no candidate achieved an absolute majority in a first round, a run-off round was to be held between the two candidates who received the largest numbers of votes in the previous round.

The key contenders in the founding elections were: Ion Iliescu's National Salvation Front; the main historical parties, the National Liberals (PNL), the National Peasants' Party (PNT), and the Social Democrats; along with the Democratic Magyar Union of Romania (UDMR). In addition, a multitude of smaller parties emerged, representing views across the ideological spectrum; all in all, more than 70 parties participated in the elections. The campaign platform of the National Salvation Front called for the abolition of the most repressive and irrational aspects of the previous dictatorship and for measured reform. At the same time the FSN pledged to protect the population from market forces. In contrast, the traditional parties proposed more rapid economic restructuring, and failed to provide the population with firm assurances that they would be protected during the economic transition. The National Liberal and the National Peasant parties labelled the National Salvation Front 'neo-communist', and charged it with hijacking the revolution.

The results of the elections of 20 May 1990 provide unmistakable evidence of the political dominance of Ion Iliescu and the FSN. In the presidential race, Iliescu won 85.1 per cent of the vote. Radu Campeanu of the National Liberal Party took 10.2 per cent, and Ion Raţiu followed with 4.3 per cent. Clearly, no individual political figure could match Iliescu. While not as lopsided, returns for the legislature also indicate the FSN's strength. The Front captured 68 per cent of the Assembly seats, and 76 per cent of those in the Senate races (Appendix 10.1).[9]

Several factors concerning the nature of popular attitudes and party support at the time of the initial transition, emerge from examination of the voting returns. Among the most striking results of the initial national vote in Romania was the strength of support for the UDMR. With a population of around two million out of over 24 million in Romania as a whole, the Magyars must have voted almost unanimously in support of the UDMR in order to give it 7.2 per cent of the total vote. Support for the UDMR was intensely concentrated in counties populated by Magyars. In 25 out of 41 counties the UDMR received less than one per cent of the vote; in Harghita, with its large Magyar population, it received 85.2 per cent. The historical parties, on the other hand, did worse than expected. The National Liberals (PNL) came in third nationally with 6.4 per cent of the vote, slightly behind the UDMR. Fourth place was not taken by the National Peasants (2.56 per cent of the vote), but by one of the ecological parties, the Romanian Ecological Movement (MER), which attracted 2.62 per cent of the vote.

Nationally, the Front gained 66.3 per cent of the vote. The FSN showed itself strongest in agricultural counties with low levels of industrialization and urbanization. It did least well in the urban setting. In contrast, the PNL did best in urban and industrial counties, and worst in agricultural ones. In regional terms, Ion Iliescu was most successful in Moldavia (94 per cent) Muntenia (93 per cent) and Oltenia (93 per cent), and least successful in Transylvania (72 per cent). Radu Campeanu's strongest showing came in Transylvania, where he won 23 per cent of the vote, presumably due to support from the UDMR. Ion Raţiu, the National Peasant Party candidate, on the other hand, did best in Bucharest, where he achieved 11 per cent of the vote, more than twice the level of the support that he polled nationally.

The election results confirmed the main political tendencies that emerged in the first months after the revolution. The FSN consolidated its early gains, while more militantly anti-communist forces remained fragmented. This outcome was in large part predetermined by the precipitate way in which the elections were held and the Front's near monopolistic access to state resources. The campaign was an unequal contest at best, pitting a cohesive successor communist party with access to state assets against a fragmented opposition. Even so, during the course of the campaign it became clear that the FSN, having successfully co-opted the symbolism of the 1989 revolution, enjoyed a level of popular support that its liberal opponents were unwilling to acknowledge.

The Emergence of Cleavage Politics and Party Formation

Bolstered by electoral success, Iliescu and the FSN government that was formed in the wake of the 1990 elections, initiated a programme of limited reform. Their policy initiatives had clear consequences for the population at large as well as at the elite level, and set the stage for the development of more intense party competition in Romania's second electoral cycle.

Within months after the 1990 election, a number of reform laws were passed.[10] Land up to 25 acres held in collective farms was slated for return to former owners. Provision was made for 30 per cent of the value of state enterprises to be distributed to the population through voucher privatization. Private enterprise was legalized. The government called for price controls to be gradually liberalized until market pricing was reached on most goods. But even the cautious reform initiatives by the FSN touched off serious political conflict between pro-reform and anti-reform forces. Social groups affected by the reforms became increasingly active in their opposition. As the year after the elections wore on, strike activity increased and demonstrations by opposition groups became an almost daily routine in the country's capital. At the same time, consensus within the ruling party broke down. As the reform process took hold, improving conditions in some sectors, but imposing costs in others, competing factions took shape within the National Salvation Front based on several alternative political strategies

(Gallagher 1995, 115–7).

Popular reaction against the National Front government and its policies reached a peak in the autumn of 1991, when demonstrations threatened public order in Bucharest for a second time since the revolution. Workers stormed through the streets demanding the resignation of President Iliescu and Prime Minister Petre Roman. Ion Iliescu, however, successfully shifted the burden of responsibility for the consequences of the reforms onto Prime Minister Roman, engineering his resignation in mid-September. Forced to leave the government, Roman became the chief representative of those in the National Salvation Front who argued that reforms should proceed both further and faster. By the spring of the following year, Roman's supporters had become confident enough to force a confrontation at the ruling party's congress. In March 1992, Petre Roman was re-elected chairman of the party. Ion Iliescu and his supporters responded by breaking off to form their own organization, the Democratic National Salvation Front (FDSN).

Thus, some two years after the initial election, the originally relatively heterogeneous communist successor party fragmented into a new reformist FSN, which entered into the spectrum of the non-governing parties, and a relatively more conservative governing party, the FDSN. Iliescu's FDSN then shifted both rhetorically and in terms of policy implementation, in the direction of Romania's coterie of 'red-brown' parties: the Socialist Labour Party (PSM), the Party of Romanian National Unity (PUNR), and the Greater Romania Party (RM).

Meanwhile, the liberal opposition parties struggled to achieve individual coherence and collective co-operation, but to little avail. Putting aside their rivalries, fourteen democratic parties came together to form the Democratic Convention and to contest local elections in February 1992.[11] This achievement raised expectations that a new degree of collaboration had been reached among regime opponents, and that this would allow them to compete successfully in national elections. However, tensions within the opposition coalition were never successfully overcome. As the second post-revolution national election campaign approached, the attention of opposition leaders shifted from efforts to defeat the government to rivalries between the main participants of the Democratic Convention: the National Liberals, the National Peasant Party–Christian Democrat, the UDMR, and the Civic Alliance Party (PAC). Ultimately the National Liberal Party determined that it could more successfully pursue its goals independently, and it withdrew altogether from the Democratic Convention.

With elections coming up, nationalist rhetoric became a progressively more strident element of inter-party debate. The presence of two extremist nationalist opposition parties – the PUNR and the Greater Romanian Party – insured that the nationalist issue remained part of Romania's political discourse. As the minority question became increasingly salient, a second shift occurred within the Democratic Convention. The UDMR removed itself from the Convention's electoral agreement, apparently in order to avoid hampering the Convention's electoral chances. The UDMR remained a member of the Convention, however, supporting its candidate in the Presidential race and pledging co-operation in the pursuit of common goals in parliament.

In the period leading up to the elections, political forces thus consolidated into two broad groupings which may be characterized as liberal–universalist and collectivist–nationalist. The relevance of this characterization can be validated through an examination of party platforms and leadership behaviour, as well as through an inquiry into mass attitudes. For purposes of this study popular attitudes were analysed through the use of a public opinion survey administered in mid-1992. The most important dimensions of differentiation that shaped party-political orientation (as indicated below) were associated with attitudes towards economic reform (privatization and income differentiation) and towards minorities (*Table 10.1*).

Table 10.1: Political attitudes and party confidence

Atttitude toward pace of privatization by confidence in party

	R^2	Beta	Significance of F
FDSN	.051	.229	.000
FSN	.030	.178	.000
RM	.027	.167	.000
PSM	.016	.133	.000
PDAR	.004	.075	.012
PNT–CD	.058	-.242	.000
CAP	.053	-.233	.000
UDMR	.023	-.155	.000
PNL–AT	.029	-.172	.000
PNL	.021	-.148	.000

Attitude toward equality scale by confidence in party

	R^2	Beta	Significance of F
FDSN	.051	.229	.000
FSN	.030	.178	.000
RM	.027	.167	.000
PSM	.016	.133	.000
PDAR	.004	.075	.012
PNT–CD	.058	-.242	.000
CAP	.053	-.233	.000
UDMR	.023	-.155	.000
PNL–AT	.029	-.172	.000
PNL	.021	-.148	.000

Minority rights scale by confidence in Party

	R^2	Beta	Significance of F
RM	.018	-.138	.000
FDSN	.015	-.129	.000
PUNR	.014	-.122	.000
FSN	.009	-.100	.0005
PDAR	.009	-.100	.0008
PSM	.005	-.080	.0077
UDMR	.143	.379	.000
CAP	.054	.234	.000
PNT–CD	.036	.192	.000
PNL–AT	.015	.127	.000

Note: The R^2 provides a measure of the relationship between a independent variable (for example, the attitude towards the pace of privatization) and a given dependent variable, in this instance attitude toward particular political parties. Beta provides a measure of how much change in the dependent variable is caused by change in the independent variable, and also the direction of change (does an increasing value in one dimension cause an increase value or a decrease in the other dimension?). The Significance of F provides a measure of the probability that a given correlation is random. By way of example, a figure of .05 would indicate that the correlation in question would have occurred by chance in less than 95 per cent of cases. In essence, this table indicates that the attitudes in question are strongly related to attitudes toward political parties, and that their effect on support for the collectivist–nationalist and liberal–universalist groupings is in opposite directions. For example, the more that respondents favour economic equality, the more positively inclined they are toward the collectivist nationalists, and the less positively inclined they are towards liberal universalists.

Source: Random national sample of 1,608 respondents taken in late June and early July 1992.

The political significance of these dimensions is immediately clear. On the three measures employed here, the direction of the relationship between attitudes on issues, and attitudes towards the collectivist–nationalist and liberal–universalist parties are consistent, and in opposite directions.

In addition to being politically relevant, these ideological dimensions are associated with historical divisions located in Romanian social structure, indicating the presence of political cleavages in the society (see *Table 10.2*). Not surprisingly, the strongest indicator of attitudes toward minorities is the divide between Romanian's majority and minority communities. But in addition to this, there are also divisions within the majority group on this dimension. While the direct effect of class and education are not significant, social status does appear to play a role. Examination of the impact of the respondents' fathers' education level produces significant results, indicating that the cultural environment of the family does effect the formation of attitudes toward minorities. Urban–rural differences are also an important determinant of attitudes toward minorities, with urban dwellers being less hostile than their rural counterparts. Attitudes toward minorities differ significantly across Romania's main historic regions as well, with areas of high Magyar population density showing higher levels of ethnic hostility. The effect of region remains strong even if one controls for the effect of urban–rural differences, and for the age and education of the population. Interestingly, attitudes toward minorities are most negative among long term residents of ethnically mixed regions rather than newcomers, indicating a long lasting historical phenomenon rather than a more instrumental effect.

Table 10.2: Political attitudes and social structure

Attitudes towards minorities

	F Ratio	F Prob.
Majority/Minority	405.3656	.0000
Class	.8389	.5221
Respondent's Education Level	.4292	.7321
Father's Education	5.0728	.0017
Urban–Rural	7.0701	.0079
Region	4.3531	.0002

Attitudes towards private property

	F Ratio	F Prob.
Majority/Minority	12.42	.0004
Class	20.5065	.0000
Respondent's Education Level	55.2005	.0000
Father's Education	33.4482	
Urban–Rural	87.0958	.0000
Region	16.3072	.0000

Note: The F ratio employs the variance of group means as a measure of observed differences among groups. The bigger the F ratio the bigger the variance, and the smaller the F ratio the smaller the variance. The F probability provides a measure of the probability that a given difference in group means is random. For example, a figure of .05 would indicate that the correlation in question would have occurred by chance in less than 95 per cent of cases.

Source: Random national sample of 1,608 respondents taken in late June and early July 1992.

Attitudes toward property are also strongly related to social structural variables. In the case of this dimension, the urban/rural cleavage stands out as the strongest predictor, with the urban population being substantially more favourably inclined toward private property. Class and education play strong roles as well. As one would expect, professionals and those with higher levels of education are more positive with regard to private property, while those with lower levels of education are less so. Finally, as in the case of attitudes toward minorities, regional differences are apparent. Here one finds residents of Transylvania, the Banat, and Bucharest more liberally inclined, while Moldovans and Oltenians appear more collectivist in outlook. This relationship remained valid when controls were introduced for education and urban/rural differences between the regions.

Table 10.3: Proximity of party support

		R^2	Beta			R^2	Beta
FSN	FDSN	.143	.37	RM	PUNR	.297	.54
					PDAR	.193	.44
FDSN	RM	.152	.39		FDSN	.152	.39
	PDAR	.145	.38		PSM	.142	.38
	FSN	.143	.37		PR	.116	.34
	PUNR	.142	.37				
	PSM	.114	.34	MER	MR	.248	.49
					PNL-AT	.223	.47
					PDAR	.211	.46
					PNL	.163	.40
PNT-CD	CAP .	427	.65		PR	.162	.40
	UDMR	.239	.49		PUNR	.150	.38
	PNL-AT	.161	.40				
	PNL	.140	.34				
	MR	.137	.54	PNL	PNL-AT	.364	.60
					MER	.163	.40
					PR	.145	.38
UDMR	CAP	.289	.53		MR	.145	.38
	PNT-CD	.239	.48		PNT-CT	.139	.37
					CA	.106	.32
CAP	PNT-CD	.427	.65				
	UDMR	.289	.53	PNL-AT	PNL	.364	.60
	PNL-AT	.178	.42		MR	.306	.48
	MR	.165	.40		MER	.223	.47
	PNL	.106	.32		PR	.215	.46
					CA	.178	.42
					PNT-CD	.161	.40
PDAR	MER	.211	.46				
	RM	.193	.44	PR	PUNR	.220	.47
	PR	.193	.44		PNL-AT	.215	.46
	FDSN	.145	.38		PDAR	.193	.44
					MER	.162	.40
					PNL	.145	.38
PUNR	PDAR	.347	.59		RM	.116	.34
	RM	.297	.54				
	FDSN	.142	.37	MR	PNL-AT	.306	.55
					MER	.249	.49
PSM	RM	.145	.38		PR	.229	.47
	FDSN	.114	.34		PDAR	.193	.44
					CA	.165	.40
					FDSN	.152	.39
					PNL	.145	.38
					PNT-CD	.137	.37

Note: The R^2 provides a measure of the association between a independent variable and a given dependent variable, in this instance attitude towards particular political parties. Beta provides a measure of how much change in the dependent variable is caused by change in the independent variable, and also the direction of change. Table 10.3 reports attitudes towards each party and correlates them with attitudes to every other party. Only the positive associations are reproduced. In essence, the analysis indicates that positive attitudes towards any party in the collectivist–nationalist grouping correlate with positive attitudes toward other parties in that grouping, but not with parties outside of the grouping. A similar phenomenon is evident in the case of the liberal–universalist camp. *Source:* Random national sample of 1,608 respondents, June–July 1992.

The coherence of the two dominate party groupings in the minds of respondents is further indicated by analysis of the relationship between respondents' attitudes toward individual political parties. This was accomplished by regression analysis, examining the relationship between support for each of the major parties and support for each of the other major parties. The results of this process, indicated in Table 10.3, are consistent with the previous analysis: supporters of any of the parties in the collectivist–nationalist grouping of parties are likely to be favourably inclined to other parties in that grouping; those positively inclined to liberal–universalist parties are likely to be positively inclined toward others in the same grouping. The validity of this association was further confirmed by performing a factor analysis on questions reflecting respondents' support for the main political parties.[12]

As Table 10.3 indicates, the FDSN was at the focal point of the collectivist-nationalist cluster of parties, with attitudes toward it and the other parties in the grouping being positively correlated. Following its rupture from the FSN, which under Petre Roman's leadership pursued a more reformist strategy, President Iliescu's FDSN became – at least implicitly – the party of the status quo, arguing for continuation of reform at a cautious pace, for a strong government sector, and for strong social protection. The remainder of the collectivist-nationalist grouping consists of four parties that occupy the political space with, or to the right of, the FDSN on the dimension of nationalism and close to the FDEN, or to its left, on the reform continuum. These include the Party of Romanian National Unity (PUNR), the Greater Romania Party (RM) and the Socialist Labour Party (PSM), and the Democratic Agrarian Party (PDAR).

While sharing some common characteristics, each of these parties has unique attributes that distinguish it from the others and make close co-operation difficult to achieve. PUNR, for example was primarily a regional party of Transylvania. The PSM, led by Ceaușescu lieutenant Ilie Verdeț, was the most obvious successor to the Romanian Communist Party and is not surprisingly staunchly collectivist. The PDAR, staffed largely by a cadre of the former regime's agricultural bureaucracy, closely associated itself with the FDSN.

The second major locus of political power, that is the liberal–universalist grouping, is located on the opposite extreme of these ideological dimensions. It consists of parties that are often identified as the 'democratic opposition', most of which participate in the Democratic Convention. These include, most prominently, the Civic Alliance Party (PAC), the National Peasant Party–Christian Democrat (PNT–CD), the National Liberal Party, (PNL), and the UDM. These parties were, in general, much more favourably inclined to rapid reform and privatization. They were also much less driven by Romanian nationalism than the former grouping.[13]

The second post-transition national elections were held in September 1992 within this context of shifting party positions. The electoral rules established by the legislature in July of 1992, reduced the number of seats in the lower house from 387 to 328, while the Senate was expanded from 119 to 143 members. A three per cent electoral threshold was adopted for participation in the legislature. Coalitions were required to achieve a higher threshold, determined by adding 1 percentage point for each participating list in the coalition, up to a maximum of 8 per cent. The actual execution of the 1992 campaign was significantly better than in the previous case. While irregularities did occur, as documented by Carry (1995), the elections were accompanied by less violence, fraud played a smaller role, and access to the media for opposition parties was much improved.

The outcome of voting in September 1992 confirmed that a considerable evolution had occurred in Romanian politics since the 1990 contest. In the presidential race, support for Ion Iliescu was substantiated as a cardinal fact of Romanian political life. With 47.2 per cent of the first round vote and 61.4 per cent in the final contest, Iliescu again dominated the field of candidates (Appendix 10.1). The Democratic Convention's candidate, Emil Constantinescu, was able to attract 31.2 per cent in the first round, but garnered only an additional 7 per cent in the second, bringing his total vote to 38.6 per cent. It was a credible showing, but the outcome clearly did not allow the opposition to threaten President Iliescu. On the other hand, the 23.7-percentage-point decline in support between 1990 and 1992 could not have been comforting to the President.[14]

Voting in the parliamentary elections reflected an even greater change (Appendix 10.1). While still capturing a plurality of the vote in the Chamber of Deputies, FDSN support fell to 27.7 per cent, as compared to the 66.3 per cent that the unified FSN won in the previous contest. Petre Roman's rump FSN accounted for only another 10.2 per cent of the vote, leaving a drop of more than 28 percentage points to be accounted for. While no definitive answer as to the destination of these votes can be given, it appears likely that they were distributed across the entire ideological spectrum. PUNR, for example, won only slightly more than 2 per cent of the 1990 vote, but more than 8 per cent in 1992. Support for the parties that constitute the Democratic Convention also increased dramatically. From a collective vote of less than 5 per cent in 1990 the combined forces captured more than 20 per cent of the legislative vote in 1992; a remarkable feat by any standards. Other parties that enjoyed slight increases include Romania Mare and Verdeț's successor Socialist Labour Party, while support for the Magyar Democratic Union remained approximately constant, as one would expect, given the nature of its constituency.

Clearly, the ideological appeal of the FDSN had proved effective in these post-communist second elections. If one considers the differential support for political parties by various social strata, the early strength of the FDSN and the difficulties facing the opposition become even more clear (*Table 10.4*). The 15 per cent of workers expressing 'very much confidence' in the FDSN in late June 1992, was nearly double the figure for any other single party; it was 8.5 per cent for the FSN. Among peasants, strong support for the FDSN was even more secure, at 24.6 per cent. Only among professionals with higher education did the FDSN fail to capture the strongest level of support, reaching only 11.5 per cent and trailing behind the Civic Alliance Party with 18.5 per cent and the PNT–CD with 16.3 per cent.

Table 10.4: Confidence in political parties by social category *

Worker confidence in political parties (%)

	Very Much	Much	Moderate	Little
FSN	8.5	22.3	26.7	42.5
FDSN	15.0	21.5	18.1	45.4
PNT–CD	7.1	10.3	21.8	60.9
UDMR	.1	6.9	15.1	72.8
CAP	6.8	14.5	19.7	59.0
PDAR	4.8	17.1	33.7	44.4
PUNR	7.9	18.9	24.8	48.3
PSM	4.2	9.6	16.7	69.6
RM	6.2	17.0	24.0	52.1
MER	4.3	19.1	29.4	47.2
PNL	6.2	12.6	25.8	55.4
PNL-AT	3.0	17.5	22.8	56.6
RP	3.6	11.5	28.1	56.9
MR	2.1	9.2	17.6	71.1

Peasant confidence in political parties (%)

	Very Much	Much	Moderate	Little
FSN	18.1	20.0	25.0	36.9
FDSN	24.6	17.2	13.4	44.8
PNT-CD	2.0	9.9	17.9	72.2
UDMR	4.7	4.8	7.6	85.0
CAP	2.4	5.7	12.2	79.7
PDAR	8.6	25.7	17.1	48.6
PUNR	9.6	13.6	19.2	57.6
PSM	1.7	3.5	8.7	86.1
RM	2.5	10.1	19.3	68.1
MER	6.3	12.5	22.3	61.6
PNL	5.1	5.1	12.4	77.4
PNL-AT	3.1	6.3	14.8	75.8
RP	2.0	9.6	25.5	65.7
MR	2.2	2.2	6.5	89.1

Professionals' confidence in political parties (%)

	Very Much	Much	Moderate	Little
FSN	2.5	12.5	27.8	57.0
FSDN	11.5	10.3	15.4	62.8
PNT-CD	16.3	20.0	22.5	41.3
UDMR	7.6	8.9	10.1	73.4
CAP	18.5	19.8	17.3	44.4
PDAR	3.8	13.9	20.3	62.0
PUNR	11.5	12.8	19.2	56.4
PSM	1.3	3.8	12.7	82.3
RM	2.5	11.4	8.9	77.2
MER	5.1	17.9	21.8	55.1
PNL	6.3	17.5	21.3	55.0
PNL-AT	2.5	22.8	30.4	44.3
RP	5.3	20.0	22.7	52.0
MR	9.1	9.1	12.1	69.1

* Data taken from a random national poll of 1,608 respondents in late June and early July 1992.

The questions concerning support for potential Presidential candidates produced even more disproportionate results (*Table 10.5*). 46.2 per cent of peasants and 31.9 per cent of workers expressed support for Ion Iliescu. In each of these categories, the only other candidate to attract more than 10 per cent support was then Prime Minister, Stolojan. Among professionals, Stolojan gained the highest level of support, 26.2 per cent, followed by Nicolae Manolescu (14.3 per cent) and Iliescu (13.1 per cent). These data confirm strong support for Ion Iliescu and the policies that he represented among a large part of the population, particularly among workers and peasants. The intelligentsia's dissatisfaction with the government and strong support for the opposition was just as clear. Given the country's demographics, however, intellectual opposition in itself could not lead to a change in regime until the opposition was able to broaden its political base.

Table 10.5: Support for presidential candidates by social category *

	Professionals	Workers	Peasants
Raţiu	10.7	9.0	1.7
Druc	2.4	0.3	1.2
Iliescu	13.1	31.9	46.2
Manzatu	0.0	1.9	1.2
Manolescu	14.3	3.1	2.3
Stolojan	26.2	15.8	11.0
Roman	1.2	2.2	4.0
Conescu	1.2	0.6	0.0
Campeanu	1.2	4.6	3.5
Nastase	7.1	5.0	0.6

* Data taken from a random national poll of 1,608 respondents in late June and early July 1992.

It seems clear in light of the data presented above that policy-relevant cleavages had already appeared within the Romanian electorate early in the post-communist transition. It is further apparent that some members of the electorate grouped political parties according to their positions on meaningful ideological dimensions.

A further concern with respect to the role of cleavages in post-communist democracies is the congruity of mass and elite attitudes. Do the positions of constituents systematically correspond with those of the representatives of the parties that they support? If this is the case, then one would be better able to argue both that party formation is proceeding, and that party competition and ideological cleavages on the mass level are mutually reinforcing (Kitschelt 1994).

A comparison of the distribution of attitudes among legislators and party supporters may shed substantial light on this issue. Despite concern among analysts about the presumably low level of political development and social atomization, a significant differentiation was evident among Romanian political parties on both of the axes described above already by the 1992 elections.

Table 10.6: Basic attitudes: legislators, party supporters, and non-supporters (group means, standard deviations, and number of cases)

Support for Private Property

		Mean	Std Dev	Cases
FDSN	legislator	1.5306	.2924	119
	supporter	1.8941	.4346	336
	non-supporter	1.7685	.5374	967
FSN	legislator	1.2015	.1380	39
	supporter	1.9374	.4863	340
	non-supporter	1.7539	.5183	964
PNT-CD	legislator	1.1673	.3456	35
	supporter	1.5693	.4546	266
	non-supporter	1.8603	.5138	1037
UDMR	legislator	1.1714	.1472	30
	supporter	1.5694	.5126	140
	non-supporter	1.8288	.5092	1163
CAP	legislator	1.1319	.2764	13
	supporter	1.5850	.4553	274
	non-supporter	1.8584	.5157	1029
PUNR	legislator	1.4147	.2193	31
	supporter	1.7522	.4419	275
	non-supporter	1.8139	.5331	1028
PSM	legislator	1.6825	.2451	9
	supporter	2.0048	.4402	90
	non-supporter	1.7858	.5178	1213
PNL	legislator	1.3036	.1937	8
	supporter	1.6414	.4714	239
	non-supporter	1.8367	.5186	1064

Attitude Toward Minorities

		Mean	Std Dev	Cases
FDSN	legislator	1.3150	.3661	123
	supporter	1.2416	.3643	329
	non-supporter	1.4694	.5353	851
FSN	legislator	1.7500	.6065	36
	supporter	1.3067	.4035	313
	non-supporter	1.4418	.5310	868
PNT-CD	legislator	1.7031	.2940	32
	supporter	1.6084	.5764	233
	non-supporter	1.3561	.4717	947
UDMR	legislator	2.8000	.2013	30
	supporter	2.1022	.6143	137
	non-supporter	1.3145	.4074	1043
CAP	legislator	1.7692	.2385	13
	supporter	1.6820	.6015	250
	non-supporter	1.3317	.4464	930
PUNR	legislator	1.0882	.1834	34
	supporter	1.1742	.2974	287
	non-supporter	1.4804	.5334	893
PSM	legislator	1.1818	.1966	11
	supporter	1.2622	.3867	82
	non-supporter	1.4167	.5102	1098
PNL	legislator	1.7143	.3037	7
	supporter	1.4304	.4864	212
	non-supporter	1.4006	.5078	968

Table 10.6 presents mean scores for legislators elected in 1992 belonging to eight of the country's most significant parties on attitudinal scales, measuring views towards property ownership (taken here as an indicator of attitudes towards economic liberalism in general) and attitudes towards ethnic minorities. The attitudes of the respondents from the 1992 public opinion survey who expressed support for those parties, and the attitudes of the respondents who indicated no support for each of the parties, are registered. On both scales, clear differences are evident between legislators associated with the ruling the Democratic National Salvation Front (FDSN), its allies (the Socialist Labour Party FDSN, and the Party of Romanian National Unity, PUNR), and the democratic opposition parties. The former grouping is less inclined toward private property, and is more hostile to minorities, while the latter group of legislators is more positive towards private property, and less hostile to minorities. On the attitude toward minorities scale, the distinction between the legislative delegation of the Democratic Magyar Union of Romania (UDMR) and the rest of field is obvious. Analysis of variance shows significant differences between parties on both scales.[15]

A comparison of party legislators' positions on the economy with those of their supporters and non-supporters indicates that party supporters in general are less positive toward private property than their respective party legislative groups. The views of the liberal opposition legislative delegations are closer to the views of their supporters than to those of non-supporters, as one would expect if party formation is actually occurring (*Figure 10.1*). This is not the case regarding the Democratic National Salvation Front (FDSN), the Socialist Labour Party (PSM) and the National Salvation Front (FSN), whose supporters are more collectivist than respondents who do not express support for those parties. But there is overwhelming evidence that supporters of these legislative groups are closer to the positions of their legislators than to the opposition party groups.[16]

Figure 10.1: Attitudes towards property in Romania: group means

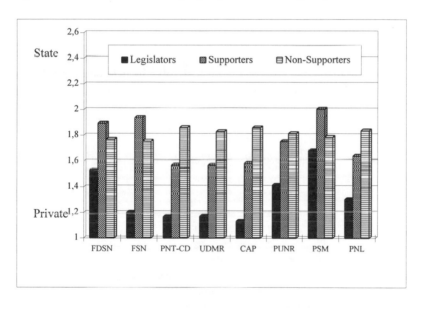

The data on attitudes towards minorities presents a somewhat different picture. Once again the scores of the liberal opposition legislative groups are closer to their supporters than to their non-supporters (*Figure 10.2*). This is also the case as regards the PSM and the PUNR, but with the direction of deviation reversed, i.e. legislators are more hostile to minorities than either their supporters or the population at large. FSN legislators here stand out, being substantially more distant from their own supporters than from respondents who do not support their party on this particular issue.[17]

Figure 10.2: Attitudes towards minorities in Romania: group means

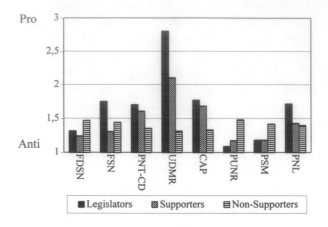

Figures 10.3 and 10.4 summarize, respectively, the data on the proximity of party legislators to their supporters, and to survey respondents who do not indicate support for the given parties (non-supporters).

Figure 10.3: Issue distance between Romanian legislators and party supporters

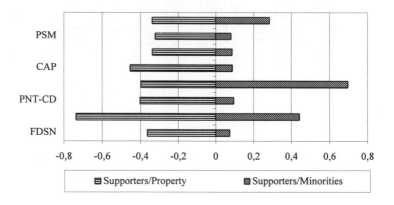

Figure 10.4: Issue distance between Romanian legislators and party non-supporters on the issues of property and minorities

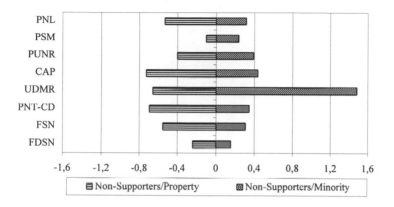

Figure 10.3 indicates that the FDSN–PUNR–PSM grouping is less distant from their supporters than are their liberal opponents, while the FSN suffers from an almost extreme divergence of opinion between legislators and supporters. Differentiation is even more evident in Figure 10.4. Clearly, the FDSN and the former communist PSM are substantially closer to the positions of non-supporters than are their opponents. Potentially, this should provide both parties with competitive advantages. The actual electoral dominance of the FDSN in comparison to the weakness of the PSM, may probably be attributed to the weak legitimacy of PSM leaders too closely associated with the Ceauşescu dictatorship, and to the additional advantages accruing to the FDSN as a governing party.

In figure 10.5 we have plotted the Party–Legislator and Party–Supporter positions spatially on both the property and attitude-toward-minority dimensions. Several critical factors can be discerned from the resulting configuration. Clearly, the Democratic Magyar Union of Romania (UDMR) and its supporters stand alone, outside the general spectrum of party competition. The tight grouping of the liberal opposition legislators along with those of the National Salvation Front (FSN) – more moderate on minority issues and less collectivist – is also clear. Equally striking is the grouping of party supporters who are significantly more collectivist than the legislative groups, while generally more moderate on minority issues than the nationalist party legislators and less moderate than the liberal party legislators.

Figure 10.5: Issue positions of Romanian legislators and party supporters

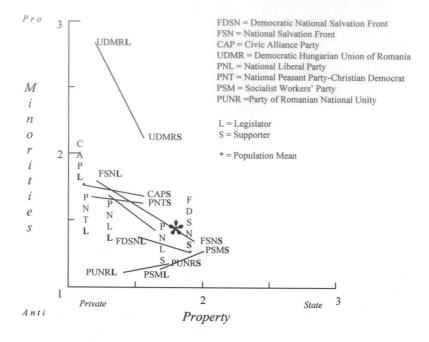

The advantage of the FDSN within the competitive environment of the early transition is apparent. Ruling party legislators are located between the more extreme nationalist-collective parties and the liberal opposition, and quite close to the supporters of both alternative groupings (as well as to the mean position of the entire mass opinion sample). The FDSN strategy, following 1990, is clear in light of this configuration. The Iliescu leadership was unlikely to lose votes to the liberal opposition – the supporters of which are actually closer to the ruling party than to their own legislative representatives on property issues – unless the FDSN were to undertake more determined reform measures or become much more moderate on minority issues. It could, however, lose substantial support to the collectivist–nationalist opposition by becoming either more moderate on minority issues or more reformist on property issues, hence it avoided movement in these directions.

Democratic Consolidation and the 1996 Elections

Romania's third set of elections, held in November 1996, was decisive. It marked the first definitive change in power since the fall of communism.

The change in leadership was fundamental, from successors of the communist regime, to proponents of reform who had been excluded from power for the first six years of the transition. The interaction between party politics and political cleavages played a clear role in the period leading up to the elections. Following 1992, President Iliescu's strategy relied upon consolidating an electoral base among peasants and workers. The FDSN appealed to the anxiety that was evident among members of these classes, concerning rapid marketization and social change. It held out the promise of relative stability and continued state protection. On the margins, the ruling party also played to the nationalist sentiments that were evident within this segment of the electorate. Following the 1992 elections, President Iliescu also formed a tacit legislative alliance with the extreme nationalist parties, whose parliamentary delegations supported Prime Minister Vacaroiu's government. In 1994 this coalition became explicit, when members of PUNR and the Greater Romania Party entered into the cabinet.

While politically expedient in the near term, this political configuration proved unworkable from the point of view of policy formation. The political and economic stagnation that so unfortunately characterized Romania in the years following the 1992 elections, can be traced in large part to the nature of the ruling party and its social base. Given the character of its party leadership and its core constituency, the Democratic National Salvation Front – re-labelled the Party of Romanian Social Democracy (PDSR) in July 1993 when it united with three smaller parties – found itself incapable of effective reform or competent management of the country's economy.

Given the character of the PDSR leadership, one can question the depth of the party's commitment to fundamental reform. Indeed, one of the primary considerations that undermined Vacaroiu cabinet's ability to govern was the continued influential role that hold-over elements of the communist regime continued to play in public life. These included managers both from the state sector enterprises who benefited from public subsidization, and the *nomenklatura* class of politically connected individuals, who were able to benefit financially from the economy's intermediate stage between market and plan, in essence trading on their access to the state.

Even those limited reforms that were undertaken by the Vacaroiu government during the 1992–96 period, however, foundered in the face of mass opposition. Repeated rounds of price reform were met by public demonstrations and strikes. In similar circumstances, centre-right governments were able to press forward with rationalization (more or less successfully, and more or less completely, depending on the case). But given the limited nature of its base, the PDSR was not in a situation to flout popular opposition. Hence price reforms were followed by wage increases, defeating the initial purpose of the exercise and fuelling inflation. The story of privatization efforts under PDSR rule, while more complex, followed much the same pattern. Initial proposals promised decisive action, but implementation was weak (complicated by the interests of the state sector managers), and when resistance was encountered, efforts foundered.

A second factor constraining PDSR rule was the party's reliance on its extreme nationalist allies for parliamentary support. An arms-length relationship in the early 1990s clearly worked to Iliescu's advantage, allowing him to garner support from the nationalist constituency, while at the same time avoiding direct association with the most extreme statements of the nationalist leaders. In 1994 the relationship between PDSR and the extremists was made more explicit through the inclusion of two ministers from the Party of Romanian National Unity in the Vacaroiu government. This was followed by the conclusion of an open agreement on co-operation with the Greater Romania Party (PUNR) and the Socialist Labour Party in January 1995.

While expedient from the point of view of domestic politics, however, this coalition proved extremely costly to the PDSR in foreign policy terms, and ultimately broke down. As Andrew Janos (1994) has aptly noted, the Central European states act under severe international constraints. In an international environment dominated by great powers whose elites are free market and politically liberal in orientation, it is extremely difficult for the leaders of small and dependent states to achieve their desired goals without some degree of ideological compliance. In the case of Romania, integration into European security structures and access to the world market were (and remain) priority goals of mainstream politicians. Achieving these goals, however, remained problematic as the international community increasingly identified President Iliescu and the PDSR with nationalist extremism. This contradictory position became progressively more difficult to manage, as Iliescu undertook to improve relations with Hungary in an effort to enhance his government's standing with Western Europe and the United States. Hence, even as the 1996 round of elections approached, the PDSR was forced to distance itself from its nationalist allies, aggravating already difficult relations with the volatile extremist leaders, and causing a breakdown in the 'red-brown' coalition.

The 1996 election results clearly testified to the erosion of support for the PDSR that occurred in 1992–96 as a consequence of its policy failures, as well as to the increased co-operation among the opposition. In the parliamentary elections held on 3 November 1996, the Democratic Convention came out a clear winner, with 30.3 per cent of the vote and 122 out of 343 seats in the Chamber of Deputies, and 30.7 per cent of the vote and 51 out of 143 Senate seats (Appendix 10.1). The PDSR, in contrast, trailed by nearly 10 percentage points, with 21.5 per cent of the vote and 91 seats in the Chamber of Deputies, and 23.1 per cent and 41 seats in the Senate. The CDR's strong plurality coupled with support from the UDMR, which took approximately 6.5 per cent of the vote, and the Social Democratic Union with approximately 13 per cent, put the opposition well over the threshold necessary to form a new coalition government under CDR Prime Minister Victor Ciorbea.

In the initial round of the 1996 presidential contest, held simultaneously with the legislative election, Ion Iliescu took the first place with 32.2 per cent of the vote. This represented a significant decline from Iliescu's 1992 performance, when he garnered 47.2 per cent in the first round. The second place position was once again held by CDR candidate Emil Constantinescu, whose vote also decreased slightly between the 1992 and 1996 contests, from 31.2 per cent to 28.2 per cent of the vote. But Constantinescu's decline was clearly accounted for in large part by the fact that the UDMR fielded its own candidate in 1996, and had not done so in 1992. In the earlier contest UDMR supporters can be presumed to have voted overwhelmingly for Constantinescu in the first round. Given this change of conditions, Constantinescu's first-round vote among non-UDMR voters can be assumed to have increased by approximately 3 percentage points.

The results of the second-round presidential contest, held on November 17, represented a decisive success for Emil Constantinescu and the opposition parties. Constantinescu's vote in the run-off increased by 26.2 percentage points to 54.4 per cent of the total vote. Despite President Iliescu's intensified efforts to play on nationalist sentiments and fear of economic change between the first and second rounds, his vote rose by only approximately half as much, 13.4 per cent, to give him a final 45.6 per cent in the final count. As in the previous competition, the role of political cleavages in producing the 1996 electoral outcome was evident. Under the conditions prevailing in 1996 however, cleavage politics did not act in the PDSR's favour. To a certain extent, the basic 1992 pattern was retained, but with a general erosion in support for the PDSR.

Exit-polling by the International Foundation for Electoral Support (IFES) and the IRSOP research organization, sheds substantial light on the mood of voters. The data indicate that, as in the earlier contest, the rural-urban division was once again significant. Rural voters favoured the PDSR over the CDR by a margin of 8 percentage points (34 per cent against 26 per cent). The peasantry provided the strongest base of support for Iliescu and the PDSR; 53 per cent of peasants voted for the PDSR, 18 per cent for the Democratic Convention. The elderly continued to support the PDSR as well giving it 42 per cent of their vote, as opposed to 24 per cent for the CDR.

Emil Constantinescu and the Democratic Convention, on the other hand, retained their hold on the upper classes, gaining 65 per cent of the vote from those with higher education. The CDR did very well among young people, who gave it 35 per cent of their vote, as opposed to 17 per cent for the PDSR. The earlier regional pattern of voting was also once again in evidence. Iliescu's vote remained strong in areas that he had dominated in previous campaigns, Oltenia, Muntenia and Moldavia. As one would expect, the Democratic Convention took urban areas, as well as Transylvania and the Banat, but with higher margins than before.

Along with declining margins of support across all categories, the factors that most accounted for the PDSR defeat were its loss of working-class vote, (as Michael Shafir 1997 points out), and support of the emerging entrepreneurial class for the opposition parties. The IFES/IRSOP exit-polling data show that workers gave the Democratic Convention 32 per cent support, well over the 21 per cent of the worker vote directed to the PDSR. This shift in allegiance was critical in determining the outcome of the election. The new middle class electorate had an effect as well. While state sector managers no doubt remained a PDSR constituency, six years of post-communism in Romania has produced a more complex economy, and increasing numbers of private owners. This group voted overwhelmingly for the Democratic Convention, giving it 48 per cent of their vote, in comparison to 11 per cent for the PDSR.

In the long term, the failure of President Iliescu and the PDSR government to press through economic reform undercut the Romanian economy's competitive position, engendering hardship for the general population, including workers, and producing the 1996 electoral backlash. This remained the case even though the policy was justified in the name of protecting workers' welfare against the ravages of unconstrained markets. By the time of the elections, 60 per cent of the voters felt that conditions in Romania had deteriorated, and in every category in which they were questioned, voters felt that the Democratic Convention would be better able to manage the country than the PDSR. The ruling party's abandonment of its coalition with the extreme nationalist parties played a role in its defeat as well. By the time that the seriousness of his situation became apparent and President Iliescu began to more actively pursue an ethnic strategy, his ability to do so was undermined, and support was not forthcoming. In essence the PDSR gave up a more extreme segment of the electorate in the hopes of broadening its appeal, but failed to attract new votes from the centre.

Conclusions

The data presented here suggest a number of conclusions. Early in the political transition both Romanian mass opinion and that of party elites (legislators) were differentiated along salient and policy-relevant ideological dimensions. Members of the general population assessed particular parties in accordance with their view on salient dimensions, and their attitudes toward a variety of parties is consistent, in accordance with each individual party's ideological characteristics. Furthermore, there was an evident coherence in the position of party legislative groups, relative to the positions taken by their supporters along the dimensions examined.

Given the nature of the cleavage structure that emerged in Romania following the 1989 revolution, the nature of early party competition is obvious. The FDSN gained control over the state at the beginning of the transition process as an implicit if not an explicit reform communist party. Initially, its leaders assumed a cautious position on economic reform issues, and then backed off from early initiatives as popular resistance to marketization and privatization became apparent. The party took up a relatively nationalist position on minority issues, which played a critical role in its legitimization strategy. The nationalism of the FDSN served to differentiate it further from the liberal parties that were its primary early opponents, while staving off the more extreme collectivist/nationalist parties.

The continual inter-elite attacks and divisions that have plagued the liberal opposition parties and created the impression of personalistic rather than issue-related politics, are also partially explained by these data. The liberal opposition legislators (with the exception of the UDMR) were apparently grouped so closely together on both issue dimensions considered here, that they felt compelled to resort to non-issue related attacks in efforts to distinguish themselves in their competition for a limited pool of potential supporters. In a similar vein, due to their intra-group competition, none of these parties moved into a less nationalist stance. Any such move risked the loss of support to other parties in the grouping that are equally pro-private property and might then be closer to potential supporters on minority issues.

The electoral behaviour, and to a certain extent the electoral fate, of parties in Romania are thus explicable by reference to the parties' proximity to each other and to their potential constituents on crucial cleavages. Whatever else, the party closest in position to the bulk of the population (the PDSR/FDSN) emerged as electorally dominant in the early phase of the Romanian transition. But both the character of its elite membership and its mass base severely constrained its ability to pursue an effective economic strategy. Consequently, support for the Romanian former communists declined within the working class, initially a key element of its electoral base. With the capacity to appeal to nationalists constrained, and unable to attract voters from the emerging post-communist social groups, the way to the 1996 regime change was opened. And so it seems indisputable that ideological cleavages emerged very early in the Romanian transition, and have played a crucial role in ongoing party competition.

Acronyms of Parties and Movements

AC	*Alianţa Civică* (Civic Alliance)
ANL	*Alianţa Naţional Liberal* (National Liberal Alliance)
CDR	*Convenţia Democratică Romăna* (Democratic Convention of Romania)
FDSN	*Frontul Democrat al Salvării Naţionale* (Democratic National Salvation Front)
FER	*Federaţia Ecologistă Romăna* (Ecological Federation of Romania)
FSN	*Frontul Salvării Naţionale* (National Salvation Front)
MER	*Mişcarea Ecologistă din România* (Romanian Ecological Movement)
PAC	*Partidul Alianţă Civică* (Civic Alliance Party)
PAR	*Partidul Alternativă Romăniei* (Alternative Party of Romania)
PDAR	*Partidul Democatic Agrar Romănia* (Agrarian Democratic Party of Romania)
PDSR	*Particucl Democraţiei Sociale din Romănia* (Social Democracy Party of Romania)
PNL	*Partidul Naţional Liberal* (National Liberal Party)
PNL–AT	*Partidul Naţional Liberal Aripa Tineretului* (National Liberal Party–Youth Wing)
PNL'93	*Partidul Naţional Liberal '93* (National Liberal Party '93)
PNT–CD	*Partidul Naţional Ţăranesc–Creştin Democrat* (National Peasant Party–Christian and Democratic)
PPR	*Partidul Pensionerilor Romăn* (The Pensioners' Party of Romania)
PR	*Partidul Republican* (Republican Party)
PS	*Partidul Socialist* (Socialist Party)
PSDR	*Partidul Socialist Democrat Romăn* (Social Democratic Party of Romania)
PSM	*Partidul Socialist al Muncii* (Socialist Labour Party)
PSMR	*Partidul Socialist Muncitoresc Romăn* (Party of Socialist Workers of Romania)
PUNR	*Partidul Unităţi Naţionale Romăne* (Party of Romanian National Unity)
RM	*Partidul Romănia Mare* (The Greater Romania Party)
UDMR	*Uniunea Democratică Maghiara din Romănia* (Democratic Magyar Union of Romania)
USD	*Uniunea Social Democrat* (Social Democratic Union)

NOTES

1. For a review of this debate and an extremely useful contribution to it, see Stephen Whitefield and Geoffrey Evans (1997). Whitefield and Evens argue convincingly for the independent role of cleavages in determining political outcomes in post-communist societies. Ellen Comisso (1997) presents a concise argument to the effect that social cleavages do exist in post-communist Central Europe, but only weakly associated with elite-level politics.

2. The public opinion survey research in Romania cited in this chapter was funded by a grant from the National Council for Soviet and East European Research, contract number 806–20. Field work was carried out by the Centre for Rural and Urban Sociology. Approximately 1,600 respondents were selected, based upon a national probability sample. A stratified sample was drawn, based on historical region and type of locality (rural, small towns, and cities). As a sampling frame, voter lists compiled for the 1990 elections were employed. Face-to-face interviews were used in this project. The questionnaire included 266 questions, and required an average time of approximately one hour to administer. Members of minority communities were recruited to administer the survey in minority districts, and in each case minority language versions of the survey instrument were prepared for the use of members of the larger minority groups. Subjects were provided with an opportunity to choose the language in which they wished to respond. The data on legislators' opinions are based on a 1993 survey of members of the Romanian parliament, conducted by William Crowther in collaboration with Gheorgeta Muntean and Informatix, AG in Bucharest. 357

members of both houses responded to the written survey; 102 responses were from the Senate, 255 were from the House. All the parties in parliament were represented in the results.

3. For a thorough treatment of the evolution of Romania's inter-war political economy, see Roberts (1951).

4. On the rise of Romanian Fascism, see Weber (1965) or Nagy-Talavera (1967).

5. On the origins and evolution of the Romanian communist movement, see Ionescu (1964).

6. The actual course of events leading to Ceauşescu's overthrow and execution, and the nature of the leadership that emerged from Romania's December revolution, immediately became the subjects of intense speculation. Cf., Tismaneanu 1990, 17–21.

7. This decision destabilized an already volatile situation, touching off a series of demonstrations both by the student movement and by anti-Iliescu political parties. In response, the FSN resorted to a combination of force and compromise. In the last week of January 1990, Iliescu mobilized supportive workers who rampaged through the capital, attacking supporters of anti-Front political parties. At the same time, limited concessions were employed to defuse opposition. The National Salvation Front agreed to dissolve itself as a government and form a new body, the Provisional Council of National Unity, which would rule until elections could be held.

8. For summaries of the programmes of these parties as well as those of the Social Democratic Party and the Ecological Democrats, see Socor 1990, 28–35.

9. Thus, even if all of the opposition groups voted as a bloc, a circumstance that was virtually unimaginable, the Front would still have controlled both new legislative bodies. In fact, on most issues the Romanian Unity Alliance (AUR) – the electoral wing of *Vatra Romaneasca* – and many of the smaller parties could be counted on to act in support of the FSN on most issues, ensuring it of control over both executive and legislative branches.

10. For a more detailed discussion of the early post communist economic reforms in Romania, see Isarescu 1992, 147–65.

11. The Democratic Convention succeeded in gaining 23 per cent of mayoral votes, in comparison with 31 per cent for the still unified National Salvation Front. More significantly, the Convention captured control of seven of the country's largest urban areas, including the capital.

12. *Factor analysis*

VARIMAX rotation 1 for extraction 1 in analysis 1 - Kaiser Normalization.
VARIMAX converged in 3 iterations.
Rotated Factor Matrix:

		Factor 1	Factor 2
V73	(FSN)	.45624	-.16666
V74	(FDSN)	.69729	-.17239
V75	(PNT)	-.12632	.81410
V76	(UDMR)	.16622	.67430
V77	(CAP)	-.11527	.82837
V78	(PDAR)	.71865	.24640
V79	(PURN)	.77177	.14958
V80	(PSM)	.58141	.05967
V81	(RM)	.74671	-.01607
V83	(PNL)	.26028	.62579
V84	(PNL-AT)	.31691	.70326

Factor Transformation Matrix:

	Factor 1	Factor 2
Factor 1	.78499	.61951
Factor 2	-.61951	.78499

13. Three other parties that played significant roles in the 1992 elections were not firmly attached to either of these groupings. Led by ex-student activist Marin Munteanu, the Movement for Romania (MR) had ties to the pre-war Legionnaire Movement. It could therefore clearly be described as nationalist, but it is also economically liberal, which puts it in an equivocal position

between two opposed blocs. Support for the Ecological Movement (MER) and the Republican Party (PR), on the other hand, did not appear to be determined adequately by the ideological dimensions identified above. Confidence in them does not correlate significantly with attitudes that distinguish supporters of the two main blocs, and their supporters were not consistent in their attitudes toward the parties that participate in the main competing coalitions (*Table 10.4*).

14. This loss, while in part explicable by migration to other parties and their candidates, must also be seen in the context of the artificially inflated support for Iliescu registered in the elections of 1990.

15. Analysis of Variance

Attitude Toward Minorities By Political Affiliation

Source	Sum of D.F.	Mean Squares	Squares	F Ratio	F Prob.
Between groups	7	67.4537	9.6362	72.8793	.0000
Within groups	288	38.0799	.1322		
Total	295	105.5336			

Support for Private Property By Political Affiliation

Source	Sum of D.F.	Mean Squares	Squares	F Ratio	F Prob.
Between groups	7	9.2347	1.3192	17.8870	.0000
Within groups	287	21.1675	.0738		
Total	294	30.4022			

16. T-tests showed differences between legislators and supporters, and supporters and non-supporters to be significant at the .05 level in every case, with regard to the property issue.

17. T-tests showed mean score differences on the scale significant at the .05 level except in the case of: FDSN legislators and their supporters; PSM legislators and their supporters; CAP legislators and their supporters; PNT–CD legislators and their supporters; and PNL supporters and non-supporters.

18. The material in this table is drawn from Bejan (1991) and Combes and Berindei (1991).

REFERENCES

Bejan, Alexandru I. (1991) 'Prezentarea şi analiza comparativă a rezultăţelor alegerilor de la 20 Mai 1990', in Petre Datculescu and Klaus Liepelt, eds., *Renasterea unei democraţii: Alegerile din România de la 20 Mai 1990*, Bucharest, Cores.

Carry, Henry F. (1995) 'Irregularities or rigging: the 1992 Romanian parliamentary elections,' *East European Quarterly*, (Spring) V. 29, No. 1.

Combes, Ariadna and Mihnea Berindei (1991), 'Analiza alegerilor', in Pavel Campeanu, Ariadna Combes and Mihnea Berindei, eds., *România înainte şi după 20 Mai*, Bucharest, Humanitas.

Comisso, Ellen (1997), 'Is the glass half full or half empty?: reflections of five years of competitive politics in Eastern Europe', *Communist and Post Communist Studies*, Vol. 30, No. 1, 1–21.

Crowther, William (1988), *The Political Economy of Romanian Socialism*, New York, Praeger.

——, and Steven Roper (1996), 'A comparative analysis of institutional development in the Romanian and Moldovan legislatures', *The Journal of Legislative Studies*, Vol. 2, No. 1 (Spring), 33–160.

Evans, Geoffrey and Stephen Whitefield (1993), 'Identifying the basis of party competition in Eastern Europe,' *British Journal of Political Science*, Vol. 23, No. 4, 521–48.

Gallagher, Tom (1995) *Romania After Ceauşescu*, Edinburgh, Edinburgh University Press.

Ionescu, Ghita (1964), *Communism in Romania: 1944–1962*, London, Oxford University Press.

Isarescu, Mugur (1992), 'The Prognosis for Economic Recovery,' in Daniel N. Nelson, ed., *Romania After Tyranny*, Boulder, CO., Westview Press.

Janos, Andrew (1994), 'Continuity and change in Eastern Europe: strategies for post-communist politics', *East European Politics and Societies,* Vol. 8, No. 1, 1–31.

Kitschelt, Herbert (1992), 'The formation of party systems in East Central Europe', *Politics and Society*, 20 (1), 7–50.

—— (1994), 'Party systems in East Central Europe: consolidation or fluidity?', paper prepared for presentation at the 1994 Annual Meeting of the *American Political Science Association*, New York, 4 September.

Lipset, Seymour Martin and Stein Rokkan (1967), 'Cleavage Structures, Party Systems, and Voter Alignments,' in Seymour Martin Lipset and Stein Rokkan, eds., *Party Systems and Voter Alignments: Cross-National Perspectives*, New York, The Free Press.

Nagy-Talavera, Nicolas (1967), *The Green Shirts and Others: A History of Fascism in Hungary and Romania*, Berkeley, CA, University of California Press.

Roberts, Henry L. (1951). *Rumania: Political Problems of an Agrarian State*, New Haven, Yale University Press.

Rogger, Hans and Eugen Weber, eds., (1965). *The European Right: A Historical Profile*, Los Angeles, CA, University of California Press.

Shafir, Michael (1997), 'Romania's road to normalcy', *Journal of Democracy,* Vol. 8 (April), 144–58.

Socor, Vladimir (1990), 'Political parties emerging', *Radio Free Europe/Radio Liberty Research Reports*, 16 February.

Tismaneanu, Vladimir (1990), 'New masks, old faces', *The New Republic,* 5 February.

Verdery, Katherine (1991), *National Ideology Under Socialism*, Los Angeles, University of California Press.

Weber, Eugen (1965), 'Romania', in Hans Rogger and Eugen Weber, eds., *The European Right: A Historical Profile,* Los Angeles, University of California Press.

Whitefield, Stephen and Geoffrey Evans (1997), 'From the top down or the bottom up? Explaining the structure of ideological cleavages in post-communist societies', mimeo.

APPENDIX 10.1: ELECTION RESULTS

PARLIAMENTARY ELECTIONS

1990 Elections
Date: 20 May
Turnout: 86.2%

House of Deputies

Party	%	Seats	Seats, %
National Salvation Front	66.3	263	67.9
Magyar Democratic Union of Romania	7.2	29	7.5
National Liberal Party	6.4	29	7.5
Romanian Ecological Movement	2.6	12	3.1
National Peasants' Party	2.6	12	3.1
Alliance for a United Romania	2.1	9	2.3
Democratic Agrarian Party of Romania	1.8	9	2.3
Romanian Ecological Party	1.7	8	2.1
Romanian Socialist Democratic Party	1.0	5	1.3
Social Democratic Party	0.5	2	0.5
Democratic Group of the Centre	0.5	2	0.5
Democratic Party of Work	0.4	1	0.2
Party of Free Change	0.3	1	0.2
Party of National Reconstruction of Romania	0.3	1	0.2
Party of Young Free Democrats of Romania	0.3	1	0.2
German Democratic Forum of Romania	0.3	1	0.2
Liberal Union 'Bratianu'	0.3	1	0.2
Democratic Union of Romania	0.2	1	0.2
Total	94.9	387	100

Senate

Party	%	Seats	Seats,%
National Salvation Front	67.0	91	76.5
Magyar Democratic Union of Romania	7.2	12	10.1
National Liberal Party	7.1	10	8.4
National Peasants' Party	2.5	1	0.8
Romanian Ecological Movement	2.4	1	0.8
Alliance for a United Romania	2.2	2	1.7
Democratic Agrarian Party of Romania	1.6	–	–
Romanian Ecological Party	1.4	1	
Romanian Social Democratic Party	1.1	–	–
Independent	n/m	1	0.8
Total	n/m	119	100

1992 Elections
Date: 27 September
Turnout: 76.3%

Chamber of Deputies

Party	%	Seats
Democratic National Salvation Front	27.7	117
Democratic Convention of Romania	20.0	82
National Salvation Front	10.2	43
Party of Romanian National Unity	7.9	30
Magyar Democratic Union of Romania	7.4	27
Greater Romania Party	3.8	16
Socialist Labour Party	3.0	13
Agrarian Democratic Party of Romania	2.9	
National Liberal Party	2.6	
Romanian Ecological Movement	2.3	
Republican Party	1.6	

Senate

Party	%	Seats
Democratic National Salvation Front	28.3	49
Democratic Convention of Romania *	20.2	34
National Salvation Front	10.4	18
Party of Romanian National Unity	8.1	14
Magyar Democratic Union of Romania	7.6	12
Greater Romania Party	3.8	6
Socialist Labour Party	3.2	5
Agrarian Democratic Party of Romania	3.3	3
National Liberal Party	2.1	
Romanian Ecological Movement	2.1	
Republican Party	1.9	

In 1992, the CDR was an electoral coalition of 12 parties, including the PNT–CD, PAC, PNL'93, PDSR, the Romanian Ecologist Party, and a number of smaller parties.

1996 Elections
Date: 3 November
Turnout: 76.0%

Chamber of Deputies

Party	%	Seats
Democratic Convention of Romania*	30.2	122
Party of Social Democracy of Romania	21.5	91
Social Democratic Union	12.9	53
Magyar Democratic Union of Romania	6.6	25
Greater Romania Party	4.5	19
Party of Romanian National Unity	4.4	18
Socialist Party	2.3	–
Socialist Labour Party	2.2	–
Romanian Socialist Labour Party	1.7	–
National Liberal Alliance	1.6	–
Pensioners' Party in Romania	1.4	–
Minority Deputies		15
Total	100.0	343

Senate

Party	%	Seats
Democratic Convention of Romania*	30.7	51
Party of Social Democracy of Romania	23.1	41
Social Democratic Union	13.2	23
Magyar Democratic Union of Romania	6.8	11
Greater Romania Party	4.5	8
Party of Romanian National Unity	4.2	7
Socialist Party	2.3	–
Socialist Labour Party	2.2	–
National Liberal Alliance	1.5	–
Pensioners' Party in Romania	1.5	–
Romanian Socialist Labour Party	1.3	–
Total	100.0	143

* In 1996, the CDR was an electoral coalition of the PNT–CD, PNL, PNL–CD, the Alternative Party of Romania, the Romanian Ecologist Party, the Romanian Ecological Federation, Civic Alliance, the Association of Former Political Prisoners, University Solidarity, Movement for Romania's Future, Association of Revolutionaries '21 December 1989', the World Union of Free Romanians, National Union of Unemployed Persons.

PRESIDENTIAL ELECTIONS

1990 Elections
Date: 20 May

Candidate	Party	% of vote
Ion Iliescu	FSN	85.1
Radu Campeanu	PNL	10.6
Ion Raţiu	PNT–CD	4.3

1992 Elections
Dates: 27 September (first round) and 12 October (second round)
Turnout: 76.3% (first round), 74.2% (second round)

Candidate	Party	% of vote First round	% of vote Second round
Ion Iliescu	FDSN	47.2	61.4
Emil Constantinescu	CDR	31.2	38.6
Gheorghe Funar	PUNR	11.0	
Caius Dragomir	SN	4.8	
Ion Manzatu	PR	3.1	
Mircea Druc	Independent	2.8	

1996 Elections
Date: 7 November (first round) and 17 November (first round)
Turnout: 75.9%

Candidate	Party	% of vote First round	% of vote Second round
Emil Constantinescu	CDR	28.2	54.4
Ion Iliescu	PDSR	32.2	45.6
Petre Roman	USD	20.5	
György Frunda	UDMR	6.0	
Corneliu Vadim Tudor	PRM	4.7	
Gheorghe Funar	PUNR	3.2	
Tudor Mohora	PS	1.3	

APPENDIX 10.2: GOVERNMENT COMPOSITION

Time	Prime Minister (Party)	Political orientation	Reason for change of Government
May 1990 – 27 September 1991	Petre Roman (FSN)	Left	Breakdown of initial ruling party (FSN) into factions. President Iliescu became leader of FDSN. Roman stepped down to lead rump FSN.
17 October 1991 – 20 November 1992	Theodor Stolojan (unaffiliated)	Left/technocrat	New elections held. PDSR controlled promulgation of post-communist constitution.
20 November 1992 – 12 December 1996	Nicolae Vacaroiu (independent, aligned with FDSN/PDSR)	Left/nationalist, PDSR controlled	Change of government following scheduled elections at end of parliamentary term.
December 1996	Victor Ciorbea (CDR)	Centre-right	

APPENDIX 10.3: THE ELECTORAL SYSTEM

Law No. 68/1992 for elections to the Romanian Chamber of Deputies and the Senate was published on 16 July 1992. It was in force for the 1996 elections. Members of the Senate and the Chamber of Deputies are elected by equal, secret, free, direct vote for a four-year term. Voters have the right to one vote for the Chamber of Deputies and one vote for the Senate. Citizens who have reached the age of 18 on election day have the right to vote. According to Article 34 of the Constitution, citizens 'mentally deficient or alienated, laid under interdiction, as well as persons disenfranchised by a final decision of the court cannot vote'. Eligibility to run for office is granted to all citizens having the right to vote and who on election day have reached the age of 23 (Chamber of Deputies), or 35 (the Senate and the office of President of Romania).

Deputies and Senators are elected from electoral districts on the basis of proportional representation. The standard for the Chamber of Deputies is one deputy to 70,000 inhabitants. The standard for the Senate is one Senator to 160,000 inhabitants. The number of deputies and senators will be in proportion to the number of inhabitants in each district. One senator or deputy will be added when more than one half of the relevant standard is surpassed. The number of deputies in a district will not be fewer than four, the number of senators will not be fewer than two. Recognized national minorities who do not elect a representative have the right to one deputy.

For the 1992 elections, 42 electoral districts were established, based on the Romanian administrative districts (judeţ). Senators and deputies were assigned to these proportionally, with a total of 328 deputies, and 143 senators. Candidates are proposed on separate candidate lists by recognized parties and other political formations. In each electoral district a party, a political formation or a coalition of these can propose for each chamber of the parliament only a single list of candidates. A party or formation can participate only in one single coalition. Individuals can participate as independent candidates only if they obtain support from at least 0.5 of the number of permanently registered voters in the district in which they wish to run. Candidates can run for the Senate or the Chamber of Deputies only in one single electoral district.

The date of elections must be publicly announced by the government at least 60 days in advance of the event. Elections must take place on a single day, and this must be a Sunday. All citizens with the right to vote shall be enrolled on permanent electoral lists in the district of their domicile. Romanian citizens living abroad have the right to be listed in the district where they were born, or where they later moved. Each voter is enrolled on a single electoral list. Voters enrolled on the permanent electoral lists will receive registration cards, which grant them the right to vote. The electoral campaign officially begins on the day that the election is announced, and ends two days before voting takes place.

Only candidates on party lists that receive a minimum of 3 per cent of the national vote may be elected. In the case of electoral coalitions, for 1992 one percentage point was added to the 3 per cent threshold for each party running in the coalition, up to a maximum of 8 per cent.

According to rules established for the 1990 parliamentary elections, 'wasted votes' are aggregated at the national level in order to achieve greater proportionality. In each constituency, an electoral coefficient is calculated by totalling the number of valid votes cast for the party lists and independent candidates and dividing this number by the district magnitude. Any 'unused' votes at the district level are transferred to the national level in which a second allocation is made using the d'Hondt method. At the national level, all party votes are combined and divided by the number of mandates not assigned at the district level.

Law No. 69/1992 for election of the President was published on 16 July 1992. It was in force for the 1996 elections. The President is elected by equal, secret, free, direct vote for a four-year term. Citizens who have reached the age of 18 by the day of the election have the right to vote, in accordance with Article 34 of the constitution. Voters have the right to cast one vote in each presidential election in accordance with Article 81 of the Constitution. Voting for President will take place in the electoral districts established for the Chamber of Deputies and Senate elections. Candidates for the presidency may be proposed by political parties or other political formations, individually or by coalitions. In order to run, candidates must be supported by 100,000 voters. Voters may support only a single candidate for election. The date of elections must be publicly announced by the government at least 60 days in advance of the event. Elections must take place on a single day, and this must be a Sunday.

A candidate who receives more than half of the votes cast in the first round is elected. If no single candidate receives a majority of the votes, a second round is held. Second-round elections will be held two weeks after the first round, based on the same voting lists as in the first round, and using the same electoral districts. Only the two candidates receiving the highest number of votes in the first round participate in the second.

APPENDIX 10.4:
THE CONSTITUTIONAL FRAMEWORK

The Romanian constitution was adopted on 8 December 1991. The form of the Romanian State is a Republic. Parliament is the supreme representative body of the Romanian people and the sole legislative authority of the country. Parliament consists of the Chamber of Deputies and the Senate. Parliament passes constitutional, organic, and ordinary laws.

The President represents the Romanian State and is the safeguard of the national independence, unity, and territorial integrity of the country. He shall act as mediator between the powers of the State, as well as between the State and society. The President is elected by universal suffrage for a term of four years. The President may preside over meetings of the government, debating matters of national interest with regard to foreign policy, defence, and public order, or other matters at the request of the Prime Minister. The President presides over meetings that he attends. The President may dissolve parliament after consultation with the leaders of both chambers if no vote of confidence has been obtained from a government within 60 days after the first request was made. During the same year, Parliament may be dissolved only once. The President may initiate referenda. The President is Commander-in-Chief of the Armed Forces. He may institute a state of emergency, but must request parliamentary approval within five days. The President may be impeached for grave acts infringing upon the Constitution, by a majority vote of the members of the Chamber of Deputies and the Senate, voting in joint session.

The Government shall ensure the implementation of the domestic and foreign policy of the country and exercise the general management of public administration. The Government consists of the Prime Minister, Ministers, and other members as established by an organic law.

The President designates the Prime Minister after consulting with the party which has obtained an absolute majority in Parliament, or if no such party exists, with the parties represented in Parliament. Within ten days the Prime Minister shall present a government list to a joint session of the Chamber of Deputies and Senate, and seek a vote of confidence.

The Prime Minister chairs and directs the Government and submits to the Parliament reports on the Government's activities. The Government shall adopt Orders and Decisions in order to organize the execution of laws passed by the Parliament. The Government exercises its term in office until validation through general parliamentary elections, or until a withdrawal of parliamentary confidence. The Government must present any information requested by the Chamber of Deputies, Senate or Parliamentary Committees, and members of the Government must attend proceedings of Parliament if requested. The Chamber of Deputies and Senate in joint session may issue a motion of censure, withdrawing confidence from the Government, through a majority of vote. Such motions are initiated by at least one quarter of the Deputies and Senators. The Government may make a programme, policy or bill, an issue of confidence before the Chamber of Deputies and the Senate in joint session. If no motion of censure has been passed within three days from such presentation, the bill or programme is considered passed, and becomes binding upon the Government.

11. Bulgaria

Georgi Karasimeonov

Cleavages reflect deep and permanent conflicts and divisions in society. But not all of them become determining factors for party formation and influence electoral behaviour.

The post-communist political system did not inherit a structurally responsive democratic party system. Favourable conditions for the development and the stabilization of a viable party system were absent in most countries prior to the communist take-over after the Second World War. Czechoslovakia was an exception to the rule.

In Bulgaria, no conditions for normal party life existed from 1923, when a military *coup d'état* interrupted the democratic process, until 1944. Authoritarian regimes followed one another. After the 1944–47 period of limited pluralism, the communist power monopoly was established and political pluralism was forcefully eliminated. At the economic level, the market economy and private property were also suppressed and state ownership established.

The communist regime attempted to regulate all societal conflicts in the name of creating a classless society, and in that process tried to 'overcome' or subdue all the cleavages typical for underdeveloped capitalism; Bulgaria was then a predominantly rural country with only a small industrial sector. It expropriated or nationalized existing private companies and politically banned all parties expressing 'bourgeois' interests. The working class became the leading 'progressive' force and the dictatorship of the proletariat took the place of the capitalist state. The class antagonism between the proletariat and the bourgeoisie was mythologized, with the aim of eliminating all real and potential 'enemies' of socialism. The constitutions of 1948 and 1971 established the leading role of the Communist Party, and – except for the agrarian party, closely linked to the communists – no other parties were allowed to participate in political life.

Although the regime attempted to create an egalitarian society and to

subdue or control the expression of conflicts, the communist society was not
without cleavages. Various cleavages appeared behind a veil of formal
political uniformity and national unity. Periodically, they were reflected in
internal party struggles and in attempts at opposition to the regime. They
did not have the same scope as in the Central European countries where
resistance to the regimes did reach large proportions, but were nonetheless a
major factor in the later transition to democracy in Bulgaria. The growth of
discontent first showed among intellectuals and among the new generation
of technocrats, which did not accept the political and administrative
monopoly of the party *nomenklatura*, especially in the late 1970s and 1980s
when the communist economic and political system entered a period of
deepening crisis.

One line of conflict was provoked by the social structure which replaced
the one based on private property. The new class structure was determined
by access to power resources at various levels in the party-state system. The
so-called 'new class', or *nomenklatura*, emerged as a specific social group,
which augmented its privileges to the detriment of other social groups.
Retaining political power, it had all but unlimited possibilities to control and
distribute economic resources. The power of the *nomenklatura* was
challenged by new party *apparachiks* and technocrats who were Western-
oriented and recognized the need for major changes in the system – changes
which were, in turn, to guarantee their future economic power. They
realized the need to transform the power monopoly of the Communist Party
into real economic power by changing property relations. Many of them
initiated limited reforms towards a market-based economy, which
challenged the dogma of state ownership.

Bulgaria experienced a sharpening of ethnic conflict in the 1980s,
provoked by the policy of forceful assimilation of the Turkish minority in
the Bulgarian nation. This policy further deepened the rift between the
nascent opposition and the regime, leading to the growing isolation of the
latter.

In the late 1980s, the conflict between modernizers oriented towards the
West, and traditionalists tightly linked to the Soviet regime became evident.
This cleavage determined the conflict between the reform communists and
the hard-liners in the Communist Party as well as the conflict between the
nascent opposition and the Communist Party machine.

The 'new working class' which emerged during the socialist era, never
experienced the contradictions inherent in class conflicts that have marked
advanced capitalist countries in their historical development. Even though
the Communist Party upheld the myth of a 'workers' state', the working
class was marked by lack of 'class consciousness' or solidarity. The
development of the rural community showed a similar pattern: in the 1950s

the majority of the population lived in rural areas following a rural life-style, but the rural strata 'melted' in the following 45 years as a consequence of rapid urbanization and industrialization processes. Its remnants today are mostly older people who hardly represent a viable social class. Consequently, communist society in Bulgaria was highly atomized; specific communitarian interests dominated and led to the formation of subgroups of a patrimonial type (family, village), intellectual circles, and so on.

The post-communist changes turned the historical development in the opposite direction – from a centralized state economy and political mono-poly to market economy and political democracy. In a relatively short span of time, new cleavages appeared that bear the mark of the radical upturn. The post-communist society in Bulgaria 'inherited' almost none of the 'historical' pre-communist cleavages. This is not the case in the Central European countries.

Some cleavages are only now emerging, some are bound to disappear, and some will appear in the future, determined by the process of transformation of society. Conflicts in non-consolidated post-communist societies differ substantially from the classical four-dimensional cleavage structure analysed by Lipset and Rokkan (1967). Political parties find themselves at the initial mobilization phase and have to establish their identities and links with the electorate. This process is fluid, because parties need time to implement their policies and test them in several rounds of elections until a certain stability of party–voter relationship establishes itself.

Excluding the Communist Party and its ally the Agrarian Party, most of the political parties at the start of the changes were what may be dubbed 'spiritual communities' – circles of friends established more on emotional than rational goals. They also tended to represent clientelist groups for the defence of particular interests. Thus, new issues and conflicts could not be absorbed or transmitted in a rational way onto the political scene, where the antinomy between the privileged and the underdogs of the old system came to the forefront in the most bitter forms. To a large extent, the new conflicts reflected clashes among elites, personal sympathies and animosities. The new political parties were thrust upon society from 'above' with little or no participation of the mass of the population, which mostly accepted the changes without any clear idea of where they would lead. New parties also sprang from the communist parties as a form of subdivisions.

Bernhard Wessels and Hans-Dieter Klingemann (1994, 12–13) have introduced the concept of 'flattened societies' for the initial phase of post-communism; when citizens were unable to define their political interests as a consequence of the fact that the location of individuals in the societal structure was determined by the state, as the largest and practically only, employer. This may no longer be the case in the Central Europe of 1997, but it remains largely true in South Eastern Europe, including Bulgaria.

Political parties in post-communist societies not only reflect conflicts; they are also agents of conflicts and shape the public agenda. Their policies and ideology, as well as inter-party relations (confrontational or consensus-oriented), are major factors in the transformation of certain conflicts and issues into cleavages. This is a consequence of the domination of 'politics' over the 'economy' at the initial phase of changes.[1]

Lipset's and Rokkan's cleavage theory was formulated on the experiences of a specific group of European countries finding themselves in similar historical conditions. Nonetheless, the methodology can be helpful in the analysis of electoral behaviour and party formation even in transitional societies, like those in Central and South Eastern Europe – with some necessary revisions. I propose a typology of cleavages which reflects the specific historical conditions in which the new democracies find themselves. As I see it, post-communist societies reveal at least four types of cleavages – residual (historical), transitional, actual, and potential.

Residual (historical) cleavages are those inherited from the pre-communist society and which, to varying extents, manifest themselves in the post-communist society. In some countries they determine electoral and party preferences. They are particularly evident in the countries of Central Europe, where the communist regimes were less able to eradicate old values and old culture, or where they accepted some elements of market economy and did tolerate forms of private property.

Transitional cleavages are those which determine political divisions and party formation at the initial stage of changes after the fall of the regime, but which later disappear or are 'swallowed' by new cleavages appearing as the post-communist societies are consolidated. They are the products of the initial 'pro-and-contra-communism' axis, which determined many of the party conflicts and divisions immediately after 1989.

Actual cleavages are new cleavages marked by the specific contradictions and conflicts of post-communist societies, resulting from the economic and political reforms. They result from changes in the social structure and property relations. To a great extent, they determine electoral behaviour and party preferences, when the major transitional cleavage based on the communism–anti-communism axis is partially or mostly resolved, and society moves on to resolve new conflicts and issues typical for the consolidation phase.

Potential cleavages represent those major issues and conflicts in post-communist societies which might transform into actual cleavages as a consequence of the evolution of the economic and political system. They are dependent on the nature of the transition and on the effect of the policies of the different political parties in power.

All of these types of cleavages are present in post-communist societies, in different proportions and guises. Their effects on the process of transition and consolidation varies between countries, depending on their development before, during and after communism.

In Eastern Europe of the late 1990s, one can find four distinct types of post-communist regimes which in a particular way reflect the different cleavages. In the first group are the regimes on the road to consolidation: Poland, Hungary, the Czech Republic, Slovenia, Estonia, Latvia and Lithuania. The second group could be defined as transitional democracies with a delayed reform movement, where the communist legacy had a strong effect on the political and economic development: Bulgaria, Romania, and Macedonia. The third group are the authoritarian democracies where there are serious deficiencies in the development of political democracy, with limited pluralism, limitations on civil liberties, and authoritarian rule: Serbia, Croatia, and Slovakia. The fourth group are the 'crisis democracies' characterised by deep conflicts, civil unrest and political instability: Albania, and Bosnia-Herzegovina.

Issues and Divisions at the Initial Stage of Transition

In most post-communist societies, including Bulgaria, the initial stage of transition was dominated by one major division and conflict. Wessels and Klingemann (1994, 12) mention a 'super issue' – reform communism versus liberal democracy – which has structured the emerging party systems in the first phase of democratization. The major issue behind that ideological confrontation was the redistribution of power resources between old and new elites, in the process of elimination of the power monopoly of the Communist Party. This transitional cleavage was, in the case of Bulgaria, revealed in the struggle between two main political blocs. On the one side were the supporters and driving political forces of the reform movement, united in the Union of Democratic Forces (UDF); and on the other, the representatives of the old system grouped around the Communist Party. The conflicts and political struggles between them determined initial party formation. Political alignments were mostly psychologically motivated, based on ideological confrontation.

Although both the anti-communists and the reform-communists understood the necessity of change, the struggle for power resources to be redistributed put them into different camps at the round-table talks which paved the way for democracy (Verheijen 1995, 105–16). Both blocs were also socially and ideologically heterogeneous, which caused several waves of differentiation and divisions within them.

The proponents of radical reforms were assembled in the Union of Democratic Forces (UDF), a coalition of new parties that sprang up in the months after the downfall of the old regime. Three major groups could be discerned. One consisted of 'historical parties', such as the Social Democratic, the Bulgarian Agrarian Peoples Party 'Nikola Petkov', the Democratic Party, and the Radical–Democratic Party, to name the most important. They were led by some of the surviving members and leaders of these parties during the pre-communist era. The second group included former dissidents who had taken part in various protest actions preceding the downfall of the communist regime. Most prominent among them were the *Ecoglasnost* movement, the Club for Glasnost and Democracy, and the *Podkrepa* trade union, most of whose leaders and members were former members of the Communist Party. The third group included newly created parties or organizations – such as the Republican Party and the Christian Democratic Party – which joined the newly formed opposition coalition, the UDF (cf. Karasimeonov 1995, 154–79).

The supporters of the Union of Democratic Forces could be subdivided into two major groups: the conservatives, i.e. the representatives of the old privileged classes marginalized and suppressed by the communists, who were longing for a 'return to the past'; and the modernists from the newer generation opting for a Westernization of society. Tactically the UDF was also divided between radicals, supporting revolutionary 'de-communization', and moderates who accepted the rules of parliamentary democracy and evolutionary change. At the beginning, the radicals, moderates, conservatives and modernists were united in one camp. Their coalition had to face a most powerful opponent, the ex-communist party, which was renamed the Socialist Party (BSP) a few months after the regime had changed.

The convergence of the groups in the UDF coalition was motivated by a one-dimensional policy and ideology – the removal from power of the former communists. All their internal differences were sublimated in the name of anti-communism and the 'liberty myth'. Most UDF factions were motivated by the perspective of gaining power – a phenomenon typical of 'outsiders' or political 'turn-coats'. The parties in the UDF were clientelist circles rather than authentic parties. Their electorates were highly heterogeneous, a fact which prompted internal differentiation and divisions as soon as the major task of eliminating the communists from power had been partly achieved.

The fact that the 'historical' parties very quickly lost their initial advantage and were marginalized, testifies to the irrelevance of the old cleavages. This was particularly true for the Social Democratic Party and the BAPU

'Nikola Petkov' which in the past had reflected, respectively, the labour/capital and the centre/periphery, rural/urban cleavages. By 1989, these 'historical' cleavages had lost their significance as determinants for party formation. When these parties opted for a more moderate policy defying the radical anti-communists, their influence dwindled dramatically and they were not able to overcome the four per cent threshold for parliamentary representation at the 1991 elections.

The communist camp was also divided into two major groups – the supporters of reform and the neo-communists, which in turn were heterogeneous. The bloc of reform supporters was divided into a radical and a moderate wing, of which the first wanted a definite engagement with democratic change and a break with the past, and the latter defended the need to keep the party together, and were keen on preserving as long as possible the party's hold on the power structures. The neo-communist camp included representatives of the 'old guard' fighting to survive and keep their privileges, as well as 'hard-liners' or Marxist ideologues. Yet compared to other ex-communist parties in Central Europe, the Bulgarian party avoided serious rifts between these rival factions and kept its relative strength and cohesion until the founding elections of 1990 and the period thereafter. It did witness an erosion of its membership, but was able to transform gradually into a parliamentary party, preserving the core of its organizational structure, and to keep a balance between the various factions from social democratic to neo-communist.

The first period of party formation was characterized by harsh confrontation between the two major political camps. It was engendered by the radicalization of the UDF after the founding elections and its attempts to implement a policy of radical 'de-communization'. This reached its peak after the second round of parliamentary elections in November 1991, when the UDF won a relative majority and formed a government with the support of the ethnic-Turkish Movement for Rights and Freedoms (MRF).

Even so, the BSP remained a powerful opponent. It was able to use the internal divisions in the anti-communist camp and 'allowed' the integration into the political system of moderate representatives of the UDF after the 1990 elections, thus lessening the pressure from the radicals. The policy of 'appeasement' was most clearly demonstrated in the support which the reform communists extended to UDF leader Zhelyu Zhelev, in the elections to the presidency in the summer of 1990. It showed the desire of the communists to compromise in order to avoid a radical 'de-communization' and achieve a consensual relationship with the opposition.

Although the confrontation between the UDF and BSP camps determined the political landscape in the following years, the 'flexibility' of the ex-communists and the internal instability of the UDF kept the political process on a peaceful track. Yet at the same time, the high level of tension between them led to bitter confrontation which blocked the reform process and delayed major changes in the economy.

The integration of the ethnic-Turkish MRF into the political system represents an interesting case of peaceful and constructive resolution of ethnic tensions, which in Bulgaria reached their peak in the late 1980s, as a consequence of the policy of assimilation initiated by the communist regime. Ethnic tensions remained a feature of the post-communist land-scape, but they did not escalate into major conflicts endangering the democratic process.

The conflict between the UDF and the BSP was reflected in various political clashes, but the main dividing line between the two concerned who should have the initiative in the reform process, and control the levers of power in a society still dominated by an all-powerful bureaucratic state. The lack of a significant private sector and the weakness of civil society at the outset of the transition process, focused the political struggle on state bureaucracy which controlled the major decision-making resources. For the UDF, de-communization mostly meant the marginalization of the com-munists in the main state structures. As long as a normal balance between the public and the private spheres remains unestablished and civil service legislation does not create the necessary guarantees against political appointments and reprisals against public officials, state bureaucracy will remain a major area of conflict between the political parties; a fact accentuated by the patronage tradition typical of Southern Europe. Those who retain control of the state bureaucracy command enormous resources and are able to determine who the beneficiaries of the reform process will be. Privatization was, of course, a particular case in point in Bulgaria.

The unresolved struggle for power between the UDF and the BSP – which continued until the parliamentary elections of 1994 – blocked not only the reform process, but kept other issues and conflicts in the shade, preventing them from becoming determining factors for electoral behaviour and party identification. It led to the persistence of a bipolar, confrontational party system and determined government formation, which was marked by instability and the lack of stable parliamentary majorities.

The third post-transition parliamentary elections in December 1994, however, resulted in a resounding victory for the socialists, and a defeat for the radical anti-communists in the UDF and their policy of radical 'de-communization'. The elections also paved the way for the emergence of new political formations in parliament, besides the three previous ones: the Bulgarian Business Bloc (BBB), a nationalist, populist party; and the People's Union, a coalition between BAPU, the main agrarian party, and the Democratic Party, which had left the UDF coalition.

Nevertheless, the socialist government which took office was unable to respond to the expectations of its electorate and began losing popular support about a year after its victory at the polls. Its main deficiencies were an inability to achieve positive results in the economic sphere, and the delay of reforms. This situation led to a deepening financial crisis and a loss of confidence among the population. Early in 1997, after month-long, unprecedented protests by the public against the worsening economic crisis and the drastic fall in living standards, the socialist government was forced to resign and agree to pre-term-elections. The April 1997 elections resulted in a radical change in the composition of parliament and in a restructuring of the political arena, with the UDF and its coalition partner, the People's Union, in the United Democratic Forces coalition, winning an absolute majority. The BSP lost a major part of its base support. Moreover, a new coalition known as the BBB – the Union for National Salvation – with the MRF as its main driving force, appeared in parliament. The Euroleft with its distinct social democratic flavour, also entered parliament in 1997.

Voting Behaviour and Citizen Values

The delay of reforms and the lack of progress in the establishment of a market economy, accompanied by a worsening economic crisis, created a situation in Bulgaria which was radically different from post-communist Central Europe, where adaptation to the challenges of capitalism had been much more successful. The fall of the socialist government in Bulgaria in 1997 marked the end of the model of development started in 1989, mostly characterized by the very strong presence of the former communist party.

Another particular Bulgarian phenomenon was the emergence of a post-communist oligarchy, composed of members of the former *nomenklatura* or their stooges, corrupt state officials and politicians, and criminal groups. This new oligarchy was the major stumbling block for reform policy and the beneficiary of the clandestine privatization of state property. It forged a policy of redistribution of national resources through newly created banks, and in bankrupt state companies which amassed bad debts. This uncontrolled absorption of national resources by the post-communist oligarchy left the country with a ruined economy and worsening living conditions.

The inability to engage in serious reforms determined the policy agenda, value orientations, electoral behaviour and party identities in late 1996 and early 1997. Most cleavages were the products of the actual social and economic situation, resulting from the failure of the political class to initiate a successful policy of transformation from plan to market.

In 1997, most of the major issues at the centre of the public agenda were the same as in the period following the change of regime in 1989. There were, however, two major differences: first, a crumbling economy and a drastic fall in living standards; and, second, the failure of the political system to produce effective governments, which brought on growing disappointment with and delegitimization of democracy.

This social and political situation led to a significant change in public attitudes. The majority of the public began to make much more rational assessments of the policy of alternative governments and parties, on the basis of their own experiences. In contrast to the recent past, electoral behaviour and party identification did not depend only, or mostly, on the import of values and evaluations from the parties. Rationalization of public attitudes and voting behaviour meant that cleavages had a stronger determining influence on citizens' political and ideological choices. Voters had a better idea of what they wanted and of how it should be achieved, and accordingly their attitude towards parties and politicians became less ideologically biased and more determined by concrete political results than before. The mood in the country clearly testifies to a general antipathy to great designs, promises and electoral programmes, and there is evidence of a more rational and sceptical approach towards the political elite.

The results of the presidential elections in November 1996 were a clear indication of the rationalization of public attitudes and behaviour. They were won by Petar Stoyanov of the United Democratic Forces by an unprecedented margin – the Socialist candidate was defeated by 60 per cent against 40 per cent. These changes were further confirmed in the parliamentary elections in April 1997.

There are a number of major cleavages and issues which can be observed in post-communist Bulgaria in the late 1990s. In different ways they are influencing electoral behaviour and party support.

New economic cleavage   One of the major actual and potential cleavages results from the radical changes in the economy and the type of economic policies introduced by the post-communist governments. They are determined by the conversion of state property to private and the contradictions resulting from that process. The transition from plan to market economy leads to fundamental changes in the social structure. Its major trait, in Bulgaria in particular, is the polarization between, on the one hand, a fast-growing class of socially marginalized and poor people and, on the other, a small, oligarchic caste of the very rich. The latter is largely comprised of heirs of the 'red bourgeoisie' who amassed their riches from covert privatization and the redistribution of state property. This process has led to the formation of a 9/10 society, with a great majority of losers and a tiny minority of winners in the transition to market economy. This cleavage reveals itself in national surveys, where the 77.3 per cent of respondents declare that the conflict between rich and poor is the major contradiction in

Bulgarian society (BBSS Gallup International Yearly Report 1995, 191; cf. *Figure 11.1*).[2]

Figure 11.1: Attitudes on political confrontation: Do you think there are serious confrontations in your country?

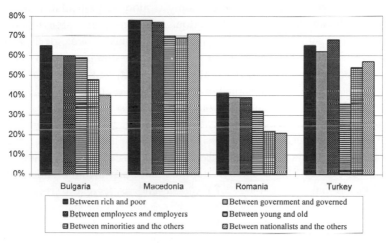

Source: BBSS Gallup Yearly Report, 1995, p. 253

This economic cleavage is qualitatively different from the class cleavage typical of the early stage of capitalism, as it is not based on a capital/labour conflict. Instead, its roots are in the massive impoverishment of great masses of people in all social, professional and age groups, and in the melting away of the 'levelled' society and the socialist 'middle' class, which enjoyed a certain stability in living conditions and security in the patronage state.

At the same time society remains 'flattened': the great majority of the population encounter similar economic conditions. This means that in the near future, the majority of the electorate will not be influenced by social status and social differences. Most citizens make the same assessment of the current economic situation and their personal financial standing. Ninety-six per cent of Bulgarians polled think the economic situation of the country is bad; 67 per cent say their personal financial situation is bad or very bad, while only 5.9 per cent declare it to be good or very good (Genov 1997, 48).

Economically disaffected voters will be greatly influenced by the effect of governmental policies on their immediate financial situation. This will be especially true for that part of the electorate not firmly attached to any of the major parties. The results of the parliamentary elections in 1997 provided ample proof of the massive change of preferences in favour of the UDF after the failure of the socialists. However, with the stabilization of the economic structure following the privatization process and the establishment of a viable market economy based on various forms of property, socioeconomic cleavages will begin to have a more determining effect on voting behaviour. When social differentiation produces more well-defined economic groups, engaged in various sectors of the economy, a more permanent structure of interests will determine party orientation. This long-term process is only just beginning and will cause a change in the dominant ideological profile of party linkages to the electorate, creating a relationship increasingly based on social and economic interests. The more abstract values associated with left or right will be complemented or replaced by economic and social cleavages and by the parties' concrete policies in response to these cleavages.

Other potential cleavages which will influence electoral behaviour derive from the conflict between the interests of private capital and the interests of the state bureaucracy, which holds in its command great resources in dominant sectors of the economy. The process of privatization undermines the decision-making parameter of the state and its representatives in the various structures. Particularly in the lower echelons of the state machinery, bureaucracy is losing some of its privileges and material benefits (including those obtained through corruption), and this obviously creates resistance.

Another conflict influencing party politics is that between the criminal groups in the 'grey' sector of the economy, prospering in economic anarchy, and economic groups willing to abide by the law. The first group has amassed its fortunes from speculation, tax evasion and various criminal activities (drugs, racketeering) and favours the 'feudalization' of the country, weak democratic institutions, and corruption in politics. The second will opt for the modernization of the country and be ready to co-operate with political groups and parties aiming for similar goals.

Ideological and political cleavages   Ideological cleavages were the major factor determining party allegiances at the start of the political transition. As mentioned earlier, the distribution of the electorate on the *pro et contra* communism axis was typical of nascent post-communist societies. Recently, there has been a growing differentiation in the ideological preferences of the electorate. The bipolar cleavage is transforming into more a complex value orientation which corresponds to particular allegiances. These values reflect attitudes toward major conflict areas such as the market economy, state property, privatization, law and order or citizens' rights.

The Bulgarian Presidential elections survey 1996 (part of the Comparative National Elections Project, CNEP) reveals that there are already some fundamental differences in value orientation between the electorate and the sympathizers and members of the major parties. UDF sympathizers are more individualistic, pro-market and anti-authoritarian, while BSP sympathizers have a more collectivist, authoritarian and nationalist outlook (*Figures 11.2, 11.3, 11.4*).

Figure 11.2: Attitude to privatization by party affiliation

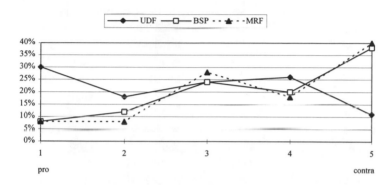

Source: Bulgarian CNEP Survey, Bulgarian Presidential Elections Survey, November 1996

Figure 11.3: Attitude to private initiative by party affiliation

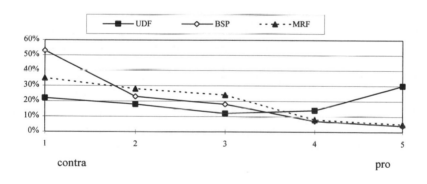

Source: Bulgarian CNEP Survey, Bulgarian Presidential Elections Survey, November 1996

Figure 11.4: Nationalist attitudes by party affiliation

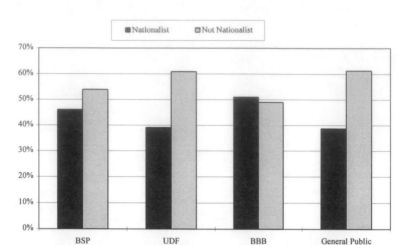

Source: *Bulgarian* CNEP *Survey, Bulgarian Presidential Elections Survey, November 1996*

Ethnic and religious cleavages   Ethnic conflicts in Bulgaria do not have the explosive character typical of other South Eastern European countries. The consequences of the assimilatory policies of the communist regime in the 1980s toward the Turkish minority were rebuffed by all major political parties and the principle of ethnic and religious freedom was established in the post-communist Constitution. Article 11 of the Constitution bans parties based solely on ethnic, racial or religious principles. This article, contested by some constitutional commentators, is a reflection of the specific internal and geopolitical situation of Bulgaria and the fears of most political parties that purely ethnic political parties (particularly parties representing the Turkish minority, encompassing some 8 per cent of the population) could endanger the sovereignty of the state. This is why the Movement for Rights and Freedoms (MRF), which originally registered itself as a 'political movement' and has its social base mainly among the Turkish population, has declared itself a national party. The subsequent ruling by the Constitutional Court allowing the MRF to participate in political life, the willingness of the MRF to integrate into the political system, and its actual participation in government formation over the past few years, have substantially reduced ethnic and religious tensions.

The majority of the ethnic Turkish population supports the MRF, and the ethnic cleavage determines electoral attitudes of both major ethnic groups in Bulgaria. However, Bulgarian nationalism as well as religious fundament-alism among the Turkish population are, for the time being, reflected only in the activity of marginal political parties and groups. Nevertheless, a change of orientation of the MRF towards a policy for national autonomy could trigger ethnic conflicts on a larger scale (*Figures 11.5, 11.6*).

Figure 11.5: Attitudes towards MRF: Does the MRF play a positive or a negative role in the country's political life?

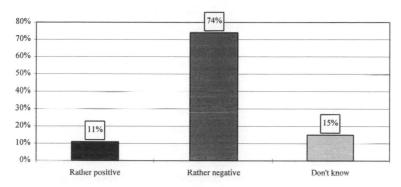

Source: BBSS *Gallup Yearly Report, 1995*

Figure 11.6: Views on Islam as a threat to national security

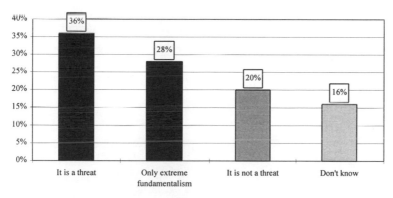

Source: BBSS *Gallup Yearly Report, 1995*

There is also potential tension with respect to the so-called Macedonian question, which is related to the fact that the newly established independent state of Macedonia has a history and culture intimately linked to that of Bulgaria. Some groups in Bulgaria, including a small party – the IMRO (Internal Revolutionary Macedonian Organization) – which is part of the governing majority, do not accept the existence of a 'Macedonian' nation.

The illegal organization 'Ilinden', on the other hand, propagates the idea of 'Greater Macedonia'.

Religion has never played a dominant role in party formation in Bulgaria, but in the aftermath of communist ideological dominance and forced atheism a spiritual vacuum has appeared, leading to growing disorientation in peoples' minds. As the dominant Greek Orthodox Church has been weakened by internal struggles, a multitude of pseudo-religious groups and sects have been able to 'invade' Bulgaria. This brings to the forefront the issue of safeguarding national identity and culture against groups and values which undermine them.

Cleavages on international policy Bulgaria's political life has been strongly influenced by its historical development and geopolitical situation. Foreign policy issues and conflicts have often determined political alignments and realignments, and the orientation of political parties.

Post-communist realities reveal similar tendencies. Two major political orientations are influencing party policies: the pro-European, integrationist; and the pan-Slavic, Russia-oriented. In the post-Cold War international setting, the NATO issue best reveals the clash between these two groups. The former orientation is represented mainly by the UDF; the latter by the BSP which is burdened by its past allegiances to Russia. A sharpening of the conflict between Russia and the West will undoubtedly have a great impact on parties' policies and their internal divisions (*Figures 11.7, 11.8*).

Figure 11.7: Attitude towards joining NATO by party affiliation, November 1996

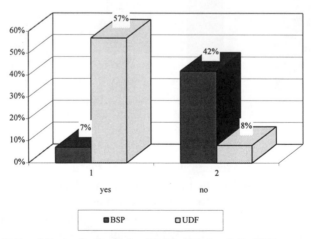

Source: National Centre for the Study of Public Opinion, Sofia 1996

Figure 11.8: General public's attitude towards joining NATO, November 1996

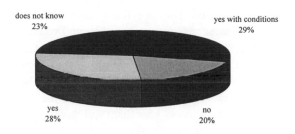

Source: National Centre for the Study of Public Opinion, Sofia 1996

The rural/urban cleavage has been of great importance in Bulgaria, determining party affiliation from the 1920s until the 1940s. The agrarian party, the BAPU, was the largest party in the 1920s, won absolute parliamentary majority in 1920 and stayed in power until 1923 when its government was brought down by a right wing *coup d'état*. In the 1940s, the BAPU was the main opposition party until 1948 when the communists rose to a position of total hegemony.

The policies of the communist regimes brought radical changes to the economic situation of the peasantry, increasingly so in the 1960s and 1970s. The modernization process, focused on industrialization and urbanization, radically transformed Bulgaria's traditional social structure. The peasantry became a minority within the population in the 1970s, and by the 1990s it was mainly composed of old people.

By and large, the rural population profited from the rise in living standards and modernization of the country and overcame the poverty of the past. This fact explains the relatively firm support of this social group for the ex-communist party after the changes in 1989. The attempts of the UDF government (1991–92) to transform property relations radically, with a return to private land ownership – in particular the restitution of land to its former owners – was the source of great conflict in rural areas. This policy generated huge unrest and a drastic fall in agricultural production and rural living standards. The congruence of nostalgia for the old times, patriarchal culture and discontent with UDF policies, generated support for the BSP among the rural population, although some of that support waned in the aftermath of the fall of the socialist government in 1997. The process of restructuring property relations with the conclusion of the programme for restitution of land, will have long-lasting consequences for the value orientations and electoral behaviour of the rural population in the coming years. As a result of a worsening demographic situation and increasing unemployment, the rural population will be particularly severely hit by economic reforms.

The generational cleavage Surveys and electoral results show very clear divisions between age groups. They are the products of divergent cultural traditions and value orientations between the older and younger generations. The former carries the values of collectivism and the patronage socialist state, and responds with nostalgia and animosity to the abrupt changes that destroy their professional and personal milieu. The younger generation (the 18–39-year age-bracket) accepts the need for radical changes in the economy and supports the values of liberalism and market economy.

Such cultural and ideological divisions lead to opposing, conflicting party allegiances. The younger generation reacts to the delay of reforms with clearly defined support for the UDF, which it perceives as an alternative to the socialist state. Consequently, those in the 18–39 age-bracket voted massively for the UDF presidential candidate Petar Stoyanov in the November 1996 elections, and for the UDF in the parliamentary elections in April 1997. Conversely, the older generation overwhelmingly backed the BSP after 1989, and remains the main strongest base of support for that party (*Figures 11.9, 11.10, 11.11*).

Figure 11.9: Main parties' electorate by age.

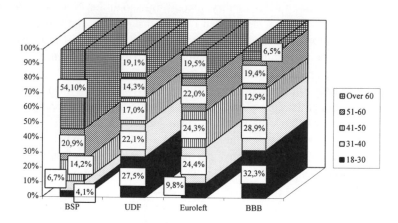

Source: Mediana Agency, March 1997

Figure 11.10: Affinity with the BSP: *How close do you feel to the* BSP?

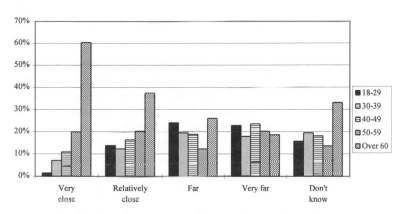

Source: Bulgarian CNEP *Survey, Bulgarian Presidential Elections Survey, November 1996*

Figure 11.11: Affinity with UDF: *How close do you feel to the* UDF?

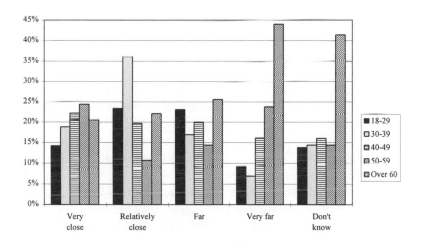

Source: Bulgarian CNEP *Survey, Bulgarian Presidential Elections Survey, November 1996*

Cleavages and the Consolidation Process

The consolidation of the new democracies will also be 'measured' by the type of cleavages they 'produce' and how they influence the policies of the political parties, i.e. how these parties are able to institutionalize conflicts resulting from cleavages.

Many cleavages in post-communist Bulgaria are cross-cutting and determine not only differences and conflicts between political parties, but provoke them in the parties themselves. This leads to internal restructuring and to various, sometimes unexpected, political alliances. A typical case was the formation of the Union for National Salvation for the 1997 elections, uniting monarchists, republicans, greens, liberals and the ethnic Turkish party (MRF). The same applies to the BSP, where at least three major factions (social-democratic, pragmatic and Marxist) compete. In the aftermath of the BSP's fall from power in early 1997 and the resulting deep crisis within the party, the social-democratic faction partly disintegrated and many of its members left the BSP to join the Euroleft, a new formation with a social-democratic orientation. That leaves the BSP with diminished influence, and the party faces the risk of marginalization if it falls under the dominance of neo-communist hard-liners. These will attempt to reaffirm their positions among the losers of the reforms initiated by the UDF government and the tight monetary policies negotiated with the IMF. This opens up the possibility of an influential social-democratic party filling the void left by the BSP.

The UDF made the decisive move from a coalition to a party in 1997. This stabilized its organizational structure and increased its effectiveness as a governing party. At the same time the UDF faces major challenges, since it will have to carry the burden of introducing reforms and legislation which will radically alter the social and economic setting.

Three minor political forces – the Bulgarian Business Bloc, the Euroleft, and the new Union for National Salvation (UNS) coalition – will try to affirm their positions in the party system. Their fate will largely depend on their capacity to respond to the new issues and major cleavages. Among them, only the ethnic-Turkish Movement for Rights and Freedom –at the core of the UNS– enjoys relatively stable, albeit shrinking, electoral support.

The various types of cleavages in post-communist Bulgaria are a prerequisite for political motivations and orientations, and party preferences. They can become determining factors of party identification only if they motivate permanent mass political interests, electoral behaviour and attachments towards one or another party. Parties in post-communist Bulgaria are facing two major challenges. First, they have to prove their ability to react to conflicts and cleavages and to respond to electoral demands and expectations. The first years of transition, characterized by the failure to introduce reforms and a deepening economic crisis, delayed the process of party identification. Although the major parties in Bulgaria did have a chance to take up positions in parliament and government – also in local governments – the period was relatively short for generating stable party preferences on the basis of comparative experience. The electorate as a whole still has only superficial perceptions of the governing potential of the major parties – particularly bearing in mind the fact that between 1989 and 1997 Bulgaria had nine different governments. Only several rounds of rotation of power consolidating the reform process, will eventually bring about more stable political allegiances and transform post-communist cleavages into more determining factors for party identification.

The second challenge faced by political parties is to establish linkage networks with all sectors of civil society, enabling them to absorb electoral demands and political interests and transform them into policy decisions. They will have to establish much more effective organizational structures and links with major interest groups (trade unions, non-governmental structures, civic organizations). Although certain primary attachments to one political party or another are in place, only time will show if they will become determining factors of a greater stability in electoral behaviour. The fact that almost 40 per cent of the electorate did not participate in the 1997 parliamentary elections – the lowest turnout in any post-communist election so far – seems to confirm that assumption.

NOTES

1. For example, laws pertaining to restitution of property, privatization laws, or legislation concerning ethnic questions, and so on, are most likely to provoke, sharpen or calm certain conflicts and issues that could evolve into cleavages. In Bulgaria, the restitution of land did become a major issue and one of the major permanent dividing lines between political parties.
2. Data show that GNP fell about 50 per cent between 1990 and 1996.

REFERENCES

BBSS Gallup International Yearly Report 1995, UNDP, Sofia.
Bulgarian CNEP Survey, Bulgarian Presidential Elections Survey, November 1996.
Genov, G. (1997), *Bulgaria Today and Tomorrow*, Sofia.
Karasimeonov, Georgi (1995), 'Differentiation Postponed: Party Pluralism in Bulgaria', in Gordon Whightman, ed., *Party Formation in East-Central Europe*, Frank Cass.
—— (1997), *The 1990 Elections to the Bulgarian Grand National Assembly and the 1991 Election to the Bulgarian National Assembly*, Berlin, Sigma.
Lipset, Seymour Martin and Stein Rokkan (1967), 'Cleavage Structures, Party Systems and Voters Alignments: An Introduction', in Seymour Martin Lipset and Stein Rokkan, ed., *Party Systems and Voter Alignments: Cross-National Perspectives*, New York, The Free Press.
Mair, Peter, ed., (1990), *The West European Party System*, Oxford, Oxford University Press.
National Centre for the Study of Public Opinion, Sofia, 1996.
Verheijen, Tony (1995), *Constitutional Pillars for New Democracies: The Cases of Bulgaria and Romania*, Leiden, DSWO Press.
Wessels, Bernhard and Hans-Dieter Klingemann (1994), 'Democratic transformation and the prerequisites of democratic opposition in East and Central Europe', Wissenschaftszentrum Berlin für Sozialforschung, FS III, 94–201.

APPENDIX 11.1: ELECTION RESULTS

PARLIAMENTARY ELECTIONS

1990 Elections
Date: 10 and 17 June
Turnout: 89%

Party	%	Seats
Bulgarian Socialist Party	47.2	211
Union of Democratic Forces	36.2	144
Movement for Rights and Freedom	6.0	21
Bulgarian Agrarian People's Union	8.0	16

1991 Elections
Date: 10 October
Turnout: 83.9%

Party	%	Seats
Union of Democratic Forces	34.3	114
Bulgarian Socialist Party	33.1	111
Movement for Rights and Freedom	7.6	25
Bulgarian Agrarian People's Union	3.9	–
BAPU 'Nikola Petkov'	3.4	–
Union of Democratic Forces–Centre	3.2	–
Union of Democratic Forces–Liberals	2.8	–
Bulgarian Business Bloc	1.3	–
Confederation 'Kingdom Bulgaria'	1.8	–

1994 Elections
Date: 18 December
Turnout: 75.2%

Party	%	Seats
Bulgarian Socialist Party	43.5	125
Union of Democratic Forces	24.2	69
People's Union	6.5	18
Movement for Rights and Freedom	5.4	15
Bulgarian Business Bloc	4.7	13
Democratic Alternative for the Republic	3.8	–
Confederation 'Kingdom Bulgaria'	1.4	–

1997 Elections
Date: 19 April
Turnout: 62.4%

Party	%	Seats
United Democratic Forces *	52.3	137
Democratic Left **	22.1	58
Union for National Salvation ***	7.6	19
Euroleft	5.5	14
Bulgarian Business Bloc	4.9	12

* Joint list of the UDF and the People's Union
** Joint list of the BSP and *Ecoglasnost*
*** Joint list for the MRF, the BAPU–'Nikola Petkov', the Confederation 'Kingdom Bulgaria', the Green Party, and New Choice.

PRESIDENTIAL ELECTIONS

1992 elections
Date: 12 January (first round), 19 January (second round)
Turnout: 75.4% (first round), 75.9% (second round)

Candidate (Party)	First round	Second round
Zhelyu Zhelev (UDF)	44.6	52.8
Vulko Vulkanov (BSP)	30.5	47.2
George Ganchev (BBB)	16.8	

1996 Elections
Date: 27 October (first round), 3 November (second round)
Turnout: 62.7% (first round), 69.8% (second round)

Candidate (Party)	First round	Second round
Petar Stoyanov (UDF)	44.1	59.7
Ivan Marasov (BSP)	27.0	40.3
George Ganchev (BBB)	21.9	
Alexandar Tomov (Independent)	3.2	
Hristo Boychev (Independent)	1.3	

APPENDIX 11.2: GOVERNMENT COMPOSITION

Bulgarian Governments since 1989

Name	Affiliation	In office	Out of office
Georgi Atanasov	Bulgarian Communist Party	November 1989	January 1990
Andrei Lukanov	BCP (later renamed the Bulgarian Socialist Party)	January 1990	August 1990
Andrei Lukanov	BCP	September 1990	November 1990
Dimitar Popov	Non-party	December 1990	October 1991
Filip Dimitrov	Union of Democratic Forces	November 1991	December 1992
Luben Berov	Non-party	December 1992	October 1994
Reneta Injova	Non-party	October 1994	January 1995
Zhan Videnov	BSP	January 1995	January 1997
Stefan Sofianski	UDF	February 1997	May 1997
Ivan Kostov	UDF	May 1997	

The 'palace coup' against Todor Zhivkov staged on 10 November 1989, initiated rapid changes towards democracy and market economy in Bulgaria. During the course of the Roundtable talks, which started at the beginning of 1990, the cabinet of Georgi Atanasov, who had been one of the main executors of the dethronement of Zhivkov, had to resign on 1 February 1990 in order to pave the way for the formation of a new government.

The national Roundtable, initiated by the representatives of the ruling party and the opposition, lasted from January until May 1990. The agreements signed by the participants in the talks were attributed legislative status. The acting National Assembly was supposed to carry out the legislative initiatives by the Roundtable without any corrections or amendments whatsoever. The main participants in the talks were the BCP (since April 1990 known as the Bulgarian Socialist Party, BSP) and the Union of Democratic Forces (UDF), an anti-communist coalition founded on 8 December 1989. The talks were held in contact groups and plenary sessions in three rounds: 22 January–12 February 1990; 12 February–30 March 1990; and 14–15 May 1990.

Meanwhile, a congress of the Communist Party was held in January 1990. Immediately after the congress a new government was formed, headed by Andrey Lukanov. It took office on 8 February 1990. Lukanov, at the time a symbol of the reformist trend within the BCP, faced potential coalition partners reluctant to join the BCP in a government of national salvation, and Lukanov had little choice but to form a one-party cabinet. By the time he handed in its resignation – on 7 August 1990 – only six months had passed, and the election campaign had been in full swing since early May.

The first free, 'founding' elections were won by the Socialist Party. It obtained 211 seats out of a total 400 in the new parliament, known as the Greater National Assembly, while its main rival, the Union of Democratic Forces, gained 144 seats. Andrei Lukanov kept trying to form a coalition government relying on a 'gentleman's agreement' with the opposition, whose leaders had promised to support a coalition government provided that one of the opposition representatives was elected President of the Republic. In September 1990, however, the BSP formed yet another one-party government, again with Lukanov as Prime Minister. In the vote of confidence, the government was supported by 234 deputies and rejected by 104.

The problematic economic and social situation, including severe deficiencies in food supply, brought down the second Lukanov government on 29 November 1990. The ensuing parliamentary crisis forced a political agreement between all political forces represented in Parliament, the main point of which was the formation of a national government for the peaceful transition to democracy, headed by the independent premier, Dimitar Popov, and backed explicitly by all political forces. The main ministries were distributed on an equal basis between the BSP and the UDF, while the sensitive Ministry of the Interior was assigned to a politically neutral cabinet member. On 20 December 1990, an eighteen-member cabinet was formed, consisting of eight socialists, three members of the UDF, two Agrarians, and five independents. The government included representatives of all parliamentary forces with the exception of the Movement for Rights and Freedoms. Though the term 'coalition' was strictly avoided, the government was generally supported in accordance with the political agreement of January 1991. It was actually a cabinet dominated by the UDF, as the key economic posts were held by its representatives.

The cabinet of Dimitar Popov enjoyed a broad parliamentary and public support and was relatively independent. It was able to embark on a programme of economic reform inspired by the recent Polish experiences. The reforms set in motion in February 1991 were perhaps the most daring in the whole of Eastern Europe. They included an almost total liberalization of prices, a high degree of liberalization of the trading and currency regime, sharp interest rate increases, and the introduction of a floating exchange rate. However, in the summer of 1991 the reform process lost momentum as structural reform did not take off. This was due to increased confrontation in the parliament and to the process of fragmentation within the UDF.

Parliament was nevertheless able to adopt a new constitution; it was enacted on 12 July 1991. Before the Grand National Assembly adjourned, it also adopted legislation providing for the restoration of agricultural land to its former owners and promoting economic reform in general, but the new laws were hardly implemented. The elections were held on 10 October 1991, and the cabinet of Dimitar Popov resigned on 5 November 1991. The elections were won by the anti-communist coalition of the UDF, but by a small margin. The UDF coalition did not have a majority in its own right and had to look for support among the only other parliamentary group with an openly anti-communist outlook, the ethnic-Turkish MRF. The MRF had no particular desire to assume ministerial responsibility, since the party was well aware that such an unprecedented position of political prominence for the ethnic-Turkish minority might arouse nationalist feelings, kindled by the main opposition party, the ex-communist BSP.

Filip Dimitrov, the leader of the UDF coalition, became Prime Minister, and he immediately initiated legislation on restitution of nationalized property and agricultural land. The programme set in motion by the UDF did lead to a resurgence of private business, but even so, privatization remained a distant goal. Powerful interests and bureaucratic snags halted privatization of state enterprises, which accounted for 95 per cent of national property, one of the highest ratios in Eastern Europe. In the area of foreign policy, the government made a *rapprochement* with the United States and Western Europe, much to the chagrin of the socialist opposition which accused the government of giving up the friendly relations with Russia.

The UDF coalition was heterogeneous, and prone to internal discord. The government faced its first open crisis in April 1992, when Dimitrov sacked the Minister of Defence, Dimitar Ludzhev, a politician with close ties to President Zhelev. In addition to this, the UDF's parliamentary coalition partner, the MRF, was becoming increasingly dissatisfied with the failure by the Dimitrov government to improve the conditions of the impoverished Turkish population and by the attempts to isolate the MRF. By September 1992, the Dimitrov government found itself in a state of siege without an absolute majority in parliament. Dimitrov decided to risk a vote of confidence in October 1992, and when the government lost the vote, it was forced to resign.

The second-largest non-socialist parliamentary formation, the MRF, was offered an opportunity to form a new government, and it nominated presidential advisor Luben Berov as Prime Minister. He was to form an expert non-party government with the aim of implementing pressing economic reforms. The government of Luben Berov received the support of a so-called 'dynamic majority' formed by the socialists, the MRF and 19 defectors from the UDF parliamentary group. Luben Berov's government was not predicted to stay in power for long; pre-term parliamentary elections were widely expected, as the government was dependent on parliamentary support from political groups which had until recently been hostile to one another. Nevertheless, the cabinet of Luben Berov was surprisingly long-lived and remained in power until September 1994, by which time even the President had withdrawn his support.

Dimitar Ludzhev, a former UDF activist, and his parliamentary group *'Nov Izbor'* (New Choice) then made an unsuccessful bid to form a government. When he did not receive the support of the two main parliamentary groups, the UDF and the BSP, the President dissolved the National Assembly and called new elections for 18 December 1994. Up to that date, Bulgaria was governed by a caretaker government of non-party officials, appointed by the President in accordance with the Constitution. The new Prime Minister was Reneta Injova, who until then had chaired the Agency for Privatization.

The elections resulted in a landslide victory for the Socialist Party, which received a parliamentary majority in its own right. Socialist leader Zhan Videnov formed a new government in January 1995. Within a few months, the new government felt the negative effects of the delayed reform and privatization processes. Under increasing pressure from the population at large as well as from the rank and file within his own party, Videnov's government was unable to pursue a coherent and consistent policy. By mid-1996, Videnov had encountered growing economic instability and popular discontent; at the end of the year he had to resign as party chairman, and in January 1997, as Prime Minister. The Socialists presented a new candidate for the premiership, but mass rallies and the opposition boycott of parliament forced them to agree to pre-term elections in April 1997. In the meantime, a caretaker government led by Sofia's popular Mayor Stefan Sofianski was appointed by the President. With the support of the International Monetary Fund, it was able to halt the downward spiral in the economy.

The elections of 1997 were won decisively by the UDF and its ally, the People's Union. A new government, led by UDF chairman Ivan Kostov, was appointed in May. It continued the stabilization programme begun by its predecessor and by the end of 1997 it could boast that it had kept the country on a course of stabilization and reforms; among various measures, it introduced a currency board which kept inflation under control.

APPENDIX 11.3: THE ELECTORAL SYSTEM

The first free multi-party elections for the Grand National Assembly were held in June 1990. The main task of the Assembly was to adopt a new Constitution and a new electoral law. The Assembly was elected through a combination of simple majority and proportional representation; the electoral system was a compromise between the political groups which had taken part in the national Roundtable talks. 50 per cent of the MPs were to be elected on the basis of simple majorities in single-member constituencies, and the remaining 50 per cent by proportional representation. Bulgaria was divided into 200 single-member and 28 multi-member districts.

During its short existence, the Grand National Assembly fulfilled its main task: the drafting and ratification of the new democratic Constitution of the Republic of Bulgaria; a new electoral law (the Law on the Election of National Representatives, Local Councillors and Mayors); and certain other basic laws. The political parties and coalitions represented in the founding parliament approved a system of proportional representation but with a 4 per cent electoral threshold. As a result of this restriction, the smaller political parties (43 parties were registered for the 1991 elections to the National Assembly) were well advised to enter coalitions. The electoral law was drafted under considerable time pressure, and the law contains significant gaps, disparities and contradictory regulations which have caused uncertainty pertaining to the electoral procedure, requiring the Central Election Commission to redouble its efforts to interpret the legislation.

The new electoral law divided Bulgaria into 31 electoral constituencies, the size and borders of which were to be determined by presidential decree. The number of mandates for each electoral region depended upon the size of the population. The 31 districts were predominantly medium-sized with 6–10 mandates each; a few were larger. The Constitution envisages a single-chamber Parliament, comprised of 240 MPs elected for a period of four years.

Any eligible individual who can collect 2,000 signatures, may run as an independent candidate in one of the 31 constituencies (The required age for candidates is 21; for voting it is 18). An independent candidate is elected if he or she obtains more votes than the regional quota (the total number of ballots cast in the constituency divided by the number of seats allotted to this constituency). This is the first step in the calculation of the outcome, and the only one that may allocate seats at the constituency level. All remaining seats are allocated on the basis of list votes aggregated to the national level. The formula used is the d'Hondt system.

Parties, independent candidates, coalitions of political parties and coalitions of parties are obliged to run on non-amendable elections lists. The voters must vote *en bloc* for a particular electoral list, i.e. vote without expressing preferences for the selection of candidates and/or the rank order of the listed candidates. The major political parties prefer non-amendable lists, since they promote discipline within the parliamentary caucuses.

The electoral legislation itself did little to ensure real or adequate proportional representation of diverse social interests in the legislative body. The 4 per cent electoral barrier proved too high for post-totalitarian Bulgaria. It favoured the two main political formations, the UDF and the BSP, which had little political tolerance for each other. A less cumbersome electoral threshold would have provided representation for political parties and social formations now largely excluded. Some analysts argue that such an amendment would have opened up the Assembly for liberal, environmental, social democratic and agrarian groups, which together enjoy the support of some 25 per cent of the electorate. Given the strength of party competition, social polarization and the complicated nomination and registration procedures, independent candidates had little chance of being elected; in fact, not a single candidate running independently was elected in 1991.

The President of the Republic of Bulgaria is elected directly by the people, and may serve a maximum of two five-year terms in office. Candidates for President and Vice President may be nominated by political parties or party coalitions, or by 5,000 voters signing a petition. The elections are carried out in two rounds, on the basis of the simple majority system. A Bulgarian-born citizen, who is at least 40 years of age, has lived in Bulgaria for the previous five years and satisfies the conditions required of prospective MPs, can be elected President.

The first local elections in democratic conditions were held in November 1991, on the basis of the law adopted by the Grand National Assembly. In 1995, a special law on local elections was adopted, introducing the proportional system for candidates to local councils. Mayors, however, are elected according to the majority principle. If no candidate in a mayoral race wins an outright majority in the first round, a run-off round is held between the three candidates with the largest vote in the first round.

APPENDIX 11.4:
THE CONSTITUTIONAL FRAMEWORK

The Constitution approved on 12 July 1991 played a major role in the transformation of Bulgaria. The founding constitutional principles are republican parliamentary rule, the sovereignty of the people, the rule of law, political pluralism and the separation of powers. The principle of separation of powers is established in Article 8 of the Constitution: 'The power of the state shall be divided between a legislative, an executive and a judicial branch'. The Constitution proclaims the supremacy of the Parliament (the People's Assembly) as a permanent, representative institution embodying legislative power. The strict application of the principle of separation of powers finds its expression in the incompatibility of the mandate of a deputy with any other state office, including a ministerial post: 'A Member of Parliament elected as a Minister shall cease to serve as a member during his term of office as Minister ' (Article 68 [2]).

In accordance with its constitutional status, the Parliament enjoys a wide range of prerogatives. The main functions of Parliament are three: legislative; creative (relating to the formation of Cabinets); and control (relating to the exercise of parliamentary control over the Government). Legislation rests with the People's Assembly, but not with the People's Assembly alone. The President of the Republic has the right to promulgate the laws passed by Parliament and to return them for a second review, and the Council of Ministers has the right of legislative initiative.

The People's Assembly elects the Government and exercises control over its activities. The permanent committees exercise parliamentary control over the government on behalf of Parliament. Parliamentary control can be preliminary (preventive), current and subsequent. The means for parliamentary control are established by the Constitution, and in greater detail, by the internal rules of the Assembly: the use of questions and interpellations by MPs addressed to the Council of Ministers or to the various Ministers; votes of no confidence, or of confidence, in the Government or its individual members; the right of inquiries and investigations on issues which concern state or social interests.

In accordance with its constitutional status the Council of Ministers (CM) 'heads the implementation of the domestic and foreign policy of the state in observance of the Constitution and the laws' and 'ensures general management of the state bureaucracy and of the Armed Forces'. The CM manages the implementation of the state budget; organizes the management of state assets; concludes, confirms and rejects international treaties in certain cases specified by law; and rescinds any illegal and improper acts by the Ministers.

The Council of Ministers consists of a Prime Minister, Deputy Prime Ministers and Ministers. The Prime Minister heads and co-ordinates the overall policy of the Government and bears responsibility for it. He or she appoints and dismisses the deputy Prime Ministers. The Ministers head the various ministries, unless Parliament decides otherwise. They are responsible to Parliament for their acts. Only Bulgarian citizens qualified to be elected to Parliament are eligible for membership in the Council of Ministers.

The Constitution itself creates the premises for the strength of power of the Council of Ministers and of the Prime Minister, who is authorized to lead and co-ordinate the overall policy of the Government. An example of the wide prerogatives enjoyed by the Cabinet is the number of legal acts which may be issued by the Government and by the various Ministries: the Government issues decrees, ordinances, resolutions, rules of administration and regulations; the Ministers issue rules of administration, regulations, instructions and orders.

Parliament is to control the Government by means of questions and interpellations, and through the Cabinet's dependence on Parliament for approval. The two-way relationship is strengthened by the opportunity given to members of the Government to take part in parliamentary proceedings and in the work of the permanent committees, where they can take the floor upon request. The procedure for the termination of the prerogatives of the Government is spelt out in the Constitution. The Government must submit its resignation in the following cases: a vote of no confidence in the Government or in the Prime Minister; the resignation of the Government or the

Prime Minister; the death of the Prime Minister; and when a newly elected National Assembly convenes.

The Constitution envisages limited prerogatives and mainly representative functions for the President of the Republic. By way of example, the President has the right to propose to Parliament a candidate for the post of the Prime Minister, but only a candidate endorsed by the largest parliamentary group and after consultations with the other parliamentary groups. The prerogatives of the President in the legislative process are limited. The President does not have the right to propose legislation and has only a suspensive veto. The application of the presidential veto is not unlimited: it is applicable only in instances of obvious violations of the Constitution and the procedures of the legislative process. A presidential veto can be overturned by a repeated majority vote in the Assembly. The Constitutional Court has the right to scrutinize the President for the legality of his actions, and may initiate proceedings against the President in cases of High Treason or violation of the Constitution.

According to Article 98 of the Constitution, the President: (1) calls elections for the National Assembly and for the bodies of local self-government; (2) has the right to address the nation and the National Assembly; (3) signs international treaties in the cases established by law; (4) promulgates laws; (5) appoints and dismisses the heads of Bulgaria's diplomatic and permanent missions at international organizations upon a motion by the Council of Ministers, and receives the credentials and letters of recall of the foreign diplomatic representatives to Bulgaria; (6) grants asylum. The President appoints four of the twelve members of the Constitutional Court. The President is the Supreme Commander-in-Chief of the Armed Forces, appoints and dismisses the High Command and presides over the Consultative National Security Council.

Within the prerogatives vested in him, the President can issue decrees, addresses and messages. Presidential decrees must be signed by the Prime Minister or by the respective Minister, excepting decrees with which the President: (1) appoints a caretaker government; (2) assigns a mandate for the formation of government; (3) dissolves the National Assembly; (4) returns a law passed by Parliament for further debate; (5) organizes the work of the offices of the Presidency and appointments presidential staff; and (6) schedules elections and referendums and promulgates the laws.

The Bulgarian constitution states that the President bears the duty to contribute to the preservation of the unity of the nation. A number of constitutional guarantees exist to that effect: the incompatibility of the presidential post with a mandate as a member of parliament, as well as with participation in the leadership of political parties. In recent years, however, some political parties, including the UDF, have called for a constitutional change strengthening presidential powers.

12. From Transition to Consolidation

Tomas Hellén, Sten Berglund
and Frank Aarebrot

The study of political cleavage formation in Central and Eastern Europe in the 1990s offers a rare opportunity to investigate the dynamics of how support for political parties is shaped by varying circumstances. In a global perspective these states are all complex, modern societies. Moreover, most of the countries emerged as independent states with relatively democratic constitutions at the time when mass politics was consolidated throughout the industrialized world in the wake of the First World War. Finally, all the states experienced profound regime changes prior to, and in the immediate aftermath of, the Second World War, as well as in the early 1990s. Central and Eastern Europe does provide students of political conflict with a fascinating laboratory for comparing the impact of very different historical and structural contexts on the patterns of political cleavages.

The current volume does not pretend to offer a final account of the conditions conducive to linking support for current political parties to societal conflicts past and present. We would nevertheless argue that the analytic contributions provided by the authors of the country-specific chapters may serve as a good starting point for future systematic, comparative investigation.

In the previous chapter, Georgi Karasimeonov presents a classification of regimes based on their degree of democratic consolidation (cf. Linz and Stepan 1996). His typology demonstrates the relatively high degree of variation among the nations covered in this volume. None of them can be classified as consolidated democracies, but most of them are indeed on the road towards democratic consolidation. Only Romania and Bulgaria are unequivocally what Karasimeonov would define as transitional democracies; Slovakia stands out as something of a borderline case, at best a transitional democracy, but perhaps an authoritarian democracy like Serbia (cf. Chapter 11). Thus, there would seem to be intimations of a North/South divide, where South Eastern Europe lags behind the Northern Tier in terms of democratic consolidation. There is, in fact, a good case to be made for the notion that the resilience of authoritarian features in the Balkans has much to do with the clientelistic heritage in that particular region.

The country-specific chapters make it abundantly clear that democratic consolidation has been possible without cleavage crystallization and a freezing of the party systems. The East European party systems remain weakly anchored in the fluid and weakly-differentiated post-communist social structure. The fact that democratic consolidation may occur in a setting of weak cleavage crystallization goes against the grain of established theory. How can this paradoxical fact be accounted for?

Chapter 2 lists several factors which go a long way towards explaining why the current, post-communist try at democracy has better prospects than the inter-war and immediate post-war experiments in democratic rule; and the importance of these factors has indeed been brought out by all the country-specific chapters.

East European political leaders and voters alike have so far vigorously pursued integration into Western political, economic and military structures. This has given Western governments and institutions strong leverage to enforce adherence to the principles of participatory democracy, the rule of law, the free market and minority protection. In short, democratic consolidation is a prerequisite for, as well as a by-product of, integration with the West. The swift and relatively smooth integration of ex-communists into the democratic framework is but one aspect of the broad commitment to democratic principles. There is a climate favouring co-optation of the organizations and individuals tainted by communism, who for their part, have all but given up their hegemonic ambitions. Moreover, the countries of Eastern Europe have successfully applied creative electoral engineering in order to avoid political fragmentation. By now, all the countries in the region have introduced electoral thresholds and several of them have electoral systems combining majority and proportional representation; designs set to produce strong and stable government and to counter immobilism.

The impact of more than 40 years of communism has also, somewhat counter-intuitively, improved the prospects for democracy. The comprehensive modernization of Eastern Europe during communism has provided a social setting more conducive to democracy than ever before. By way of example, the high level of education (Berglund and Aarebrot 1997, 93; Lewis 1994, 132) makes it inconceivable for the countries of contemporary Eastern Europe to restrict balloting in a way similar to Hungary in the inter-war era, when rural voters had to state their voting preferences openly or were not allowed to vote at all (Rothschild 1974, 160). Another aspect of communist modernization conducive to democracy, was the emergence of social groups with interests – at least potential – which political parties could set out to represent. The post-communist societies have sometimes been referred to as 'flattened societies' (Wessels and Klingemann 1994); they were certainly marked by class differences, but did not have an independent middle class in the Western sense. Nevertheless, these flattened societies contained embryos of a modern class structure. Of particular importance are the well-educated middle strata which may develop into a Western-style propertied middle class.

Civil society alone did not bring down Soviet-style communism, but the increasing strength of autonomous organization in Eastern Europe throughout the 1980s and the early 1990s is easy to document and was certainly an unintended by-product of communist-initiated modernization. It is no coincidence that the transition was violent and/or an elite-level affair in the least modern societies, where civil society was not developed enough to challenge clientelistic structures. While the peoples of the Baltic republics organized a 'singing revolution', and the Czechs and Slovaks embarked on their Velvet Revolution, the transfer of power was a backroom affair in Bulgaria and Romania; in Romania, eventually spilling over into a regular shoot-out between competing factions of the beleaguered regime.

Cleavage Typologies: Three Different Approaches

The seminal Lipset–Rokkan classification scheme (Lipset and Rokkan 1967; Rokkan 1970; 1975) draws on a wide range of historical data mainly from Western Europe; it identifies manifest cleavages rooted in the long-running processes of national and industrial revolution, such as urban/rural, centre/periphery, church/state, labour/capital and social democracy versus communism (*Figure 12.1*).

In Chapter 2, the editors take an intermediate position on the relevance of historical cleavages in contemporary Eastern Europe. They were repressed during several decades of dictatorship before, as well as after, the Second World War; they may re-emerge, but not necessarily in the same form. By way of example, the rural–urban dimension has been thoroughly transformed by communist-style modernization. Collectivization of agriculture reduced the farmers to workers, and to all intents and purposes wiped out the constituencies of the inter-war agrarian parties, with the exception of the peasant parties of Poland and Slovenia. Advocating privatization of agricultural land has not been a successful strategy for the reborn agrarian parties of the early 1990s; agricultural workers have adjusted well to being workers rather than farmers, and they are now rallying to parties associated with the defunct communist regimes, which serve as parties of rural defence.

Figure 12.1: Cleavage typologies and their origins

Origins	Lipset and Rokkan	Karasimeonov	Editors	Cleavages discussed in country-specific chapters
Pre-war social structure	MANIFEST • urban–rural • centre–periphery • Church–State • labour–capital • social democracy–communism	Residual (Historical) Cleavages	*Historical* • core populations versus minorities • religious–secular • urban–rural • workers–owners • social democracy–communism	• ethnic/linguistic • religious • urban–rural • regional • left–right
Contemporary social structures		Actual Cleavages	*Contemporary* • national versus cosmopolitan • protectionist versus free-market • generational	• mode of distribution • rent-seekers versus wage-earners • education • generation
Regime transition from authoritarian to democratic		Transitional Cleavages	*Transitional* • apparatus versus forums/fronts	• communist regime versus civic forums/fronts • apparatus versus civil society • professionals (competence) versus dissidents ('amateurs')
Long-term developmental trends	LATENT	Potential Cleavages		

Figure 12.1 provides an overview of the scope of conceptual variations in the usage of terms related to the cleavage concept throughout this volume. First, Lipset's and Rokkan's distinction between manifest and latent cleavages is taken as a point of departure. We would argue that this book deals primarily with cleavages manifested through the representation of and the electoral support for political parties. Thus, Figure 12.1 indicates that latent cleavages – or, in Karasimeonov's typology: 'potential cleavages' – are not subject to investigation by the authors. Secondly, we have classified the categories proposed by Karasimeonov and ourselves in terms of their respective origins. We would argue that some of the manifestations of

political parties in contemporary Eastern Europe originate from social conflicts present already in the inter-war period. As mentioned above, these 'historical' or 'residual' cleavages are not necessarily represented by the same parties or even by the same ideologies today as after the First World War. In fact, in most cases it is new parties which today capitalize on old societal cleavages.

Another set of manifest cleavages is derived from contemporary social conflicts. Such cleavages are referred to by the editors as 'contemporary' cleavages; by Karasimeonov as 'actual' cleavages. Lack of precedence from the inter-war period is the common denominator behind this class of conflicts. Finally, both the editors and Karasimeonov have defined a class of manifest 'transitional' cleavages. These are conflicts related to the dramatic days and months following the fall of the Iron Curtain and the collapse of the Soviet Union. In order for a cleavage to be classified as transitional, parties which still identify themselves with the early popular fronts or, conversely, with the besieged pro-Soviet communists, must be present on the parliamentary level throughout the 1990s.

In the right-hand column of Figure 12.1, we have listed terms for classification of cleavages employed in the various country-specific chapters. Thus, we will argue that, despite some terminological ambiguities, a conceptual consistency exists throughout the volume.

The relevance of the left–right dimension is an important finding in the country-specific chapters. The party systems in all countries, with the exception of Estonia (and, possibly, Latvia; cf. *Table 12.1*), are structured along a left–right dimension, either explicitly or implicitly. As convincingly demonstrated by Zdenka Mansfeldová's chapter, Czech voters place the parties and the parties place themselves explicitly along a socio-economically defined left–right continuum. In the remaining countries, the political parties somehow end up on a left–right scale anyway. This is emphatically brought out by the chapters on Lithuania and Hungary. The legacy of communism in Eastern Europe has added one important component to the left–right cleavage: the conflict of interest between winners and losers in the transition process, between what may be classified as wage-earners and rent-seekers. This component has some features in common with the Lipset–Rokkan labour/capital cleavage, which also revolves around questions of distribution and redistribution. Yet it is important not to overstate the particularity of the East European case. The left/right or labour/capital cleavage in Western Europe has undergone a profound change since Lipset and Rokkan developed their classification scheme in the 1960s. The welfare state has contributed to a weakening of class linkages, and created a growing constituency of subsidy-seekers who use political parties to extract resources from the state. With the public sector accounting for more than half of GDP in many West European countries, the state has seen fit to take over many of the distributive functions formerly attributed to private capital.

Several parties compete for the different segments of the rent-seeking electorate in Eastern Europe. The rent-seeking electorate has occasionally found representation through the ex-communist parties, but some of the former ruling parties have developed into paragons of pro-market virtue – the Lithuanian Democratic Labour Party (LDDP) is a case in point; as evidenced by William Crowther's chapter on Romania, legislators affiliated with the three main communist party-derived formations (FDSN, FSN, PSM) are more pro-market than the population average. All East European parties, including the ex-communists, are in constrained by voters conditioned to seeing the state as a source of subsidies, and by external economic constraints, as well as by the need to make a clean break with communism and the planned economy.

In several of the countries where the immediate post-transition constellation was one of 'Us versus Them' – the popular fronts against the *nomenklatura* – the post-communist countries have gone through a metamorphosis and acquired genuine democratic credentials. This tendency is particularly strong in Poland, Hungary, Slovenia and Lithuania. Slovakia is a deviant case in the Central European context, as the Public Against Violence was soon co-opted by the former *nomenklatura*, creating a setting resembling the Romanian configuration. In Estonia and Latvia, the former communist organizations have been all but eradicated from the parliamentary arena, although many members of the disbanded *nomenklatura* remain active within newly established parties. All things considered, the post-communist trauma seems to be receding, and with it the transitional cleavages it created.

Since the collapse of communism, the issues of nationalism, ethnicity and race have been of less importance than might be expected, given Eastern Europe's legacy of ethnic politics. Even so, it is legitimate to ask whether this will be a permanent state of affairs. The countries in South Eastern Europe are as ethnically heterogeneous as they were before the Second World War, and the Baltic states even more so; Polish 'anti-Semitism without Jews' (Lendvai 1971) and anti-German resentments in the Czech polity are manifestations of ethnic cleavages which lost most of their underlying substance during the ethnic cleansings of the 1940s. External constraints, operative on the elite level, may go a long way towards accounting for the limited degree of exploitation of ethno-linguistic cleavages. EU and NATO intervention has certainly played a major role in defusing, or at least suspending, the Trianon issue between Hungary and her neighbours.

Identity politics is an important feature of state- and nation-building, and it still plays a role in Eastern Europe. State- and nation-building was not completed by the end of the inter-war era, and communism slowed down the process. In this respect, the Baltic states had the dual disadvantage of being not only communist but also under direct Soviet rule and subject to intense attempts at Russification. It should therefore come as no surprise that identity politics plays such a prominent role in these countries, in Estonia to the extent of overshadowing other cleavages.

Contemporary Cleavage Structures in Eastern Europe

Capitalizing on the conceptually consistent pattern defined in Figure 12.1, we will seek to define and compare the cleavage patterns for all the ten countries analysed in the previous chapters of this volume. In order to do so, it is necessary to define a set of historical, contemporary and transitional cleavages at a rather high level of abstraction. We do this in order to be able to compare variations in cleavage patterns across the countries of Eastern Europe. The results are reported in Table 12.1 below.

The first five cleavages are historical, closely related to Lipset's and Rokkan's classification of 1967:

- *Core populations versus ethno-linguistic minorities* Here we refer to political parties which are clear-cut representatives of a linguistic or ethnic minority, or to any party appealing to the core population by negative references to national minorities;
- *Religious versus secular* This dimension is captured by parties seeking to gain votes by defending religious values or by parties attacking religious values and arguing for a secular society;
- *Urban versus rural* This cleavage is manifested by parties which represent cities or rural areas and have some roots in the politics of the inter-war era;
- *Workers versus owners* This cleavage, also known as labour/capital or left/right, manifests itself through parties which derive their support primarily from within organized labour, or from within employers' organizations such as federations of industry. Traditional social democratic parties would be typical examples;
- *Social democrats versus communists* This cleavage is tapped by parties derived from the traditional conflict between internationalist and nationally-oriented socialism.

The next three cleavages are contemporary:

- *National versus cosmopolitan* At the poles of this cleavage we find parties with the nation-state as the focal point, and parties strongly oriented towards international co-operation as a way of solving political problems. To be listed as an exponent of this cleavage, nationalist or cosmopolitan rhetoric must be a dominant feature of the party's appeal;
- *Protective versus free market* At one end of this spectrum are parties which try to preserve subsidies for unprofitable industries; at the other are parties which launch themselves by arguing that the free market will benefit the country, irrespective of negative short-term consequences such as unemployment and social tension;
- *Generational* This cleavage is manifested by parties which derive their support from people with a common generational experience, such as pensioners and youth.

Finally, we have listed one transitional cleavage:

- *Apparatus versus popular forums/fronts* In order for this cleavage to be manifest, the party system must include parties which are derived from the old communist ruling apparatus, or parties which represent a direct continuation of the early anti-communist popular forums and fronts.

For a cleavage to be listed as relevant in Table 12.1, a party representing it must have returned at least five per cent of the vote in recent general elections (see the first appendices to the country-specific chapters). The same party may be salient as a mobilizing agent on more than one cleavage. For a party to be considered 'mobilizing' on the basis of a historical cleavage, it is not necessary for it to have had organizational continuity since the inter-war and immediate post-war eras. Cleavages do not have to be bipolar in order to be registered as salient for any specific country: it is sufficient for the party system to include a party, or a group of parties, seeking to capitalize on one end of a given dimension. For example, a country is considered to have a religious/secular cleavage, if it has a religious party polling more than five per cent of the vote; a secular counterpart is not necessary.

If each significant party in a country attempts to mobilize voters on the basis of the same position on a given cleavage, we do not classify that cleavage as salient. For example, in countries where all relevant parties are in favour of NATO and EU membership, the national versus cosmopolitan cleavage is not considered salient.

Following these rules of classification we arrive at the pattern of salient cleavages presented in Table 12.1. A '+' marks a salient cleavage, whereas a '+' within brackets indicates marginal salience relevant to one of our criteria.

Table 12.1: Patterns of cleavage types in Eastern Europe based on parties represented in national parliaments after 1989

		Est	Lat	Lit	Pol	Cz	Slk	Hun	Sln	Bul	Rom
HISTORICAL	Core population versus ethno-linguistic minorities	+	+				+			+	+
	Religious versus secular	+		+	+	(+)	+	+	+		
	Urban versus rural	+	+		+			+	+	(+)	+
	Workers versus owners	(+)	+	+	+	+	+	+	+	(+)	+
	Social democrats versus communists		+	+	(+)	+		+	+	+	+
CONTEMPO-RARY	National versus cosmopolitan	+				+	+	+	+	+	+
	Protectionist versus free-market	+	+			+	+	+	+	+	+
	Generational							+	+		
TRANSITIONAL	Apparatus versus forums/fronts	+		+	+	+			+	+	+

Est: Estonia; Lat: Latvia; Lit: Lithuania; Pol: Poland; Cz: Czech Republic; Slk: Slovakia; Hung: Hungary; Sln: Slovenia; Rom: Romania; Bul: Bulgaria.

Much has happened in Eastern Europe since 1989–90. Political life no longer revolves around the pros and cons of Soviet-style communism. Cleavages long suppressed and manipulated by the communist and pre-war authoritarian rulers have re-emerged, and new cleavages specific to post-communist societies have appeared. The countries of contemporary Eastern Europe all have a multi-dimensional cleavage space. Table 12.1 strongly suggests the presence of a North–South dichotomy, with the Northern Tier –

encompassing Estonia, Latvia, Lithuania and Poland – having the most simple cleavage structure. The manifestation of a larger number of what we refer to as 'contemporary cleavages' accounts for much of the greater complexity of the cleavage structure in our six southernmost countries.

A word of caution might be appropriate at this stage. Table 12.1 tells us which cleavages are represented by the relevant parties in each of the ten East European countries; it does not convey any information about cleavages represented by non-relevant parties, i.e. parties polling less than 5 per cent of the valid votes cast. More important still, the table does not say anything about the relative importance of the various cleavages identified. And not all cleavages are of equal importance.

We know from Mikko Lagerspetz' and Henri Vogt's analysis that contemporary Estonia is uni-dimensional to all intents and purposes. Identity politics is pervasive to the extent that Estonia might even be classified as a case of non-party politics. This of course does not preclude the existence of enough actors in the market to fill a few more cells in the matrix than the crucial first cell. Similarly, Hermann Smith-Sivertsen convincingly demonstrates that contemporary Latvian politics may be reduced to two salient cleavages: ethnic inclusion versus exclusion, and the disadvantaged strata versus professional elites. Of these two, the latter hardly registers in our matrix because of the electoral weakness of the relevant parties (LSDSP, LSDP/LDDP). Darius Žeruolis and Gábor Tóka deliberately refrain from identifying dominant cleavages in Lithuania and Hungary, respectively, but they offer ample evidence as to the existence of an underlying left–right dimension. This dimension is much more explicit in the Czech Republic, as brought out by Zdenka Mansfeldová, who also makes a highly interesting comparative analysis with the other half of the defunct Czechoslovak federation. She describes Slovakia as marked by a complex and multi-dimensional conflict between modernizers and traditionalists. Attitudes towards the communist past is one important aspect of this dimension, and in Romania and Bulgaria this division still serves as the main differentiating criterion between political parties. In Poland, the coalition of post-Solidarity parties (AWS) recently managed to revive the main transitional cleavage of the early 1990s, but Marian Grzybowski's analysis makes it clear that Polish politics has a strong undercurrent of left–right differentiation. Drago Zajc's interesting contribution on Slovenia also highlights the importance of a distributive dimension in Slovenian politics, but not to the exclusion of other cleavages, as evidenced by Table 12.1.

Nor does the table indicate how major cleavages interact, but we know from the country-specific chapters that they tend to be cross-cutting rather than reinforcing. In contemporary Eastern Europe, it is possible for a devout Catholic peasant to be a card-carrying member of a socialist party. In a similar vein, it is nowadays possible – indeed even commonplace – for ex-communists to have a cosmopolitan and free-market orientation. The ethno-linguistic cleavages, however, define much more watertight compartments. Ethnic parties normally poll the bulk of their respective constituencies, as demonstrated by the ethnic parties of Slovakia, Bulgaria and Romania. But the data at hand also provide indications of an increasing flow of votes across ethno-linguistic boundaries, particularly in Latvia, and also to some extent in Lithuania; and in Bulgaria and Romania, the salience of the ethno-linguistic dimension has recently diminished as a result of a process of co-optation encouraged and applauded by the international community.

The Normalization of Eastern Europe

It is standard operating procedure to conclude a volume like ours with an evaluation of the prospects for democracy in Eastern Europe. This is easily done. The reader will undoubtedly have noticed that the vast majority of our indicators pull in favour of democracy. Seven out of the ten countries in our sample qualify as being on the road towards democratic consolidation: only Romania, Bulgaria, and particularly Slovakia, lag behind. Yet even the laggards in our sample have made considerably more progress on the bumpy road towards democracy than the majority of the states within the CIS and the former Yugoslav federation. It would nevertheless be foolhardy to exclude the possibility of setbacks. Democracy is not a one way street.

The countries of Eastern Europe do in fact have features which may turn out to be problematic for democratic consolidation in the long run. As evidenced by the country-specific analyses in this volume, cleavage crystallization remains far from complete and the linkages between parties and voters are weak. The net result is party system fluidity and a high degree of electoral volatility. These are weaknesses which can be offset by what we have referred to as 'creative electoral engineering' – but only to a degree, as shown by the surprising success of outsiders like presidential contenders Stanisław Tymiński in Poland, George Ganchev in Bulgaria or Valdas Adamkus in Lithuania; or, for that matter, of parties such as the Czech Republican Party, the People's Movement for Latvia (Siegerist Party), and Poland's Party of Friends of Beer and Party X. As if this were not enough, there is the potential explosiveness of ethnic and national grievances, currently checked by pressure from the international community, and by a strong wish on the part of East European leaders to bring their countries into the European Union and NATO.

The problems of the new democracies in Eastern Europe are closely monitored by Western political science, and frequently discussed on the implicit assumption that West European democracy may be taken for granted and serve as a model. This attitude may be captured by substituting the West for the Soviet Union in an East German communist party slogan of the 1950s (Leonhard 1994): 'Who learns from the West learns how to triumph'. We believe things are slightly more complicated than that.

Contemporary Western Europe is in fact beset by many of the problems encountered in the East European context, albeit in different forms and to a different order of magnitude. Most of Western Europe is in the middle of a transition process of sorts. Harsh economic realities undermine the welfare states which were built from the 1950s and onwards, on the dual assumptions of continuous growth and the primacy of politics. The increasing inability of the welfare state to deliver on its outstanding promises erodes the legitimacy of the political system as well as attachments to political parties. This has not yet reached alarming proportions, but it is worth noting that Western Europe includes countries who exhibit levels of dissatisfaction with democracy comparable to some of the more extreme East European cases. As of 1994, the proportion of voters dissatisfied with democracy in Italy and Greece approached the 30–35 per cent levels registered in Hungary and Bulgaria, the most extreme cases of dissatisfaction in Eastern Europe as of 1995. In a similar vein, it may be noted that the level of dissatisfaction with democracy was of the same magnitude (11–14 per cent) in Britain, France Belgium, Romania, the Czech Republic and Slovenia (Eurobarometer No. 39, 1994; Central and Eastern Eurobarometer No. 6, 1995). Moreover, there is ample evidence of decreasing levels of party attachment in Western Europe (cf. Schmitt and Holmberg 1995; Biorcio and Mannheimer 1995). There is even a case to be made for the notion that Western Europe is currently undergoing a process of party system 'unfreezing'. The Italian case is, of course, the most pronounced, but as a rule, established parties have found it increasingly difficult to defend their position against new political entrepreneurs such as the Greens in Finland, Sweden and Germany, or against various kinds of populist movements such as the Progress parties of Denmark and Norway, the Austrian Freedom Party (FPÖ) and the National Front of France.

Last but not least, the breakdown of Soviet-style communism has had an impact on Western Europe well beyond the obvious economic and strategic implications. With the spectre of communism removed from the political agenda, the conceptual and ideological space in Western Europe was substantially reduced. It is probably premature to proclaim the demise of ideology in Western Europe, but like their East European counterparts, West European parties face the necessity of reformulating and rethinking their ideological positions. There is thus, a very strong case to be made for broad all-European comparative research, as opposed to more narrow East–East and West–West comparative research designs.

REFERENCES

Berglund, Sten and Frank Aarebrot (1997), *The Political History of Eastern Europe in the 20th Century: The Struggle Between Democracy and Dictatorship*, Aldershot, Edward Elgar.

Biorcio, Roberto and Renato Mannheimer (1995), 'Relationships Between Citizens and Political Parties', in Hans-Dieter Klingemann and Dieter Fuchs, eds., *Citizens and the State*, Beliefs in Government Volume 1, Oxford, Oxford University Press.

Lendvai, Paul (1971), *Anti-Semitism without Jews: Communist Eastern Europe*, Garden City, Doubleday.

Leonhard, Wolfgang (1994), *Spurensuche: 40 Jahre nach Die Revolution Entläßt Ihre Kinder*, Cologne, Kiepenheuer & Witsch.

Lewis, Paul G. (1994), *Central Europe since 1945*, Singapore, Longman.

Linz, Juan and Alfred Stepan (1996), *Problems of Democratic Transition and Consolidation: Southern Europe, South America and Post-Communist Europe*, Baltimore and London, Johns Hopkins University Press.

Lipset, Seymour Martin and Stein Rokkan (1967), 'Introduction', in Lipset, Seymour Martin and Stein Rokkan, eds,, *Party Systems and Voter Alignments*, New York, Free Press.

Rokkan, Stein (1970), *Citizens, Elections, Parties: Approaches to the Comparative Study of the Process of Development*, Oslo, Universitetsforlaget.

—— (1975), 'Dimensions of State Formation and Nation-Building: A Possible Paradigm for Research on Variations within Europe', in Charles Tilly, ed., *The Formation of National States in Europe*, Princeton, Princeton University Press, 562–600.

Rothschild, Joseph (1974), *East Central Europe Between the Two World Wars*, Seattle and London, University of Washington Press.

Schmitt, Hermann and Sören Holmberg (1995), 'Political Parties in Decline?', in Hans-Dieter Klingemann and Dieter Fuchs, eds., *Citizens and the State*, Beliefs in Government Vol. 1, Oxford, Oxford University Press.

Wessels, Bernhard and Hans-Dieter Klingemann (1994), 'Democratic transformation and the prerequisites of democratic opposition in East and Central Europe', Wissenschaftszentrum Berlin für Sozialforschung, FS III, 94–201.

Name Index

382   *Name Index*

384   *Name Index*

Subject Index